Shock the World

SHOCK THE WORLD

UConn
Basketball
in the
Calhoun
Era

Peter F.
Burns, Jr.

NORTHEASTERN
UNIVERSITY PRESS
BOSTON

NORTHEASTERN UNIVERSITY PRESS

An imprint of University Press of New England

www.upne.com

© 2012 Peter F. Burns, Jr.

Manufactured in the United States of America

Designed by Eric M. Brooks

Typeset in Fresco Plus Pro by Passumpsic Publishing

University Press of New England is a member of the
Green Press Initiative. The paper used in this book meets
their minimum requirement for recycled paper.

Library of Congress Cataloging-in-Publication Data
Burns, Peter F.
Shock the world: UConn basketball in the Calhoun era /
Peter F. Burns.
    p. cm.
Includes bibliographical references and index.
ISBN 978-1-55553-777-7 (cloth: alk. paper)—
ISBN 978-1-55553-793-7 (ebook)
1. University of Connecticut—Basketball. 2. Connecticut
Huskies (Basketball team) 3. Calhoun, Jim. 4. Basketball
coaches—Connecticut—Biography. I. Title.
GV885.43.U44B87 2012
796.323'630974643—dc23   2012008458

5 4 3 2

Contents

Preface

Hurricane Katrina displaced me from my New Orleans home in the fall of 2005. In search of a distraction from the devastation to the place I called home since 2001, I decided to write a book about something I knew and loved. My friend John Roger Thomas said that if he wrote a book based upon those criteria, he would have written an autobiography. For me, that subject was UConn men's basketball.

Since Jim Calhoun became coach in the spring of 1986, I felt like I was a part of UConn basketball. The Huskies are my team and Calhoun, who reminds me of my father in many ways, is my coach. I received two degrees from UConn's political science department and I was in and around the university from the start of the Chris Smith era to the end of the Donyell Marshall one. I attended Calhoun's first Big East game, his first Big East tournament game, the Lyman DePriest game against BC, UConn's first Big East tournament championship (I stormed the court), The Shot against Clemson, and the program's first and third national championship games. Despite this connection to UConn and an affinity for the program, my outsider status allows me to tell a complete story about UConn basketball under Jim Calhoun. I am not Calhoun's friend or employee and I won't need access to him or UConn basketball in the future. This book provides the highs and lows of the Calhoun era.

Speaking of access, I did interview Calhoun twice for the book—ish. I asked Calhoun questions at his reunion games in 2006 and 2010. I tried to get a one-on-one interview on several occasions, but every time I called or emailed the office I was put on a maze that led nowhere. Twice, I asked Calhoun personally for an interview—once after the game at Indiana and again in 2010—both times he gave his office number to me and both times I just couldn't arrange an interview. The questions I asked Calhoun, the interviews I conducted, and the thousands and thousands of stories I read about the coach allowed me to write a definitive biography of the Calhoun era.

I interviewed many people who know Calhoun, and the picture they drew of him is someone who is loyal, guarded, a belonger (the late Dave Solomon's word), private, knowledgeable about many things, and deeply committed to his family, friends, players, and the University of Connecticut. He is also demanding, tough, hard to please, and a yeller (during games). He's no-nonsense. I asked Calhoun's former player and assistant coach Steve Pikiell, now head coach at SUNY Stony Brook, what Calhoun did especially well as a coach. "Everything," Pikiell said. That's my assessment too.

Acknowledgments

I have too many people to thank for this book. Staff members at the New Orleans Hornets, Detroit Pistons, Charlotte Bobcats, Boston Celtics, and Dallas Mavericks allowed me to interview NBA players. Peter Gold of Gold, Orluk & Partners provided access so that I could ask questions to former players at Calhoun's reunion games. Melanie Detziel and Ed Ryan of the *Daily Campus* provided pictures. Kristin Eshelman of the Dodd Center is an example of a high-quality employee at UConn. She was first-rate in helping me secure photos from the early Calhoun era. I wish to thank Betsy Pittman, the interim curator at the Thomas J. Dodd Research Center, University of Connecticut Libraries. The photos used from the Dodd Center were published with permission. Fanbase.com, Uconnhuskies.com, UConn men's basketball media guides, and Espn.com provided important statistics and game information. Peter F. Burns, Sr., Pat Burns, Patty Burns, Ed Thorndike, and Holly Thorndike provided room and board for me as I traveled to Connecticut to conduct interviews and get pictures. Jillian Liese, Matt Thomas, and Tom O'Keefe read drafts of the book; Ed Kislik read the entire manuscript and provided detailed comments in three days. Each reader improved the book. Wendy Porche, Mike Berner, Sean Gorman, Terry Burns, Cliff Burns, John Erlingheuser, Greg Stamos, Tom Polo, Danny Polo, Michael Polo, Paul Polo, Joe Trippi, Zane Gould, Adria N. Buchanan, Pat Sweeney, and many of my students at Loyola University New Orleans also provided information, encouragement, advice, or all three. Matthew Lutts of AP Images and Robert Chong of Getty Images assisted with pictures. Steve Hull and the staff at the University Press of New England and the Northeastern University Press were professional and more than helpful. Chris Fettweis read several complete drafts of this book. I am indebted to him forever. However, if you feel that the book could use several pages on the 1997 NIT consolation game, blame Chris.

Thomas V. O'Keefe, Jr., my uncle, is the biggest UConn fan I have met. Tommy graduated from UConn in 1969 and fell in love with the team in the first place because Wilbur Cross High School's Dom Perno, who like my uncle is a native of New Haven, starred for UConn in the early 1960s. My uncle loves to tell the story of meeting Sandy Fishman while they played intramural basketball at the field house in 1966. Fishman told my uncle that he was going to play basketball at UConn. My uncle said, "You are playing basketball at UConn." "No, no," Fishman said. "I am going to play for the varsity team." Fishman not only made the varsity team but he averaged 1.3 points in his two-season, 25-game year career at UConn. Tom scored four goals and had seven assists in his UConn hockey career from 1967 to 1969. He went to the penalty box on many occasions and felt shame. Tom would have made it to the Iron League if scouts came to his games. This book is dedicated to Tom O'Keefe, who knew that UConn was great in everything before everyone else did. No matter what, he will always love UConn.

> You can change wives; you can change religions;
> you can't change teams.
> TVO'K (November 7, 2011)

Shock the World

Hopefully, When It's All Said and Done, You'll Say, "He's Pretty Good"

It was the worst of times, it was the worst of times.

Spring 2010.

Reporters, so-called experts, and pundits started to write the epitaph for the Calhoun era of UConn men's basketball. The university had yet to offer a new contract to its longtime coach, who assured everyone that his new deal was around the corner. Calhoun missed seven games and 23 days of work for unspecified health reasons in 2010. The program faced an NCAA investigation and almost certain punishment for use of an intermediary to sign a recruit. Other teams used the coach's uncertain future and the NCAA investigation to steer recruits away from UConn.

The Huskies had just completed an 18–16 season, which ended in the second round of the NIT. In modern-day Connecticut basketball, that result was a disaster, especially when Maya Moore and the women's team hadn't lost a game in two seasons. Kemba Walker was the team's lone returning star, but could he carry a team that included seven new players? Calhoun had coached great players in the past—Donyell Marshall, Ray Allen, Emeka Okafor, Ben Gordon, and Rudy Gay, among others—but not since Caron Butler in 2002 would he rely as much on one player to carry a team as he would on Walker in 2011.

A headline in the *Wall Street Journal* asked, "Last Stand for UConn's Calhoun?" At the same time, the *Sporting News*'s Mike DeCourcy wrote that the 2010 recruiting class, which included one top 100 player, combined with the loss of three seniors put UConn in jeopardy of missing the NCAA tournament in consecutive years for the first time since 1989, Calhoun's third season in Storrs. *Sports Illustrated*'s Seth Davis wrote that "the trend lines around his [Calhoun's] program were heading in a bad direction long before Friday's revelations [about recruiting violations]. At the very moment when UConn basketball needed a fresh jolt, it was delivered a devastating blow. I suspect it will be a long, long while before it fully recovers." Earlier in the season, Davis encouraged Calhoun to quit, writing that "the game of college basketball will miss [Calhoun] when he retires, but his family will miss him more if he keeps putting this kind of toll on his body. So please, coach, get out while you still can. The sideline is no place for a good man to die."

In the season after these predictions about Calhoun were made, UConn received no votes in the Associated Press's preseason top 25 poll, but won the Maui Invitational, the most prestigious preconference tournament in the country. The team rocketed to number seven in the AP poll the next week—the second highest jump for any school in history—and made it as high as number four during the season. After this strong start, however, the Huskies lost nine conference games and finished ninth in the Big East. They dropped seven of their last 11 and four of the final five games. Despite the team's struggles, Calhoun touted Walker as the best player in the nation.

Then, UConn won five games in five days at Madison Square Garden to win its record-tying seventh Big East Tournament title. The Huskies were the first team to *play* five games in five straight days in a conference tournament, and beat four top 25 teams in consecutive days.

UConn followed the five wins in New York City with six more to take the program's third national championship. Calhoun was right: Walker was the nation's best player. Walker shattered the Big East Tournament record for points by 44, beat Pitt at the buzzer, and made important plays at the end to defeat Syracuse and Louisville. He captured the most outstanding player award for the NCAA tournament.

Calhoun showed his brilliance in the tournament runs. He called time-out at the right moments, had the correct matchups on the floor, and designed plays and strategies to allow his team to win. Calhoun built a Hall of Fame career on such moves.

At the White House ceremony to honor the 2011 national champions, President Barack Obama had to explain why he picked Kansas—and not UConn—to win the national title. At first, he blamed ESPN's Andy Katz, who told him that UConn had no chance. Then, Obama said that teams like UConn "shocked the world" and busted many brackets.

Shocked the world?

Maybe.

But the conference tournament and national championship runs in March of 2011 weren't as shocking as the overall transformation the program made in the Calhoun era. A quarter century earlier, the UConn basketball program was a mess with few advantages and Jim Calhoun, then head coach at Northeastern University in Boston, knew it. . . .

In the movie *Major League*, Charlie Donovan, general manager of the Cleveland Indians, calls Lou Brown and says, "Listen, Lou, I hope you're sittin' down 'cause I got an offer you probably been dreamin' about your whole life. . . . Would you like to manage the Indians this year?" When he receives the call, Brown is working at Tire World in Toledo and in the middle of taking a customer's order.

"I don't know," Brown says in a voice that sounds affected by equal parts yelling and cigarettes. "Lemme think it over, will ya, Charlie? I got a guy on the other line about some whitewalls. I'll talk to ya later." Brown hangs up.

That scene resembles the exchange between UConn athletic director John Toner and Northeastern University basketball coach Jim Calhoun in the spring of 1986. Like Brown, Calhoun had worked in the minor leagues forever. Like Donovan, Toner thought Calhoun wanted the chance to coach in the big leagues. Like the Cleveland Indians, UConn was a last-place team with little hope of improving. Like Brown, Calhoun said, "Lemme think it over, will ya?"

When he thought it over, Calhoun turned down the job 15 times . . . in his mind. He repeated the following questions; each time he answered them, he decided to stay in Boston.

Would top high school basketball players come to UConn,
a program that lacked tradition and a national name?

The name UConn meant nothing to the nation's elite high school players. If they wanted to play for a Big East school, the country's best preferred Georgetown, Syracuse, St. John's, and Villanova. From the start of Big East conference play in the 1979–1980 season through the 1985–1986 season, the one before Calhoun arrived in Storrs, UConn went 9-48 against these teams.

The name UConn also meant nothing to the nation. In a 1987 episode of *Cheers*, Rebecca mentions that she attended the University of Connecticut. She doesn't say she went to UConn because, at that time, few outside the state knew what those letters meant. In response, Norm says that he and the other guys at the bar were such big fans of the Connecticut football team, the "Fighting Insurance Salesmen."

In the fall of 1987, few in the United States knew that basketball was the university's athletic specialty. Few knew that the Husky served as the school's mascot. Nobody cared. Any basketball coach would struggle to entice top players to an invisible university and program.

The term "regional power" is often used to characterize UConn basketball before the Big East began play in 1979. Under Coach Hugh Greer, the team compiled a 286-112 record from 1946 to part of the 1963 season, and it won the Yankee Conference 12 times, including 10 in a row, in a span of 13 seasons. The

Big East Conference (37–61)

Big East Conference Tournament (1–7)

NIT (2–6)

NCAA Tournament (4–14)

Yankee Conference included the universities of Rhode Island (URI), Maine, Vermont, and New Hampshire, which weren't basketball powerhouses in any period.

UConn spent four weeks in the AP top 25 before Toner asked Calhoun to become head coach. It went 2-6 in the NIT and 4-14 in the NCAA tournament before the spring of 1986.

The team lost both of the NIT games it played while a member of the Big East conference and it hadn't appeared in the NCAA tournament since the Big East began play in 1979-1980. Its lone appearance in the Elite Eight came in 1964 after Dom Perno stole the ball in the waning minutes of the Sweet 16 game against Bill Bradley's Princeton team in Raleigh, North Carolina. Two days later, Duke scored more points in the first half than UConn did for the entire game and beat the Huskies, 101-54.

In the years before the 1986-1987 season, UConn won some memorable games; several fine basketball players wore the UConn uniform but none dominated college basketball or went on to brilliant NBA careers. A handful of good coaches such as Greer, Fred Shabel, and Dee Rowe guided the team, but equating these successes to the accomplishments of a basketball power, regional or otherwise, is an overstatement.

*Would top high school basketball players — even ones
from Connecticut — ever want to live in Storrs?*

As a land-grant institution, UConn emphasized agriculture and Storrs, a rural area with livestock and rolling hills, was a perfect location for the school. A couple of gas stations, a few strip malls, and trees — lots and lots of trees — make up the scenery on the way to the university. Cows greet visitors who enter the campus on Route 195. Storrs was an isolated town that lacked a movie theater, clothing store, McDonald's, or other amenities one would expect to find in a college setting.

At the time that Toner and Calhoun talked, students had few options for fun on campus, save the bar scene, and even those choices were limited. Ted's and Huskies were about the only places to go out in Storrs. There are only so many times anyone — even a college student — can listen to "Joy to the World" by Three Dog Night at Ted's without getting bored after a while.

If students had cars — only juniors and seniors were allowed to have them on campus — they could drive 15 minutes to the East Brook Mall in Willimantic. There, they could eat at Papa Gino's, ride the iron horsey for 25 cents, or go outside and watch the leaves change colors. That's about it.

Boston is more than an hour's drive from Storrs, New York City more than two hours. Students can make the round trip from UConn to one of these cities in a single night, but the journey is long and inconvenient. Even Hartford isn't that close to Storrs. The capital of Connecticut is a 36-minute drive from campus, but the ride seems longer.

UConn was what is known as a suitcase school, one from which students went home every Thursday night or Friday afternoon and returned Monday morning. Even though 15,000 students attended UConn, a person could walk through the central part of campus on weekends and not see an undergrad.

If basketball players liked isolation, limited entertainment options, rolling hills, cows, trees, and temperatures that would make Lambeau Field shiver, then Storrs was for them.

In the first ten years of the Big East conference, Boston College and Villanova thrived with players from Connecticut. John Garris of Bassick High School in Bridgeport, John Bagley of Harding High in Bridgeport, Jay Murphy of Meriden, and Hartford Public High School's Michael Adams are members of the Boston College Varsity Club Hall of Fame. Harold Pressley of Saint Bernard in Uncasville, John Pinone of South Catholic High School in Hartford, and Trumbull High's Harold Jensen starred for Villanova. At Pitt, Bridgeport's Charles Smith was a freshman All-American in 1985, an All-American in 1987 and 1988, and Big East player of the year in 1988.

In 1997, Dick "Hoops" Weiss of the *Daily News* in New York compiled a list of the top 50 all-time players in the history of the Big East; six players came from Connecticut, but only Chris Smith (46) played for UConn. Charles Smith (8), Pinone (14), Bagley (20), Adams (28), and Pressley (47) also made the list.

Colleges and universities throughout the country came to Connecticut to recruit star players. Mike Gminski of Masuk High School in Monroe led Duke to the NCAA finals in 1978 and played in the NBA for 14 years. In 1980, Rod Foster of St. Thomas Aquinas in New Britain led a Larry Brown-coached UCLA team to the national final against Louisville. Wes Matthews, a high school teammate

**CONNECTICUT HIGH SCHOOL BASKETBALL PLAYERS
WHO LEFT THE STATE IN THE PRE-CALHOUN ERA**

Mike Gminski
Masuk High School, Monroe
Duke (1976–1980)

Jay Murphy
Maloney High School, Meriden
Boston College (1980–1984)

Wes Matthews
Harding High School
Wisconsin (1977–1980)

Michael Adams
Hartford Public High School
Boston College (1981–1984)

John Bagley
Harding High School, Bridgeport
Boston College (1979–1982)

Harold Pressley
St. Bernard High School, Uncasville
Villanova (1982–1986)

John Pinone
South Catholic High School, Hartford
Villanova (1979–1983)

Charles Smith
Harding High School
Pittsburgh (1984–1988)

Rod Foster
St. Thomas Aquinas High School,
  New Britain
UCLA (1979–1983)

of Bagley's at Harding, starred for the Wisconsin Badgers and played in the league for nine years. A recruiting base existed in Connecticut, but history suggested that these players would leave the state for a real team on a real campus.

Would the university support a first-class operation of any kind?

The University of Connecticut treated basketball as if it were another extracurricular activity. A lowest-bidder mentality permeated the UConn athletic program, which made decisions based upon which hotel chains or uniform companies offered the cheapest prices. The university located parents and friends of players in the worst seats in the arena. The recruiting budget was meager and the basketball offices were cramped and came equipped with rotary, rather than push-button, phones as late as spring 1986.

In 1986, UConn's new president, John T. Casteen III, created a task force on athletics. Casteen, the former dean of admissions at the University of Virginia, saw Ralph Sampson's teams bring notoriety, enthusiasm, money, and interest to that institution. He wanted to replicate that experience at UConn.

The task force included the complaint that plans were not in place for a new sports center or for the renovation of the current athletics infrastructure.

UConn's basketball facilities weren't even state of the art for the 1950s, when most of them were built. The roof of the field house—where the team practiced and played some of its home games—leaked. Coaches put towels on the floor to prevent players from slipping and the court from warping. They steered recruits away from the field house for fear that the facility would discourage players from signing with UConn. The locker room needed a lounge, new carpeting, and updated pictures of games and players.

The basketball court sat in the middle of other activities at the field house. As the basketball team practiced, sprinters and even casual joggers ran around it and pole vaulters jumped over it. The coaches raised a curtain around the court to spare players from running hundreds of feet to get loose balls.

The task force pointed the cannon at Toner, the athletic director at UConn since he stepped down as the school's football coach after the 1970 season. Toner announced his resignation in January of 1987. In his 18 years on the job, Toner got UConn into the Big East, hired two Hall of Fame basketball coaches, and started and oversaw the construction of Gampel Pavilion.

Earl Kelley epitomized the dysfunctional nature of UConn athletics at that time. Heavily recruited out of Wilbur Cross High School in New Haven, Kelley earned Big East rookie of the year honors in 1983 and would become the only UConn player to lead the team in scoring for four years. On April 4, 1985, Kelley and five friends threatened to hurt two students if they did not lead them to Gregory Johnson, who allegedly had stolen 10 dollars, a gun, and some knives from Kelley's room. Kelley and company forced one of the students into a van and ordered him to take them to Johnson. Kelley, his friends, and the abducted student looked for Johnson at his dorm room and a bar on the edge of campus. The abducted student escaped at the bar.

Kelley received a reduced charge of disorderly conduct, which came with a three-month, suspended jail term and a year's worth of probation. The university claimed that Kelley had violated its student conduct code. The crowd at Kelley's disciplinary hearing was so large—about a hundred students and dozens of reporters—that the university moved the venue from the Wilbur Cross library to Jorgensen auditorium. Kelley said he didn't have the gun when the police confiscated the pistol. Besides, he said, the gun—a pre-World War II Spanish-made automatic—didn't work.

The dean of students found Kelley guilty of physical assault, harassment, and endangering. The dean banned Kelley from the dorms and cafeterias but allowed the point guard to continue to play. Seven weeks after his hearing, Kelley flunked off the UConn team. At the time, he averaged 19.6 points and ranked fifth on UConn's all-time scoring list.

Along with Corny Thompson, Kelley was UConn's best Big East player before Calhoun arrived. No one in the program, athletic department, or university could handle him. Kelley's academic probation—and the team's seven-game season-ending losing streak without him—led to Head Coach Dom Perno's resignation.

The task force revealed that the basketball program mirrored other areas of the university. In the 1980s, UConn's campus—not just its basketball facilities—looked and felt like the 1950s, when most of the newest academic buildings, too, had been constructed. Except for the Wilbur Cross library and its gold cupola, none of the buildings on campus distinguished UConn from other schools.

At the time that Calhoun considered the UConn position, most of the university's buildings needed new roofs, plumbing, electrical wiring, air conditioning systems, or some other major improvement. The condition of the campus showed that the governor and State Legislature—the entities responsible for funding the university—were either ignorant about or apathetic toward UConn.

Why leave the regional powerhouse you created?

After stints as an assistant coach at his alma mater, American International College (AIC), and head coach at Old Lyme High School (Connecticut), Westport High School (Massachusetts), and Dedham High School (Massachusetts), Calhoun became Northeastern's head coach in 1972. He took that program from Division II to Division I and compiled a 250–137 record. Calhoun earned the New England coach of the Year and the Kodak District I coach of the year honors three times each; he led those Huskies to five NCAA tournaments in a six-year period. Through the 2010–2011 college season, Calhoun had won more games than any coach in the history of Northeastern basketball.

In 1981, 11th-seeded Northeastern defeated Fresno State, the sixth seed in the NCAA tournament. The next year, Northeastern, again the 11th seed, beat sixth-seeded St. Joe's. The Huskies lost to third-seeded Villanova in double overtime in the next game. In a preliminary-round game in 1984, Northeastern defeated LIU-Brooklyn, but a buzzer-beater by sixth-seeded VCU's Rolando Lamb at the Meadowlands ended the season for Calhoun's 11th-seeded Huskies.

In the spring of 1986, Calhoun's Northeastern program was much stronger than the program in Storrs. Future Celtic and NBA all-star Reggie Lewis had finished his junior year, and the following season Northeastern was poised to win 25 games, be ranked among the nation's top 25, and be the coach's best team. Calhoun grew up in and around Boston, and loved Fenway Park, the Red Sox, and the Boston Pops. Home games were Calhoun family reunions. Northeastern University tenured Calhoun and promised the athletic director's position to him when he retired from coaching.

Calhoun's Northeastern teams "were a trademark of his personality," said Mike Gorman, the play-by-play announcer for the Big East network from the start of the league until the early 1990s. "They were fierce," he said. Gorman — who also started as the television voice of the Boston Celtics in 1980 — believes that college teams adopt the personality of their coach and pro teams resemble their best players. The Celtics were Larry Bird's team; the Spurs assumed Tim Duncan's personality; Kobe ruled the Lakers; and Michael Jordan molded the Bulls into his image. Northeastern teams were a trademark of Calhoun's personality. They were driven to succeed, fierce, and hard-nosed, just like their coach. "They had no one over six foot eight and finished in the top three in rebounding in the nation every year," Gorman said.

Toner became impressed with Calhoun while he watched Northeastern beat UConn in the championship game of the 1985 Connecticut Mutual Classic. When Perno resigned in the spring of 1986, Toner remembered how much he liked Calhoun's team. He wanted the Northeastern coach to take over the UConn program.

. . . but what about all those advantages?

Calhoun realized that UConn offered advantages that Northeastern could never provide. The Huskies of Storrs were the only college basketball team of note in Connecticut and shared major league status with the Hartford Whalers. Calhoun called Northeastern basketball the 10th sports story in a nine-sports-story town.

In the late 1980s, 20 to 25 daily newspapers covered UConn's home games and 14 traveled with the team. UConn basketball was — and continues to be — among the most covered college teams in the nation. St. John's late sports information director Katha Quinn referred to the media that followed UConn as "the Horde." She came up with the term because she would shoehorn more than a dozen UConn beat writers into the snuffbox called Alumni Hall.

Calhoun was impressed that the fans filled the Hartford Civic Center for the final home game of the previous season. If people got excited over a team that won three conference games, he thought, they'd turn maniacal if teams challenged for Big East titles. Add to that equation the State of Connecticut's wealth, and Calhoun figured that his program would also enjoy financial support.

Bobby Knight told Calhoun to take a job at a state school if he wanted to leave Northeastern. Be the head coach at the "University of Somewhere," Knight said. A state university had far more resources than those with which Calhoun operated at Northeastern.

The Big East gave Calhoun a chance to recruit the best players and compete for national championships. Northeastern lacked the exposure and potential players that the Big East provided.

As bad as UConn's facilities were in 1986, Calhoun would move upward in venue if he came to Connecticut. Northeastern played in the 6,000-seat Matthews Arena, which opened in 1910. UConn played its Big East games at the Hartford Civic Center, which held more than 16,000 fans. Calhoun realized that "there never was going to be a big arena, big crowds" at Northeastern. "Plucky Northeastern always would be plucky Northeastern." Just because UConn lost in the past didn't mean it couldn't win in the future, Calhoun thought. He felt that he became "too settled" at Northeastern. It took two days for him to get over his team's loss to Oklahoma in the 1986 NCAA tournament. That defeat should have caused weeks, if not months, of misery, the coach said.

The other finalists for the UConn head coaching job were Fairfield University coach Mitch Buonaguro, who was a former assistant to Rollie Massimino at Villanova, and Canisius College head coach Nick Macarchuk. The inclusion of Macarchuk put UConn assistant coach Howie Dickenman in a difficult position. Dickenman was the only member of Perno's staff to stay on after the head coach resigned. His father coached Macarchuk in high school at Norwich Free Academy in eastern Connecticut. Before he came to UConn in 1982, Dickenman served as Macarchuk's assistant at Canisius in Buffalo for five seasons. The two were close, but Dickenman maintained loyalty to UConn. He treated the three finalists as equals.

The final candidate to be interviewed, Calhoun came to Storrs and met with President Casteen for two hours on May 13, 1986. By the end of that day, he received an offer to become UConn's new head coach; he told Toner that he would make a decision by 2 p.m. the next day. When that deadline approached, Calhoun asked for an extension until 10 p.m. that night.

That evening, Calhoun and his wife Pat attended the New England Gridiron Club dinner, where he received a clock for coach of the year honors. The Northeastern coach knew everyone in the room. That overfamiliarity bothered him. When he returned from the dinner, he asked for another extension—this time until 8:45 the next morning. He discussed UConn's tentative offer with others, including Big East commissioner Dave Gavitt and Syracuse coach Jim Boeheim, who told him that the proposed contract was too low and that Calhoun's compensation needed to match what other Big East coaches earned. Based on that advice, Calhoun rejected the initial offer. He would serve as the test case for whether UConn was serious about moving up in class.

UConn upped the offer, and Calhoun signed a seven-year contract. As he understood it, he had three years to clean up the mess and three more to win. The university would buy him out if UConn didn't win within six years. Calhoun's initial base salary of $66,520 increased to $70,000 on July 1, the start of the state's new fiscal year. Benefits, including a country club membership, a car that assistant coach Dave Leitao called a "Dodge Shitbox," membership to the university faculty club (not quite the Oak Room at the Plaza Hotel), and revenues from basketball camps and equipment endorsements increased the new coach's salary to about $125,000 per year.

Calhoun was surprised by how upset his Northeastern players were when he told them of his decision to take the UConn job. Northeastern sophomore Kevin McDuffie, a six foot seven, 235-pound, power forward who banged into competing rebounders and got the ball for Reggie Lewis, had been the object of his coach's scorn on several occasions. Each time Calhoun said tough things to him, McDuffie smiled and said, "Aw, yeah, coach, that's alright." McDuffie cried when Calhoun announced his decision to leave. Reggie Lewis told Calhoun to do what was best for the coach and his family. Lewis was on his way to play with a college all-star team in Japan at the time Calhoun made his decision.

Most of these Northeastern players hated Calhoun at one point or another because of the way their coach drove them, but they came to love Calhoun, who acted as their father figure and taught them about hard work and life.

At the press conference to introduce him as the new UConn coach, Calhoun said, "My teams are family oriented. We care about each other and they want Coach to do whatever is best for Coach and the coach's family. Hopefully, I'll bring the same thing here."

Recruiting was Calhoun's number-one priority. "I expect to see less of Jim now," said his wife Pat on the day her husband was hired. "I know UConn needs players," she continued, "and that means he's going to spend some extra time recruiting." Calhoun called recruits as soon as he accepted the position. He told the media, the fans, and coaches of other programs that "Connecticut's borders are closed," which meant that he intended to keep talented players from leaving the state.

"I really think it's a doable situation," Calhoun said of his ability to transform UConn basketball. Mike Gorman thought that Calhoun took the UConn job with a chip on his shoulder, a good chip. The new UConn coach, who got

Day 1, May 15, 1986. Calhoun didn't smile much in his first season. Calhoun with sons, Jeff (*far left*) and Jim Jr. (*far right*), and wife Pat at his introductory press conference.

University Photograph Collection, Archives & Special Collections at the Thomas J. Dodd Research Center, University of Connecticut Libraries. Photo published with permission.

little respect as the coach of low-profile Northeastern, wanted to show that he was better than the coaching giants at Georgetown, St. John's, and Villanova.

Calhoun felt that UConn would experience success with him as its head coach, but he didn't know what that meant. Would success mean NCAA tournament berths? Challenging the league's big four teams? Big East championships? Sweet 16 and Elite Eight appearances? National championships? Calhoun wasn't sure.

After he heard all this optimism, Phil Chardis of north-central Connecticut's *Journal Inquirer* asked at Calhoun's introductory press conference, "Do you know what you're getting yourself into?" The crowd laughed. Calhoun did not. "Anybody who doesn't do their homework is a fool," the new coach said. Calhoun thought he knew the challenges: recruit players to the middle of nowhere to a program with little appeal; change the culture of the basketball team, athletics department, and university; marshal the resources of a wealthy state; increase fan interest, and, of course, win games.

Days after taking the UConn job, Jim and Pat flew to Puerto Rico for the Big East meetings. When they arrived in their room, they exhaled and looked at each other and Jim said, "Holy shit, what did we get ourselves into?" Then he laughed. Later, Calhoun admitted to Chardis that he didn't know what he was getting himself into.

Twenty-six years after Calhoun told those in attendance at his first press conference at UConn, "Hopefully, when it's all said and done, you'll say, 'He's pretty good,'" he had guided the Huskies to three national championships, seven Big East tournament championships, and 10 regular season conference titles. Calhoun took UConn to 18 NCAA tournaments. So far, his teams have compiled a 46-14 record in the NCAA tournament, including 13 appearances in the Sweet 16, nine in the Elite Eight, and four Final Fours. The coach's over-all record at UConn is 627-244, and the Huskies have averaged 24 wins per season during this period. Prior to Calhoun's arrival, a UConn team never won more than 23 games in a season. Calhoun is also a Naismith Hall of Famer with a career record of 875-381.

Thirteen former Huskies appeared on NBA rosters on opening day of the 2009-2010 season; by comparison, Duke and UCLA had 14 pro players and 13 former North Carolina Tar Heels played in the NBA. UConn's NBA players included all-stars Ray Allen, Richard "Rip" Hamilton, and Caron Butler.

Connecticut basketball never saw success like this before Calhoun arrived.

In 25 years at Connecticut, Calhoun changed a basketball program, a university, a state, and college basketball. He willed a program to national prominence. Bobby Knight, Mike Krzyzewski, Dean Smith—and many other great coaches—cannot make this claim. They took over national programs with winning traditions and an infrastructure to facilitate greatness. Not Calhoun. He inherited a sunken ship. Because of his accomplishments, Jim Calhoun should be regarded as the greatest program builder of all time and the best college basketball coach of his era.

This book explains how he did it.

1

BUILDING A PROGRAM FROM SCRATCH

I Don't Want My Managers
to Have to Clean Up Puke

As the 1986–1987 Huskies walked into the first practice in the Calhoun era at UConn, Guyer Gym was hotter than usual. The windows had been taped shut, newspapers blocked all views, and large garbage pails dotted the gym floor. The doors had been barred so that no one could get in; no one could get out, either. The windows behind the baskets were caged, which gave a prisonlike motif to Guyer. The curved ceiling and structure made the place feel like a Quonset hut. When people complained that UConn basketball had subpar facilities, they had Guyer Gym in mind. The players wore gray t-shirts and tiny shorts. They weren't worthy of official practice gear. They saw no basketballs. At 3 p.m. on October 15, 1986, Coach Calhoun entered Guyer Gym, slammed the door shut, and his era began.

Greg Economou, a walk-on in his first season of basketball after two years on the baseball team, talked to Calhoun before the season. The meetings were cordial and Economou regarded Calhoun as a nice, reserved man. The person in front of Economou now was not the one he met before the season began. This guy was all business.

Calhoun told his new charges that UConn was not the most talented team, but it would be the hardest-working team in the country. Then, he said, "I don't want my managers to clean up puke, so if anyone had to puke, use the pails."

To start practice, Calhoun told the players to run dozens of laps at "full fucking speed" around the gym, which held four basketball courts. That distance was the warm-up. Calhoun held a list of the drills he wanted to run. Between activities, players got little to no rest time and had to run another two to three laps around Guyer. Dean Smith conducted practice in the same way at Carolina. During the few seconds of break at Guyer, many players puked or dry-heaved into the trash cans. As the players sprinted around the courts, Calhoun consulted the list of basketball drills. When the players returned, the next activity began.

As his heart raced while he ran around and across Guyer Gym, Economou saw that his new coach devised down-to-the-second plans for basketball drills, running exercises, and water breaks. To intensify practice and create hardworking players, Calhoun kept everyone moving. On day one, he went to ludicrous speed.

Assistant Coach Dave Leitao transformed into a mad man during the Guyer Gym practice. "Down! Up! Down! Up!" Leitao yelled as the players ran in place, fell, and rose in response to his commands. Then, Coach Leitao ran a foot-fire drill, in which players pumped their feet up and down as if their lower extremities were ablaze. "Start again. Too slow," Leitao said.

"It was like death," freshman point guard Tate George said of the practice. He remembers how hot Guyer was that day and how often players threw up. The most difficult part of the first practice was that "no one could tell you what to expect. Everyone was there for the first time. We didn't have someone [a player] who could say, don't worry, only twenty minutes left." At that time, George said that he didn't understand what it meant to be committed. He would learn.

Calhoun had a long way to go and a short time to get there. He wanted to do what they said couldn't be done. The initial practices started a culture of hard work into which future Husky players stepped.

Another assistant coach, Glen Miller, played at UConn in the early days of the Big East and transferred to play for Calhoun at Northeastern. He said that the first practice established expectations for a work ethic and commitment level. It showed the players what it meant to be a Calhoun-coached Husky. It set the tone for a season and a program.

The players in the basketball torture chamber that day shared similar feelings and emotions — pain, anxiety, and resentment. They started to develop a strong dislike for their new coach and his relentless style. This anger created a shared experience among the players, each of whom had now been Calhouned. For the rest of their lives, these players had a common bond; they were a family created by a crazy coach, who was more like a fox than they knew. These players would share this experience with future Huskies who participated in Camp Calhoun.

At age 15, Calhoun was catching fly balls in center field before a Babe Ruth all-star game when a neighbor yelled over the center field fence, "Jim, your father's dead. You better go home." The future UConn coach learned of his father's death in the same way—shouted out by a neighbor—that his father found out about Calhoun's grandfather's passing. Fred Herget, Calhoun's basketball coach at Braintree High School, just south of Boston, was the only person in Calhoun's house after Calhoun's father died of a heart attack. He taught his player that a basketball coach could be a surrogate father to his players and that a basketball team is a family. Herget cared about Calhoun as a basketball player and a person and he acted as Calhoun's father figure until he died of cancer in 1985.

The 1986–1987 University of Connecticut Huskies. Calhoun's first team in Storrs.

Many of Herget's players didn't understand or appreciate their coach's tactics until after they graduated. "He was so tough on me," Calhoun said of his high school coach. "I can honestly tell you — [I] hated him." Calhoun appreciated the effects of Herget's style after he graduated from high school. He said Herget "was always my best friend until the day he died. He was a wonderful person. But he was the toughest person ever, ever, in my entire life."

Mark Twain once said, "When I was a boy of fourteen, my father was so ignorant I could hardly stand to have the old man around. But when I got to be twenty-one, I was astonished by how much he'd learned in seven years." Players felt the same way about coaches Herget and Calhoun. On the first day of practice and throughout their playing days, many UConn players disliked their coach. After they left Storrs, they appreciated what his style did for them as a team, as players, and as people.

A small wooden box sits on Calhoun's desk with the words "the secret to success" etched on top. The answer — "Hard work!" — sits inside. Calhoun developed his work ethic in and around his hometown of Braintree, Massachusetts. Calhoun's father taught the future coach about hard work. He traveled around the world five times with the Merchant Marine.

When Calhoun graduated from high school, he attended Lowell State — later renamed UMass Lowell — but withdrew to provide for his mother. He worked as a stonecutter and got up for work at five each morning. From this two-year experience, Calhoun learned that he didn't want to be a stonecutter for the rest of his life, but he also gained appreciation for hard work.

Calhoun approached his work as a basketball coach with the mind-set of a stonecutter. On day one, he began to teach his players how to work like stonecutters—long, hard, and under extreme conditions.

Calhoun learned how to develop a program from Herget. Like any college coach, Herget recruited his talent. As Braintree's director of recreation, Herget scouted players on the city's courts. He discovered Calhoun as the future coach played in the Braintree parks as a tall but awkward sixth-grader.

Herget put his players on summertime shooting regimens, which included taking two hundred shots every day. He monitored player development in the summertime because he hired most of his players to work in the city recreation department. Herget made sure that Braintree installed lights on the courts at French's Common behind City Hall so that players like Calhoun could play after dark in the summer.

Inspired by his mentor, Calhoun made sure that the UConn basketball program operated in a first-class manner in everything it did. Parents and friends of players received game tickets in prime locations in the arena. Eventually, though, the athletic department would move them to the side of the court opposite the UConn bench because Calhoun's language was too graphic during games.

Calhoun developed a basketball infrastructure at UConn. He transformed a squash court to a lounge for basketball players so they could study in the field house. He wanted his players to attend study hall in or near the gym after a hard practice. The new coach knew how a real basketball facility and program operated and for the time being, he improvised. If he couldn't have a basketball arena with a study hall, he was going to make one.

While he was the coach at Northeastern, Calhoun visited Chapel Hill, North Carolina, for a week to learn how Dean Smith and his coaching staff created the Carolina family. Smith was the father of a program. Carolina basketball had a familial atmosphere to it.

When Calhoun came to UConn, he sought to build a program, not just a team. Regardless of wins and losses, the first team established the foundation for the future. That team needed to be tough, resilient, and hardworking because Calhoun wanted his program to embody these qualities. Calhoun wanted his UConn teams to be a family and the Big East's version of Carolina.

Calhoun had never lost more than 15 games in any year at Northeastern. He had become allergic to losing—and he wouldn't enjoy his first season at UConn.

We Need a Couple of Guys to Get Us through the Rest of the Season

"They won't lose twenty games, I guarantee you that," said Karl Fogel, Calhoun's assistant for seven years and successor at Northeastern, before his former boss started in Storrs. Early in the season Calhoun said, "If it were up to me, we'd play this season in a five-hundred-seat gym and all the reporters would stay home." He knew.

In Calhoun's first game, an exhibition, UConn lost to the Melbourne (Australia) Tigers, 100–92, at the field house. The night before, Boston College, which experts predicted would battle UConn for the bottom spot in the Big East, beat the Australians by 22 points. Melbourne's Andrew Gaze, who would lead Seton Hall to the national championship game two seasons later, scored 42 points against UConn.

As Calhoun stood before the media for his first postgame press conference at UConn, he said, "We've worked four hard weeks, and it didn't look like it. To break it down technically would be insulting your intelligence."

The players came to a different conclusion. We scored 92 points, that's a lot, good for us. As the players dressed and the managers collected the uniforms in the UConn locker room, Calhoun barreled in and told the equipment manager to "get the practice stuff ready." The entire team and the managers did a double take. What? Continuing a strategy he used at Northeastern, Calhoun held a practice after a game to address unacceptable play.

The players returned to the court 15 minutes after the game ended. Parents, friends, the media, and workers, among others, were still in the building when the team went back on the floor. The cleanup crew, in the process of raising the hoops to the rafters to prevent students from playing on the main court, lowered the baskets for the team to use.

When the UConn team hit the court, Calhoun informed his players that they would learn how to play defense if it took all night. For the next couple of hours, the team ran every defensive drill known to mankind and some Calhoun devised along the way. Calhoun coaches to perfection. He believes that if he gives in on perfection, then he doesn't serve his players well as basketball players or as people. Calhoun despises laziness and mental mistakes.

One miserable defeat after another characterized Calhoun's first year at UConn. After UConn beat the University of Massachusetts (UMass) by four

Calhoun's first game at UConn. Melbourne (Australia) Tigers 100–UConn 92. November 13, 1986, Field House, Storrs, Connecticut.

in Calhoun's first regular season game as the Huskies' head coach, it lost the next game by two in overtime at Yale. Storrs legend has it that following the game, Calhoun told his team, "They kicked your ass and now they're going to the library."

During halftime of a road loss, Calhoun kicked a roll-away chalkboard, which flipped upon impact and trapped the coach's foot within it. Calhoun lost his balance and fell to the floor—the entire chalkboard followed. Boom! There sat the UConn coach in a chalkboard sandwich.

Not one player made a sound.

No laugh.

No snicker.

No smirk.

Nothing.

That's how scary it was to play for Calhoun, said one player there at the time. The players waited for Calhoun to get up and finish yelling at them.

Howie Dickenman has said that Calhoun is so intense that the coach often doesn't hear anyone or anything during the game. Calhoun exhibited this intensity well before he arrived in Storrs. During games as a high school player, to encourage his teammates to play harder, Calhoun would snap their jockstraps and say, "Get off your ass!"

On December 9, 1986, Dickenman missed the only game during his 14-year tenure as UConn's assistant and associate head coach. Instead of accompanying the team to Boston University, Dickenman delivered a national letter of intent to a recruit in New Orleans. About 15 minutes after the scheduled start of the UConn-BU game, Dickenman called a friend in Connecticut to find out the score.

The coach's friend said the game was not on TV or the radio. Convinced that his friend was wrong, Dickenman asked, "Are you sure you had the right station? Did you try all the channels?" "Howie," his friend said, "it's not on." It wasn't.

On the way to play BU in Boston, UConn had faced a Mercury Bobcat on the Massachusetts Turnpike near the town of Auburn, and as would happen often that season on the court, the Huskies lost. As UConn traveled east on the icy Mass Pike en route to the game, Watson "Watt" Wordsworth, the team's bus driver, screamed, "Oh my God! Oh my God!" as he tried to avoid the Bobcat, which had crashed into the guardrail and stalled in the middle of the highway with no lights on.

The team bus rammed the car. It fishtailed and pinballed from the median, to the side of the road, and back to the median, where it stopped. Wordsworth stood up, said, "My God, I killed her," and ran off the bus. Calhoun thought the bus had killed a woman, who let out a piercing scream. As it turned out, the woman was not in her car at the time that the Huskies' bus smashed it. Her scream was so loud because she was outside awaiting help.

At a rest stop on the Mass Pike not far from the site of the accident, Calhoun called BU to postpone the game. At the end of the conversation, however, Calhoun slammed down the phone, boarded the bus, and told his players that the game was on and that they were going to kick BU's ass.

BU officials told Calhoun that UConn had a contractual obligation to play the game. They said, "We want to play the game even if we have to play at midnight." One BU player referred to this game as "Custer's last stand," and said, "I don't know if everyone knew it, but [BU coach Mike] Jarvis really wanted to win bad." Jarvis, who coached the junior varsity team at Northeastern when Calhoun was the head coach, had a tenuous relationship with Calhoun before this game.

The *Boston Globe*'s Joe Burris wrote that a personality mismatch between the coaches created some of the tensions during the 1972-1973 season when Calhoun served as Northeastern's head coach and Jarvis coached junior varsity. Calhoun had trouble recruiting Cambridge Rindge & Latin (CR&L) players when Jarvis was that school's head coach. According to one of his assistants, Calhoun and his staff were bothered when Patrick Ewing—who played for Jarvis at CR&L—listed BU but not Northeastern as one of the five schools he might attend. The rivalry intensified when Calhoun and Jarvis coached Northeastern and BU, respectively.

The players waited aboard the first bus, which was no longer fit to drive, for about two-and-a-half hours for a second bus to come from Storrs. UConn arrived at 8:50 for the 8 p.m. game, and BU gave the Huskies less than 30 minutes to warm up. BU claimed that the window to televise the game was about to close and that the game needed to be played immediately. As a compromise, Calhoun bought an extra 10 minutes.

During the game, benches cleared after UConn guard Phil Gamble exchanged elbows with a BU player. The players pushed each other all the way to the hockey boards at BU's arena, but no one was ejected.

At the half, UConn's statistician told Calhoun that the official scorer had shortchanged UConn by two points; the media and everyone else at courtside said the same thing. Calhoun lobbied for the points but stopped when the official scorer began to cry. "What was I to do?" Calhoun asked. "Punch her? She cried and left."

After waiting on the frigid Mass Pike for two hours, UConn players gave new meaning to the cliché ice-cold shooting. They shot 36 percent from the floor and 57 percent from the foul line. Gamble finished his UConn career with a 40.6 shooting percentage from three-point range, but that night he missed all of his 11 shots from the field. Cliff Robinson scored 26 but missed 14 of 20 free throws. When asked about the effect of UConn's trip on the Huskies' performance, Jarvis responded, "Are we trying to find excuses for UConn?"

After the game, an 80-71 BU win, Calhoun vowed never to return to BU, and to this day, UConn has not played the Terriers in Boston.

In the same year, its third year in Division I, the University of Hartford, which played some of its games in the Hartford Civic Center in an attempt to improve its stature, defeated UConn in the Connecticut Mutual Classic. "They beat us, simple as that," Calhoun said. "We'll soar. Give us time and support and we'll soar." A coach needed imagination, vision, and resiliency to make this claim.

The 61-53 loss to Providence College at the Hartford Civic Center on January 24, 1987, is not memorable for what happened on the court. PC played in the

Final Four that season, and UConn was the worst team in the Big East. Robinson and Gamble became ineligible after this game. UConn had a higher academic eligibility standard than the NCAA. These two players were unable to raise their respective cumulative GPAs high enough to remain eligible.

Robinson and Gamble accounted for 44 percent of the Huskies' offense in UConn's first 16 games of the 1986–1987 season. Calhoun pleaded their case before a university appeals board, which denied the coach's request for the players' reinstatement. "You are nothing but accountants, not educators," he said.

According to Calhoun, Robinson and Gamble had received bad advice. An academic advisor assigned a pre-med biology course to the players because it fulfilled a requirement and fit their schedules. Calhoun called this unbelievable. Robinson and Gamble continued to practice with the team, but sat out the rest of the season.

Calhoun thought that UConn may not have enough players to field a team. He told the coaches of other sports at UConn that he needed bodies. If you have any athletes who want to work out for four for five weeks, send them my way, he said. On the day Robinson and Gamble became ineligible, Calhoun said, "We'll look in the cafeterias and dorms. There has to be people. We need a couple of guys to get us through the rest of the season." Bobby Knight at Indiana and Coach K at Duke didn't need to make similar solicitations.

In Calhoun's first season, UConn lost 10 games by 10 points or more and seven of those defeats were by at least 15 points.

Two of UConn's three conference wins showed that Calhoun could motivate and coach. In the first game without Robinson and Gamble, freshmen guards Tate George and Steve Pikiell scored 15 and 14 points and played 38 and 40 minutes, respectively, to lead the Huskies to a six-point victory over BC before about 3,300 at Boston Garden.

During the first half against Seton Hall at the Hartford Civic Center, Seton Hall's Mark Bryant knocked Steve Pikiell and Greg Economou out of the game. Bryant, a six foot nine, 245-pounder, played monster for Seton Hall. As the conveyor belt to UConn's bench and training table rolled, Calhoun turned to assistant coaches Dickenman and Bill Cardarelli and asked what he should do. Calhoun had five players left who were neither hurt nor walk-ons. Hey, you make the big bucks, you decide, the assistants said.

Calhoun walked down the thin bench and summoned Brian Hall into action. Hall, a goalie on UConn's soccer team and a finalist for Mr. Basketball while a high school student in South Dakota, answered Calhoun's call for players after Robinson and Gamble could no longer play. With a soccer goalie and former baseball player on the roster, the running joke became that UConn had more athletes from other teams than they had basketball players. Calhoun didn't laugh.

Hall told Calhoun that he could kick the ball in the basket against Seton Hall, if necessary. Calhoun laughed, but only after the game. Hall played 60 seconds as the *MASH* unit patched up another player.

This game was senior day for Gerry Besselink, who was playing his final home game. Besselink made a free throw with 45 seconds to go to extend UConn's lead to two. He grabbed 13 rebounds against Seton Hall and averaged a team-high 10.7 rebounds per game for the season. Not until Emeka Okafor in 2004 would another Husky average double digits in rebounds. After the Huskies stole the ball from the Pirates, UConn had its third conference victory of the season, its ninth and last win overall: UConn 56–Seton Hall 54.

The UConn players celebrated at center court before they went to the locker room. The 8,130 fans asked for a curtain call until UConn came back to the court and bowed. The players—including Robinson and Gamble in regular clothes—returned to the team's free throw line and waved to the fans, who chanted "Gerry . . . Gerry" and "UConn . . . UConn." The fans haven't responded that way to a UConn win since that day.

Commenting on the crowd's reaction, Calhoun said, "It was terrific. Five times to the NCAA tournament [as coach at Northeastern] and I never felt the way I felt during that." Calhoun wants to win every game, but this one was special. "Somebody said I have two wishes left . . . and they're right, I used one today."

In the last game of Calhoun's first season, against eighth-seeded BC in the Big East tournament, ninth-seeded UConn led until 10 seconds remained, when Boston College took the lead for good: BC 61–UConn 59. In the locker room after the game, Calhoun promised his team and coaches that UConn would never have another 9–19 season.

Tate George was the object of Calhoun's wrath in the 1986–1987 season. When any of Calhoun's teams make a mistake, the coach often blames the point guard, even if that player did nothing wrong. Tate found that out. "A lot of us didn't have our fathers in the household, so you go from having your mother raise you to having a man screaming in your face; it doesn't go over very well when you're the man of your household." And scream, Calhoun did. George took a couple of years to realize that he shouldn't take Calhoun's words or actions personally.

George had "a lost feeling" when Calhoun remained silent. Typically, he wished that his coach would shut up, but when Calhoun went quiet, George didn't know what to do. In the BU game, Calhoun said nothing and decided to "let us run ragged," George said. The point guard realized how much he needed his coach as a result of this tactic. "When a father figure doesn't reprimand you," George said of the silent treatment, "you don't know whether you are doing right or wrong."

> **CALHOUN RULES**
> Make and Keep
> Bold Promises

In the summer after his freshman year, George received frequent reminders from everyone that Yale and Hartford had beaten UConn during the season. He knew that Calhoun would hold him responsible for the way UConn played. George realized that it was up to him to make sure that the Huskies never lost to these teams again.

For the first of two summers, Calhoun told George that he would recruit a replacement for him unless the player's performance improved. Years later, George realized that his coach said these kinds of things to keep him motivated and make him better. He also knew that Calhoun was serious: if George couldn't lead the team to victory, Calhoun would find someone else who could.

Many players can't recall seeing a happy Jim Calhoun. If a player averaged 10 points a game, the coach wanted 14 the next year. This attitude allowed Calhoun to become the best developer of talent in college basketball. Under Calhoun, for example, Reggie Lewis went from receiving scholarship offers from only Northeastern and Towson State to being the 22nd pick of the 1987 NBA draft.

Pikiell averaged 8.2 points in more than 30 minutes per game, which exceeded the player's expectations. When Pikiell visited his coach's office at the end of the basketball season, he discovered that Calhoun wasn't satisfied with this performance. Calhoun told Pikiell that he needed to emulate Billy Donovan, who had just led Providence to the Final Four and was about to begin a 44-game career in the NBA.

At the season's conclusion, UConn's 9-19 overall record and its 3-13 conference mark indicated that the Huskies remained in the Big East's basement. The number of losses tied the most defeats in a season, set by the 1968-1969 team, which went 5-19. UConn was so bad in the 1986-1987 season that Calhoun recommended that each player hand, not pass, the ball to the next player to avoid turnovers. His strategy was to hang on for 35 minutes and try to win in the end.

Calhoun was cut from his eighth grade basketball team. Despite more talent and greater personal success in football and baseball, basketball was

Calhoun's favorite sport. "From [the day I was cut], I didn't put the ball down," said Calhoun. "I would shoot in the rain. My parents would scream for me to come out of the cold. It might have been two degrees, but it didn't matter because I had to sink the next shot." Two years after getting cut, Calhoun earned the rare distinction of making the varsity team as a sophomore. This man knew persistence.

Calhoun finished eight marathons, four each in Boston and New York. As he ran across a bridge during one New York Marathon, he stubbed his toe on a grate that was covered by AstroTurf. He noticed that his running shoe turned red and figured he had broken the skin on his toe. The pain was sharp and Calhoun didn't realize that all five toenails were broken. What do you do when you break all your toenails while running a marathon? "You just keep going," said Calhoun, who finished the race.

At one point at least during his first season in Storrs, Calhoun told his wife that he thought he'd "made a huge mistake by taking the UConn job." He said, "We are out of here. We are *out* of here." His old job looked better than his current one. Reggie Lewis and Northeastern beat defending national-champion Louisville in the Great Alaska Shootout, won 27 games, and captured the America East regular and postseason titles. Lewis won conference player of the year for the third consecutive season. He finished as Northeastern's all-time leading scorer. At the time of his graduation, Lewis's 2,709 points were good for ninth on the NCAA all-time scoring list.

Calhoun referred to his first year as UConn coach as the lowest moment in his life, but he couldn't quit until he turned the program into a winner. To accomplish that task, Calhoun employed the mentality of a marathoner, not a sprinter. Like he did as a high school basketball player and New York City marathon runner, Calhoun kept going.

3

You've Got to Learn How to Win

When Calhoun and his staff recruited in the coach's early years in Storrs, they sold recruits on the idea of competing against the country's best players, like Alonzo Mourning, Derrick Coleman, and Malik Sealy. Georgetown, Syracuse, St. John's, and Villanova had established stars including Patrick Ewing, Dwayne "Pearl" Washington, Chris Mullin, and Ed Pinckney. Calhoun and his coaches turned UConn's lack of tradition into an asset: "Come to a place where you're not going to be the next something. Come to a place where you can be the first. This can be your stage," Calhoun said.

Not everyone viewed the Big East as an advantage for UConn. Before Calhoun arrived and even in the early days of the coach's tenure, many fans wanted to return to playing against the universities of Rhode Island, Maine, Vermont, and New Hampshire. They believed that Georgetown, St. John's, Syracuse, and Villanova would beat UConn forever. Calhoun did not.

Before a December game against Purdue in 1986, the nation's fourth-best team at that time, Calhoun compared his team to the Boilermakers: "We're at least two good recruiting years away from being on a level with them." Less than a month later, he told a reporter, "You need stuff for your paper. I need players." Calhoun believed then and continued to adhere to the principle that good players make good coaches. Without talent, UConn would continue to lose.

In the staff's first full recruiting period, Dickenman pursued six foot eleven center Sean Muto of Mechanicsburg, Pennsylvania. As Muto approached UConn for his on-campus visit, he told Dickenman that the ride to Storrs wasn't that bad. Dickenman asked why the recruit assumed the worst. Another Big East coach told Muto that he needed to take a helicopter to get to UConn. Muto attended the site dedication ceremony for the Gampel Pavilion. He and Calhoun went to a Lionel Richie concert at the Hartford Civic Center. That's probably why Muto selected St. John's.

Calhoun and his staff turned Storrs's rural character into an asset: come to UConn, they said, the only Big East school not in a city. Come to UConn, and enjoy a college campus away from the dangers of urban America.

Calhoun regarded Muto's decision to eliminate PC, BC, and Seton Hall before UConn as a good sign. He said, "As long as we're second, as long as we keep doing what we're doing, we'll get kids." He believed.

In year one, the new program landed a top 100 recruit from another part of the country. To Calhoun, Lyman DePriest's recruitment "made a statement that the University of Connecticut could go into a city like Detroit and get one of their top players."

When Dickenman told DePriest, the 72nd-rated senior by recruiting expert Bob Gibbons, that he coached at UConn, the player said, "Alaska?" DePriest wanted to play in the Big East. He starred on a defense-oriented team in high school and Calhoun emphasized defense. "This is a team sport, and what you have, we could use here," Calhoun told him. The UConn coach wanted DePriest's toughness. He got it.

Robinson, Gamble, and George impressed DePriest, who saw an opportunity to play right away at UConn. Iowa, Iowa State, Michigan State, and Wisconsin also expressed interest. PAC-10 schools and some others recruited him to play wide receiver in football, another sport at which he excelled in high school. DePriest wanted to play basketball in college. In his senior year of high school, he suffered a high-ankle sprain during football season. Afraid about the lingering effects of the injury on his college basketball prospects, DePriest signed with UConn as soon as he could.

Calhoun used the Big East to recruit John Gwynn from DeMatha High School in Hyattsville, Maryland. Under Hall of Fame coach Morgan Wootten, DeMatha produced many collegiate and professional stars, including Adrian Dantley, Danny Ferry, and Sidney Lowe. Gwynn, who grew up in the Washington, DC, area, wanted to play for Georgetown, but Coach John Thompson had no interest in him. North Carolina State, Maryland, and some other Atlantic Coast Conference (ACC) schools were among Gwynn's choices. Gwynn choose UConn because the Huskies played in the Big East.

Chris Smith, of Kolbe Cathedral in Bridgeport, was the state's primary prospect in 1987, even though he was still a junior. If Calhoun wanted to close Connecticut's borders, he had to keep Villanova, Boston College, and other Big East teams from landing Smith.

In 1987–1988, Gamble and Robinson's grades improved and they reestablished academic eligibility. Calhoun begged them to stay. Despite the suspensions and the attractiveness of these players to other schools, UConn's two best players remained in Storrs.

In UConn's January 16, 1988, game at Syracuse, Robinson made a free throw with two seconds left in regulation to win the game, 51–50. UConn held a Syracuse team that averaged 95.5 points per game to 50, the fewest points scored by the Orangemen in a home game since they moved into the Carrier Dome in the fall of 1980.

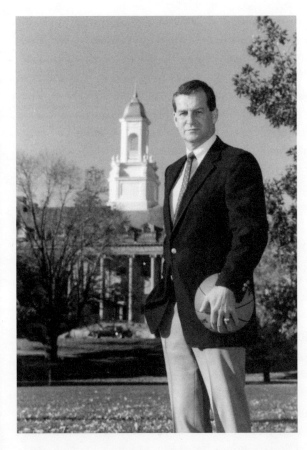

Calhoun looks ready as he prepares for his second season. Fall 1987. Wilbur Cross building on the UConn campus, Storrs, Connecticut.

University Photograph Collection, Archives & Special Collections at the Thomas J. Dodd Research Center, University of Connecticut Libraries. Photo published with permission.

The Huskies took the four-hour bus trip back to Storrs after the game. A downed tree closed Route 195, the major access road to campus, and the UConn bus turned around and took Route 44 to get home. The team arrived on campus at about 6 a.m.

As part of standard operating procedure, the players waited in front of their lockers to get the week's schedule. Calhoun would inform them of times for practice and study hall. If UConn could beat ninth-ranked Syracuse on the road, Calhoun told his team, then the players could exert more energy and effort to defeat the rest of the teams in the Big East.

Practice starts in an hour.

This 7 a.m. practice rivaled the first-day Guyer Gym experience. It focused on running. Most practices included short breaks between drills. Not this one. Don't get happy after a big win, Calhoun said. We can do better.

Cliff Robinson was the first Husky to receive Calhoun's version of the star treatment. "You must be ready to practice when I walk through the curtain at three," Calhoun said to his team. One day, Calhoun walked through the partition and saw something that alarmed him. "What are you doing?" Calhoun asked Robinson. "I am tying my shoe," Robinson said. "Ok," Calhoun said. "I'll tell you what, why don't you go and wait in the stands." As Robinson watched from the bleachers, his teammates ran eight suicide sprints. They paid for his mistake.

As a program in progress, UConn lost several close games in Calhoun's second year, the worst of which came against 12th-ranked Syracuse at home in February. Syracuse's center, Rony Seikaly, a 54 percent free throw shooter, made two at the line to tie the game. UConn used its last two time-outs to set up the final play. Eight seconds remained.

As he struggled to inbound the ball at midcourt, UConn's Jeff King panicked and threw the ball to Syracuse's Stevie Thompson, who thunder-dunked the ball to win the game for the Orangemen. Because one pass shifted them from the verge of victory to a defeat, the Huskies took a while to recover from this loss.

Despite this defeat, the UConn program progressed in Calhoun's second year. UConn increased its number of league wins by one from the previous season; it beat Syracuse and Georgetown. Half of UConn's losses in the conference came by six points or fewer. After a last-second defeat at Georgetown, Robinson said, "I guess you can say that we can play with everybody in the Big East. But that's not a good feeling when you're not winning."

In March of 1988, the NIT selected UConn as part of its tournament field. In the first-round game at West Virginia, Tate George sent the game to overtime when he hit an off-the-glass shot late in regulation. UConn won, 65-57. Afterward, Calhoun told his point guard, "The game never should have come down to the last shot; you led us down the wrong path."

"If you did something well," George said, "it was never quite good enough for Coach Calhoun," who worked players to the point of mental and physical exhaustion without so much as a pat on the back or a nod of approval. Just when the player was about to crack, Calhoun said something to encourage him. Economou remembers when Calhoun told him that he was important to the team. Before that little talk, Economou heard little from the coach. After that, he wanted to continue to run through the wall.

Dave Solomon, who covered UConn and the New York Giants for the *New Haven Register*, said that Calhoun reminded him of former Giants coach Bill Parcells. According to Solomon, both men had a gift to drive players to the point where they hate the coach but then they could reel them back to the happy family.

Players get better because they want to prove Calhoun wrong. "Coach tears you down and picks you up," said George, "but he didn't let you fall too far." Calhoun told George to "prove to me that you can play. Show me."

After the win at West Virginia, UConn beat Louisiana Tech at the Hartford Civic Center to advance to the NIT quarterfinals. The Huskies couldn't host VCU in Hartford because the Civic Center had booked the *Muppet Babies*. VCU's home—the Richmond Coliseum —had scheduled a George Thorogood and the Delaware Destroyers concert for that night.

NIT officials and the two teams concluded that UConn's field house would be the site of the quarterfinal game. UConn had won its previous 21 games in Storrs, but it beat U.S. International, Delaware State, Maryland Eastern Shore, and St. Copious of Where? during that stretch. It hadn't played a team as good as VCU.

"It was about a hundred and fifty-five degrees inside," Dickenman said of the field house that night. Future play-by-play man Joe D'Ambrosio estimated the temperature to be at least 90 degrees. "I can still remember Jim Calhoun taking off his jacket, and he never did that," he said. The heat shouldn't have bothered the Huskies, who had practiced in more intense conditions in that building.

That night's attendance—4,801—was the largest to watch a game at the field house. UConn sports information director Tim Tolokan noticed a haze that hung over the court that night and asked the director of the field house about it. "Tim, the crowd is making so much noise that they are shaking the dust off the rafters," she said.

The crowd that night showed the program what a home-court advantage felt like. It chanted "UConn, UConn, UConn" throughout the game and repeated "Final Four" near the end. "All UConn has to do is play here more often," VCU's coach said of the field house. "I think they could beat a lot of people here."

In the spring of 1988, this 72-61 win ranked in the top five victories of all time for the program. Winning was new. The students ran onto the court to congratulate the players at the game's conclusion.

The Huskies met BC in the NIT semifinals at Madison Square Garden. BC guard Dana Barros had made at least one three-point shot in each of his previous 39 games—an NCAA record. He made five in the first half against UConn. His back-to-back threes at the end of the half gave the Eagles a 41-33 advantage. Barros scored 22 of BC's 41 points in the first half.

Calhoun's first star, Cliff Robinson, and his first big win at UConn. UConn 72–VCU 61. March 25, 1988, Field House, Storrs, Connecticut.

University Photograph Collection, Archives & Special Collections at the Thomas J. Dodd Research Center, University of Connecticut Libraries. Photo published with permission.

Accounts vary on what happened at halftime. Dickenman's version is that he, Calhoun, and Leitao talked strategy and the head coach concluded that DePriest—the team's toughest player—would guard Barros. DePriest's strength would allow him to get physical with Barros. UConn player James Spradling said that Lyman was built like a linebacker, and hit like one too. Ever the bulldog, Coach Dickenman would tell DePriest to ram into players in practice. More than once, Spradling was on the end of DePriest's physical play. "Do it again," Dickenman instructed and DePriest hit harder each time. The physical tests taken in Calhoun/Dickenman-coached practices served UConn well against BC on this night.

Calhoun said, "Who is going to guard this guy?" "Motherfucker" or other variations of that word may have been used in this question. In his account, DePriest stood up and said, "I'll take him." He had no idea that Barros scored that many points in the first half.

Both versions confirm that Calhoun told DePriest, "Lyman, no screens, no picks. Run through every one of them. Don't let Barros touch the ball." In the first half, BC players acted like concrete barriers that enabled Barros to catch the ball without a defender near him. In the second half, DePriest disintegrated one BC screen after another and the Eagles' picks weren't as square or solid as they had been earlier in the game. During timeouts, DePriest waited for Barros outside BC's huddle. It worked. "Barros gave up. He slowed his pace," DePriest said. Because Barros stopped trying to score, DePriest had a much easier time guarding him in the second part of the half. Barros had two points on two shots in the second half; UConn won by six.

ALL–CALHOUN ERA, BEST DUNK
- - - - - - - - - - - - - - -
Lyman DePriest on Perry Carter UConn vs. Ohio State March 30, 1988 NIT Finals, Madison Square Garden

Robinson scored 29, but DePriest was the game's star. The 1988 NIT semifinal is "The DePriest Game." "The game turned me into a defensive specialist," DePriest said. He became the bar against which other great Husky defenders would be measured in the future. To this day, Calhoun regards DePriest and center Rod Sellers as the toughest players he coached and characterizes DePriest as his toughest defender.

Before the NIT finals, Calhoun told the Huskies that they were one of six teams still playing and practicing—the two NIT finalists and the Final Four teams were still alive. Calhoun said the picture of the NIT winner goes into the Basketball Hall of Fame in Springfield, Massachusetts, for perpetuity and that he wanted his players to have that honor.

Early in the final game against Ohio State, Lyman DePriest noticed that Perry Carter—who had spurned Calhoun and signed with Ohio State instead of UConn—was distracted on defense and he dunked in Carter's face. With 15:21 remaining in the game, the Huskies trailed by six and Robinson sat on the bench with four fouls. Ohio State coach Gary Williams thought that Robinson's absence would allow his team to win. Calhoun did too; he was scared to death. His team wasn't.

In about eight minutes, UConn tied the score at 46. With less than five minutes left, it had an 11-point lead and a death grip on the NIT championship, which it won by five. Gamble scored a game-high 25 points and was named the most valuable player of the tournament.

"You've got to learn how to win," Calhoun said after the team's victory. The NIT exposed UConn to winning. UConn fans stormed the floor and MSG security, not used to this kind of hysteria for the NIT, needed 15 minutes to get the students off the court.

The team bus rolled up to the tollbooth on the East Hartford side of the Charter Oak Bridge at 2:30 a.m., and two toll takers pounded on it in excitement. They were forerunners to much larger crowds that greeted national championship teams in the future. The NIT championship was the biggest thing that happened to UConn basketball since the Huskies beat Hofstra in double-overtime and advanced to the Sweet 16 in 1976.

UConn had made its first postseason, national tournament since it lost in the first round of the NIT in 1982. It notched its first postseason win since a victory at South Florida in the opening round of the 1981 NIT. UConn made the NIT quarterfinals for the first time since it lost a heartbreaker to Boston College in 1974, and it won that tournament for the first time in program history.

The Huskies had never won more than two games in a single national, postseason tournament until they notched five to capture the NIT. They finished the season at 20-14, the program's first winning record in five seasons and its first 20-win campaign since 1980–1981. UConn had also won its first Big East tournament game since the conference's initial tournament in 1980.

The NIT championship didn't turn UConn into a national power. CBS televised none of UConn's games in the next season. The Huskies needed to convince CBS that it deserved to be on the network's limited regular season television schedule. The 1988 season did not ignite Huskymania. UConn's NIT Final Four games weren't sellouts (10,453 in the game versus Boston College and 13,779 against Ohio State), and one would have expected UConn fans to pack Madison Square Garden if hysteria were in full bloom. Despite improvements on and off the court, UConn basketball was still a work in progress

When a program starts with nothing, an NIT championship is gold. Calhoun needed to build off this title and win Big East championships, qualify for the NCAA tournament, and win games there. UConn wasn't ready for that, but the program had the right trajectory.

Had the program advanced far enough to close the borders?

4

The Most Important Recruit in UConn Basketball History

Chris Smith from Kolbe Cathedral High School in Bridgeport tested Calhoun's "borders are closed" strategy. Villanova and Boston College wanted him, and in the past one of the two would have gotten him. Calhoun and his staff started to recruit Smith as soon as they took over. They realized that a rejection by Smith would damage their ability to sign top-rated players from inside and outside Connecticut.

Calhoun, Dickenman, and Leitao went to Bridgeport in September of 1987 to sell Smith on UConn. In Smith's mother's living room, the coaching staff tried to convince Smith, his mother, Lola, and Jo-Anne Jakab, Kolbe Cathedral's athletic director and an advisor to the star player, that Smith could help build a program at UConn.

The Smiths didn't know where UConn was. Lola expressed reservations about the academic setbacks faced by UConn basketball players. Once Smith figured out where UConn was, he wasn't impressed. "The first time I went into the field house," he said, "I couldn't believe it. I'm thinking to myself, 'This is Big East basketball?' There were birds flying around inside, other teams practicing at the same time. It was crazy." Despite these drawbacks, Smith liked UConn's coaches and players.

Throughout his years of extensive recruiting, Dickenman kept three-by-five index cards on every player he recruited. He doesn't need the cards, though, because he seems to remember everything. On Smith's card, Dickenman wrote, "Mom not sold," and she did not see UConn as a "name" school. He wrote that Chris liked UConn a lot.

Dickenman connected with Jakab; both were Central Connecticut graduates. Jakab said to the Smiths at the meeting among the player, coaches, and family, "Chris, you should go to UConn." Dickenman thought that the location of Smith's high school — 33 Calhoun Place — indicated that Smith would sign with the Huskies.

The day before Smith visited UConn, Dickenman and Leitao drove to the Mark Furniture Warehouse in Vernon to get new couches, furniture, and fixtures for the basketball office. "Can you get it there in a day?" Dickenman asked the sales representative. "We need it tomorrow and it needs to be new." Everything had to impress Smith.

Dickenman suggested to Jakab that Smith visit Villanova during a weekend on which the Wildcats had a home football game. As it turned out, the Wildcats played UConn on that particular Saturday. What a coincidence.

Smith visited Boston College during the basketball team's exhibition opener. Dickenman thought it would be good for Smith to see the crowd and the relative enthusiasm at BC games. He knew that other New England schools lacked the fan base and attention that UConn received. When Smith went to the BC game, two tumbleweeds sat in the stands. "It worked out real well," Dickenman said.

Smith recognized the opportunity UConn and Calhoun presented to him. At the press conference to declare his intentions to sign with UConn, Smith said, "I'm from Connecticut. I might as well stay home and be part of it. Hopefully, some day I can lead them to the NCAA championship." A national championship? The Huskies hadn't qualified for the NCAA tournament since Smith was a second-grader.

Smith gave an identity to UConn. He dribbled the ball in a distinctive manner: low to the floor and side-to-side. His dribble came with a lot of wrist action, so much so that it appeared as if Smith was carrying the ball with each dribble. Today, every player dribbles this way, but at the time, Smith was unique (although Laura Lishness, the point guard on UConn's women's team and a year older than Smith, dribbled the same way). Elite players who competed with and against Smith in the summer knew UConn because that team had the kid with the distinctive dribble.

Dickenman realized the effect of Chris Smith one day while he was in the Detroit airport. As Dickenman engaged in conversation, someone asked him what he did, and Dickenman said he was an assistant coach for UConn. The person moved his feet apart and imitated the Smith dribble.

Calhoun had closed the borders.

5

We Weren't Just a Gnat Anymore

In its poll before the start of the 1988–1989 season, the *Sporting News* ranked UConn the 12th best team in the country because the Huskies had returned their core from the NIT championship team and added Smith. UConn appeared ready to qualify for the NCAA tournament for the first time since 1979, its last year in the Eastern College Athletic Conference (ECAC), as well as to contend for its first Big East championship. The fans expected as much.

It was not yet to be; the close losses that characterized the previous season reemerged and were even worse in this campaign. These two years of narrow defeats served as growing pains for a program on the rise.

During the regular season, UConn led at Georgetown until the last minute but lost by four. PC beat UConn by two in the Hartford Civic Center and four in Providence. The Huskies lost in overtime at Villanova and by three to number-12 Seton Hall, which finished the season as the national runner-up.

Calhoun said that the 1988–1989 season was his hardest at UConn because he knew the program had made progress. "We weren't just a gnat anymore," he said. "We started to get real close to folks. And we had some real, real tough games where we just didn't get over the top. But progress had been made. We knew we could do it. And, to be honest, I was a little taken aback by people saying, well, he's good enough to get us going but he really can't get it."

UConn finished the Big East regular season in seventh place with a record of 6–10 and 16–11, overall. The season ended at the field house, where the University of Alabama at Birmingham (UAB) defeated UConn in the NIT quarterfinals. "In retrospect, you had to go through one of those seasons where you were close, but not close enough," wrote Calhoun. "Then the choice became building on that, or being discouraged by it." The choice was clear by the end of January 1990.

In June, the NBA invited Cliff Robinson and other probable first-round picks to attend the draft at Madison Square Garden. In his senior season, he averaged 20 points and 7.4 rebounds per game. His six foot ten frame, long and lanky body, and athletic game made many think he could excel in the NBA. None of the teams that picked in the first round held this opinion. Robinson was the last invitee sitting in the Green Room at Madison Square Garden. The commentators and cameras focused upon Robinson, who left

Madison Square Garden with slumped shoulders and head down before his name was called. The Portland Trail Blazers used a second round pick, the 36th overall, to draft him.

Of all the players drafted that year, Robinson would have the longest NBA career, retiring after the 2006–2007 season at the age of 40. At worst, Robinson is the fourth best player from that draft, which included Shawn Kemp, Tim Hardaway, and Vlade Divac. The NBA gave its Sixth Man Award to Robinson in 1993. Robinson played in the 1994 All-Star game and made All-NBA defensive second team in 2000 and 2002.

Despite falling to the second round, Robinson was UConn's highest NBA draft pick since center Thomas "Toby" Kimball was selected 25th in 1965. Kimball was the lone UConn player to remain in the NBA for longer than one season before Robinson, who played in 1,380 NBA games, 513 more professional games than *all* the pre-Calhoun pro players from UConn combined.

During the mid-1980s, better high school players began to select colleges based upon which coach could get them into the pros. Robinson, a legitimate All-American candidate, gave a reputation to Calhoun and UConn as a coach and program that produced top-flight NBA players. Robinson started to make UConn more attractive to elite players who wanted to earn megamoney as pros.

UConn's top recruit from the high school class of 1989 was Scott Burrell, an all-state player in basketball and baseball from Hamden, Connecticut. He was also a standout quarterback. Ron Carbone, Burrell's high school football coach, said, "I'll never forget this one pass he completed. The ball traveled over seventy yards in the air. I think it had frost on it when it finally came down." The football programs at Notre Dame, Penn State, and Miami took an interest in Burrell, but because of the physical pounding he had taken, he retired from football after his junior year in high school.

Dickenman wanted Burrell in the worst way. One day, he read a column that explained why Burrell should attend UConn. Shortly after that, Dickenman took his copy of the newspaper and drove to 331 Evergreen Avenue in Hamden. He still remembers this address off the top of his head. Dickenman put the newspaper under Burrell's doormat and drove to the nearest pay phone. The message was short: "Scott, the newspaper man just delivered your paper to your door. You may want to check under the mat."

The University of Miami was Dickenman's first obstacle. Burrell, a professional pitching prospect who threw in the 90s, considered playing baseball at Miami. In November, however, he signed with UConn to play basketball, which he called his hobby. Dickenman didn't have Burrell yet. In June, he had to compete with the Seattle Mariners, which used the 26th pick overall to take Burrell in the first round of the 1989 major league draft. After the draft, Burrell wasn't sure what he was going to do. Calhoun was certain.

The UConn staff called Burrell six to seven times a week and told Scott that he would be better off if he played baseball and basketball at UConn, competed in the Cape Cod baseball league in the summer, and waited three years to get redrafted. Calhoun thought that Burrell would have the opportunity to play basketball in the Olympics, come close to completing his degree, and develop his baseball skills in three years as a UConn baseball player. He told Burrell that a $100,000 bonus wouldn't amount to much after taxes and three years.

Calhoun knew Burrell and his family better than anyone he had recruited at UConn. He understood that Burrell's parents wanted their son to get a college degree. Sam, Scott's father, had coached Yale's freshman baseball team from 1968 to 1979 and, at the time, was Hillhouse High's baseball coach and an assistant coach for the Yale football team. He delivered the same message to Scott: "You can't dribble a basketball or throw a baseball all your life. You need an education to fall back on."

Burrell decided not to sign with Seattle and instead he tried his hobby in Storrs. He didn't play baseball at UConn but was redrafted by the Toronto Blue Jays in the fifth round of the 1990 draft. Burrell would play in the Blue Jays' organization for two summers. With Burrell, Smith, George, DePriest, Gwynn, and Sellers on the team, UConn would be competitive in 1989–1990. The addition of another player moved the team from the middle of the league to places imagined in dreams.

For the 1989–1990 season, UConn did not return a player who had averaged double-digit scoring in the previous year, but Rod Sellers thought that Gamble and Robinson's departure would help the team. The year before, UConn had relied on them. If the offense didn't depend so much on two players, Sellers reasoned, then Chris Smith may have averaged around 15 points. Sellers went into the season believing that a more-balanced offense would prevent opponents from closing in on one player.

"Every game we lose will be because of what you do," Calhoun said to senior Tate George before the season started. If George didn't play well enough, then Calhoun would start Smith at the point. Calhoun also told George, "This program will take off or you will set it back." Statements like this one made George feel pressure on and off the court at all times.

To show that he was a leader that year, George assumed responsibilities that no other Calhoun-coached player had taken on at UConn. He ran the study

halls and picked up players who were where they weren't
supposed to be. George wanted to keep Calhoun's pressure
off the younger players to hold the team together. According
to George, many of the newer players allowed him to lead.

UConn was 11-2 in the early part of the season, It beat
teams from the ACC, Southeastern Conference (SEC), and Atlantic 10 — but
lost both of its conference games. Boos shook the Hartford Civic Center after
a 64-57 loss to Villanova in December. In more than two decades of covering
UConn basketball, Joe D'Ambrosio said the loudest boos directed toward the
Huskies at a home game came on this night.

In its first game of the new year, UConn lost to 16th-ranked St. John's by 31.
The coach's defensive staple — the 2-2-1 press — wasn't working and the staff
questioned whether to scrap it. "Let's do it better," Calhoun said. The press
stayed. The Chicken Little fans, as Calhoun referred to a large subset of the
UConn fan base, assumed the sky was falling. Wasn't it?

Not to Rod Sellers, who felt that UConn was a good team that hadn't played
its best.

UConn followed an 18-point home win versus Pitt with a 17-point road
victory over Villanova. For most of its next game at Seton Hall, UConn appeared to be on the way to its third straight double-digit win. UConn used
its 2-2-1 press to lead by 16 points with a little more than eight minutes left
in regulation. Scoring droughts hurt UConn throughout the season, and one
in this case allowed Seton Hall to cut its deficit to one with 38 seconds left.
In the past, the Huskies would have lost this kind of game. Freshman Nadav
Henefeld made two free throws to put UConn up by three with 32 seconds to
go; after Seton Hall's Michael Cooper missed a shot — he had connected on
eight in a row — Henefeld fired a pass to Rod Sellers, who rammed the ball
home to seal a win.

The Huskies' three-game conference winning streak marked a first since
the end of the 1982-1983 season.

Then the big boys came to town.

UConn beat Syracuse, the nation's fifth-ranked team, by 11 on ESPN's *Big
Monday*. As UConn fans left the Civic Center following this game, they realized that a Husky win over the Orangemen was special, but not uncommon.
Defeating Georgetown and St. John's — in a seven-day span, no less — would
let everyone know that UConn had changed to an elite team in the league, at
least for one season. At this time, Calhoun was 1-5 against both Georgetown
and St. John's as UConn's head basketball coach.

The *New York Times* rated Georgetown as the nation's fourth best team in its preseason poll because sophomore Alonzo Mourning and junior Dikembe Mutombo had returned. In his freshman year, Mourning (six foot ten) averaged 13 points, seven rebounds, and five blocks per game. Mutombo (seven foot two) blocked two shots a game and redirected many more. UConn would guard these giants with players between six foot five and six foot nine.

When the referee tossed the ball to start the UConn-Georgetown game, the Hoyas were the nation's last unbeaten team. With 1:21 remaining in regulation, the Hoyas' Mark Tillmon stood at the line to shoot two free throws to try to put Georgetown up by one. He missed the first . . . and the second. After that break, Henefeld, Gwynn, and DePriest made seven of eight free throws and UConn won by five.

Henefeld had made five three-pointers, including one to give a 63–60 lead to UConn with 3:31 remaining. Boeheim thought Georgetown and Syracuse would have beaten UConn were it not for Henefeld, a player who changed the UConn program. His story with UConn began in April of 1989, when he visited Storrs for five hours.

Five hours.

Henefeld, a native of Israel, had just concluded a two-day trip to St. John's, which he didn't like. Marv Kessler, a former coach in Israel and at Adelphi University, called Calhoun and said that Henefeld "didn't like St. John's and he didn't think he liked [St. John's coach Lou] Carnesecca, but he loved basketball. . . . Why don't you have him up, he's only going to be here a few more days." Kessler said, "He's good, this kid. Six foot seven. A forward. Handles the ball. Larry Bird." When Calhoun heard Larry Bird, he decided to look at Henefeld.

Leitao picked up Henefeld in New York at 5:30 in the morning, and by nine that night, Nadav was on a plane back to Israel. Henefeld had served three years in the Israeli army, but he played ball more than he played soldier. He wrote 20 letters to American universities but received little feedback. Kessler opened doors for Henefeld at St. John's and UConn.

For Henefeld, Connecticut looked and felt more like a university than St. John's, a commuter school. "I talked with Coach Calhoun and the other coaches and saw the beautiful campus; I said to myself, 'This is the place for me.' St. John's was nice, but if I went there I would have had to live in an apartment, and I wanted to stay in a dormitory. . . . I wanted to experience college life," Henefeld said.

No one from UConn had seen Henefeld play in person. Calhoun did so in July 1989 at the Maccabiah Games in Tel Aviv. Henefeld was named the most valuable player of that tournament. When he returned, Calhoun told his wife

By the time Gampel Pavilion was complete, UConn had climbed from the bottom to the top of the Big East.

Pat that Henefeld "is one of the most interesting players I've ever seen. On offense and defense, he makes everybody else on the team better." With that said, Henefeld had his scholarship.

NCAA rules prohibited Henefeld from practicing as he waited two months to become eligible. Henefeld received a high enough score on the SAT to compete and he holds the distinction of playing in a game—UConn's first exhibition game, against Marathon Oil—before he practiced.

Henefeld played angles well; he was where he was supposed to be. In UConn's first game against Georgetown, Henefeld dominated Dikembe Mutombo despite standing seven inches shorter than the Hoyas' center. Mutombo's line: two points, seven rebounds, and zero blocks in 12 minutes.

Henefeld complained to Calhoun that the media paid too much attention to him and not enough to his teammates. He didn't say much otherwise. Henefeld was quick, but not fast. On defense, he played near the ball. On offense, he knew who to get the ball to and who wasn't hot.

Calhoun told Henefeld to shoot more, but Nadav preferred passing. He complimented Henefeld during the season more than any other player he has coached at UConn, except perhaps Kemba Walker. Calhoun calls Chris Smith the most important player in program history, but Nadav Henefeld can also make a serious claim to that title.

Beyond the importance of any one player, Sellers said that the team's closeness turned these Huskies into a winner. More than half of the team lived in the same dorm, McMahon Hall, which stands next to Gampel. No matter where they went, the Huskies had seven or eight of their teammates with them. On Saturday nights after games, the team would be together at Ted's or Huskies. After the players spent time with their girlfriends on Sunday morning, they got together that night.

After UConn beat Central Connecticut by 22 in the final game at the field house, St. John's came to Storrs for opening night at Gampel Pavilion. Big East founder Dave Gavitt had referred to UConn basketball as a sleeping giant when the Big East was formed because the school was the only public university in the league and the fan base was rabid. The Huskies had hit the snooze button before the Calhoun era began. In much the same way, Gampel Pavilion was a sleeping giant. In 1983, the state promised to build a $14 million sports complex at UConn, with 1985 its projected opening date. The university broke ground for the complex on June 29, 1987. Governor William A. O'Neill recognized that the project was vital and the construction continued. No O'Neill, no Gampel Pavilion.

The first game at Gampel showed how far UConn had traveled as a program and as a team. The Huskies' facilities were now as good as or even better than most in the conference and the 1990 team was better than most in the conference. UConn avenged its 31-point loss to St. John's with a 14-point victory. In 25 days, it had improved by 45 points. The Huskies won 12 of their first 14 games in the new on-campus facility and through the 2010–2011 season, they would go on to post a 138–20 record at Gampel.

The opening of Gampel and the month of January 1990 closed the "Building a Program" part of the Calhoun era. The new coach had changed the culture, developed an infrastructure, and showed he could win. Toughness, hard work, and an allergy to losing characterized the new culture. UConn basketball now had a state-of-the-art facility and an academic support system that kept players eligible. In January 1990, the Huskies beat Villanova, Syracuse, Georgetown, and St. John's. Up to that point, the program had never beaten these four teams in the same season.

2

DOMINANT BUT NOT GREAT ENOUGH

6

I Know It Sounds Crazy, but I Never Thought We Were Going to Lose

All Big East schools receive a limited number of student tickets for the Big East tournament. Before the 1989 tournament, a few dozen UConn students showed for the lottery. The UConn athletic ticket office distributed the tickets and laid out the procedure for picking up tickets in New York if UConn defeated Seton Hall in the first game. "If UConn wins two games," a representative from the athletic ticket office said—and then he began to laugh and the students followed. UConn basketball was no longer a joke in 1989, but a Big East finals appearance was, well, laughable. Before the 1990 tournament, students filled the bleachers on one side of the field house to get their tickets for the Big East tournament. This time, the students outnumbered the tickets. No one laughed when the ticket office explained the procedures for championship Sunday. Still, the question remained: would UConn win the conference tournament for the first time in school history? Everyone seemed to be asking this question, including the players.

In 1989, Seton Hall, the second seed, faced seventh-seeded UConn. A year later, the teams flipped seeds. UConn played Seton Hall in the first game on Friday at noon. At the time, Madison Square Garden was undergoing renovation that would eliminate its infamous blue seats, change the red, green, yellow, and orange seats to purple and teal, and create luxury boxes behind one basket. Because the crowd for the noon game typically arrives late, spectators could hear workers talking to each other, drilling, and sawing as UConn played Seton Hall. The construction served as a metaphor for the UConn program. By the time the Garden's renovations were complete, UConn's transformation to king of the league and national power would also be finished.

At Madison Square Garden for the 1990 Big East tournament, fans could buy shirts with the logo of the league's traditional powerhouses: Georgetown, St. John's, Syracuse, and Villanova. If anyone wanted to show allegiance to the league's other teams, they could purchase a shirt with a silhouette of a basketball player on the front and the name of the school—in generic letters—running down the side. This would be the final year that UConn fans couldn't buy gear with the Huskies logo at the Garden. Before the Dream Season, beyond the UConn Co-op, people couldn't buy much of anything with UConn, the

The 1989–1990 University of Connecticut Huskies. The team that produced the Dream Season. Sitting on the sidewalk (*left to right*): Tate George, Chris Smith. Sitting on the wall (*left to right*): Lyman DePriest, Steve Pikiell, John Gwynn, Scott Burrell. Standing (*left to right*) Rod Sellers (*second from left*), Toraino Walker, Marc Suhr, Nadav Henefeld, Dan Cyrulik, Murray Williams, Jim Calhoun.

University of Connecticut, or Jonathan the Husky on it. No market existed for these items. UConn was not a brand name.

UConn used the defensive hammer to pound its opponent in the Big East tournament quarterfinals. Seton Hall turned the ball over 14 times in the first half on the way to 24 in the game. UConn converted its 17 steals into 24 points and won by 18.

Throughout the season, UConn employed the 2-2-1 press to steal the ball 484 times in 37 games, two shy of Oklahoma's 1988 national record of 486. Oklahoma played two more games in 1988 than UConn did in 1990. Henefeld broke the mark for most steals in a season by a freshman in men's NCAA Division I basketball (138), a record that still stands.

Mourning, Mutombo, and the Hoyas were up next in the tournament. In this game, Georgetown led by six at the break; UConn had lost every game in which it trailed at the half during the season. With a little more than 13 minutes remaining in regulation, UConn was down by eight but turned that deficit into a six-point advantage with 5:38 left.

A film of UConn's second-half defense against Georgetown should be on exhibit at the Hall of Fame in Springfield, Massachusetts. UConn held Georgetown to five points over a 12-and-a-half-minute span in the second half. It converted Georgetown's 19 turnovers into 24 points and won by five.

As John Thompson shook Jim Calhoun's hand after the game, he described UConn's team and that win as "magnificent." In response, Calhoun said, "There's no one I'd rather beat" than you.

UConn had no time to celebrate its victory over the nation's fifth-ranked team because it needed to prepare for the next day's Big East tournament championship game against the country's fourth-ranked team—the Syracuse Orangemen.

When Calhoun put Gwynn into the game at the 14:50 mark of the first half, he set the timer and—ding!—Syracuse's 17-5 lead shrank to 25-19. During that streak, Gwynn scored half of his 16 points.

On the way to New York City for the 1990 Big East tournament, John Gwynn had asked Tate George, "How good do you think we are?" George thought the team could be really good, but he told Gwynn, "Every other team has a guy they can go to coming off the bench. We need you to be that guy. You must have spurts."

People referred to Gwynn as the Microwave, a nickname for the Detroit Pistons' Vinnie Johnson, who, like Gwynn, came off the bench and produced instant offense.

Gwynn complained to George about his playing time. Don't worry about that, George said. If you get five minutes, take five shots. For the season, Gwynn averaged 10.6 points in 17.2 minutes; he came off the bench in every game. Gwynn wanted to start, but Calhoun liked to have scoring energy off the bench. George told Chris Smith to pass the ball to Gwynn whenever possible. He saw deference as the best way to improve Gwynn's confidence.

Deference worked.

In the Big East tournament final game, after Syracuse had tied the score at 57, Gwynn untied it with a three-pointer. Not long after this shot, UConn held a one-point advantage when Gwynn hopped, skipped, and jumped into the left side of the lane, hit a left-handed layup from his hip, and was fouled by Syracuse's Dave Johnson. Gwynn's free throw extended UConn's lead to four and Syracuse never recovered.

Gwynn was a great finisher who made circus-style layups throughout his career at UConn. "I'd go in on anybody. [Kareem] Abdul-Jabbar, [Hakeem] Olajuwon, I'd take it in on anybody," Gwynn said. "I knew it would go in" — Gwynn said of his layup against the Orangemen — "because it always does in practice."

"Smith and George, I figured, are going to hurt us, but Gwynn beat us," Syracuse coach Jim Boeheim said. Smith, George, and Gwynn were the first UConn players to make the all-tournament team. Gwynn became the first nonstarter to earn this distinction. The three-guard attack — established by George, Smith, and Gwynn — became a staple of UConn's teams in the future.

At the game's conclusion, many of the UConn students who had rushed the court two years before to celebrate an NIT championship did so again, but this time, the Huskies were one of the favorites to make the Final Four. Destination: Denver.

The NCAA tournament selection committee designated the Huskies as the number-one seed in the East and chose Boston University, led by Mike Jarvis, as UConn's first-round opponent. This game was the first between the two teams since the bus accident on the Mass Pike in 1986. The media loved this matchup more than they did the average one-versus-16 affair.

Prior to the season, UConn fans were like uncooked popcorn kernels that needed heating. With each win, the heat increased, and pop . . . pop . . . pop . . . more dormant UConn fans and people who didn't even know the university existed became energized. Once UConn captured the Big East tournament, the popcorn kernels blew the lid off of the pot and spread throughout the state.

During the days between the Big East and NCAA tournaments, signs were everywhere along Route 44 and other highways and roads in Connecticut. Often, they had balloons and inspirational messages attached to them. Many thanked the team for a great year. The basketball office at UConn became inundated with emotional cards and thank-you letters. The $15 face value for tickets for UConn's NCAA tournament games at the Civic Center escalated to between $50 and $150 on the street, but many fans decided to keep the tickets and attend the game. A student ticket to UConn's NCAA tournament games in Hartford was as hard to get as a golden ticket to Willie Wonka's factory. Veruca Salt's father would have had to pay big time for these tickets. Students filled the entire field house to get one of 50 tickets available to them. Scalpers, Slugworth, and representatives of Henry Salt's peanut-packing company waited in the field house and offered cash for the tickets, but most students kept their seats.

Close to five thousand fans attended UConn's open practice at the Civic

Center before the BU game. Governor O'Neill declared game day "UConn Basketball Day" to honor the Big East champions. Fans mobbed the UConn players at the Marriott in Farmington, which served as the team's hotel. They pounded on the Husky bus and blocked its entrance to the Hartford Civic Center before UConn's game at the NCAA tournament. The bus radioed into the Civic Center, circled the building, and let the players off on the side of the arena.

With 17 minutes to go in its first-round game, UConn trailed BU by three points. Then, in one stretch, UConn outscored the Terriers 21–1. In the game's final 16-plus minutes, BU scored 11 points. Smith called UConn's second-half performance "the best defensive output we've had all year." The final: UConn 76–BU 52.

In the second-round game, Cal scored the first basket before UConn ran off 17 straight points. The Huskies led by 16 at the half and won by 20. The Golden Bears averaged 13 turnovers for the season. Against UConn, they committed their 13th turnover with eight minutes left in the first half. Of UConn's 2-2-1 full-court press, one Cal player said, "We expected them to press, but not that hard. By the time you got across half-court, you were exhausted."

Clemson, UConn's next opponent, overcame a 19-point deficit against La-Salle in the round of 32 to advance to this Sweet 16 game in the Meadowlands. It featured Dale Davis and Elden Campbell—also known as the Duo of Doom. Davis and Campbell would play 16 and 15 seasons, respectively, in the NBA. When Sellers walked onto the floor to play against the Duo, he said, "Man, these guys are big." But the Huskies led by nine at halftime, and the team had won all 29 games when it led at the half. With six minutes left to play in this contest, the Huskies led by 14. As he sat on UConn's bench, Coach Leitao thought this game seemed too easy for UConn. Winning in the Sweet 16 was supposed to be hard. Elite Eight, here UConn comes.

Not so fast.

Clemson's presses converted UConn's 19 turnovers into 21 points. Throughout the Brendan Byrne Arena, fans jumped off the UConn bandwagon. Some complained that UConn played too many freshmen, such as those who helped the Huskies win the Big East tournament. Others screamed at Calhoun.

The UConn coach must have felt the heat. Calhoun took off his sport coat during the second half and he kept it off as the game's climax approached.

The Clemson game's final minutes set up Tate George to be the goat of the game and the ultimate villain for the year. George had silenced the so-called Tater Haters during the season by leading UConn to the Big East championship. With 21 seconds to go, UConn was up by two as it attempted to inbound a pass. George and Clemson's Derrick Forrest fought for the ball off the inbounds pass, which went out of bounds off of George. Strike one. With 12 seconds left, Clemson looked for Davis or Campbell but when UConn's defense collapsed toward the middle, the Tigers swung the ball to David Young, who connected on an open three-pointer from the corner to give a one-point lead to Clemson.

The Huskies hadn't trailed since the score was 7–6. UConn called time-out, and on its next possession, George missed from 16 feet away. Davis, who had blocked two of George's shots, redirected this attempt. George said he was gun-shy because of the earlier blocks. Strike two.

Clemson's Sean Tyson grabbed George's miss and was fouled with 1.6 seconds to go. He missed the front end of the one-and-one and UConn collected the uncontested rebound and called time-out. The Huskies trailed by a point, but one second remained in the game, possibly the season.

UConn's sports information director, Tim Tolokan, sat across from the Husky bench as Clemson's comeback took shape. He knew a loss would devastate his close friend, so he button-hooked around the arena to meet Calhoun as soon as the UConn coach would shake Clemson coach Cliff Ellis's hand and head to the locker room. He wanted to provide moral support and professional cover for his friend.

In the Clemson huddle, Ellis said, "No fouls." He figured that free throws were the only way UConn could win. Ellis instructed Campbell to guard the inbounds passer.

On the UConn side, the players held their heads down as they walked toward the bench. Sellers looked at the score, ran the last 10 minutes back in his mind, and thought, "You can't be serious . . . we blew this." Tate George figured his "career could be coming to a rotten end after so much sweetness."

When the Huskies reached the sideline, they heard something that surprised them: optimism. "Come on, guys, get your heads up," Calhoun said. "We have a second left. We're going to win," he said. The coach knows when to scream and yell and when to relax his teams and this night was no exception.

Calhoun told his players that they had enough time to win the game. "I know it sounds crazy," he said later, "but I never thought we were going to lose." For assistant coach Glen Miller, Calhoun's presentation of the play convinced the players that the game was not over.

The coach called for "Home Run," a play in which Burrell throws a court-length pass to any open UConn player. Calhoun asked, "Scott, can you make this pass?" Burrell, the quarterback who had thrown the 70-yard passes, said yes.

Calhoun called for his guards to crisscross and get to an open space on the floor. The team worked on this play every day, but it always put two seconds on the clock. Burrell didn't know if the play could be completed in half that time. Smith was Burrell's first option. George was the decoy.

As the team broke the huddle, George said to Burrell, "Throw the ball to me. I'll catch it; I'll catch it . . . I'm the senior; I missed the last shot; let me take the last shot."

With Campbell in his face, Burrell threw a pass to George. According to Calhoun, "Scott threw it to the corner and led Tate. Very few guys I have ever seen threw it that well. Usually, it curves, but it was amazing how well-thrown the ball was."

George received the pass with his back to the basket. As he turned to shoot, he noticed that Sean Tyson, the Clemson defender closest to him, had backed off. George could hear the Clemson players and coaches screaming, "Don't foul! Don't foul!" Pictures of George shooting the ball show Tyson moving away from the shooter with his hands in the "I didn't touch him" position. If you want to see passive in action, watch Tyson on this play.

After George shot the ball, Tyson blocked his vision.

The roar from the crowd let George know that he made The Shot. When the ball went in, the amazement could be heard throughout Brendan Byrne Arena. When the ball went in, Calhoun hopped from the UConn bench past half court but stopped when he saw the dejected look on Ellis's face. He turned serious as he outstretched his arms and tilted his head as if to say, what are you going to do? Calhoun sympathized with Ellis. He had been there.

When CBS's cameras found Calhoun amid the on-court chaos after the shot, the UConn coach was greeted by Tolokan, who had anticipated the despair of a funeral but got the joy of a wedding. Calhoun hugged Tolokan so hard that it looked like he was throwing a punch into him. "We're playing another game," Tolokan said to Calhoun.

The players ran around the court and didn't know who to grab and hug. When Sellers reached Burrell, the man who had thrown the best pass in UConn basketball history couldn't breathe. "What's wrong?" Sellers asked. "Coach D was choking me," Burrell said. After George sank the shot, Coach Dickenman stormed the court, found Burrell, and hugged him so tightly around the neck that he nearly asphyxiated his player.

A UConn loss after giving up a double-digit lead with less than 10 minutes to play would have marred this season, and it is doubtful that people would

ALL-CALHOUN
ERA, BEST SHOT
- - - - - - - - - - - - - - - -
Tate George
UConn vs.
Clemson
March 22, 1990
NCAA East Region
Semifinal
Brendan Byrne
Arena, East
Rutherford,
New Jersey

apply the term Dream Season to this campaign. UConn's first appearance on prime time national television would have ended in disappointment. This victory was more important for the long-term success of the program than any other the Huskies have played since. Several other games come close, but this one set the standard.

The Shot solidified the beauty of this season, and it furthered UConn's national presence. All the recruits who watched this game saw UConn in a positive light. CBS, ESPN, and other national sports programs continue to show highlights of this play. The Shot made UConn a brand name. And then there was Duke.

In the Elite Eight matchup against the Blue Devils, the Huskies overcame a nine-point second half deficit to tie the score when Chris Smith hit a three with nine seconds to go. If Smith had missed that shot, the Dream Season would have ended in regulation. Ahead 78–77 in overtime and seconds away from UConn's first Final Four, George intercepted a pass from Duke's Bobby Hurley to Phil Henderson, but the ball bounced out of bounds off his leg and the Blue Devils retained possession. In front of the Duke bench, George crouched over with knees bent, elbows together, and fists clinched. He looked like he might vomit.

Calhoun saw George dribbling that ball all the way to Denver, the site of the 1990 Final Four. Duke coach Mike Krzyzewski stood in George's shadow and spun his arms to indicate traveling on UConn's point guard. Krzyzewski called for anything that would help at that moment.

After George's near steal, Duke called time-out with 2.6 seconds remaining in overtime, at which point assistant coach Leitao looked up from the UConn huddle and saw a fan's sign that said the Huskies were on their way to the Final Four. For the first time, Leitao realized how close the team was to that goal. That sign made Leitao nervous.

On the ensuing play, which took place in front of Duke's bench, UConn decided not to guard the inbounder, Duke sophomore Christian Laettner. Calhoun wanted to avoid a game-ending layup by Duke. If the Blue Devils were going to win, Calhoun reasoned, they would have to hit a jumper outside of 15 feet with limited time left.

Calhoun guarded against the high-percentage shot in favor of a low-percentage one. For DePriest—one of UConn's five defenders on the floor for the final play—the objective was clear: don't let the ball get inside. When Krzyzewski noticed that UConn had dropped five men into coverage, he called

Jim Calhoun, Chris Smith (no. 13), and Tate George (no. 32) talk about The Shot with Dick Stockton (right) and Hubie Brown (left). UConn 71–Clemson 70. March 22, 1990, Sweet 16, Brendan Byrne Arena, East Rutherford, New Jersey.

for "Special," a play in which Laettner would inbound the ball to Brian Davis, who would return the ball to Laettner for the shot.

As Coach K had diagrammed it, Laettner got the ball back from Davis and took a 15-footer to try to win the game. He double-clutched as DePriest streaked by to try to block the shot. Sellers didn't see whether Laettner made the basket; he had his back toward the hoop as he guarded Alaa Abdelnaby. He raised his arms in victory because he didn't think that Laettner could make that shot. His arms fell when he saw DePriest fall to the court in agony.

The outcome stunned the UConn players, coaches, and fans, who hadn't experienced defeat in more than three weeks. As the players watched from their knees in front of the bench, they collapsed like dominoes when Laettner's shot went in. So horrified, Dickenman turned away from the court.

Two nights before, Tate George was the hero of college basketball and the darling of the state of Connecticut. On this Saturday afternoon, he wore the goat's horns. If the ball hadn't bounced out of bounds off his body, UConn would have been on its way to Denver.

In the bowels of the Brendan Byrne Arena following the game, a teary-eyed Calhoun said he would coach in the Final Four someday. He talked about the only starting point guard he had coached at UConn. "I should say that Tate George is as good a player as you're going to see. If you think he's a good player, and if you would have had the privilege of being around him for four years of coaching him, then it would have made you a much better person. He epitomizes what we want UConn basketball to represent. I've been waiting four years to say that," said Calhoun. He told George "not to let that last attempt define your life," a message George never forgot.

George had gone through Calhoun's gauntlet. On the other side of a Husky's playing career is an appreciative coach who compliments his former players. When he reflected upon Calhoun's effect on him, George said that you "don't realize how important [Calhoun] is as a man in your life when you are in it." George became the first UConn player to be taken in the first round of the NBA draft.

As he sat in his expansive and unfurnished office in the new John Paul Jones Arena more than 15 years after this game, Virginia head coach Dave Leitao concluded that it was Calhoun's reactions to moments like the one George experienced in 1990 that made the coach so special. Leitao also experienced a humbling moment as a Calhoun-coached player in the NCAA tournament. In the waning seconds of the first overtime against Villanova in the second round of the NCAA tournament in 1982, Leitao missed two shots from within six feet that would have moved Northeastern into the Sweet 16. Northeastern lost that game in three overtimes, 76–72.

"In retrospect, missing those shots was good for me," said Leitao, who explained that the dose of humility helped him overcome future disappointments. Leitao, who coached with Calhoun for 16 seasons, said that, as a player, you don't always understand Calhoun or the coach's tactics, but you can't argue with the results and you notice that you always improve. For Leitao, the wins and the championships at both Northeastern and UConn were great, but the life lessons that Calhoun teaches his players and coaches were most special and important.

UConn learned about the Duke Rules in this game. The Huskies shot 12 free throws; Duke took 32. Laettner shot one fewer free throw than the entire UConn team. He scored nine of his 23 points from the free throw line.

The Huskies called Laettner "the dirtiest player we ever played against." According to Sellers, "Christian Laettner is one of the all-time greats. He was skilled, had a nice touch, and used his body well. But he was as dirty as he was good." Laettner elbowed opponents in the back as they ran away from a play or down the court. He hit players who were nowhere near the action. Sellers told Laettner to stop the dirty play. "You are too good for that," the

Connecticut center said. In the next season, Sellers would do something about a Laettner cheap shot, but in 1990, Laettner sent Sellers and the Huskies home brokenhearted.

At an impromptu rally at Gampel Pavilion held as soon as the team bus arrived on campus, Calhoun's voice cracked and his eyes filled with tears as he told the crowd, "Five hours ago, Christian Laettner broke our hearts. You people have put them back together."

As bad as the loss to Duke was for UConn and Calhoun, the season had changed the program. The team's accomplishments—winning the Big East regular and postseason titles for the first time in school history, qualifying for the NCAA tournament for the first time since 1979, and advancing to the Elite Eight for the second time in school history and the first time since 1964—made that year a Dream Season, one that would transform UConn from Big East doormat to national power and showcase Calhoun's greatness to the college basketball world. In 1990, he was named coach of the year by the Big East and every service that gives such an award, including the Associated Press, United Press International, CBS Television, the *Sporting News*, and *Basketball Weekly*. After his Georgetown team lost to UConn in the Big East semifinal, John Thompson said, "Calhoun has done one of the most exceptional jobs I've seen in eighteen years of coaching."

Huskymania erupted in 1990. For three months, UConn basketball occupied the people's attention in the state, and after that season, the fans expected a Dream Season every season. Not too many states hold parades for teams that lose in the Elite Eight, but the state of Connecticut honored the 1989–1990 UConn team with a parade in Hartford.

With low expectations and few previous successes, this team captivated the state for the first time. Each play, each game, each win heightened interest in these Huskies. UConn had now experienced, rather than just imagined, success in the Big East and the NCAA tournament. The program's flower bloomed for the first time, and that process makes this year the most special season in Huskies' history.

7

Oh, UConn, That's the Place Where They Made the Buzzer-Beater

The Dream Season allowed Calhoun and his staff to move to a national recruiting campaign. UConn's first recruiting class after the Dream Season included Kevin Ollie from Crenshaw High School in Los Angeles, Arizona player of the year Brian Fair from Phoenix, Florida player of the year Rudy Johnson from Jacksonville, Nantambu Willingham from Atlanta, and Donny Marshall from Federal Way, Washington.

Ollie turned down Arizona and UCLA to come to UConn. "I probably wouldn't have been interested in UConn if they weren't in the national spotlight that year," he said. When Ollie visited Storrs, he saw a family disguised as a basketball team. He watched the Huskies practice together, leave Gampel together, and hang out together.

Calhoun made the family culture, Ollie said. Calhoun ensured that the players stayed together as much as possible. Ollie remembers sitting with teammates in hotels, attending plays together in New York, and doing lots of things as a group. Ollie came to UConn with seven other players from different regions of the country. The new Huskies couldn't go home on the weekends, so they hung out with each other. The lack of distractions in Storrs helped create the bond and the family during the Calhoun era.

According to Donny Marshall, "When I told people I was going to UConn, they'd say, 'Oh, UConn, that's the place where they made the buzzer-beater.' Before that, I don't think they would have known anything about UConn. And I doubt I would have even considered it, either."

Fair, a Syracuse fan who wore number 31 because he idolized Dwayne "Pearl" Washington, became familiar with UConn by watching *Big Monday* on ESPN. He couldn't refuse UConn's scholarship offer because he wanted to play in the league with "the tough teams."

During the time he recruited Rudy Johnson, Dickenman was speaking to Pete Abraham, the UConn beat writer for the *Norwich Bulletin*, who was scheduled to appear that night on *Sports Talk* with Arnold Dean on WTIC Radio in Hartford. Dickenman told Abraham that Johnson was visiting that evening and that he wanted him to somehow announce that "Connecticut needs a long, six-foot-six player who can run the floor and drive." You need to say that at 7:17 p.m., Dickenman said. Johnson's connecting flight from Philadelphia was set to arrive at seven. Dickenman knew the two would be done with baggage and back in the car at 7:17. Deal.

Abraham delivered. Dickenman heard it and marveled at the writer's execution. Johnson did not hear it. His plane was circling overhead because of thunderstorms in the Hartford area. It didn't matter. Johnson signed with UConn anyway.

After the first signing period for the high school class of 1991, experts contended Ollie, Fair, Johnson, and Marshall, all of whom were ranked within the top 70 in the country, put the Huskies behind Kansas for the best class of recruits.

Donyell Marshall waited to commit. A six foot ten forward from Reading, Pennsylvania, with a Kevin McHale wingspan, Marshall was a McDonald's All-American. *USA Today* named Marshall its Pennsylvania player of the year. As a senior in high school, Marshall averaged 25 points and 13 rebounds a game.

In the fall signing period, which took place between November 14 and 21, 1991, Marshall planned to commit to Syracuse, but his mother talked him out of it. She didn't know which coach she liked the best, but at that time Marshall said his mother "wasn't feeling Coach Boeheim." After eliminating Syracuse, Marshall almost signed with Maryland, which was on probation at the time. His desire to play in the NCAA tournament right away led Marshall to reject the Terrapins. As it had with Nadav Henefeld, UConn's location worked in Calhoun's favor. The 1991 McDonald's All-American game was played in Springfield, Massachusetts. At the urging of Coach Calhoun, Marshall visited UConn on his drive back to Reading from the McDonald's game. This marked Marshall's second trip to Storrs. He attended UConn's exhibition game against Marathon Oil at Gampel Pavilion in November of 1990.

Marshall received an unprecedented reception for a recruit during his official visit. Stories in various papers alerted Huskymaniacs that this big-time recruit would be at the game. The fans made signs welcoming Donyell to UConn and they chanted his name during the game. The attention still wasn't enough to convince Marshall to select UConn.

During his second visit, Marshall talked to Scott Burrell and Oliver Macklin and watched some of the UConn-Seton Hall baseball game at J. O. Christian Field. Marshall felt no pressure from the coaches on this visit. He said their tendency to stay back helped him make a decision.

Before the Dream Season, Donyell had never heard of UConn; after that season, the media exposure, the program's new winning tradition, and an instant bond with the current players put Marshall on the brink of becoming a Husky. On his way back to Reading, Donyell made his family friend promise that he would take Marshall's mother to at least four games a year. The friend said yes. And, in Donyell's words, "that was the end of the story."

8

I Hope People Took Some Polaroids Tonight

Nadav Henefeld returned to Israel to play professional basketball after the 1990 season. Calhoun's only one-year star, Henefeld made UConn's all-century team and Dick Weiss named him the 41st best player in the history of the Big East. Henefeld helped create a program and his influence taught Calhoun to go to Israel to get talent. In the first five seasons after Henefeld's departure, three Israelis — guards Gilad Katz and Doron Sheffer as well center Uri Cohen-Mintz — played for UConn. Henefeld starred for Maccabi Tel Aviv in the Israeli and European professional leagues from 1990 to 2001. During that time, his teams won 11 titles in Israel and one in Europe. Seven years after Henefeld's retirement, the *Jerusalem Post* characterized him as "the greatest defensive player Israeli basketball has ever seen."

Without Henefeld, UConn finished in the upper-middle and middle of the pack in the Big East conference in 1991 and 1992, respectively. Both teams secured invitations to the NCAA tournament. Though they didn't replicate the magic of the 1989–1990 season, they continued to establish UConn as a higher-level program in the Big East and the nation. The 1990–1991 Huskies advanced to the Sweet 16 before Duke, the eventual national champion, eliminated them.

Smith was UConn's best player in his final two seasons as a Husky. In his farewell performance at Gampel Pavilion, Smith scored 32 points and became UConn's all-time leading scorer. Following the game, a 21-point win over PC, Calhoun said, "I hope people took some Polaroids tonight because you're not going to see the likes of him around here again." To this day, Smith remains UConn's all-time leading scorer.

UConn's biggest win in Smith's last two seasons came against Shaquille O'Neal's LSU Tigers at the Minneapolis Metrodome in the opening round of the 1991 NCAA tournament. The subtitle of this game could have been "The Game Plan," because Calhoun designed a psychological and tactical strategy that, according to starting point guard Steve Pikiell, allowed UConn to win before tip-off.

UConn came into this game after a 19-point loss to Georgetown in a Big East tournament quarterfinals game in which Calhoun received two technical fouls, and the automatic ejection that comes with them, with 7:32 remaining in the first half. Following the game, Calhoun said, "I've said some things that

I should have been thrown out for, not only out of gyms, but possibly states and possibly countries." On this night, Calhoun believed that the officials should have been "looking into about section 219 [of Madison Square Garden] as opposed to looking at the coach."

In the week leading up to the LSU-UConn game, the 19-year-old All-American O'Neal said, "If I were Jim Calhoun, I'd put four guys on Shaquille O'Neal." He had missed two weeks because of a hairline stress fracture on his left leg, but was expected to be at full strength by game time.

Calhoun played the underdog card against LSU: "People don't think we have a chance. I do. We've played pretty well the last couple weeks. People are calling us a disappointment, but did you know this is the first time in twenty-six years that UConn has sent teams to the NCAA back to back? I take great satisfaction in our group."

Rod Sellers's friends told the UConn center that Shaq would eat him up. Sellers wasn't so sure about that. The SEC was an athletic conference, not a physical one, he figured. O'Neal can't be more physical than Alonzo Mourning, Sellers said. Mourning would shoot a jump hook and slap Sellers on the way down. In Big East games, one opposing player would hit Sellers with an elbow and another used his forearm. After conference games, Sellers had bruises on every part of his body, including underneath his calves.

Calhoun wanted to press LSU, a high-scoring team. He saw that LSU was susceptible to the fast break, so if the Huskies had the opportunity, they were to push the ball up the court. Another key was to attack the Shaq and hope for foul trouble. O'Neal bit on pump fakes, so UConn coaches told their players to use as many against him as possible.

On tape, LSU looked like a one-man team. The Tigers didn't shoot well, so Calhoun listened to O'Neal; he put four guys—Sellers, Burrell, DePriest, and power forward Toraino Walker—on Shaq. The game plan worked: UConn won 79-62. LSU coach Dale Brown kept O'Neal in the game "because if we took him out, we probably would've had our asses whupped by forty more than we were." O'Neal finished with 27 points, most of which came while the Huskies held a big lead. No other LSU player scored more than seven.

Sellers was right: O'Neal was big and agile but not as physical as Mourning, Pitt's Brian Shorter, or the other centers in the Big East. Sellers said he could have played another 40 minutes after the LSU game; he needed to get iced down after Big East games.

Dale Brown recognized the brilliance of Calhoun's game plan: "We've been a horrendous perimeter team. . . . Why more people didn't play us this way is beyond my imagination. We seldom got pressed." Calhoun said, "I'm not sure there have been many times we've executed the game plan as perfectly as we did tonight."

After a win over Xavier in the round of 32, UConn met Duke again. This time, Duke was the superior team, but this game included the most controversial event of the last two years of the Smith era. As Rod Sellers cut across the lane, Laettner hit him with what Sellers called a "vicious blow to my head." Sellers never saw it coming. He was dizzy, his tooth was stuck to his cheek, and he began to bleed. He went to the bench, where the trainer said, "He got you good." Sellers agreed.

A short time later, Calhoun walked over to Sellers and asked, "Ready to get back in?" A woozy and now stunned Sellers said yes. As Smith and Duke guard Bobby Hurley scrambled for a loose ball on the floor, Laettner joined the scrum. Upon seeing Laettner on the court, Sellers couldn't resist. He pounded Laettner's head into the Silverdome floor.

The referees didn't call a foul on Sellers, but the NCAA Division I championships committee reviewed the play and suspended Sellers for UConn's first-round game in the 1992 NCAA tournament. Of the process the NCAA used to suspend Sellers, Big East commissioner Mike Tranghese said, "It's setting a bad and dangerous precedent if you rely on isolated shots on television to make a decision like this." Commentators Dick Vitale and former N.C. State coach Jim Valvano, among many others, opposed the decision, which the *Washington Post*'s Michael Wilbon called "the worst penalty in recent memory."

In the Elite Eight in 1992, Laettner stomped on the abdomen of Aminu Timberlake after the Kentucky defender hit the floor while trying to guard the Duke star. Laettner received a technical foul for the stomp. He admitted he "made a mental note to try to get [Timberlake] back and be physical with him" after the Kentucky player had "pushed him down" earlier in the game.

Len Elmore, CBS's color commentator, said, "I don't know if he [Laettner] did it on purpose or not." Without hesitation, play-by-play man Verne Lundquist said, "Yeah, he did."

In response to that incident, Wilbon wrote, "Laettner has elbowed and kneed many a player in his four years at Duke. He has cold-cocked teammates in practice. Kenny Blakeney's introduction to Laettner during a recruiting trip as a DeMatha senior was a fist in the chest, before as much as 'hi' had been uttered. If it took until Saturday's foot to the chest to figure out Laettner is mean as a viper, you're way behind the game. He's as surly as he is talented." If you didn't know any better, you would have thought that Sellers wrote these words.

The NCAA did not suspend Laettner as it did Sellers. It said that Sellers committed a flagrant foul whereas Laettner's was a contact technical. What? The Black Coaches Association complained that the NCAA applied its rules in an inequitable manner because Sellers, an African-American, received a punishment when he fouled Laettner, who is white. The NCAA's executive director denied that race had anything to do with the different decisions. "I think to put this in a racial context is unfortunate," said Bill Schultz, who used the racial composition of the championships committee to explain why the committee's decision wasn't racist. Three of the seven committee members were black.

The NCAA doesn't punish Duke players on the court. It wouldn't do so off the court either. Especially Laettner.

Sellers and Laettner saw each other several times after the incident, but they discussed the matter once. At the NBA combine in Chicago, Sellers admitted that he went overboard. He and Laettner agreed that the incident was part of the game.

Calhoun stopped appearing on the *Mike and the Mad Dog* radio program in New York for five years after co-host Mike Francesa referred to Rod Sellers as a dirty player. The UConn coach was upset that Francesa had commented on one of his players without consulting him first.

Calhoun maintained close contact with Reggie Lewis, who played in the NBA All-Star game in 1992. During one of the Celtics games he attended that year, Calhoun was excited to see Lewis play defense. After a playoff game against the Indiana Pacers, Calhoun said to Lewis, "You actually guarded Reggie Miller."

With Smith, UConn became one of the five best teams in the Big East, made it to three consecutive NCAA tournaments, and advanced to the Sweet 16 and Elite Eight. Despite this unprecedented success, the UConn basketball program was still a work in progress when Smith left after the 1992 season. It followed the Big East tournament championship with consecutive one-and-done performances at the Garden. UConn posted losing records against Georgetown, Syracuse, and St. John's in Smith's career. The Huskies hadn't won at Georgetown or St. John's in league play.

During the Smith era, the team struggled to score on a consistent basis. To make UConn a juggernaut, Calhoun needed to recruit scorers who played nose-to-nose defense. As it turns out, he already had.

9

Calhoun Taught Me Everything

When Donyell Marshall and his fellow freshmen tried to walk into the locker room at Gampel Pavilion in the fall of 1991, Calhoun blocked their entrance. Then he said, "You can't just walk in here. You have to earn it. You aren't as good as everyone says you are. You aren't as good as you think you are. If you are that good, prove it." Calhoun gave small gray t-shirts and shorts to each player. The players had to earn their practice uniforms as well. They had to earn everything.

The new players and their teammates didn't touch a ball for the first two or three days of practice. The heat and steam poured out of Guyer's pipes as Calhoun told his new players, "I'm not the guy who came into your living room. This is a whole different coach."

The new players joined the family in mid-October 1991. They had now experienced Guyer Gym, the short shorts, and the first days of having to prove themselves for the rest of their time in Storrs. They had been Calhouned.

Calhoun's first big recruiting class went 35-23 in its first two years. Its Big East record was 19-17. That record would have delighted Huskies' fans in the middle 1980s, but after the Smith years the results were far from acceptable for Calhoun or the UConn Nation.

After Providence beat UConn, 73-55, in the quarterfinals of the 1993 Big East tournament, the Huskies lost to Jackson State in overtime, 90-88, in the opening round of the NIT at Gampel Pavilion. Jackson State's Lindsey Hunter scored 39 points to beat UConn. "We couldn't stop him," said Ollie of Hunter's performance, which the UConn point guard referred to as "a show." In the locker room after the game, players hung their heads and mourned a difficult end to a disappointing season. When they looked up, they saw a teary-eyed Coach Calhoun; they started to cry as well. The coach vowed that UConn would never experience another season like the one that had just ended. The addition of a legend helped Calhoun look prophetic.

On September 10, 1992, the first day of the fall signing period for basketball recruits from the high school class of 1993, Howie Dickenman planned to be in Baton Rouge, Louisiana, to deliver a national letter of intent to Kirk King, the 35th-rated player in the nation. Instead, he and the rest of the passengers waited on the tarmac in Nashville. While on board, Dickenman learned that his flight to Baton Rouge had been canceled. Because of a class field trip, King wouldn't be available the following day, so Dickenman had to go elsewhere.

Dickenman asked the Delta flight attendant to look at the Official Airline Guide for flights to other locations. With his Rolodex mind at work, the UConn assistant coach figured he could fly near the hometown of another recruit. As the flight attendant rattled off possible destinations, Dickenman asked, "Did you say Columbia, South Carolina?" The flight attendant said yes. Dickenman wanted to go there. Visions of a six foot five guard from Hillcrest High School in Dalzell, South Carolina, danced in his head. The player's name?

Ray Allen.

The following day, Dickenman landed in Columbia at 9:30 a.m. and arrived at Hillcrest High School at 11 a.m. Unannounced, he asked the Hillcrest varsity coach if he could speak to Allen. Dickenman and Allen talked in a classroom in Hillcrest High for about a half hour. In high school, Allen earned the nickname Candy Man because his game was so sweet. As a senior, he averaged 25 points and 10.5 rebounds per game and led Hillcrest to the state title.

Before this meeting, Allen disliked UConn because it had beaten home-state Clemson, but Tate George's shot was the only thing that he knew about the program. Like DePriest and others before him, Allen figured that UConn meant Yukon. "We all thought that," Allen said.

As the conversation progressed, Dickenman asked about Allen's three sisters. What are their birthdays, he asked. Throughout the recruiting process, Dickenman spent time with Allen's sisters, and he can still recall their birth dates. Allen's sisters appreciated Dickenman; they hung up the coach's coat when he attended their brother's games.

Allen found Dickenman to be curious, but not obnoxiously so. The UConn assistant asked how Allen was handling the recruiting process. Unlike other recruiters, he did not criticize other programs or denigrate other coaches. He was not overbearing. Other coaches and programs guaranteed a starting spot to Allen; they told the high school star that he would become *the* man on their campus as soon as he arrived. They promised to turn Allen into an NBA player. Dickenman, Leitao, and Calhoun told Allen that he had potential and that hard work would allow him to improve. They didn't mention the NBA.

John Wooden had approached Bill Walton in the same way that Calhoun and his staff recruited Allen. At Walton's dinner table, Wooden told the Helix High School star and his family, "You're the player we want. We won't give you

Donyell Marshall helped turn UConn into a powerhouse. Marshall is guarded by future Arizona coach Sean Miller in a 10-point Connecticut win over Pitt at the Hartford Civic Center on January 14, 1992.

University Photograph Collection, Archives & Special Collections at the Thomas J. Dodd Research Center, University of Connecticut Libraries. Photo published with permission.

anything. We're not going to promise you that you'll start but we think you can. But you're going to have to earn it." Like Calhoun, Wooden was the only coach to talk in this way to his star recruit.

Calhoun's players need talent and a thick skin. If a player needs coddling, Camp Calhoun isn't the place for him. Allen wanted to be challenged. He appreciated Calhoun's direct approach, questioning style, and hard-to-please demeanor. Many of the best recruits want bouquets. None are forthcoming from Calhoun, who offers praise about as often as John "Bluto" Blutarsky passed a class at Faber College.

For Allen, UConn's approach was refreshing. Dickenman delivered the pitch: UConn is in the most televised conference in the country; UConn focuses on academics; UConn isn't in the city, like other schools. This spiel didn't feel like a pitch to Allen. Dickenman and Calhoun appeared to be genuine and honest.

Throughout the conversation, Allen's eyes stayed fixed on Dickenman. Allen told Dickenman he had received brochures from dozens of programs, including East Carolina University, but he couldn't see himself in an ECU uniform.

As Dickenman left Hillcrest High School on the day he met Allen, he passed

Dominant but Not Great Enough | 69

Dave Odom, Wake Forest's head coach, who was with his top assistant. When Dickenman got back in the rental car, he pumped his fist in victory; he believed that being the first to see Allen was a win in an important recruiting battle.

He was right.

Dickenman returned to Hillcrest two weeks later, September 25, 1992. He recalls the date for two reasons: he remembers everything and that is the date of his father's birthday. Allen wasn't there when Dickenman arrived. He never missed school, but he was at the hospital that day for the birth of Tierra Rayanna, his daughter.

Throughout the recruiting period, Dickenman called Allen on a regular basis. On most occasions, he phoned Ryan's Steakhouse, where Allen washed dishes. Dickenman was the only coach to call there. To complete the circle, he visited the recruit in South Carolina on the last official day of recruiting. When he returned to Connecticut, Dickenman told several people including his good friend and women's coach Geno Auriemma and Phil Chardis that he had a feeling that Allen would be a Husky.

Ray Allen is a renaissance man. The son of an Air Force mechanic, he lived in California, Germany, Oklahoma, and England before he moved to Shaw Air Force Base in rural South Carolina. He lived global politics. When he was four and living in Germany, a local girl with whom Allen played was pulled away by her brother who said, "You can't play with the Americans." Allen grew up on military bases; when he lived overseas, Allen learned that "there was always a hatred toward Americans."

Allen plays the piano and cut his own hair prior to each televised game in college. He was so competitive at ping-pong that his friends started to call him Forrest Gump, who played for the U.S. Army table tennis team. Allen also considers himself to be an elite Yahtzee player. One summer during his college days, Allen washed cars at a dealership; by summer's end, he had sold five cars.

Dickenman's pursuit of Allen illustrated how recruiting happened in the early 1990s and how it has changed since. "I dealt with Ray," Dickenman said. He also talked to Allen's parents and high school coach. Now, Dickenman said, coaches must deal with the recruit's AAU coach or "his guy." This indirect method makes recruiting much more difficult.

Throughout the recruiting process, Allen met one young coach after another who marketed their respective programs to the point where Allen was unable to tell whether they were selling their university or a pre-owned Mercedes Benz. These slicksters, as Allen called them, were often successful at convincing young and naive high school players that the yellow brick road lay ahead. Allen didn't believe the slicksters and wanted something different. Dickenman showed him that UConn was different.

Calhoun had never seen tapes of Allen. He went to South Carolina to meet Ray's family and see Allen in action. Allen knew little about UConn's head coach. When he saw Calhoun for the first time, Allen thought that Calhoun fit the part of an old-school, hardnosed coach. "Okay, this guy's an older coach," Allen thought, "he can't be like the other younger slicksters." He wasn't. Calhoun, who wore a tie dotted with basketball-playing shadowy stick figures, preached from the "you've got potential, but you need to work hard" bible. No promises.

"I am who I am, and I'm not Popeye. I'm pretty satisfied with myself," Calhoun once said, and Allen appreciated this approach. "When he comes to recruit you," Allen said of Calhoun, "maybe the things he says aren't much different from the things other coaches say, but the way he says them is different. First of all, you have to listen real hard just to hear what he says—him talking so fast with that Boston accent—but you feel that he means it. He doesn't try to be hip or cool, like a lot of the coaches. He's just himself."

Allen scored nine points with Calhoun in attendance, and this performance made it hard for the UConn coach to get a feel for the player's game. Dickenman insisted that Allen was a player. Calhoun believed.

After he visited the Storrs campus, Allen wanted to play for UConn. Connecticut was a basketball school. Allen wanted to leave the South. He liked that UConn had a campus and wasn't situated in a city. "If we weren't winning, [Storrs] might be a problem," Dickenman said. "But because we're winning, we're now selling that we're the only school in the Big East that is not really in the city. There is some uniqueness to that." Winning turned Storrs into an asset.

The UConn players were close, like a family, Allen thought. They hung together because they had similar interests, came from across the country, and attended a university located on a farm. Calhoun promoted this family concept by requiring the team to work out together at 5:30 a.m. and eat breakfast together at 7:30 a.m., before classes began. The results showed.

In the recruiting process, Calhoun links old to new. Scott Burrell mentored Allen when the high school senior visited Storrs. They became very close friends even though they never played with each other.

Allen visited Kentucky and Alabama. He noticed that the players weren't as tight on these teams as they were in Storrs. The coaches at these schools didn't approach Allen with the same warmth he received from Calhoun, Dickenman, and Leitao.

Other schools didn't see in Allen what Dickenman recognized. Virginia expressed initial interest, but then sent a letter that stated, according to Allen, "they had checked their personnel and realized they already had somebody with my talents, so they were terminating me (as a prospect)." Its decision bothered Allen, who achieved revenge when he scored 20 and 24 points, both game highs, in his two games against the Cavaliers. UConn crushed Virginia both times: 77–36 in 1993 and 76–46 in 1996.

Calhoun doesn't get enough credit for being the game's best developer of talent. According to future associate head coach George Blaney, "One of Jim's great talents is [that] he recognizes what a player can be like in two years down the road, rather than what a player is right now. . . . That only comes from an ability to evaluate." Blaney said. "There are very few coaches around the country who know how to really evaluate."

Allen didn't make the McDonald's All-American game and recruiting expert Bob Gibbons rated Allen as the sixth best guard and 30th best player among that year's high school seniors. Gibbons ranked Kirk King as the 35th best senior. *Hoop Scoop*'s first-team All-Americans included Rasheed Wallace and Jerry Stackhouse (who both attended the University of North Carolina), Ronnie Henderson and Randy Livingston (LSU), and Dontonio Wingfield (University of Cincinnati). Allen made the eighth team; King was on the 12th team.

Even after Allen committed to UConn, Gibbons ranked Kansas, Duke, Indiana, and LSU as the top four recruiting classes in the early signing period. He put UConn ninth on that list. *Hoop Scoop* claimed that St. John's, which had signed James Scott and Roshown McLeod, recruited the best class in the Big East.

The 1993 recruiting class continued UConn's commitment to national and international recruiting. Gibbons referred to Calhoun's successful recruitment of King as UConn's "great invasion of the South by going into LSU's backyard to sign [a player] that Dale Brown really wanted."

Allen added scoring punch and sizzle to a UConn team in desperate need of both. Doron Sheffer provided leadership, experience, savvy, clutch play, and a winning attitude, all of which were characteristics that the 1992–1993 team had needed.

Sheffer, the son of a diamond mogul from Ramat Efal, a five-hundred-family village outside Tel Aviv, came to the United States after his three-year mandatory military service in Israel. He wanted to play in the NBA and had rejected a six-figure contract in Israel to play college basketball in the United

States. Sheffer wanted to play at Kentucky, but he couldn't take an entrance exam early enough to be considered for UK; he picked UConn instead.

At the time he came to UConn, Sheffer held a more prominent place in Israeli basketball history than Nadav Henefeld. The legend of Doron Sheffer, also known as the Ice Man for his expressionless face during games, began when Sheffer scored 24 points en route to the State Cup tournament championship for Hapoel Galil Elyon. It blossomed when Sheffer, an amateur, led Galil Elyon to an upset victory over Maccabi Elite Tel Aviv in the Israeli basketball championships in 1993.

At the age of 20, Sheffer was the Israeli league's most valuable player. Many refer to Maccabi as the Celtics of Israel, but that characterization isn't fair to Maccabi, which won every Israeli championship from 1970 through 1992 and 1994 through 2007. The person responsible for this monumental, unprecedented, and never duplicated victory now played for UConn. Because of his international experience and age, NCAA rules limited Sheffer to three years of eligibility. Sheffer began his UConn career at the age of 21.

As Calhoun gained one future NBA great, he would soon lose another. Reggie Lewis collapsed on the court of the Boston Garden during a playoff game against the Charlotte Hornets on April 29, 1993. He returned to play in that game on two separate occasions. In a May 23, 1993, article about Lewis's condition, *Sports Illustrated*'s William Oscar Johnson wrote, "So what does it all mean? About the only thing one can say for sure is that the questions remain almost as puzzling as they were the night Lewis collapsed against Charlotte. Can Lewis ever play again? Should he? Should the Celtics let him? What are the legal ramifications? The medical? The financial? The telltale heart pounds on and on."

Calhoun and Leitao saw Lewis at Brandeis University on July 14, 1993. They noticed an uncertainty and tentativeness in Lewis that they had never seen. Calhoun was convinced that Lewis would try to play again. Two weeks later, Lewis died of a heart defect on the Brandeis court while he practiced his shooting before a pickup game. Calhoun gave a eulogy at Lewis's memorial service. At a ceremony to honor Lewis at the Basketball Hall of Fame in the summer of 1994, Calhoun said, "At fifty-two years of age, Reggie Lewis is my hero."

When Calhoun played at Braintree High School, Coach Herget required the team to do things together. Calhoun felt that his team didn't win as many games as it should have during Donyell Marshall's sophomore year because the players weren't close enough. He changed that and returned to Herget's lesson that a team is a family. Calhoun required players to take teammates with them wherever they went. If Donyell wanted to attend a movie or a concert, for example, at least one teammate needed to go with him. Calhoun fosters, commands, and does everything he can to keep the players together as much as possible. He tells his players, "These are your brothers. These are the guys you are going to be with. These are the guys who are going to make a difference in your life."

The 1994 team bonded; wins followed.

Two games in 1994 showed UConn's resiliency. UConn led at Providence College by five with 18 seconds to go in regulation. Seven seconds later, Donny Marshall committed a foul. No big deal. Marshall smiled and clapped, much like his coach would when he disagreed with a call. Bang. Referee John Cahill assessed a technical foul to Marshall. The officials had warned Donny to stop refereeing the game at least two times earlier in the contest. Donyell loved Donny but after the technical the entire team including its All-American player wanted to strangle the other Marshall.

Providence made three of the four free throws and trailed by two. Because of the technical, it retained possession and hit a three-pointer to take a one-point lead with 8.8 seconds left. Timeout, Connecticut.

At the time, Ollie thought that his coach was going to kill Donny. If we lose this game, Ollie thought, I am not sure Donny's going to make it out of that locker room. As Ollie prepared to stop a fight in the locker room, Calhoun asked him to save Donny and UConn altogether.

Ollie had been benched with 14:11 left and didn't reenter until 1:20 remained. He hadn't attempted a shot during the game; Allen and Sheffer had played better than he had in this game.

Calhoun had plenty of weapons from which to choose for the final play. Donyell Marshall and Ray Allen had scored 28 and 20 points, respectively. Neither would touch the ball. Instead, Calhoun put Ollie back in the game and told his point guard, "Take the ball hard [to the basket]. . . . I want you to lay the ball up." "The best thing I have found in that situation is just to go to the hole," Calhoun said later. He figured that UConn would get a basket, a foul, or an offensive rebound.

Ollie took the inbounds pass, flew up the floor, got into the lane, and banked in a shot. Providence missed its final attempt; UConn won by a point. Donny lives. The outcome showed that Calhoun-coached teams are not out of many games even when victory seems impossible.

What kind of a coach inserts a player who hasn't taken a shot and asks him to make a game-winner? A brilliant one.

Like Tate George before him, Ollie learned to accept the responsibility that comes with playing point guard for Jim Calhoun. Before an NCAA tournament game against Cincinnati in 1995, Calhoun knew that UConn's opponent would win if the Huskies committed turnovers. "Don't turn the ball over; that's your responsibility," Calhoun said to his point guard. Following the UConn win, Ollie, who scored 13 points, had nine assists, and committed one turnover, said, "The pressure was on me. I knew. Coach told me that."

"Coach is demanding, which made me a better person and basketball player," Ollie said. Ollie couldn't slack off for one day while he ran Calhoun's team. Ten years after Ollie left UConn, Calhoun noted that his former point guard "puts the onus on himself. What an unusual, unusual philosophy." Calhoun helped instill this attitude in Ollie.

Calhoun put a demand on Ollie's potential. The coach didn't turn the team over to Ollie until the point guard proved himself. "He was always bringing in guys to take my spot," Ollie said of his coach. "So I had to continue to raise my level and continue to compete to the best of my abilities." This kind of challenge enabled Calhoun to develop Ollie into an elite college player and an NBA regular.

The victory over PC was UConn's 16th in 17 games. The 1993–1994 Huskies won more games by the end of January than the previous year's team had won all season.

Many subplots dominated UConn's game at Boston College on February 9, 1994. Billy Curley's flirtation with UConn four years earlier and his futility against the Huskies served as the lead to this drama. UConn recruited the six foot nine player who came from Calhoun's neck of the woods in Duxbury, Massachusetts. Curley played basketball the Calhoun way: tough. His decision came down to UConn, BC, Villanova, Notre Dame, or Michigan.

Dickenman and Calhoun viewed Curley as a central piece of UConn's future. At the time UConn recruited Curley, the Dream Season had yet to start, the team came off a somewhat disappointing 1988–1989 season, and the recruiting class led by Donyell Marshall was more than a year away.

Curley's father, a BC graduate, wanted his son to attend his alma mater. On the Sunday before the fall signing period commenced, the *Boston Globe*'s Bob Ryan, also a BC grad, called Curley "the most important basketball recruit in the history of the school." Ryan wrote, "It's quite possible that the course of Boston College basketball for the duration of the twentieth century now depends on the whim of a high school senior from Duxbury."

Ryan's column included direct quotes from Boston College coach Jim O'Brien about Curley's potential impact on BC basketball. O'Brien told Ryan, "We are very close to being a good team. Billy Curley could be the guy to put us over the top. We're telling him he could be for BC basketball what Doug

Flutie was for BC football. There's no question he comes in and starts, and would be our best player." O'Brien made these remarks despite NCAA rules that don't allow coaches to comment on a player before the recruit signs a national letter of intent. UConn and Villanova complained to Big East commissioner Gavitt about O'Brien's comments. O'Brien pleaded ignorance. The NCAA authorized Gavitt, as league commissioner, to resolve the matter. Gavitt concluded that O'Brien hadn't done anything wrong.

Dickenman waited and waited on the day Curley was to make his decision. That evening, he was talking on the phone with Calhoun when the head coach's line clicked; Curley was on the other line. Calhoun told Dickenman that he would call him right back. Dickenman waited, and waited, and waited.

When Calhoun called back, he said, "BC." Upon hearing the news, Dickenman dropped to a knee as if he had been kicked in the gut. He took the loss of Curley harder than every other rejection he had received from a player in the Calhoun era.

More than four years later, UConn traveled to Chestnut Hill for a conference matchup against BC. This game at Boston College marked the final opportunity for Curley and BC's other seniors to defeat UConn. They entered the game 0-7 against UConn in their careers; the Huskies had won the last 12 meetings against the Eagles.

As a blizzard developed outside, the Eagles took a 51-33 lead with 17:30 remaining in regulation. At the time, Donyell Marshall feared that his team would be the one to lose the streak. "We rebuckled ourselves and came back," Marshall said. "We just never gave up," said Ollie, who contends that Calhoun's personality instilled resilience in the team. "We could have easily given up considering how much we were down . . . but we came back."

With 5.5 seconds left and the score tied at 79, Ollie blocked Howard Eisley's shot from behind. He gathered the ball and dribbled down the court; Donyell raced with him. Marshall watched a replay of this game on ESPN Classic in 2010 and had forgotten about this play. He yelled, "Throw me the ball," at the television when he rewatched the game. It didn't help. Ollie threw late and behind an open Marshall with 2.2 seconds to go. Donyell came in too fast and clunked a layup as time expired.

BC led 86-83 with 53.6 to go in the first overtime, but Donyell Marshall's three-pointer tied the score with 35 seconds left. Marshall remembered that shot. He scored a game-high 33 points and had 10 rebounds. Curley air-balled an open shot as the horn sounded with the score tied at 86.

In the second overtime, with BC down by three and time about to expire,

UConn's defense forced the Eagles' Marc Molinsky to take a two-point shot instead of a three. Molinsky misfired anyway as the buzzer sounded: UConn 94–BC 91. After Calhoun shook hands with the BC coaches, he pumped his fist and showed a bit of a smile. At the time, Calhoun said the win was one of the top two or three he had at UConn.

Curley scored 32 points (a career high), grabbed 16 rebounds (tied for a career high), and had six assists. Following the game, he did not speak to the press. Before he told the media, "Sorry, not tonight," Curley cried uncontrollably in the locker room. Dickenman had no sympathy for him.

UConn pounded most of its opponents in that season. Following the Huskies' 41-point win at Virginia, Coach Jeff Jones apologized to his team's fans for having to sit through that game. The Huskies beat Villanova by 24, St. John's by 15, and Georgetown by 12.

Despite UConn's lopsided wins, Calhoun continued to discipline the team when he sensed poor play. In the first half of a CBS game against St. John's at the Hartford Civic Center, Calhoun benched Donyell for not boxing out. As he crouched beside Marshall, Calhoun said, "Play harder." After the game, Calhoun said, "The reason I got on Donyell is because I'm like a proud father. We're on CBS. I want Donyell to look great. Donyell is great. I want everybody to see that." Marshall regarded Calhoun as "a father figure I probably didn't have growing up."

Throughout the Calhoun era, players echoed Marshall's sentiment about the role that the UConn coach played in their lives. Chris Smith said that Calhoun is "a hard person to play for and anybody would tell you that; but as far as off the court, I've always looked at the program and Coach as family. If you stayed with the program you can call on Coach and he is there for you." Gerry Corcoran, who played for Calhoun at Northeastern, regards Calhoun as "a tough coach, but more than that, he taught us how to be men . . . he was like a second father to me. Over a four-year period of my life, I spent more time with him than I did with my father. He had a huge impact on me."

Calhoun once invited Rod Sellers into his office and talked about time management, homework, smart decisions with women, and accountability. Sellers's father had died when he was 12, so the first time he heard these kinds of things from a man, they came out of Calhoun's mouth. The same held true for other players, including Lyman DePriest, whose father died when he was young.

Joe Sharpe, UConn's basketball trainer for nine years, said that Calhoun nurtures everyone around him. People see Calhoun on the sideline during games, but they don't watch the coach in his office or on buses and planes, where the coach discusses more than basketball. Calhoun encouraged Sharpe, who started at UConn at the age of 24, to think about his financial future. "You have thirty years to work," Calhoun would say. "Where do you want to be financially at that time?" Calhoun discussed real estate and stocks as possible options for Sharpe, who had lost his father at age 13.

In turn, Sharpe encouraged Calhoun, whose arthritic knee made him retire from running, to take up weight training and biking. The two biked together around the Willimantic area and on the back roads that had little traffic. One time, Sharpe and Calhoun biked so far that they had to call Calhoun's wife Pat to come and get them. They didn't have bike lights and the sun was about to set. Jim and Joe loaded the bikes onto Calhoun's Ford Expedition and away they went.

Sharpe, who now serves as the head athletic trainer for the NBA's Oklahoma City Thunder, remains close to Coach Calhoun and his family. He thinks about Calhoun more than he lets the coach know. Sharpe believes that he wouldn't have made it as far as he has without serving under Calhoun in his first job.

In 1993–1994, UConn went 16–2 in the Big East, and finished a league-record three games ahead of second-place Syracuse to claim the conference's regular-season title. It won all of its 15 home games. It went from being unranked at the start of the regular season to the nation's second-ranked team by the end. It won the program's first games at St. John's in New York and Georgetown at the USAir Arena in league play. It swept Georgetown and St. John's for the first time in program history. The 1994 team beat St. John's as many times in one season (three) as Chris Smith's teams had in four.

Despite all of the wins and achievements, two defeats tarnished the 1994 season. In the Big East tournament quarterfinals, UConn lost to Providence, 69–67. Then, in the East Region semifinal, UConn played a bizarre game against Florida in the Miami Arena. The game started at about 11 p.m. Coach Leitao recalled that the team hung around and waited all day and didn't eat its pregame meal until 7 p.m. During the game, UConn did not play well, and it lost Donny Marshall to an ankle injury.

Donyell Marshall was fouled in the act of shooting with 3.4 seconds remaining and the score tied at 57. At the time of the foul, Leitao, who saw Marshall make 20 out of 20 from the line against St. John's earlier in the season, would have bet his mortgage that Donyell would make at least one free throw. After Marshall missed the first, Florida called time-out to make Marshall think about the second.

As Donyell stood at the line awaiting the ball to take the shot, two Florida players, Craig Brown and Dan Cross, switched sides along the lane, and Brown said to Marshall, "The whole world is watching you shoot this free throw."

With 15,000 Florida fans screaming at Marshall, Donyell's second free throw went in and popped out. After Florida missed a half-court shot at the buzzer, the game went to overtime, which the Gators dominated. Fans criticized UConn for blowing a 10-point lead in the second half, committing 23 turnovers, and scoring 26 points after halftime.

When the Huskies returned from Florida, Dickenman said the "whole state was a funeral home." The day after the men's loss, Rebecca Lobo and the women's team were eliminated in the Elite Eight by eventual national champion North Carolina. On that same night, Dickenman and a friend ate at Rossini's Restaurant in East Hampton. As Dickenman enjoyed pasta and wine, he heard it. One waiter said to another, "Can you believe he missed those free throws. I could have made one free throw. Anybody can make one free throw." Dickenman's meal was ruined. Check please.

The missed free throws affected how people perceived Marshall's career. When UConn fans think of the school's greatest player, Donyell's name rarely comes up. Karl Hobbs played at UConn and coached on Calhoun's staff from 1993 until 2001. He believes that Donyell Marshall was the best player in the Calhoun era. "Maybe it's because Donyell was on the team when I began to coach at UConn," Hobbs said, "but he dominated every game on both offense and defense." In 2010, Hobbs hired Marshall to be his assistant coach at George Washington University.

Marshall was so good in 1994 that Calhoun said the similarity between Donyell and Reggie Lewis was "really scary."

When asked about his favorite games at UConn, Marshall responded, "Probably every game my junior year." That's a logical answer considering that Marshall's 1993–1994 season was the best in UConn basketball history until 2011. He was the first Husky to break 800 points in a season (855), averaging 25.1 points per game, the most in the Calhoun era. He broke the 30-point mark eight times and scored 20 or more points in 23 consecutive games, also a program record. Chris Smith and Richard Hamilton are tied for second on that list with seven straight games of 20 or more points.

In three games against St. John's in the 1993–1994 season, Donyell scored 42 points twice and 29 points in the other game. Marshall had the flu during his 29-point game. The second time Donyell scored 42 against St. John's, he set the Big East tournament record for most points in a game. That record still stands. The 42 points also place Donyell in a tie with Cliff Robinson and Kemba Walker for most points in a game during the Calhoun era.

Calhoun did not judge Marshall on two free throws in Miami. After the Florida game, he said, "Donyell Marshall is a large reason why we were still playing tonight. He has made a lot of wonderful shots. He has done too much for us to be concerned about two missed free throws. I love him to death."

Marshall made the All-American team, earned All-Big East honors for two consecutive years, and was named the 1994 Big East player of the year and the league's best defender. Marshall moved UConn back into the conversation of elite teams in the nation.

Marshall gave up his last year of eligibility and entered the NBA draft. The Minnesota Timberwolves took him with the fourth pick. The Timberwolves also selected BC's Howard Eisley, who told Donyell that he hated UConn and especially his team's double-overtime loss to the Huskies. In his 15-year NBA career, Marshall played in 957 games and averaged 11.2 points and 6.7 rebounds in 26.2 minutes per game. Jason Kidd (second pick), Grant Hill (third pick), and Juwan Howard (fifth pick) are the only players selected in the 1994 draft to have longer NBA careers than Marshall.

Marshall learned that players "don't appreciate the yelling and screaming and [Calhoun] getting on you until after you leave. When you leave you realize what he was doing and what it was about and you appreciate it more." Calhoun "taught me everything," he said. The coach showed his star player how to play the game and how to be respectful.

Take a look at Calhoun-coached players in the NBA, Marshall said. "We were all taught to play a certain way; we all come out and play tough. We might not be the greatest defenders, but we play tough and as hard as we can. We try to play the right way," he said. Marshall is convinced that UConn players tend to have prodigious careers because Calhoun taught them how to play hard and tough.

In the spring of 1994, as Marshall was about to begin his career in the NBA, Calhoun had his successor and an entire team built around him for the 1995 season.

10

He's Going to Be a Special, Special Player

Calhoun brought Donyell Marshall, Kevin Ollie, and Ray Allen to media day at the first round of the 1994 NCAA tournament in the Nassau Coliseum. In the past, Calhoun had only taken seniors to this event, but without a single one on the team, he selected two juniors and a freshman. He wanted to prepare Allen to take over as team superstar.

At the 1994 Olympic Festival in St. Louis, Missouri, a competition of amateurs that featured most of the events from the summer Olympics, Allen scored 101 points in the four-game tournament to break Shaquille O'Neal's scoring record of 98.

Before the 1995 season, Calhoun said, Allen is "the next guy in line in the program, and we've been fortunate enough to have guys like Cliff Robinson, Tate George, Chris Smith, and Scotty Burrell and Donyell, and we said he'd probably be the heir apparent. We like to have a guy we feature sometimes, and we think that makes everyone else better."

Teams could not rest for a second against UConn in 1994–1995. UConn's "don't blink or you'll miss it" attack doomed Seton Hall's Danny Hurley, brother of Bobby, at the Meadowlands in 1995. With UConn ahead 83–81 and less than 25 seconds remaining, Donny Marshall launched a Burrell-like pass to Allen on the inbounds play. Allen caught the ball, dunked on Hurley, and was fouled. The three-point conversion ended the scoring for the game. UConn struck so quickly that Hurley and Seton Hall argued that the official had given the ball to Marshall before the Pirates' defense could get ready. UConn's superior speed and quickness decided many games that season.

A microcosm of UConn's pressure defense came against Georgetown during the semifinals of the 1995 Big East tournament. Georgetown led 73–72 after Sheffer made two free throws; 4:12 remained. On the ensuing inbounds play, Georgetown called two time-outs to avoid a five-second violation. On the same possession, Allen Iverson, who could score in a straitjacket, couldn't get off a shot before the 35-shot clock expired. The Huskies used their defense to convert a three-point deficit with about 7:30 remaining to a seven-point win.

Several victories during the regular season marked the progress of UConn's transition to a juggernaut. UConn beat Duke by four in the inaugural Great Eight in the Palace of Auburn Hills in suburban Detroit. The Blue Devils had won all four previous meetings against UConn. Allen scored a game-high

26 points. "He's going to be a special, special player," Calhoun said of Allen. "He's got a lot of work to do on his game, but he's pretty special right now." It's never enough.

Coming into the first Syracuse contest in the 1994-1995 — an ESPN *Big Monday* game at Gampel — both teams were 7-0 in the league. UConn was ranked second in the nation, Syracuse was sixth. The Huskies were undefeated and the Orangemen had one loss.

Syracuse hadn't been to Storrs since 1972, and Coach Boeheim wanted to keep it that way. He preferred the Hartford Civic Center to the claustrophobic confines of Gampel. He feared his team would be intimidated in an on-campus facility in which the student section looked down (literally and figuratively) on his team.

"Gampel was a great building to do a game," said Mike Gorman, who called Big East games there in the first years of the arena's existence. Gampel's intimacy appealed to Gorman. "The bright lights and smaller setting meant that everyone could see you and you could see everyone," he said. This intimacy served as a stark contrast to larger and darker conference arenas, such as the Capital Centre outside Washington, DC, Madison Square Garden, the Meadowlands, and the Spectrum in Philadelphia.

Gorman saw the Huskies' games as a cultural event and the entertainment for the week for those in attendance. "The crowd lifted you up with them," Gorman concluded. That's what scared Boeheim.

For most of the game, Boeheim's fears appeared unfounded. His team held an 11-point lead with 11:40 remaining in regulation. Calhoun called a time-out and preached defense. He put the press on, and the Huskies went on a 20-6 run, during which Allen got hot. "Everything I shot felt good," he said. Nineteen of Allen's 31 points came in the second half, and the Huskies won the game, 86-75. Allen considers this game and the one the following year against Villanova at Gampel as the two most memorable in his UConn career.

In the rematch about three weeks later, UConn handed Syracuse its second conference loss of the season, going on a 9-0 run near the game's conclusion to win by seven. On the basis of this win and its overall record, UConn received the program's first number-one ranking in the Associated Press poll. It became the first school to have the top-ranked men's and women's basketball teams at the same time.

Spread over two seasons, the Huskies became the first Big East program to win 18 consecutive regular season conference games. UConn was also the first team in Big East history to capture outright regular season titles in consecutive seasons. It became the first Big East program to defeat Georgetown three times in the same season. UConn joined Syracuse as the only other Big East team to win five consecutive games against Georgetown. After UConn eliminated Georgetown from the 1995 Big East tournament, John Thompson sought out seniors Kevin Ollie and Donny Marshall, congratulated

them on the victory, and told them, I hope I never have to see you fucks again.

UConn was now the Beast of the Big East.

As the king-father of the UConn family, Calhoun likes to control his team's environment. The UConn men's and women's teams played a doubleheader against the Kansas Jayhawks at the Kemper Arena in Kansas City, Missouri, on January 28, 1995. They traveled together to the games, which the top-ranked and eventual national-champion women's team won by 10 points over its 13th-ranked opponent. A CBS audience watched Kansas's seventh-ranked men's team beat the second-ranked and unbeaten Huskies by 29 (88–59). After a 10–0 Kansas run, the Huskies trailed 38–18 with about six minutes left in the first half and got no closer than 19 for the rest of the game.

After the game, Calhoun said, "We played awful. We played as poorly as we can play. . . . I didn't realize we could play this poorly." He also said, "I just talked to our athletic director and we are not dropping basketball at the University of Connecticut. They never considered it for the women, but for five minutes at the conclusion of this game there was some discussion." When a reporter asked Calhoun his opinion on whether UConn should keep men's basketball, the coach smiled and said, "About 50-50."

His comparison between the men's and women's teams created problems for Calhoun, who was asked later to clarify his statement. He insisted that he loved the women's team and did not direct his comments toward the female players.

After he watched the crowd leave a women's basketball game at Gampel, Calhoun told Malcolm E. Moran of the *New York Times* that UConn would need to build "a day care center and senior home" for its women's fans. The *Dallas Morning News*'s Steve Richardson was in the room at the time and reported Calhoun's quote. UConn president Harry Hartley—a friend to both women's coach Geno Auriemma and Calhoun—said that a dynamic tension existed between the two coaches. Those words chilled an already cold war.

In 1999, Leigh Montville, a UConn graduate and *Sports Illustrated* writer, wrote that Calhoun and Auriemma weren't friends because of the age difference between the two. Geno had kids of Little League age while Calhoun prepared for his first grandchild. The coaches agreed with Montville's reasoning for their lack of friendship, but before Auriemma won his second national title in 2000, he said, "We had won the national title in '95, and the men still hadn't ever won it. You show me any school where that's the case, and I'll show you a little friction."

Both men addressed their so-called rivalry in their respective books. Calhoun wrote first: "Read my lips: I don't hate Geno Auriemma."

Calhoun didn't hate women's basketball either. He said that he and Auriemma weren't friends, but neither are most coaches at big-time universities. Calhoun disliked comparisons drawn between the men's and women's programs. He wanted to be compared to men's programs, not the women's team. In an earlier *Sports Illustrated* piece, Calhoun told Montville that if he had a daughter, he would want her to play for Geno.

Auriemma disputed President Hartley's claim of a dynamic tension between the two coaches. "Where did that come from?" he asked. The tension is one-sided, Auriemma wrote. At the end of his book's section on Calhoun, Auriemma wrote that he was fed up: "I am sick of talking about him, to tell you the truth. We've made it work here. We don't have to be best friends—and we're not. We both work here. We both support the university. That's all I am going to say about it."

At the end of 2009, a reader asked Mike Anthony, the *Hartford Courant's* beat writer for men's basketball, about the relationship between Calhoun and Auriemma. Anthony wrote, "The relationship is about the same it's been for the last, oh, 20 years: frosty. It's a non-relationship. . . . I hardly ever see Calhoun and Auriemma together and assume they're cordial to one another, but they are complete opposites, seem to harbor grudges, don't deal with each other and don't have to. It's too bad, but it is what it is."

Other people with knowledge of the subject say Calhoun believes he has a harder job than Auriemma. Geno recruits elite students who are among the highest-rated basketball players in the country. Tamika Williams, Anne Strother, Tina Charles, and Maya Moore were Gatorade national players of the year. They are the female equivalents of Al Harrington, LeBron James, Greg Oden, and Kevin Love. Calhoun has never had a Gatorade national player of the year on his team. Calhoun hasn't coached the same level of high school talent as Auriemma.

Calhoun takes players who come from poor neighborhoods, tough circumstances, and some don't have fathers in their lives. He must mold these men into a team. For his part, insiders say, Auriemma thinks that Calhoun is out of control and is not as good a spokesperson for the university as he is.

In 1994–1995, UConn finished the regular season with a 23–3 record and a 16–2 mark in the Big East. It lost to Villanova, 94–78, in the Big East tournament finals. The NCAA tournament selection committee awarded the second seed in the West to UConn.

In his first years at UConn, Calhoun coached blue-collar teams, which consisted of good athletes who were not among the cream of the crop out of high school. Calhoun made these players better. When the UConn program took off, Calhoun polished the diamond-studded talent he brought to Storrs. Despite UConn's greater access to the country's better players, Calhoun continued to take raw athletes whom he needed to teach and develop.

When Howie Dickenman recruited Donny Marshall, he told Calhoun about this phenomenal athlete from Federal Way, Washington. "Jim, this guy runs the floor better than anyone I have seen," Dickenman said. "Can he shoot?" Calhoun asked. "Jim, this guy can jump," said Dickenman. "Can he rebound?" Calhoun questioned. "Jim, he hustles on every play," Dickenman said. "Howie, you do know that I'm the basketball coach, not the track coach, don't you?" Calhoun said.

Marshall, a six foot six forward whose physique reflected an overdose on push-ups, sit-ups, and pull-ups, was the kind of multitalented athlete against whom teams need to compete in modern collegiate basketball. As a ninth-grader, Marshall cleared six feet, five inches, in the high jump, an achievement that would have earned him the silver medal at the state meet that year. As a high school soccer player, Marshall made the all-state team and scored 25 goals in his senior season, the most in the state of Washington.

During the 1995 NCAA tournament, Calhoun said, "No big guy in America, no three [small forward], no four [power forward] or five [center] guys in the country can run with Donny Marshall." After watching Marshall score 22 points against his team in the first round of the 1995 NCAA tournament, Tennessee-Chattanooga forward Brandon Born said, "I've never seen anyone run the court like him."

Marshall neutralized the top scorer on the opposing team. Not a power forward by trade, Marshall defended Syracuse's John Wallace, one of the country's best players at this position, who made four of his 16 shots and scored a season-low 10 points.

After Marshall's first year, Calhoun told the freshman that he "probably wouldn't play, it might be best to go back to the Pac-10, play for Washington State." Challenged by Calhoun's words, Marshall said, "I'll be your captain and I'll play in the NBA some day." Both of his predictions came true.

Marshall returned to Federal Way during the summer after his first year at UConn. He played basketball five hours a day, six days a week against Seattle SuperSonics rookies and first-teamers like all-stars Shawn Kemp, Detlef Schrempf, and Xavier McDaniel. Marshall had worked intense hours in the past. During soccer season in high school, he practiced basketball for an hour or two in the morning before first period started.

When Marshall returned for his sophomore season at UConn, his teammates noticed a difference. "When [Donny] came back that first fall, we knew something happened. He came alive," said Ollie. Calhoun's prove-me-wrong attitude helped develop many players. Donny Marshall was one of them.

When Marshall began to play organized sports, his older brother and father figure told him to be the aggressor on the field or the court. Marshall's brother said to Donny, "If you go out on the floor and aren't the enforcer, someone else would be. You have to be the intimidator and intimidate others, or you'd be intimidated." In high school, Marshall referred to this aggressive, intimidating style as "Marshall Law." To commemorate this brand of basketball, and to let his high school opponents know that he was going to bang into them, Marshall had LAW shaved onto the back of his head.

Sans the Law hairstyle, Marshall employed an intimidating style at UConn. In the semifinals of the 1995 Big East tournament, Georgetown's Othella Harrington delivered an elbow to Marshall, who went to the floor and then to the bench to recover. In the previous season, a Harrington elbow had knocked Marshall out of a game. Marshall had enough. When he returned to action in the 1995 Big East semifinals, Marshall looked for Harrington. After two minutes, he found him. Marshall drilled Harrington at midcourt and received a flagrant foul.

Because Marshall expressed his emotions on the court and played a physical game, supporters of opposing teams and members of the media outside Connecticut vilified him. They complained that Marshall mugged for the camera, patted himself on the back after a good play, and bowed to the crowd after road wins.

Donny Marshall dominated the first three rounds of the 1995 NCAA tournament. Every time Maryland peeked at UConn's lead in the Sweet 16 game, Marshall knocked the Terrapins back. He looked like he was going to take UConn to the Final Four in his hometown of Seattle.

In the Elite Eight, however, UCLA's Toby Bailey (who scored a career-high 26 points) and Tyus Edney (22 points) beat UConn down the floor and scored too many easy baskets. The Huskies came as close as four points with a little more than 12 minutes remaining, but an 8-2 UCLA rally ended the Huskies' season. UCLA was on its way to the program's 15th Final Four and 11th national championship: UCLA 102–UConn 96.

Junior center Travis Knight called this the best game in which he played at UConn. He liked the up-and-down pace and appreciated the beauty of two running teams scoring close to two hundred points. For Knight, the elegance of this game differed from Big East slugfests, which are sometimes hard to watch and even more difficult to play.

ALL–CALHOUN ERA, FOURTH BEST INDIVIDUAL SEASON FOR A PLAYER
- - - - - - - - - - - - - - - -
Ray Allen
1994–1995

Following his team's victory, UCLA coach Jim Harrick said, "I thought today we had a player [Edney] that was a little better than everybody on the floor. Except for Ray Allen." Allen scored 36 points — 18 in each half. In his 23 seasons as a college coach, Harrick had never seen a player come off double staggers — screens by two players — and shoot the ball like Allen.

The loss to UCLA ended the UConn careers of Kevin Ollie and Donny Marshall. In Ollie and Marshall's final two years, the Huskies won 57 games and lost 10, an 85 percent success rate. In Big East games during those two seasons, UConn went 32-4, an 89 percent winning percentage.

Ollie played for 11 franchises in a 13-year NBA career, one shy of the record, 12, a distinction held by three players. Undrafted out of UConn, Ollie played four seasons for the CBA's Connecticut Pride before he went to the NBA. "Without [coach] pushing me, I don't think I would have had the resiliency I had in the pros, because he was always pushing me," Ollie said in the summer after he retired from pro basketball. Ollie played in 662 NBA games and averaged 3.8 points over his career.

Ollie served as coach on the court and mentor off of it. In 2003, Cleveland signed him to teach rookie LeBron James how to play in the NBA. The Oklahoma City Thunder signed Ollie to mentor point guard Russell Westbrook, a star in the making in the shadow of Kevin Durant. In the summer of 2010, Calhoun hired Ollie as an assistant coach.

When Marshall and Ollie graduated, UConn was the Big East's most dominant team, but it had not won the Big East tournament since 1990. UConn was now 0-2 in Elite Eight games under Calhoun, and the whispers that the coach could not win the so-called big one grew louder.

One week and a day after UCLA eliminated the Huskies, the UConn women's team completed an undefeated season and beat Tennessee in the national championship game. The men's team started an interest in the school; Rebecca Lobo added to the passion.

After Calhoun's first season at UConn, State Representative Tom Ritter of Hartford invited Calhoun and the Huskies to the Capitol. "For what?" Calhoun asked. "Because we want to honor you," Ritter said. "Honor us? We went 9-19." Ritter said that some of the members of the Connecticut General Assembly were alumni and they wanted to meet the coach and the team.

On April 25, 1995—the day that the UConn teams visited state legislators at the Capitol—Connecticut's state senators and representatives fell over themselves to meet Rebecca Lobo and Ray Allen. Governor John Rowland announced his support for UConn 2000, a $1 billion legislative package to modernize the university through construction of state-of-the-art facilities and rehabilitation of old buildings.

UConn 2000 aimed to reverse the brain drain, in which talented high school students from Connecticut pursued their degrees outside the state. The men's and women's basketball teams made UConn 2000 a reality. According to the *New York Times*, "Despite initial skepticism, the program sailed through the Legislature, thanks to a well-orchestrated lobbying campaign and, in no small measure, to the wave of 'Huskymania' that swept the state as the women's and men's basketball teams pursued national championships." An Associated Press story stated, "University administrators have often said that UConn's basketball success helped UConn 2000 garner acceptance in the Capitol." In UConn's case, basketball led to educational gains.

As he stood before the State Senate on Husky Day in 1995, Calhoun defended his program against critics who said it couldn't win the big one. In his short remarks in the Senate chambers, Calhoun told legislators about his team's recent accomplishments: 28 wins for the year, back-to-back conference championships, a six-point loss to the eventual national champions, and five players with GPAs of 3.0 or better. The defense rested.

In Connecticut in 1995, national championships were the new standard. The women had theirs, where was Calhoun's? The coach who had already performed the greatest turnaround in college basketball history had to defend 25-plus-win seasons, Big East titles, and Elite Eight appearances.

11

Ray Allen, One of the Greatest

After the 1995 season, Allen and Sheffer considered pro careers but decided to return to Storrs. Allen didn't feel he was ready to go to the NBA after his sophomore year. Still insistent on playing in the NBA, Sheffer rejected an offer to play professionally in Israel.

Destination: the Meadowlands, site of the 1996 Final Four, became a mandatory mission. Anything short of playing in the final weekend of the college basketball season would be a disappointment, and concerns about Calhoun's ability to win the so-called big one would be more than validated in the minds of many of his detractors and even some of his supporters.

Calhoun acknowledged the challenge: "Our goal is to win a national championship. Just getting to the Final Four probably at this stage wouldn't be enough. Getting there in 1990 might have been fine. But I don't think that would be the goal now."

In less than a decade, Calhoun had changed the culture of UConn basketball. The Huskies had a first-rate program. Gampel Pavilion dwarfed Guyer Gym and the field house. An academic program kept players eligible, although Calhoun received criticism for an insufficient graduation rate. Calhoun attracted the best players Storrs had ever seen and developed them into future NBA stars. UConn won . . . a lot.

The program that couldn't beat Yale in 1986 needed a national title 10 years later. John Wooden made it to his first Final Four and won his first NCAA tournament in his 16th season at UCLA. Calhoun didn't have that much time. Anyone who paid attention to UConn basketball wanted a national championship *now* or, as Charleston Chiefs goalie Denis Lemieux said in *Slap Shot*, "right fucking now."

UMass and its superstar, Hartford's Marcus Camby, distracted UConn. Supporters of the two schools, located an hour and 15 minutes away from each other, argued over which team was superior. When the media asked UConn athletic director Lew Perkins about Madison Square Garden's desire to host a game between the two teams, he replied, "People are calling us from everywhere. There isn't an arena in the country that's not interested."

Calhoun clashed with UMass coach John Calipari. Calhoun canceled the series between the two schools after the 1990 game, and Calipari taunted him for that. Calipari called UMass the king of New England basketball after his team became the region's first to gain the top spot in the college rankings. That proclamation irritated Calhoun, who said that Calipari didn't know enough about New England basketball to make such a claim. Calhoun referred to Calipari as "Johnny Clam Chowder," because the UMass coach, a native of western Pennsylvania, didn't even know how to pronounce "clam chowdha." If Calipari didn't know clam chowder, how could he say anything about New England?

Calhoun called the confrontation inevitable because he and Calipari competed for the same territory. He said that a generational difference — Calhoun is nearly 17 years older — increased the tension. In 1995, a New England sportswriter said the Cals couldn't stand each other. He figured that Calhoun hated Calipari in part because the UMass coach reminded him of Geno Auriemma.

After the 1996 season, UConn and UMass signed a contract to play a multiyear series of games in the two states. On the day the deal was announced, Calipari left UMass for the NBA. In the 10 games played between the two teams since the start of the 1996–1997 season, UConn holds a 9–1 record over UMass.

UConn dominated its opponents in 1995–1996. After demolishing Texas Christian by 26 in its opening game, sixth-ranked UConn lost its next contest, 101–95, in overtime to 10th-ranked Iowa in the semifinals of the Great Alaska Shootout. Some around the UConn program said this was the most upset they had ever seen Calhoun after a game.

The loss to Iowa was bad news . . . for the Huskies' opponents. In the next game, UConn pummeled Bobby Knight's Indiana Hoosiers by 34. Allen scored 29 points in this game and was named the tournament's most valuable player, despite UConn's third-place finish in the Shootout. UConn's victory over Indiana started a 23-game winning streak. The Huskies led the entire second half of every game in this stretch.

At this point in the evolution of the program, UConn had elite scorers like Allen and Sheffer, stud athletes like Kirk King, Ricky Moore, and Rudy Johnson who could outrebound and outrun the other teams, and Travis Knight, who played his position well. Every Husky who played during this era could defend his opponents. With these combinations, UConn scored lots of points and held opposing teams to lower-than-normal totals.

After UConn's 79–61 victory over Florida State, Seminoles' coach Pat Kennedy addressed his team's performance in an ad in the *Tallahassee Democrat*. More than a year later, Kennedy said he wrote the letter to let "our boosters know how sorry I was at the way we played." Jeff Jones, who apologized to Virginia fans after UConn's 41-point win in 1993, witnessed another Cavalier bludgeoning at the hands of the Huskies; this time UConn won by 30.

In January, UConn's *Big Monday* game against Villanova was canceled because of a snowstorm in Connecticut. It was played the next night on ESPN2. Ray Allen wanted revenge for the previous year's defeats to 'Nova. Prior to the game, he took shots in front of the students who had been let into Gampel. He missed most of his attempts.

Recognizing that his star player was overstimulated, Calhoun called Allen to the sideline and said, "You can't win the game in the first 38 seconds." After Allen missed his first three shots, Calhoun put his star on the bench to cool him off. When Allen returned less than a minute later, he scored 22 points in the first half and made a critical basket with the shot clock expiring late in the game to stunt a Villanova comeback. UConn won, 81–73.

UConn dominated on the road to the point where the other school's fans booed their teams and then left well before the clock expired. The 1995–1996 team set the school record for victories and became the second UConn squad to win 30 games. Like the 1993–1994 team, it won all 15 of its home games. It went 27–2 in the regular season and set the team record for winning percentage (.944) in a single Big East season. At the time, Calhoun regarded this team as the best he had ever coached.

By season's end, the Big East's MVP award came down to Ray Allen and Allen Iverson of Georgetown. They were the most prolific and high-profile stars the Big East had produced in one season since Georgetown's Patrick Ewing and Chris Mullin of St. John's battled each other.

After Georgetown pounded UConn in the lone regular season meeting between the two teams, many speculated that Iverson would win the league's most valuable player award. In that game, Iverson scored 26 points, stole the ball eight times, and had six assists. Ray Allen played his worst game of the season to that point and scored 13.

Calhoun believed that his Allen deserved the most valuable player trophy because Ray had a greater effect on his team's success than Iverson had on his. UConn lost one Big East game and captured the conference regular season title. In what Big East commissioner Mike Tranghese described as the closest MVP vote in the history of the conference, Allen, as in Ray Allen, was named the MVP at a ceremony attended by neither Georgetown coach John Thompson nor Iverson.

Allen dominated in his junior year. Against Rutgers, he made nine of his 14 three-point attempts as part of a 39-point performance. More than 10 years later, Calhoun regarded this game and Donyell Marshall's 42 points against St. John's as the best single-game performances during his 20-year tenure at UConn. In 1996, Calhoun called Allen the best player he had ever coached.

Prior to UConn's first game in the 1996 Big East tournament, Adrian Griffin, the best player on Seton Hall, the Huskies' opponent in the quarterfinals, said, "If we stop Ray Allen, we'll see if the rest of their role players step up." He saw. Allen shot four for 17 from the field and scored 11 points. UConn won by 21. Travis Knight scored 12 points, assisted on four baskets, and set a program record with 19 rebounds in a Big East tournament contest.

In UConn's game against Syracuse in the semifinals of the 1996 Big East tournament, Ray Allen scored 29 and the Huskies won, 85–67. Three weeks after UConn dominated Syracuse, the Orangemen would play Kentucky in the NCAA tournament finals.

Ray Allen got excited when he saw his name and Allen Iverson's on the Madison Square Garden marquee the night of the conference championship game. With 4:46 remaining in the game, Ray couldn't have been all that excited. Georgetown's Jahidi White just made a basket, Knight fouled out as a result of the play, and the Hoyas led 74–63. Georgetown's Victor Page waved his arms so frenetically that he nearly took off in flight. UConn's starting backcourt had scored four points in the half and Allen hadn't made a field goal since 7:41 remained in the first half.

"They are really playing well," Dick Vitale said of the Hoyas.

The victim of what he considered two questionable calls, Knight sat on the bench with a blank look upon his face.

On UConn's ensuing possession, freshman Ricky Moore fed King for a one-handed layup, and UConn trailed by nine with 4:24 left. John Thompson decided to hold the ball, kill time, and let Iverson or Page create offensive opportunities as the shot clock expired. A Georgetown foul followed by two free throws by King cut the deficit to seven. 3:45 remained.

When ESPN returned from a commercial break, Brad Nessler and Vitale described the story of the night. Allen had scored 12 points in the first 11 minutes of the game but managed three — all from the free throw line — in the next 25. He was 0 for 13 from the field in that time.

The Hoyas turned over the ball when the shot clock expired and Jerome Williams's shot shook the backboard but missed the rim. 3:08 remained. Allen missed an open three-pointer, but King grabbed the ball and shot it up and in with one motion, and pumped his fist. UConn now trailed, 74–69, with 2:49 left. More than a minute later, Sheffer's free throws narrowed the gap to three; 1:43 remained.

Vitale continued to condemn Ray Allen as the game came to a close. He criticized Allen's jump-shooting and even his dribble. "I love Ray Allen, I've seen his talent," Vitale said after he commented that Allen dribbled the ball too high. He praised Iverson, who was outplayed by Allen. Ray Allen scored more points, shot a better percentage from the floor, turned the ball over less, and had more rebounds and two fewer assists than Iverson. No mention of Iverson. Instead Allen was the focus of the criticism.

Ricky Moore continued to defend Iverson, who missed again as the shot clock was about to expire. Moore got the ball, blew past Iverson, but missed a layup. King dunked the rebound. Georgetown's lead was one. 1:04 remained. King finished the game with 20 points and nine rebounds, eight of which came off the offensive glass.

Georgetown's full-court pressure troubled Calhoun, who, on the day of the championship game, tried to figure how to beat the trap. During UConn's pregame practice, Ricky Moore broke the pressure by dribbling through or by defenders. After watching Moore solve the press, Calhoun said, "Why don't you do that in the game. Go right through the press." He turned to the players and asked them if Moore could break the press on his own. The team yelled, "Yes!" After watching Moore's performance in practice throughout the season, the players called him "Jesse Owens," in reference to the freshman's ability to run by everyone who defended him.

With 45.3 seconds left, Page missed the front end of a one-and-one. He neither smiled nor pumped his fists. Down 74-73 and with the ball in hand, UConn called time-out. 38.1 seconds remained.

"Weave it to Ray," Calhoun said. The coach told Moore to get the ball to Allen, who would cut behind the point guard, take a pass, and head to the basket for a shot. Everyone else was to clear out of Allen's way. As he listened to Calhoun explain the play, Allen thought, "Wow, this is great to know that Coach has faith in me." Without regard for the shots he missed in the second half, Allen walked back onto the court and thought, "It's winning time."

Moore dribbled to the wing opposite UConn's bench, where he handed the ball to Allen, who semicircled the top of the key. Iverson guarded him. Allen stopped his dribble to the right of the free throw line near UConn's bench. He went up, considered a pass to Rudy Johnson in the corner, but Jerome Williams cut off his passing lane. Now he had to shoot the ball on the way down. He pumped his legs like he was riding a bicycle as he pushed the ball toward the hoop. The ball floated toward the rim as Allen applied the softest of touches. It went in.

Allen got what he termed a "lucky roll." Georgetown's Thompson said that Allen "hit the kind of shot we wanted him to take—falling, off balance, and it winds up going in the basket. What are you going to do?" With Allen's field goal, the only one he scored in the second half, UConn took a one-point lead. The crowd roared. 13.6 seconds remained.

Georgetown inbounded the ball to Iverson, who was met by Moore as he came into the front court. With 6.6 seconds remaining, Iverson missed an off-balance, fade-away jumper from the free throw line as Allen, Moore, and Sheffer covered him. Jerome Williams grabbed the rebound in the paint. He hurried himself and Rudy Johnson's hands-straight-up defense caused Williams to miss a short shot with 2.7 seconds left. The ball went out of bounds off of UConn, but time had expired: UConn 75–Georgetown 74. Ray Allen impersonated Steve Martin's dance in *Parenthood*. He ran, marched, and danced—all in the same motion. He flew past his coach.

Page won most valuable player of the tournament, but it was Moore's play that changed the outcome of the finals. The writers had voted before Moore and King rewrote the ending of the game. Moore made six of his 12 shots and scored 14 points (12 in the second half). Thanks in large measure to Moore's defense, UConn held Georgetown scoreless for the final 4:46 of play.

Moore separated his shoulder in the first half of UConn's first-round NCAA tournament win over Colgate and sat out the rest of the postseason. After wins in the first two rounds, top-seeded UConn made its third consecutive appearance in the Sweet 16. At the University of Kentucky's Rupp Arena, the Huskies faced the fifth-seeded Mississippi State Bulldogs. In the SEC tournament finals, Mississippi State had defeated Kentucky, a team that would go on to win the NCAA championship that year.

Bizarro is one of Superman's enemies. He's the anti-Superman. Bizarro wears a backward S, is ugly, stupid, and unethical. These are things that Superman is not. The Bizarro Huskies played in the 1996 Sweet 16 contest. All the things that the UConn team was in 1995–1996, it wasn't on that night. The 1995–1996 team liked to run and attack. Against Mississippi State, UConn scored no points on the fast break. The 1995–1996 team scored 83 points per game. On this night, it managed 55. Mississippi State forced the Huskies to play at molasses speed.

Calhoun told his players to "Push it!" but UConn's attack was hurt by Moore's absence. Without him, Sheffer and Allen played extra minutes and struggled for open shots. Calhoun said that UConn lost some zip and never was the same after Moore got hurt. According to Knight, the team didn't know how to adjust without its speed and spark plug.

Allen scored 22 points, but made just 36 percent of his attempts from the field. For the season, he shot better than 45 percent from the floor *and* three-point range. Against Mississippi State, he missed six of his final seven shots, including a three-pointer that would have tied the game with 12 seconds to go.

Dreary and overcast weather greeted the team when it returned to Connecticut. As Howie Dickenman drove away from Gampel, he saw Ray Allen on the corner and asked if he needed a ride. Allen accepted a lift back to the Clubhouse Apartments, where he lived with Travis Knight. Dickenman, who claimed he could get from Bradley Airport to the UConn campus in 15 minutes (the 37-mile trip takes at least 40 minutes), took his foot off the gas to drive Allen home.

In the car, Dickenman said, "You have a big decision coming up. For whatever it's worth, do what's best for Ray Allen. Ignore what others say. Don't please anybody but yourself."

Dickenman pulled into the driveway of the complex and saw Allen take his gear out of the backseat and walk along the sidewalk and up to the apartment door. As Allen put the key in the lock, Dickenman, sitting alone in his car, said, "Ray Allen, one of the greatest." Allen disappeared through the door as tears formed in Dickenman's eyes. Dickenman figured that he would never again see Ray Allen in a UConn uniform.

He was right.

Dickenman still tears up when he tells that story.

On April 22, 1996, with Jim Calhoun at his side, Ray Allen told a small audience at Gampel Pavilion that he would enter the NBA draft. The Minnesota Timberwolves selected Allen with the fifth overall pick. They traded Allen's rights to the Milwaukee Bucks for Stephon Marbury.

In his first 14 seasons in NBA, Allen would go on to average 20.2 points per game and play in nine All-Star games. He would be part of a gold-medal Olympic team in 2000 and a world championship Celtics team in 2008. In 2011, Allen would surpass Reggie Miller as the NBA's all-time leader for three-pointers made.

In the summer of 2006, the Boston Celtics acquired Allen from Seattle. Allen joined Kevin Garnett and Paul Pierce to form the new Big Three for the Celtics. Allen and Garnett knew each other from South Carolina. They were on the same AAU team and played together in other venues. As 16- and 17-year-olds, they had traveled to Columbia, South Carolina, and played pickup games against the Gamecocks team, which included future NBA players JoJo English and Jamie Watson. "We would go in and dominate them," Allen said.

Allen brought Garnett to the UConn game at North Carolina State in December of 1992; they went into the UConn locker room afterward. Dickenman

Ray Allen never left UConn. He recruits players for his former coaches and returns to Storrs on a regular basis. Here, he waves to the fans at UConn's first night celebration on October 14, 2011.
Ed Ryan/ *The Daily Campus*

gave a program to Garnett, and based upon the wide-eyed look he received, he was certain that this was Garnett's first college game. To this day, Calhoun wonders what his program would have been like had Garnett joined Allen in Storrs. When Garnett and Allen played together as pros, they helped the Celtics win that franchise's 17th NBA title and appeared together on the *Late Show with David Letterman* to discuss the championship.

Allen made more than one old-school reconnection when he went to Boston. During the 2008 championship run, an old friend occupied Allen's personal seats at the TD North Garden. Howie Dickenman attended many of the playoff games that season, and he was there when Allen and the Celtics beat the Lakers to take the NBA championship. He congratulated Allen in a champagne-filled Celtics locker room after the game.

Allen remains close with several of his UConn teammates and friends. Donny Marshall, Burrell, Ollie, and Allen live in Connecticut in the summer

Two eras ended in 1996—the Ray Allen era and the Howie Dickenman era. Calhoun called Dickenman his "right hand man" and said that Howie "did as much as anyone to build our program." Dickenman and Calhoun on the sidelines in UConn's first game at Gampel, January 27, 1990.

University Photograph Collection, Archives & Special Collections at the Thomas J. Dodd Research Center, University of Connecticut Libraries. Photo published with permission.

and play golf together. Allen has talked to many recruits on behalf of the UConn coaching staff. He recruited for Dickenman at Central Connecticut State University, for Leitao at Virginia, and for Hobbs at George Washington. Dickenman once called Allen when Joe Seymore, one of his recruits at Central, said that the former UConn star was his favorite NBA player. At the time, Allen, Burrell, and Natambu Willingham were golfing in Las Vegas. Allen was happy to speak with Seymore, who went on to average 8.1 points in his 124-game, four-year career under Dickenman at Central Connecticut.

Like Allen, Dickenman left UConn in 1996. As head coach at Central Connecticut, his alma mater, Dickenman would lead the Blue Devils to the program's first three NCAA tournament berths. Calhoun referred to Dickenman as his "right-hand man," and said that Dickenman "did as much as anyone to build our program."

"Those are my guys," Allen said of his UConn coaches toward the end of the 2009-2010 season. "They have a lot to do with where I am today." Allen and his former coaches continue to talk about basketball and life. Allen values their opinion.

As a second-round pick for the Los Angeles Clippers, Sheffer became the first Israeli taken in the NBA draft. Because he thought his chances to make the Clippers were close to zero, Sheffer signed a contract worth a reported $400,000 per year to play with Maccabi Elite, the same team for which Nadav Henefeld starred. According to Eli Groner of the *Jerusalem Post*, Sheffer had "the most storied college basketball career of any Israeli ever."

The Chicago Bulls used their first-round pick, the 29th overall, to take Travis Knight, making him Calhoun's fifth first-round pick at UConn. Knight never played a game for Chicago, but earned a championship ring as a member of the 2000 Lakers, and joined Burrell as the second Husky to play on an NBA championship team. Knight left the Lakers when Rick Pitino and the Celtics offered him a seven-year, $22 million contract. He played 371 games over six seasons in the NBA.

Allen, Sheffer, and Knight took three-quarters of the team's offense and 60 percent of UConn's rebounding with them when they left. One starter remained. It appeared unlikely that a player as talented and as accomplished as Ray Allen would ever wear the UConn jersey again. It seemed even more remote that a set of players as good as the ones who just left Storrs would play for UConn in the future.

The Ray Allen era in UConn basketball was glorious to most but disappointing to those who accepted nothing less than a national championship. During Allen's three years as a Husky, UConn won 87 percent of its games, 90 percent of its conference contests, three regular season conference titles, and one tournament championship in the Big East. With Allen, UConn never lost two or more games in a row and was in first place from the beginning to the end of the star's career.

Critics bashed the Huskies, who were called the best team from December to early March and one of the biggest underachievers in sports. One writer concluded, "Huskies coach Jim Calhoun can't win the big one because he can't get his team to the big one." Despite the glory of the Ray Allen era, the new expectations left many saying, "Those teams did well, but . . ."

3

NATIONAL CHAMPIONS

12

You Learn from Losses, but after You Get Three or Four, the Learning Stops and the Misery Starts

Donyell and Donny Marshall, Kevin Ollie, Brian Fair, and Rudy Johnson set the standard for the best UConn recruiting class in the Calhoun era, but the 1996 class approached this bar. Calhoun said that the 1996 recruits were more ready to contribute than the players from the 1991 class.

UConn's 1996 recruits included Kevin Freeman, who was ranked among the top 35 high school seniors. Freeman, a six foot six, 220-pound, swingman, left Longmeadow High School outside Springfield, Massachusetts, after three years and attended Paterson Catholic in Paterson, New Jersey, for his senior year.

Freeman teamed with Tim Thomas, the nation's number-two high school prospect, to form the core of one of the best high school teams in the country. In his one year in New Jersey, Freeman learned how to play outside a star's spotlight. At Longmeadow, Freeman was *the* man and the best prospect in Massachusetts. Tim Thomas was *the* man at Paterson Catholic. Freeman averaged 22 points and 13 rebounds per game at Paterson. The experience of shining outside the spotlight would help Freeman in college.

UMass, Boston College, Seton Hall, UCLA, UNLV, Minnesota, Pittsburgh, Duke, and Rutgers were on Freeman's list of potential schools. Freeman waited until the spring signing period to make his decision, but in the end chose UConn, he said, because of its history of winning and its aggressive and uptempo style of basketball. The closeness of the UConn players impressed him.

When Jake Voskuhl entered Strake Jesuit High School in Houston, he was six foot five. By his senior year, he was nearly seven feet and weighed 245 pounds. The *Houston Chronicle* regarded Voskuhl as "the best passing center in the state." In his senior year, he averaged 10.6 points and 15.1 rebounds per game. At six foot eleven, Voskuhl was a giant but his bright blond signature haircut and boyish looks gave him a gentle appearance. On the court, however, he was not gentle. By the start of his senior year, he had earned the nickname The Hammer for his physical play inside and setting screens on the perimeter. Strake won the Texas Christian Interscholastic League state championship in each of Voskuhl's four seasons. Voskuhl would go on to play the same role for UConn, which beat DePaul and Purdue among others to sign him.

The biggest catch that year was Richard "Rip" Hamilton, who fans and recruiting experts predicted would be UConn's next star. Hamilton's father had earned the nickname Rip when he ripped his diapers as a child. He passed the nickname to his son, who grew to be a six foot six guard in his hometown of Coatesville, Pennsylvania.

Hamilton was the second best high school player in the Philadelphia area. The best was the nation's top recruit, a guard from Lower Merion, Pennsylvania, also six foot six, named Kobe Bryant. Hamilton, a second-team *Parade* magazine All-American, a top 20 prospect, and Calhoun's second McDonald's All-American, averaged 24 points and 14 rebounds per game as a high school senior. One scouting expert characterized him as the "No. 1 sleeper in this class."

In the pre-Calhoun era, Hamilton would have played for Villanova. He grew up cheering for Villanova when Rollie Massimino coached the Wildcats. Hamilton didn't know about UConn until Donyell Marshall, from nearby Reading, starred for the Huskies. Because he and Marshall had similar backgrounds, Hamilton figured that he could fit in and flourish at UConn, as Marshall had a few seasons earlier. After Marshall left UConn for the NBA, Hamilton continued to follow the Huskies and the program's next star, Ray Allen.

As part of his trip to visit Hamilton, Karl Hobbs flew to the Philadelphia airport, where he planned to rent a car to drive to Coatesville. One problem: all the cars were rented. Hobbs thought about a cab ride, but figured that the 40-mile trip would be too expensive. He began to panic. This was his last opportunity to visit Hamilton's home. "We do have something, sir," the rental car employee said. "How about an eighteen-passenger van?" Knowing that Rip was special, Hobbs rented the van.

Hamilton's father thought that the UConn assistant had driven one of the university's surplus vans from Storrs to Coatesville. "Doesn't Connecticut have any money?" Big Rip said. "Can't you afford a car?" This was his car.

Hamilton waited until the spring signing period to commit, having made official visits to UConn and Clemson. During Hamilton's trip to UConn, the Huskies treated him as if he were already on the team. Hamilton ate with the team at Calhoun's restaurant, Coach's Bar and Grille, prior to the Virginia game at the Civic Center. When Hamilton returned to Coatesville, he knew he would wear the Connecticut uniform the following season. UConn's star power, success, and national television exposure drew him to Storrs.

During Hamilton's first month on the team, Calhoun said that a chair could score double-digits against Hamilton. The coach's style has always been to break down players, then build them up; Rip was next. Hamilton was skinny, almost scrawny, but his endurance would make a pogo stick envious. He had no limitations on offense.

Despite the prominence of the players Calhoun brought in and the size of the 1996 recruiting class—seven altogether—the experts rated UConn's class as the fifth best in the nation and third in the Big East behind Syracuse and Villanova.

During the Calhoun era, older players taught newer ones about the program's culture. For the 1996-1997 season, the UConn team lacked a returning star or core player who could teach the freshmen. Year one of the Rip Hamilton era must be seen in this context, one in which a new UConn team learned how to win and play for Calhoun. Coming into the season, Calhoun had never started more than one freshman at a time. For the 1996-1997 season, he started three: Hamilton, Voskuhl, and Freeman.

After losing its first game to Indiana in The Classic at the RCA Dome in Indianapolis, UConn won 11 of its next 13. Leading up to a game at the Civic Center against number-one and unbeaten Kansas, Calhoun told his wife that he thought UConn could win the Big East because no team in the conference scared him.

The season turned because of $370 plane tickets. On January 16, 1997, three days before Kansas came to town, UConn suspended Kirk King and Ricky Moore. In the fall of 1995, they had received free plane tickets from a wannabe agent from Wolcott, Connecticut, which is an NCAA no-no. After its investigation, the NCAA banned King from playing for the remainder of the 1996-1997 season and suspended Moore for five games. The NCAA concluded that no one on the coaching staff or in the university administration had any knowledge of these wrongdoings.

King received the harsher punishment because he lied about taking the ticket and, as a senior, he knew the trip violated the rules. The NCAA figured that Moore, a freshman at the time, didn't understand the implications of his actions. It denied UConn's appeal for a leaner sentence and ended Kirk King's collegiate career.

Calhoun made sure that King stayed with the family, though. Because NCAA rules stipulate that players without eligibility can be student coaches, Calhoun named King as a student assistant; King went to practice, sat on the bench, and traveled with the team for the rest of the season.

At the time of these suspensions, King was UConn's leading rebounder (7.6 rebounds per game) and third leading scorer (11.8 points per game) and Moore, the team's point guard and top defender, led the team with 91 assists; he scored 8.2 points per game as well.

Calhoun often employs an us versus the world approach. "They" don't think we can win, but I do. For the Kansas game, Calhoun focused his team on winning the game. These are the cards we were dealt, Calhoun said, let's play them. Before the game, Calhoun told his team that he was excited about this "great opportunity for us. . . . I'm telling you they are the best and you can beat them."

Calhoun replaced his team's fast-paced, push-it tempo with Pete Carril's Princeton spread offense and a game of kill the clock. The strategy worked. UConn stalled, hit shots right before the shot clock expired, and slowed the Kansas offense.

The Hartford Civic Center rocked more than it ever had. Many season-ticket holders regard this game as one of the most exciting UConn games they ever attended. The Huskies built a 23-7 lead seven minutes into the contest. Led by All-Americans Raef LaFrentz, Jacque Vaughn, and Paul Pierce, Kansas cut UConn's lead to three at the half; they ignited several runs that gave the Jayhawks a 41-34 lead with about 17 minutes remaining. UConn tied the game at 53 and 55. Kansas took the lead for good with under 4:30 to play, and this hidden classic went the way of the Jay (Kansas 73-UConn 65).

Even with the dark times that UConn faced against Kansas on this day, Calhoun kept championship dreams in sight. He told his team "to look at how Kansas handled things down the stretch. I told them to take a lesson from a great basketball team." UConn lost its next three games.

As the Huskies struggled in the regular season, Calhoun told them that postseason berths, especially ones in the NCAA tournament, were the rule in Storrs. He warned his players that they didn't want to be the ones who broke the program's streak of national postseason play, which the 1988 NIT champs had started.

Over the course of that first season, Hamilton developed into a star. Against Kansas on CBS, he started at point guard and outplayed Vaughn. Hamilton set career highs for points (21) and assists (8) in that game. Vaughn, who nursed a strained left knee at the time, scored nine and had five assists.

After the game, the media asked Hamilton what it was like to play against Kansas and Vaughn and he said, "I'm not intimidated by anyone. When the ball is thrown up, I feel I can play with anyone." Hamilton's performance earned praise from Kansas coach and future Hall of Famer Roy Williams, who said, "That's a freshman . . . who got . . . twenty-one against us and we're pretty doggone good defensively."

In its 13-point loss to Seton Hall on senior night at the Civic Center, UConn played with little passion. It was the Huskies' fourth straight defeat. After the game, the players took solace in knowing that one of the academic year's biggest parties was taking place that night in Storrs. As they waited to head back to campus, team trainer Joe Sharpe told the players that they were not to go to their dorm rooms when they returned to campus. Instead, they were to wait at their lockers for a team meeting.

NCAA rules do not allow a team to hold a practice on game day, so Calhoun waited until midnight. Hamilton had his eye gouged during the game. He told Sharpe that he couldn't practice because his eye was "messed up." Sharpe agreed. "Give him some goggles," Calhoun said. The UConn coach told his trainer to return to the court only if he brought Hamilton with him.

Hamilton donned Kareem-style specs and he and Joe Sharpe joined the team on the court. Attendance at this session was mandatory. No student party for the team. Instead, the Huskies were about to party Calhoun-style, like it was 1986.

Calhoun was irate that his team had neither rebounded nor defended. So, the two-hour practice consisted of one-on-one and box-out drills. Calhoun served as referee, so few fouls were called. The practice included running and puking.

At one point, Calhoun gathered the team at midcourt and told his players, "Get the fuck out of my face in three seconds or we will be practicing for another half hour." The players scattered. According to Calhoun, "The only unfortunate thing about the practice was that whoever we would have played at that point in time, we would have beat. Rashamel Jones hit eight of his first nine jump shots."

After the practice, Voskuhl phoned his father, a former star at the University of Tulsa, to tell him to compile a list of schools to which he could transfer. "I couldn't take it anymore. I'd had it," Voskuhl said. His father told him "to calm down, call again the next day, wait until the end of the season to make a decision." By that time, Voskuhl had cooled and decided to remain in Storrs.

Calhoun wanted to make the NIT so that his team could learn how to win. He said, "It's very difficult to grow as a team in losses. You learn from losses, but after you get three or four, the learning stops and the misery starts."

UConn did make the NIT in 1997, and beat Iona, Bradley, and defending NIT champion Nebraska at Gampel. Hamilton scored 25 and 24 points in UConn's first two games. In the next game, Nebraska guard Tyronn Lue scored 14 points and made all four of his three-point attempts in the first half, which ended with his team up by nine points. To stop Lue, Calhoun called on senior Dion Carson, who held Lue to six points on two of eight shooting in the second half. Hamilton made 12 of his 14 shots en route to a career-high-tying 31 points and UConn won by nine. As a result of that tournament, Calhoun said that "Rip went from a good young player to a different level." The Gampel wins put the Huskies into the NIT semifinals at MSG, where they lost in overtime to Florida State. In the consolation game, UConn beat Arkansas by 10.

The 1997 NIT provided five more games of experience to the young players; Calhoun used the extra games and practices to try to improve upon the team's weaknesses, including its inability to close out opponents. The NIT taught the young Huskies more about how to win, a bonus that carried UConn a long way in the next few seasons.

"Nineteen ninety-seven was a rough year for us," Moore said. "But you have to go through some things in order to get better, basketball-wise." That season started a three-year journey.

By the time the 1996–1997 season ended, optimism had spread throughout Husky Nation. All five starters returned; each was an underclassman. Calhoun felt that the Huskies needed a floor leader. He likened his returning team to a group trapped in the desert in search of water.

Who would quench that thirst?

13

The Kid Comes with a Bag of Tricks

During a game while Ricky Moore served his suspension, Calhoun told Karl Hobbs that the team needed a point guard for the following season. "There are only two out there," Hobbs said to Calhoun. Khalid El-Amin, who played for North High School in Minneapolis, and Baron Davis of Crossroads High School in Santa Monica, California, were the highest-rated guards in the class of 1997. Hobbs's mission was to get one of them. He went to Santa Monica first.

With Duke and UCLA as his top choices, Davis didn't consider UConn. He signed with UCLA. Minnesota, here we come.

Hobbs and El-Amin knew each other. Hobbs had recruited Lamar Odom, who played with El-Amin in the summer. Odom and El-Amin hung out with each other. On many occasions, Odom handed the phone to his friend so that he could talk to Hobbs. Even with this relationship, Hobbs wasn't sure that the star point guard had an interest in UConn.

El-Amin led North to an undefeated season in his sophomore year in high school. His coach said, "He's like having two coaches, except that one is playing, running the show on the floor." When the state tournament concluded, El-Amin was named its MVP.

During the summer between his sophomore and junior years in high school, El-Amin was named the best of the 100 underclassman at the prestigious ABCD basketball camp in Teaneck, New Jersey. At ABCD, El-Amin played with Richard Hamilton and Kevin Freeman.

El-Amin committed to the University of Minnesota on at least two occasions, reopened his recruitment after each commitment, and added Kansas, Georgetown, and Cincinnati to his list of possible schools. After he saw El-Amin in a high school all-star game in California, Hobbs called Calhoun and said, "Hey, let me tell you one thing we definitely don't want?" "What's that?" Calhoun said. "We definitely don't want Khalid El-Amin to go to Georgetown. The kid comes with a bag of tricks," Hobbs said.

El-Amin had more followers than the Pied Piper. His actions off the court made news. As a junior, he married a college sophomore. He divorced his wife during his senior year and fathered a child, Tezzaree, with another woman. Later that season, El-Amin was benched at the start of a critical game late in the season because he was late to several practices and missed one outright. The next season, his parents suspended him four games for poor grades.

In El-Amin's junior year, North lost one game before it entered the 16-team tournament as the favorite to repeat as state champions. With 5.5 seconds left in the quarterfinals and his team down by one, El-Amin dribbled twice and launched a 23-footer just before the clock hit double zero. The ball went in, of course. For the game, El-Amin scored 41 points, a career high; his nine three-pointers set the state-tournament record.

As a senior, El-Amin averaged close to 20 points, along with four rebounds, seven assists, and three steals per game. Under El-Amin's leadership, North became the first Minnesota high school in close to 30 years, and the second in history, to win three consecutive state titles.

UConn did not appear to be a perfect fit for El-Amin because Ricky Moore was set to return for his junior year. At El-Amin's house, Khalid asked one question: "Coach, are you bringing me in to back up Ricky Moore?" Calhoun said that he recruited El-Amin to get a basketball player and leader. He knew that if El-Amin attended UConn, neither he nor Moore would sit on the bench. He had played three-guard lineups in the past.

The UConn program is a rarity because its recruits play with team members during visits. These scrimmages test the recruits. The recruiting visit allows current players to judge whether the recruit would fit in at UConn. During one particular recruit's trip, the UConn players found out that the recruit was a member of a gang. Ricky Moore told Calhoun, "You cannot recruit this guy." Calhoun listened.

When UConn beat writers and others came to watch El-Amin scrimmage during his official visit, they said, "This is Khalid El-Amin? The best point guard in the country?" El-Amin's appearance stunned them. Even Kevin Freeman, who hosted El-Amin during the guard's visit to Storrs, noticed that the skinny and athletic El-Amin with whom he played at the ABCD camp had gained some weight. El-Amin was listed as five foot ten and about 190 pounds, but people thought he looked pudgy.

That morning, the team went through a workout, in which it ran Cemetery Hill. When the players returned to Gampel, they were led by El-Amin, who chose the teams and dictated how the teams would shoot for possession of the ball. In seven years of watching high schoolers play on their official visits to Storrs, Joe Sharpe never saw any recruit take over a workout like El-Amin did on that day.

When the scrimmage games started in Gampel, everyone knew that El-Amin's weight had no effect on his ability to play. Khalid directed the players on the basketball court, distributed the ball with precision, scored and coached when necessary. At one point, Freeman didn't anticipate a sharp pass from El-Amin, who told him, "You have to step to the ball, K-Free."

El-Amin's team won every game.

The members of the 1996–1997 team bonded with El-Amin, who felt like he was already their teammate. They told Calhoun to get this guy. Following the scrimmage, El-Amin announced that UConn was "very high on my list now." He eliminated the University of Minnesota from consideration. On his 18th birthday, El-Amin woke up with a Kansas hat, a Georgetown hat, and a UConn hat on his dresser. Later that day, in front of family, friends, fans, media, and at least six television cameras outside North's gym, El-Amin put on the UConn hat.

Calhoun's trip to Minnesota and El-Amin's visit to Connecticut were the deciding factors in El-Amin's decision. At the press conference to announce his selection, El-Amin was asked about whether he would play much on a team that already had a point guard. UConn "needs a *lead* guard," said El-Amin, who thought that he and Ricky Moore could work well together. "Ricky can score and defend. I think I can do some of those things too. Both of us on the floor together—we'll cause trouble for some people."

Calhoun now had the leader of the band.

During a time-out against URI in the preseason NIT in UConn's third game of the 1997–1998 season, Calhoun told his team that he wanted two layups. Bang. Bang. The Huskies made two quick baskets and Calhoun felt someone pat him on the back. It was El-Amin. "Good call," he said. "No one's ever done that before," Calhoun said of the patting. El-Amin said that his coach "allowed me to be me . . . but he didn't have much choice in that matter."

Calhoun's former players had never seen a Husky have carte blanche to shoot. Tate George spoke with Robinson and Gamble about El-Amin and they asked, "'Who the hell is this kid, taking all these shots?' We never had an opportunity to do that," George said. "I had to wait my four years. It's just a sign of the times." It was also a sign of El-Amin's uniqueness.

Calhoun needed his new point guard to fit in to his system. El-Amin couldn't do whatever he wanted. Calhoun benched El-Amin after a sloppy practice and pulled him from another game after El-Amin attempted to dribble past every defender on the other team. But still, Khalid El-Amin was different.

Early in the 1997–1998 season, it became apparent that as El-Amin went, so went UConn. In the semifinals of the preseason NIT against Florida State, he shot 17 percent from the field and 22 percent from three-point range and the Huskies lost by seven. In the next game, against Arizona State, El-Amin scored

The kid with the bag of tricks. Khalid El-Amin leads UConn over Stanford.
UConn 76–Stanford 56. February 7, 1998, Gampel Pavilion, Storrs, Connecticut.

University Photograph Collection, Archives & Special Collections at the Thomas J. Dodd Research Center,
University of Connecticut Libraries. Photo published with permission.

a career high 29 points and the Huskies won by 21. At home, he torched West
Virginia for 29 points on 12 of 18 shooting and UConn buried the Mountaineers by 13. In the rematch in Morgantown, El-Amin was not so awesome — 7
points — and UConn got crushed by 18.

El-Amin was the team's leader, but Hamilton was its star. Hamilton became
the second UConn sophomore after Ray Allen to reach a thousand points. In
1998, Calhoun regarded Hamilton as "a top twenty-five player. . . . Next year,
he can be a top ten or top five." Calhoun's comments reflected a strategy to
keep his star, who would surely be tempted to leave for the pros after the season. Hamilton joined Chris Mullin and John Bagley as the only sophomores to
win conference player of the year honors.

The 1997–1998 Huskies played old-school Calhoun basketball: tenacious
D and track-meet O. UConn displayed this brand of basketball to a national
audience against ninth-ranked Stanford in Storrs. Heading into the game,
most reporters questioned whether UConn could match Stanford's starting
frontcourt, which stood at seven foot one, six foot nine, and six foot seven. The
game was no contest: UConn 76–Stanford 56.

At one point during the game, Stanford went without a point for more than five minutes and in the second half, it went 11:11 without a field goal. Its 56 points were the lowest for the team in two years. Under Calhoun, UConn may hold a record for eliciting apologies from other coaches directed to their fans. Stanford coach Mike Montgomery said, "I'm sorry we didn't play better. They were fired up. I thought they were the aggressor."

Calhoun referred to the game as "a peek at the future." He had his eyes on 1998–1999, when the team would be a year older and have played a full season together. He was concerned that the team might not stay together.

UConn beat St. John's by 29 at Gampel in the season finale to win the conference's regular season title. El-Amin torched St. John's for 29 points. During one stretch in the second half, he outscored St. John's 11–0. After the game, Calhoun tried to get the team to think about the NCAA tournament and next season: "This team is good enough that it's going to be judged probably in the NCAA tournament—and hopefully come back next year and do some things, too."

In the Big East quarterfinals against Providence, UConn led by two with 3:39 to go, then surged to win by nine. UConn beat Rutgers by 14 in conference tournament semifinals. Afterward, Rutgers star Geoff Billet expressed his admiration for the standard that UConn set under Calhoun. "I saw exactly who we want to be," Billet said after the game. "We're both state schools. We have similar facilities. If I could pick a role model for us, it would be Connecticut." Ten years earlier, no one wanted to be like UConn.

In the Big East tournament final against second-seeded Syracuse, the Orangemen led 48–39 with 9:35 remaining in the game. Calhoun called time. El-Amin had missed 11 of his 12 shots. After the time-out, he hit a three-pointer that started an 11–0 Husky run. With UConn ahead 52–51, Voskuhl grabbed an offensive rebound, which he fired to El-Amin, who begged for the ball in the corner. Bang. El-Amin's three put UConn up by four with 3:03 to go in regulation. Syracuse never got closer than that: UConn 69–Syracuse 64.

Parents often measure their children's height with markings and dates on the wall. In many ways, Calhoun did this in the Richard Hamilton years. After each win or major event, the coach evaluated how much the team had grown and how far it needed to go. He wanted to win the Big East tournament so that the team could see how much it had grown.

Against Syracuse, El-Amin didn't shoot well, launched several bad shots, and, at times, established a pace that was too fast for his teammates. When the outcome of the game was in doubt, El-Amin played better than anyone else. He earned the Big East tournament's most valuable player honors.

In second-seeded UConn's first game in the NCAA tournament at Washington, DC's MCI Center, Fairleigh Dickinson's Elijah Allen scored 43 points, but that wasn't enough, as Hamilton and El-Amin scored 30 apiece to lead the Huskies to an eight-point victory. With the win, UConn moved to 7-0 in first-round NCAA tournament games under Calhoun.

UConn advanced to the Sweet 16 after it beat Indiana by 10 points. El-Amin scored 22 and had a career-high-tying eight assists. Reporters asked him if he was surprised that UConn went from the NIT the season before to the Sweet 16, and El-Amin said, "They didn't have me last season. I'm not being boastful, but that's how I feel."

For most of its Sweet 16 game, UConn controlled 11th-seeded Washington. The contest was played in front of a small crowd at Greensboro Coliseum because at least half of the fans left after North Carolina beat Michigan State in the first game. UConn led 64-55 with 10:16 left but the Huskies would score 11 points for the rest of the game.

Donald Watts, the son of former NBA star Slick Watts, made a three-pointer with Moore in his face to give Washington its first lead of the game. Only 33.2 seconds remained. Calhoun called UConn's final time-out with 29.1 seconds to go and decided to play for the last shot; he figured his team was too tired to stop Washington if time remained on the clock.

El-Amin held the ball far from the basket for about 15 seconds. Voskuhl went from the post to the top of the key to set a screen for El-Amin, who made his move with 12 seconds left. The pick-and-roll was on. As El-Amin dribbled along the right side, two Washington defenders converged on him. After setting the screen, Voskuhl moved down the center of the lane, got open, and received a pass from El-Amin.

Voskuhl's shot tap-danced on the left and then right side of the rim and bounced away. The ball was batted into Hamilton's hands with 5.5 seconds remaining. He shot and missed. El-Amin climbed the beanstalks to tap the ball back to Hamilton, who was standing near the dotted semicircle in front of the free throw line.

"Okay, you missed the first one," Hamilton said to himself. "This one, don't worry about how much time is on the clock; just shoot it like you would shoot any jump shot." It seemed to the UConn star like he had the ball for 15 minutes.

Hamilton set himself as best he could, took a step back with his left leg, and put up what could have been UConn's final shot of the season. Momentum carried Hamilton to the floor and he started to slide past the free throw line as the ball traveled toward the basket. When the shot went through the net, Hamilton sat at the top of the key. His teammates soon joined him there.

The game-winner against Washington was Hamilton's first career buzzer-

Dynamic duo to the rescue. Khalid El-Amin and Richard Hamilton celebrate
after Hamilton made a buzzer-beating shot against Washington in the Sweet 16
in Greensboro, North Carolina, on March 19, 1998, to give UConn a 76–75 win over
the other Huskies.

AP Photo/Alan Marler

beater at any level. The weekend before, he and Freeman watched NCAA tournament games and Rip told his best friend and roommate that he wanted to make a buzzer-beater.

When the Huskies returned to their locker room, Freeman wasn't with them. Freeman's body had cramped up and he went down near the UConn band. Doctors estimated that Freeman had lost between eight and nine pounds during the game, and they administered an IV to replace his fluids. He would be ready for UConn's next game.

"We came here to play Carolina," Calhoun said after the Washington game. As soon as UConn reached the regional finals for the third time under Calhoun, the media retrieved the "Jim Calhoun has done everything but get UConn into the Final Four" stories. And there were lots of them.

Fans received Carolina blue and white pompons as they entered the Greensboro Coliseum for the UConn-UNC game. All the businesses and buildings outside the arena had Carolina blue signs in their windows.

After an 11–2 UConn run, the Huskies trailed 59–58 with 5:37 remaining. Then, Hamilton launched a three to try to give a two-point lead to UConn. He missed and Antawn Jamison dunked on the other end to put Carolina up three. El-Amin missed a three to tie the game on the next possession; the Huskies never recovered and lost by 11.

According to El-Amin, "When we cut the lead to one, we got antsy and excited. I guess we showed our age there. We didn't really execute when we were down one and three. . . . That was the game there." Ricky Moore said that UConn could have won the game. The UConn players wanted a national championship.

14

We're Having a Special Season

With the sweat from the Carolina game still on his body, Rip Hamilton began to field questions about his future plans. Rip was torn. He had to weigh NBA money against the prospects of a national championship.

Calhoun knew that UConn would be top 20 good without Hamilton, but Final Four special with his star. At first, he tried the hard sell on Hamilton. If you aren't a lottery pick, teams won't invest in your success, he said to Hamilton. If players are good enough to make big money, Calhoun tells them to go. If players aren't guaranteed a high spot in the draft, Calhoun encourages them to stay. The UConn coach believes that team success leads to personal success for his players. If UConn won the national championship, he told Hamilton, then his draft stock would be even higher.

Calhoun backed away once he made his pitch that Hamilton would make much more money with another year of college. He didn't want to push Hamilton to jump to the NBA just to prove him wrong.

The tension reached its peak inside Gampel Pavilion, where Calhoun used team manager and Rip's friend Josh Nochimson (remember that name) to communicate with Hamilton. Nochimson conveyed messages between Calhoun at the court level and Hamilton, holed up in the video coordinator's room on the lobby level. Back and forth they went. Calhoun and Hamilton avoided each other. That process became almost comical to the coach. Almost.

Kobe Bryant and Ray Allen provided information to Hamilton about what to expect in the NBA. Hamilton recorded the advice and information on note cards. The NBA players reiterated Calhoun's point: if you aren't sure that you're going in the lottery, stay at UConn.

"I hate to tell you this, Coach, but he's gone. Believe me, he's gone," Hobbs told Calhoun in the weeks between the end of the season and the time Hamilton made his decision. Hobbs recruited Hamilton and the two became almost like family. He grew close to Hamilton's mother and father. He told Hamilton's parents that they should write a book on how divorced parents should raise their children. He found a unique bond among Rip and his parents despite the challenge and agony of divorce. If anyone knew Hamilton, it was Hobbs.

Calhoun called a meeting among his staff, Hamilton, and Freeman, who said he "wanted to be more involved" and considered transferring if his best friend turned pro. Hamilton "was out the door. He had already said goodbye to Karl Hobbs and Dave Leitao when he came into my office," Calhoun said. The coach wanted to reiterate that UConn could get to the Final Four and win if they stayed.

In that meeting, Calhoun told the two players that UConn would win the national championship if they returned. According to Calhoun, about 20 minutes after the session started, Hamilton "was screaming 'National championship! National championship!'" Calhoun believed that it was advice from NBA players—it's better to be a lottery pick than a late first-rounder—that ultimately swayed Hamilton. After a discussion with Calhoun about his future and with the news that his buddy was coming back, Freeman decided to stay as well.

Hamilton also chose to return because the players on the team were like his family. The 1998 team was close and Hamilton knew he and his new family could continue to accomplish great things in the next season.

Then, the storybook season of 1998–1999 began with what appeared to be a nightmare. Hamilton was one of three college players invited to try out for the 1998 USA Basketball Men's World Championship Team. He broke his foot on the first day of the tryouts. After surgery, however, doctors speculated that he would be ready for UConn's first official practices in mid-October.

NCAA rules allow teams to take one overseas trip to play every four years. Calhoun decided that UConn would play in London and Israel in the summer of 1998. Returning players participated in a 10-day minicamp of practices in Storrs and competed against professionals overseas. The UConn team was already close; the trip allowed the players to grow closer. Before the Huskies left, they visited Joe McGinn in the hospital. McGinn had served as UConn's manager from 1992 to 1995, when he attended the university as an undergraduate. Even after he graduated, McGinn never left the family. McGinn had battled kidney disease since the age of three and one of the ramifications of the condition was stunted growth: McGinn stood at five foot two, 118 pounds. Most experts believed McGinn would not live past the age of 16, 18 tops. Despite his health limitations, McGinn was a good athlete. He once made 27 consecutive free throws to win a free throw–shooting contest; he served as captain of Bristol Eastern High School's golf team; and he captured the Junior Golf Championship at the Pequabuck Golf Club.

McGinn and Calhoun talked on the phone on a regular basis. The UConn coach liked that McGinn was a redheaded Irishman who loved the Red Sox and the Huskies. Calhoun appreciated McGinn's personality. He liked fighters; McGinn was one. McGinn would say to Calhoun, "Yeah, Roger Clemens . . . He's not going to Toronto for the fucking money. He just wants to be a Canadian. Yeah, Bobby Valentine is the guy the Mets need. Yeah, he's a real fucking genius Calhoun." The coach liked that. McGinn appreciated that Calhoun treated him as if he were without illness.

Because of circulation blockage from the knees down, McGinn's doctors concluded that the amputation of his legs was the best choice. McGinn's parents called upon Calhoun to tell their son about the doctors' recommendations. The players visited McGinn in the hospital after the surgery. McGinn inspired others. Players thought they were tired in practice until they looked at McGinn, who was fighting kidney disease for as long as he could remember. If he can fight, so can I, the players thought, and they tried harder.

In late August 1998, the Huskies trailed Peristeri, a top professional team from Greece, by 11 with 7:40 to play. They used pressure defense to get within one with 4:40 remaining. Peristeri took a 76–71 lead with 2:38 left, and the Huskies looked cooked again. Not quite. UConn's press forced Peristeri to turn the ball over and El-Amin scored five points during the decisive run; his shot gave UConn the lead for good with 21 seconds remaining: UConn 82–Peristeri 76.

When the UConn players returned to the locker room, they celebrated like they had won the Big East championship. Calhoun said UConn played "the best game of our year — the entire year — that nobody knows about." The game taught UConn that it could come back against any team under any conditions.

As the team came back to the States, Calhoun said, "Some kids made great strides on this trip, and I'd say Kevin tops the list." At the London Towers Invitational, Freeman scored 25 points and pulled down 13 rebounds. UConn won by 21. Freeman had another double-double (14 points and 10 boards) in a win over Maccabi Raanana in Israel and close to another (21 points and nine rebounds) in a win over a team from Greece.

The summer trip taught UConn how to play and win without Rip Hamilton. If Hamilton couldn't play because he was hurt or in foul trouble, or if he had a subpar game, this UConn team experienced what it was like to thrive without him.

The previews of the 1998–1999 season tended to include Duke, Stanford, UConn, Kentucky, Michigan State, and Maryland within the top five or six. Duke, the preseason number one, featured player-of-the-year candidates Trajan Langdon (14.7 points per game and 39.5 percent three-point shooting in 1997–1998) and Elton Brand (13.4 points and 7.3 rebounds per game in 1997–1998) as well as William Avery, Shane Battier, and Chris Carrawell. Duke added Corey Maggette, a McDonald's All-American from Fenwick High School in Oak Park, Illinois.

After Duke lost by a point to Cincinnati in the last second at the Great Alaska Shootout, UConn became the new number one, a position it last held during February of Ray Allen's sophomore year. On February 18, 1995, Villanova had beaten UConn by 23 points at Gampel Pavilion to end the Huskies' one-week stay in the top spot. This time, the team hoped to keep the position for longer, but, as Calhoun said, "If we are there on the twenty-ninth or thirtieth of March, then it will be something." For now, it meant very little.

Michigan State, ranked number nine but fresh off a 73–67 loss to Duke, visited Gampel Pavilion in early December for a CBS game. Before its home games, UConn played a recording of ring announcer Michael Buffer declaring, "Le-e-e-t-t-t-t-t's get ready to rumble," and a bell rang in the background to signify the start of a fight. Against Michigan State, Buffer made the announcement in person.

At first, UConn was not ready to rumble. Freeman scored the game's first basket, but then the Spartans rattled off 11 straight points. Calhoun called time-out and cursed Buffer and the distraction he thought the ring announcer presented. Buffer hasn't returned to a UConn game since. He might be banned from the state.

During time-outs, Calhoun yells, ridicules, counsels, motivates, devises strategy, stays silent, and does a variety of other things. Regardless of the coach's tactics, UConn responds well when Calhoun calls time-out. This game was no different. UConn turned an 11–2 deficit into a 14–13 lead. It never relinquished control after it went ahead 34–32 with 1:50 remaining in the opening half: UConn 82–Michigan State 68. The players did not make a big deal about the victory. Calhoun had conditioned them to think about a national championship.

For the Spartans, preseason All-American point guard Mateen Cleaves shot 13 percent from the field and 14.3 percent from three-point range. Ricky Moore guarded Cleaves from Bradley International Airport on Friday afternoon until the Spartans left Connecticut after the game. Michigan State coach Tom Izzo said that Moore defended Cleaves better than anyone else. Moore's defense became a weapon in the 1998–1999 season. Calhoun disagreed with Moore when he heard his guard say that his defense was worth a 40-point scoring night. More like 50, Calhoun said.

Gampel Pavilion's opening in January of 1990 had marked the transformation of UConn basketball. After its win over Michigan State, UConn had won every game at Gampel since a January 29, 1997, loss to Providence. Calhoun appreciated the importance of the Gampel crowd: "We've created an atmosphere here. I think the students do that. I think the team does that. I think our winning has done that. I think there's a lot of reasons why there aren't many basketball places like this in America. This is a very special place for basketball. There's not much question about that."

In its December 12, 1998, game at 20th-ranked Pitt, UConn trailed 68–62 with less than a minute to play. Then El-Amin, who went scoreless in the first half, made a three-pointer to cut the deficit to three. Pitt fans taunted El-Amin before, during, and after the game, spewing racial epithets and mocking his weight. "What was said to him shouldn't be said to any person," Calhoun said. El-Amin said the remarks were "personal comments."

With 18 seconds to play, Pitt's Ricardo Greer made one of two free throws to give a 69–65 lead to Pitt. With Pitt fans chanting "Overrated" — clap, clap, clap-clap-clap — toward the number-one-ranked and undefeated Huskies, sophomore guard Albert Mouring made a fade-away three-pointer from 22 feet to cut the Pitt lead to one. Nine seconds remained as the Pitt fans pushed their way toward the court to rush the floor. They were about to celebrate their team's first victory over a top-ranked team in the 48-year history of the Fitzgerald Field House. On the inbounds play, Pitt's Vonteego Cummings overthrew his teammate. Freeman recovered the ball in UConn's backcourt and passed to Mouring, who put the game into El-Amin's hands. El-Amin jetted into the lane and hit a five-foot shot with two seconds remaining. Pitt missed a desperation shot at the buzzer: UConn 70–Pitt 69.

El-Amin jumped onto the scorers' table and indicated to the fans that UConn was still number one. Calhoun grabbed El-Amin off the table and said, "You are going to walk off the court in a classy manner." Calhoun gave five seconds of frustration to El-Amin. "I wasn't going to give him six," he said.

At this point, the game felt more like World Wrestling Federation action than basketball. Fans threw bottles, chewing gum, and pennies onto the court; Ricky Moore's lip was cut in the chaos. When asked if he was hit by plastic bottles, Calhoun said he had the welts to prove it. Afterward, he claimed that the team's temporary locker room lacked adequate heating and that the security staff should have prevented objects from being thrown onto the floor. The Pitt athletic director said that the locker room had heat, and he could not confirm that fans had thrown anything onto the floor.

Of UConn's win and El-Amin's postgame dance, even the hometown *Pittsburgh Post-Gazette*'s Ron Cook wrote, "It's not every day that you see a visiting player come into the home team's building, make the game-winning shot and jump on the scorers' table to taunt the fans with No. 1 gestures. Connecticut's Khalid El-Amin did yesterday. And he was completely justified."

On January 20, UConn beat Miami by two in overtime for its 16th straight win, a program record for most wins to start the season. With the victory, Calhoun tied Hugh Greer for the most wins (286) in UConn history. Following Auburn's loss to Kentucky, UConn was the last undefeated team in Division I.

St. John's had lost 92–88 in overtime to number-two Duke on the previous Sunday at the Garden on CBS television. Now it now faced number-one UConn for a Saturday game, in the same building, on the same channel. The media hyped the contest as the biggest conference regular season game since Patrick Ewing's Georgetown Hoyas played Chris Mullins's St. John's Redmen in 1985.

In first-half play, UConn scored 16 of the game's first 19 points, but St. John's took a 43–38 lead into the locker room. UConn trailed at the half for the fourth game in a row. Lavor Postell helped St. John's grab 13 offensive rebounds in the first half. Bootsy Thornton, who scored 40 points against Duke, had 12 in the opening half against UConn. For the Huskies to win, they needed to stop Postell and Thornton.

St. John's took a 10-point lead with 17:30 left. Calhoun called time-out. CBS's Verne Lundquist said that Calhoun's face was so red that it looked as if the coach had been hung upside down. The rage didn't work. Calhoun called another time-out 24 seconds later after Reggie Jessie put in another St. John's offensive rebound to extend the Red Storm lead to 12.

Calhoun went silent. He approached the huddle and said, "Think about this. Think about what you are doing." El-Amin knew UConn had time to come back, but understood that the deficit could not grow any larger than 12.

It didn't.

Calhoun put Moore on Thornton and Hamilton on Postell. Thornton went scoreless from then on and St. John's did not have an offensive rebound in the game's final eight minutes. UConn went on a 10-0 run to cut the deficit to a single basket. Moore stopped a St. John's three-on-one break, kept the ball from going out of bounds, flew up the floor, and made two free throws after he was fouled. Calhoun walked onto the court and high-fived Moore. A Voskuhl dunk put the Huskies ahead with 4:41 to go. St. John's never recovered.

St. John's player Ron Artest claimed that his team quit and choked under the pressure. He referred to UConn as "one of the more arrogant teams that we play, [but] they just always back it up. They kicked our butts." He looked forward to a rematch, which would have to take place in the conference tournament, if at all.

UConn was about to enter its 10th consecutive week as the number-one team in the AP poll; it had defeated five ranked teams during the season. The week ahead presented two more tests—against 16th-ranked Syracuse at the Hartford Civic Center on Monday and at fourth-ranked Stanford on Saturday—but this team was ready. It believed it could beat any team under any conditions.

Seven hours before the Syracuse game, UConn announced that Hamilton and Voskuhl were out of that night's contest. Against St. John's, Hamilton suffered a contusion of his right thigh, which limited his ability to plant his leg and move. Reports speculated that Voskuhl had a stress fracture in his left foot because he experienced three or four similar injuries while in high school. Voskuhl was scheduled to go to Houston that Wednesday to meet with his doctor, a world-renowned orthopedic surgeon.

The same lineup had started 36 consecutive games, of which UConn had won 34. The losses came to UNC in the 1998 Elite Eight and at West Virginia on February 11, 1998. With Hamilton and Voskuhl not in uniform, UConn fell to Syracuse: Orangemen 59–Huskies 42. On this night, UConn, which came into the game averaging 83.9 points per game, scored the fewest points in a game in the Calhoun era.

Calhoun demands that his team get all the loose balls; he views this as a sign of outhustling and being tougher than the other team. On this night, Syracuse got all the loose balls. Following the game, Calhoun said, "Players other than Hamilton and Voskuhl are allowed to get loose balls."

UConn's loss combined with Duke's annihilation of seventh-ranked Maryland meant that the Blue Devils replaced the Huskies as the number-one team in the country. Most people in the national media probably regarded Duke as the better team, but UConn had stayed in the top position because of its undefeated record. After its loss to Cincinnati, Duke destroyed every team it played. It beat number-three Kentucky by 11 at the Jimmy V Classic in the Meadowlands, number-four Maryland by 28, and number-10 UNC by 12. St. John's had been the only team to sniff Duke since November.

Doomsday for UConn was supposed to take place Saturday February 6, 1999, in Palo Alto, California. Stanford wanted revenge for the 20-point humiliation it suffered the previous year in Storrs. It thought that jet lag and the game's starting time of 9 a.m. Pacific Standard Time were the primary reasons for its demise in 1998.

The Stanford players and coaches incorporated "Beat the University of Connecticut" into their team goals, which hung inside their locker room. Now, Stanford had a weakened UConn in its sights, but the Huskies weren't as depleted as Stanford had expected.

Voskuhl suffered from a bruised foot, not a stress fracture; his doctor cleared him to play. The Cardinal returned a huge frontline and UConn needed Voskuhl's height, bulk, and talent to neutralize Stanford's inside dominance. All season, the offense ran through and around Voskuhl's screens.

During a practice before the Stanford game, Hamilton fell to the floor when he attempted to fight through a screen. He estimated that he was at less than 80 percent capacity on the day of the Stanford game. Calhoun wanted him to spit on the injury and play. That didn't happen.

The schedule said that UConn was playing Stanford, but for those in uniform that day, the game was a trip back to London and Israel. The Huskies needed that experience against the nation's fourth-ranked team. Calhoun realized that if UConn was going to beat Stanford, El-Amin would need to play well. He challenged his point guard before the game. The coach asked El-Amin, "Is the fire still in the belly? I've done eight hundred of these. It's still in mine." El-Amin said yes and his play indicated that the fire still burned inside him. He took Calhoun's words as a threat that he never wanted to hear again.

He didn't.

El-Amin knew he should have been more aggressive against Syracuse. The coach motivated Khalid to score more often to compensate for Hamilton's absence. Calhoun told his team to push the ball up the floor and outrun the big and slow Cardinal.

The plan worked. UConn took a 24–8 lead 12 minutes into the game; El-Amin scored 16 points in the first half. Stanford coach Mike Montgomery said that it was next to impossible to simulate UConn's quickness in practice. Calhoun had watched Arizona and Cal trap Stanford and realized that the Cardinal didn't like pressure. So, it was pressure and a trap that Stanford got.

Stanford trailed by four at the half and kept the game close until the end. In the final 1:34, UConn made 12 of its 14 free throws and sealed an 11-point win.

At the game's conclusion, Calhoun hugged Voskuhl, whose 20 minutes, four points, four rebounds, and two blocks helped UConn control the middle. Then, El-Amin received a Calhoun embrace.

Hamilton returned in the next contest but UConn played ho-hum basketball in most of its final six games of the regular season. Two games after the Huskies struggled to beat Seton Hall on the road, UConn lost to Miami, 73–71, at Gampel Pavilion. The Huskies weren't aggressive on defense and weren't potent on offense. The nation took notice: the AP dropped UConn from second to fourth behind Michigan State, Auburn, and Duke.

UConn doubters forgot the debate about whether the Huskies were in the same league as Duke. At this point, they questioned whether UConn was as good as Miami. Jim Calhoun and UConn had to defend a spectacular record once more.

In the late 1980s and early 1990s, Syracuse and Georgetown would play the final Big East regular season game at the Carrier Dome, televised by CBS. By 1999, UConn had replaced Georgetown as conference heavyweight, and it traveled to Syracuse to take on the Orangemen.

In what UConn regarded as a "statement game," the fourth-rated Huskies pounded Syracuse, 70–58. El-Amin said, "We wanted to tell people that we're still here, that we're still the number-one team to beat." The 1999 Huskies became the first Big East team to win all its conference road games.

As he addressed the beat writers before the trip to the conference tournament, Calhoun said, "We're twenty-five and two, we're having a special season." The fans' and media appetite for victory was so large that this record put Calhoun in the position to defend that record.

Richard Hamilton was named Big East co-player of the year along with Miami's Tim James. Miami had two first-team all-conference players, UConn had one. Khalid El-Amin made the second team, but no other Husky player was on any of the three teams. Etan Thomas of Syracuse, not Ricky Moore, was named the defensive player of the year. Calhoun thought that Freeman should have made one of the top three teams and that Moore should have been defensive player of the year. Before UConn's first game in the Big East tournament, Calhoun called a special team meeting to use the slights to motivate his players.

In the quarterfinals against Seton Hall, UConn trailed by a point with 1:44 remaining. Freeman told his teammates that UConn could be the ones going home. Hamilton tried to give a two-point lead to UConn when he launched a three-pointer on his team's next possession. He missed. With UConn's national championship hopes bouncing off the rim, Freeman dunked them through to give a 51–50 lead to the Huskies. His two-handed stuff staked UConn to a three-point advantage with 29 seconds left in a game that felt about as comfortable as a dentist's visit to UConn fans.

With two seconds left and his team down 57–54, Seton Hall's Gary Saunders wanted to make the first and miss the second of two free throws to give his teammates a chance to tip in the rebound and tie the game. He made the first but put the second one in by accident. UConn didn't have to inbound the ball.

A great team can have its two main scorers go cold, play the antithesis of its style, and still win. UConn did those things against Seton Hall. At this point, it had beaten top-ranked teams by blowouts and in overtime; it throttled most bad teams but escaped others. Of his team, Calhoun said, "They have a belief that you're not going to lose, and after twenty-five wins, our kids certainly believe that." Teams that don't think they can lose are hard to beat.

In the Garden's John Condon Memorial Press Room and in the arena's various corridors, both writers and basketball fans noted that UConn didn't have the scoring power to win a national championship; if the Huskies could beat Seton Hall by only three, they couldn't knock off the current Duke squad, which now hit legendary status as one of the greatest college basketball teams of all time.

In its first game at the ACC tournament, Duke destroyed Virginia, 104-67. Virginia coach Pete Gillen described Duke as "a wrecking machine." At MSG and throughout the country, UConn naysayers viewed the Huskies as a wrecked machine.

As Calhoun waited in the hotel lobby for the team bus before UConn's second conference tournament game, he received word from his daughter-in-law Jennifer—a former team manager—that Emily Calhoun, the coach's first grandchild, had been born. Jennifer called while doctors stitched her up; the doctors asked why she needed to call at that moment and she said, "Coach has to go to the game." The birth was more exciting than the game that night: UConn 71-Syracuse 50.

Coworker and close friend Tim Tolokan describes Calhoun as a private person in a public position. Most people never see the private Calhoun, the one who kisses his sons, sings Broadway songs in his car, or feeds organic apples to deer in his yard. People don't get to see the Jim Calhoun who meets his friends at Foxwoods Casino at 2 a.m. the morning after his son gets married. That Jim Calhoun reflects on his life and the future of his two sons. He fears that males have not lived long in his family and has said that his goal in life is to make sure that everything will be alright for his children.

After the Syracuse win, at 9:30 p.m., the coach spoke to his son by cell phone in front of the media and said, "You kids did great today. Love you. Bye." Calhoun carried a picture of Emily in his suit pocket for the remainder of UConn's games. Many people who have been around Calhoun on a regular basis say they have never seen the coach happier than when he found out he was a grandfather for this first time.

In the Big East championship game, UConn, the nation's second-ranked team, scored the first 13 points against number-10 St. John's and the tailor started to sew the team's conference tournament championship banner: Huskies 82-Red Storm 63. UConn's large contingent at the Garden chanted, "We want Duke, We want Duke."

The players wanted Duke too.

The 1997–1998 and 1998–1999 Huskies joined Patrick Ewing's Georgetown Hoyas of 1983–1984 and 1984–1985 as the only teams to win the Big East tournament in consecutive years, but this group of Huskies became the first team to win the conference regular season and tournament titles in back-to-back years. A reporter asked Calhoun about the significance of this achievement. "It means an awful lot of good players come to Connecticut. I've been blessed with having some tremendous players play for us," Calhoun said. While making his remarks, Calhoun pointed at former Husky Scott Burrell, who visited the locker room after the game. The family supports its members.

Another family member visited the Huskies at the same time as Burrell. His name: Joe McGinn. Players stopped their interviews to talk to him. Making it to the game was not easy. Ricky Moore embraced McGinn; he knew that his friend was suffering, but McGinn didn't want the attention. He told Moore, "Hey, this is your third Big East championship." That was the last time Moore saw McGinn.

According to the head of the NCAA tournament selection committee, UConn was the second best team in the nation; Duke was number one. The 1998–1999 Duke Blue Devils joined UNC (1957), Duke (1963), and NC State (1973 and 1974) as the only teams in the 46-year history of the ACC to win every conference game in the regular season and league tournament. The 1957 Tar Heels and 1974 Wolfpack went on to win the NCAA tournament.

At this point, Calhoun was arguably the best coach to never take his team to the Final Four and the UConn program had the most NCAA tournament appearances—20—without a trip to the Final Four. When asked about the lack of a Final Four appearance on his resume, Calhoun said, "We've got one of the best programs in the country. I don't need [the Final Four] to legitimize myself as a coach. I'd love for it to happen for me, for the kids, the program, the state, but there are no guarantees. But if we keep going at this level, I think we'll walk across that wire without falling."

On Selection Sunday after UConn received the number-one seed in the West, Calhoun and McGinn discussed the brackets for about 20 minutes. This was a ritual for the two. Convinced the Huskies would make it to St. Petersburg, Florida, where the Final Four was to be held that year, McGinn told ESPN, his employer at the time, that he needed vacation time during the Final Four weekend. He did this more than a year in advance. McGinn filled out the brackets and put Duke, Ohio State, Michigan State, and UConn into the Final Four. He picked UConn to win the national championship.

15

This One's for Joe

Welcome to the Duke Invitational. Only one team in this dance can party like it's 1999. Only one team has the stuff of an NCAA champion. No team has looked this good coming into March since those days of yesteryear, before cable, when Kareem Abdul-Jabbar was Lew Alcindor and UCLA wrecked the rest of the country and owned March like the wind. This year . . . everybody is playing for second. It is Duke and it is the field of 63. It is Duke against Duke.

Steve Kelley, *Seattle Times*, March 9, 1999,
the day after Selection Sunday

On the Monday after the seeds were announced, the Las Vegas Hilton and the MGM made Duke a 3–5 favorite to win the Final Four. In other words, a person would have to bet five dollars on Duke to win three dollars. Duke was the biggest favorite in 10 years. Bill Guthridge, then head coach at North Carolina, had watched dominant basketball for more than three decades in Chapel Hill. He had coached Michael Jordan at Carolina but even he was enamored with Duke. "They are head and shoulders above everyone else," he said.

The UConn team and coaching staff felt disrespected by the Duke worshipping. They were the best team in the country. Calhoun had told them. The nation deified the Blue Devils and Calhoun made sure that his team did not join that number. The Huskies believed they could win the national championship even if that meant they had to defeat Duke.

Two days after the brackets were announced, Joe McGinn died of a heart attack at the age of 26. He was sleeping in his mother's arms at the time. The UConn team learned of McGinn's death when it arrived in Colorado. Calhoun had taken the team two thousand feet above Denver to the U.S. Air Force Academy to practice in higher altitudes. Because of the upcoming game, Calhoun and his team could not return to Connecticut. Instead, they set up a memorial service at the Air Force Academy.

Calhoun had his Big East championship watch hand-delivered to McGinn's family, who put it on their son's wrist for burial. The casket included McGinn's lucky UConn hat and sweatshirt and a Huskies flag. Dickenman, who called

McGinn every day and sometimes twice a day, served as a pallbearer. El-Amin and the team dedicated the rest of the season to McGinn.

Calhoun suffered virus-like symptoms on game day and watched the opening game from his hotel room in Denver. This wouldn't be his last health-related absence from an NCAA tournament game. UConn beat the University of Texas at San Antonio by 25. Calhoun returned for the next game, and the Huskies beat New Mexico by 22. In Phoenix, in the Sweet 16, UConn beat Iowa by 10. Again, the program was on the doorstep of a Final Four.

Prior to 1999, Calhoun was 3–3 in the Sweet 16 and 0–3 in the Elite Eight. The UConn coach said that he had won big games, including more than five hundred overall and four Big East tournament championships. This time, though, those numbers weren't good enough.

Former Florida State University football coach Bobby Bowden, who seemed to win every game unless it was against Miami, said that the "big game" is always the one you lose, and not the others that you win. At this point, the same applied for Calhoun.

In the Elite Eight, UConn played 10th-seeded Gonzaga, a team Calhoun compared to the 1987 Providence College Friars, which three-pointed their way to that year's Final Four. Concede an easy basket over an open three, he told his team. All threes had to be contested. Gonzaga's precision passing, smart decisions, and open shots bothered the Connecticut coach. At 1 a.m. on the Friday before the game, Calhoun called Tom Moore, an assistant coach since the 1994–1995 season, and asked, "What do you think?" Moore hesitated and said, "Jim, they run good stuff."

The UConn-Gonzaga game had six lead changes and 11 ties; UConn's biggest lead was six, Gonzaga's four. With a little less than two minutes left, UConn led by two, 61–59. As the Huskies passed the ball on the perimeter to try to kill some of the clock, El-Amin dropped the ball, which trickled out of bounds. The last time El-Amin had turned it over like that was never. That play scared Freeman, who began to think the Final Four wasn't meant to be for UConn.

Matt Santangelo was fouled and the 78.2 percent free throw shooter went to the line to try to tie the game with 1:33 left. He missed the front end of the one-and-one, and the ball was batted out of bounds. The call could have gone either way. UConn ball. Maybe destiny wasn't so anti-UConn after all. Gonzaga extended its defense and tried to force a turnover. The time ticked away . . . 1:23, 1:22, 1:21 . . . but the game was still scary as far as UConn was concerned . . . 1:10, 1:09, 1:08. . . . Then, El-Amin hit Hamilton, who had slashed toward the lane. After one dribble, Hamilton found Voskuhl, who made an uncontested layup. UConn was up four with one minute and counting.

On the next possession, Gonzaga's Quentin Hall swished a three-pointer. "Oh no," Calhoun thought, as he started to believe that maybe a trip to the Final Four was not meant to be.

El-Amin was fouled with 34.4 seconds left. He had missed all 12 of his shots from the floor and finished with five points, the third-lowest point production for his college career. But with the game in doubt and the pressure as high as it could get, El-Amin delivered. His two free throws gave UConn a three-point lead, 65–62.

If you want to see the best defense UConn has ever played, watch the film of how the Huskies swarmed Gonzaga on the next possession. The Zags came close to a backcourt violation when Santangelo was trapped under UConn's basket and threw a pass toward midcourt. Hall saved the ball to Richie Frahm, whose shot was short, but UConn batted the rebound out of bounds — 16.4 seconds till St. Pete.

UConn's defense grew more intense. Santangelo threw up a double-clutched two-point attempt that bounded high off the glass and came down to Freeman, who was fouled.

Ever since he was a kid in the playground, Freeman imagined shooting big free throws. He couldn't get much bigger in the free throw department than hitting one to take his team to the program's first Final Four. As Freeman's free throw was in flight, Calhoun did a short skip on the sideline. In. Freeman made the second shot, stole the inbounds pass, and flung the ball in the air.

Destiny wore a UConn jersey on the day of the Elite Eight. Calhoun had emphasized defense since Andrew Gaze's Australian team tortured the Huskies in his first game at UConn. Now, his team's defense brought him to the Final Four.

Hamilton scored 21 points on nine of 16 shooting. At one point during the second half, he ripped off eight straight points. For his efforts, Hamilton was named the MVP of the West regional.

Jim Jr. and Jeff Calhoun cried in the stands, as did many UConn fans at Phoenix's America West Arena and throughout the country. The painful endings to glorious seasons sweetened this victory. Calhoun the elder did not cry. When the game ended, he received a bear hug from Leitao, a man he considers to be his third son. After the coach finished his interview with CBS television, the players dumped Gatorade on him.

The moment's significance hit Calhoun when he climbed the steel steps to cut the net. The ladder symbolized the mountain Calhoun and UConn had scaled to reach the program's first Final Four. It was steep and, at times, the Final Four seemed like Mission: Impossible.

"I took a deep breath and gave myself those five minutes," Calhoun said of the first time he cut down the nets to send his team to the Final Four. He equated losing in the Elite Eight to purgatory—not quite heaven, not quite hell. "Gonzaga freed him," Dave Solomon of the *New Haven Register* said of the effect of the Elite Eight win on Calhoun.

Calhoun was happy, but not content. The entire year, UConn's goal was to *win* the Final Four. Nothing that happened in Phoenix changed the mission.

The players cried when they returned to the locker room and found a picture of Joe McGinn taped to each locker. Calhoun said, "This one's for Joe," and he began to cry, a new sight for even the longtime beat reporters.

Almost as soon as the game ended, Calhoun called the McGinns to tell them that they must come to the Final Four. He would pay all the expenses. The McGinns accepted when Calhoun told them that they couldn't say no to family. Calhoun said that telling McGinn about the amputation option was far more emotional and difficult than making the Final Four.

Hamilton and Freeman realized the enormity of the Final Four accomplishment the day after UConn beat Gonzaga. They received a call in their room on South Campus and couldn't believe who was on the other end: Jay-Z. The rapper was performing at the Hartford Civic Center that night as part of the "Hard Knock Life" tour. Jay-Z had called to ask Rip if he could wear a replica of Hamilton's number-32 jersey onstage. Of course, Hamilton said yes. He and Freeman attended the concert.

Jim O'Brien left BC after he battled the administration over the admission of basketball players. He took Scoonie Penn, his best player and the 1995–1996 Big East rookie of the year, with him to Ohio State. NCAA rules require transferring players to sit out a year and the Buckeyes went 8–22 without Penn. With him, Ohio State's record jumped to 27–8 heading into its game against UConn. O'Brien entered the national semifinal on an 18-game personal losing streak against Calhoun.

For Calhoun, the mission was clear: Stop Penn. Ohio State had its version of the dynamic duo. Michael Redd, a six foot six sophomore who would go on to a strong NBA career, averaged 21.0 points and six boards per game in 1998–1999, but Calhoun knew that Penn was the head of the Ohio State dragon.

Moore shut down Penn; UConn beat Ohio State, 64–58. Penn went three for 13 for the game and scored 11 points. "Moore is the best defensive player I've coached," Calhoun said. Penn admitted that Moore took away his game: "He just didn't let me breathe the whole time. . . . I was waiting for him to turn his head the wrong way. He never did." Penn joined Mateen Cleaves of Michigan State, Jason Hart of Syracuse, Arthur Lee of Stanford, and a long list of prolific guards who Moore shut down in 1998–1999 alone. Hamilton and El-Amin outscored Penn and Redd, 42–26.

And then, there was Duke.

16

We Shocked the World!

After UConn beat OSU but before the second national semi-final game, reporters asked El-Amin about Duke. He finished his extra-large nachos and a big Coke from the concession stand at Tropicana Field and then talked about the Blue Devils, who were about to play and beat Michigan State in the second national semifinal. To him, Duke was another team in UConn's way of a national championship. "I think we bring a different challenge to Duke, and I think it's going to be difficult for them to match up with us," he said. Duke hadn't heard this kind of rhetoric from any of its previous victims, er, opponents. What's more, the UConn players believed El-Amin.

"We feel we're capable of beating Duke. Why wouldn't we feel that way?" El-Amin said. When he was told that Kareem Abdul-Jabbar thought Duke would win in a blowout, El-Amin said, "I think his opinion was a wrong one." Maybe it was Roger Murdock, the pilot from *Airplane*, who made that prediction.

The other part of the dynamic duo believed too. Hamilton said, "The one thing that St. John's did was play them like they were any other team. They didn't look at it like, 'This is Duke, the number-one team in the country.' They played them like they would anyone else." That's how Calhoun approached the game—Duke is just another team.

"We all knew we were going to win that game. Both teams were number-one team in the country . . . and we weren't getting a whole lot of credit for it because of the players that Duke had," Hamilton said.

"We knew we were going to win. We had been down so many times by five or six points, and came back to win. We were the Chicago Bulls of college basketball. Confident, but not cocky," said Kevin Freeman. The Huskies believed they were invincible.

Duke had stolen UConn's spotlight during the season. "You keep hearing it's Duke and sixty-three other teams. Any time you hear that, you want to go out and keep playing," Freeman said when the Final Four was set.

The media and Las Vegas thought UConn should fear Duke. One columnist wrote, "Take it to the bank: pigs will do calculus before Connecticut beats Duke in tonight's championship game." Duke joined the 1984–1985 George-town Hoyas as the heaviest favorites in the history of NCAA championship games, at 9.5 points.

Duke put a lot of talent on the floor and the bench. Its roster included seven McDonald's All-Americans, four of whom didn't start. In the entire history of the UConn program, four McDonald's All-Americans had played for the Huskies. If you looked only at high school talent, the national championship game would have been the mismatch everyone predicted.

The lines makers and so-called experts didn't think UConn could stop Elton Brand, Duke's six foot eight, 260-pound, center who was the national player of the year and a double-double machine. Brand averaged 17.8 points and 9.7 rebounds. His shoulders were as wide Tennessee and his hands the size of trash can tops.

Teams had to make a choice against Duke: stop Trajan Langdon and get beaten on the inside by Brand or concentrate on the center and get bombed from the outside. Calhoun concluded that Brand was the head of Duke's dragon. Duke struggled when a foul-troubled Brand sat on the bench for 11 minutes against Michigan State; Calhoun noticed. He had watched eight or nine Duke games during the season; each time, he wrote notes on blue index cards, which went with him to St. Pete. Calhoun decided to double down on Brand every time the center received the ball. He did not want to rotate defenders. Instead, he assigned the biggest player, usually Freeman, to join Voskuhl or backup center Souleymane Wane in the double team.

Duke played quicker when William Avery dribbled the ball up the floor. Stop that, Calhoun said.

Duke players switched who they covered on pick-and-roll plays. Calhoun used Duke's defensive strategy to UConn's advantage. He ran plays where Hamilton screened Brand to cause the Duke center to leave his man and defend Hamilton.

In a team session the night before the championship game, Assistant Coach Tom Moore dissected videotape of Duke and talked about the Blue Devils' strengths. He praised Brand as the best player UConn may have faced all season, Avery as the best point guard, Chris Burgess as the best defensive forward—and Calhoun had enough. He did not want thoughts of Duke's dominance to creep into his players' heads. Duke wins too many games before the contest starts. Not this one.

"Our assistant coach seems to agree with everyone else that Duke is a hell of a team," Calhoun said. "Everybody thinks Duke's great—and it has been, for thirty-two straight games. But do you know what? In those thirty-two games, Duke hasn't faced the University of Connecticut." Calhoun was right. Duke hadn't seen a team with UConn's character, quickness, and battle scars.

"You're going to beat Duke," Calhoun said. Then he told them how they would do it.

In addition to the Brand plan, the "believe you can win" attitude, and the demystification of Duke, Calhoun played another angle. Avery had been Ricky Moore's protégé in the playgrounds and gyms in Augusta, Georgia. They played together at Westside High School for two years. UConn's message to Moore was clear: you own Avery. Moore now viewed Avery as an "enemy," and said, "William hasn't faced anyone who plays defense like I do."

The players returned to the Hyatt Regency West Shore at about 5:40 on the Sunday night before Monday's game and 6 p.m. was the cutoff time to see friends and family. After 6 p.m., it was teammates only.

As he thought about the game in his hotel room, Moore kept hearing people say that UConn had no chance against Duke. These predictions motivated Moore, and when the UConn co-captain had a purpose, he felt like he could do anything.

Freeman and Hamilton went to a nearby Red Lobster, where they sat in the back and watched the women's national championship game. Duke was trying to become the first school in history to win both the men's and women's basketball tournaments in the same season. That feat, as it turned out, would be five years away. Freeman and Hamilton thought Duke's loss in the women's game was a good sign.

When he returned to his room, Freeman put on his game jersey, which he wore to bed.

CBS's Bonnie Bernstein interviewed Calhoun and El-Amin outside the UConn locker room before game time. At the conclusion of the interviews, El-Amin looked into the camera and said, "We plan to shock the world." El-Amin had not planned the comment. "It's what came into my head . . . it was the right phrase at the right time," he said.

Ten years prior to this game, UConn struggled to win a game in the Big East tournament. An NCAA tournament berth seemed unattainable. Fast-forward 10 years and the Huskies had four Big East tournament championships, six regular season titles, and eight NCAA tournament appearances. In the NCAA tournament, they advanced to the Sweet 16 seven times, the Elite Eight four times, and the Final Four once. The world should have been plenty shocked already.

In the locker room before a game, Calhoun is at his most calm. "He's not rah-rah," said former athletic trainer Joe Sharpe of Calhoun's pregame approach. Despite the magnitude of the national championship game, Calhoun remained composed before his team hit the court. The team knew it could beat Duke; it just had to execute the game plan.

As he led the team onto the court, El-Amin dribbled with one hand and signaled to the UConn fans to cheer louder with the other. The Husky Nation followed El-Amin and escalated to the sound of a Boeing 747. Sharpe couldn't believe the number of UConn fans in the sections behind the team's bench. He figured that more UConn fans were at this game than at the ones at Gampel.

On the eighth anniversary of its upset of UNLV, Duke tried to set a record for most victories in a season — 38. It stormed out to a 9-2 lead, one that could have become unmanageable if it grew any larger. The Huskies fought back to take a 15-13 lead with a little more than 13 minutes to go in the first half. The game remained close for the rest of the half and Duke led by two at the break. That score was good news for the Huskies, who were 9-0 on the season when they trailed at halftime. "Keep doing what you're doing," Calhoun told his team in the locker room. "Keep playing hard; stay with it; keep moving the ball; and play tough."

The big-little mismatches, the double-teams on Brand, and having Langdon take the ball up the court all worked in UConn's favor. UConn was in good shape and Calhoun knew it.

With four minutes left in the college basketball season, the score was tied at 68. At that moment, El-Amin said to Hamilton, "It's winning time." Rip agreed.

Hamilton sank two free throws with 3:50 left and Moore stripped the ball from Avery on the other end to set up one of the biggest shots in UConn history.

Avery guarded Hamilton while Brand played Voskuhl. In front of the UConn bench, Voskuhl set a screen for Hamilton — and as Calhoun had detected in one Duke game film after another — the Blue Devils switched. Now, Brand covered Hamilton. Brand responded late to Moore's pass to Hamilton, who hit a three-point jumper from the corner to extend the lead to five with 3:29 left.

That shot provided a cushion that UConn used for the rest of the game. Points are tough to come by in the late moments of tight national championship games. Special players score them.

Carrawell missed a jumper. Battier jumped straight up, tipped the ball to himself as he stood between Freeman and Moore, and in one motion threw the ball to Langdon. Bang. A three-pointer. The four-point lead was down to one.

A long minute and 44 seconds remained. In an instant, UConn went from having a four-point lead and the ball to a one-point advantage. With time expiring on the shot clock and 1:16 left in the game, Moore passed to El-Amin. As soon as El-Amin got the ball between the half-court line and the top of the key, Voskuhl walked over to the ball to set the screen. After Duke's defensive switch, Brand guarded El-Amin as the shot clock showed eight seconds. El-Amin stutter-stepped, blew past Brand, and made a short shot to extend the lead to three with 1:05 left.

More than seven years after this game, Calhoun would rank this shot as one of the best plays made during his career at UConn.

Less than six seconds later, Duke Rules reappeared. Moore breathed on Avery and received his fourth foul. Avery made both free throws to bring his team within one (75–74) with 54 seconds left.

UConn emptied the shot clock on its next possession but settled for an El-Amin air ball. Duke now had possession, down one, with a chance to win. Twenty-five seconds remained.

Duke did not call time-out. Calhoun put Moore on Langdon, who had scored 25 points on seven for 15 shooting. Krzyzewski wanted Langdon to beat Moore one-on-one. As Langdon approached him, Moore wanted to press up on him and force the Duke star to take a bad shot. Langdon tried to take Moore on the left side of Duke's basket across from his bench. He ran into the lane and traveled. 5.4 seconds remained. Time-out, Duke.

"I'm really surprised that they tried to challenge the number-one defender in the NCAA tournament so far," said CBS commentator Billy Packer. Calhoun had the right matchup. Krzyzewski didn't.

When CBS returned from the commercial break, the camera showed Krzyzewski's wife Mickie and the couple's daughter. Mickie shook her head while her daughter had her head in her hands. She bawled and her hands shook as she wiped away her tears. As CBS ran a slow-motion shot of Coach K's daughter crying, CBS's Jim Nantz said, "The Krzyzewski family trembles."

On the inbounds play, Avery fouled El-Amin and told the Connecticut point guard that he would miss the free throws. That must have been a joke.

El-Amin had one thought in mind: make the first free throw. He had missed both of the free throws he had taken earlier in the game, but the NCAA championship wasn't on the line then. Duke's Grim Reaper swished the first shot. El-Amin's second free throw pinballed the rim and fell into the basket as Calhoun did a one-legged hop on the sideline to make sure the ball went in.

Ahead 77–74, UConn was 5.2 seconds away from a national championship. At Tropicana Field, many UConn fans hugged each other; others resisted. They had seen lucky buzzer-beaters by Duke in the past.

Duke inbounded the ball and again refused to call time-out. Coach K didn't want to give UConn an opportunity to regroup and reset its defense.

As Langdon dribbled along the left sideline, Calhoun followed. UConn's co-captain Rashamel Jones kept Langdon in front of him and forced Langdon to the sideline, where Moore, El-Amin, and Hamilton met him. Moore stuck out his leg, Langdon fell to the floor, and time expired. Now near half-court, Calhoun hopped to Dave Leitao and the two hugged.

El-Amin sprinted away from the pile with his index finger extended. He ran toward the Huskies' bench, but reversed course and headed to the scorers' table at center court. El-Amin told Jim Nantz, "We shocked the world!"

Hamilton's most vivid memory of the national championship was of El-Amin running around saying, "We shocked the world, We shocked the world." Despite being named the most outstanding player of the final game and making one clutch basket after another, Hamilton said he will always remember El-Amin's words and actions following the game.

El-Amin and Hamilton scored UConn's last 11 points, combining for 26 of UConn's 40 points in the second half. They did what others before them couldn't: lead UConn to a national championship and play big in the biggest games.

Elton Brand put up impressive numbers for the game — 15 points, 13 rebounds — but he didn't dominate. He grabbed as many rebounds in the first half against Michigan State as he had all game against UConn. Two Huskies harassed him every time he touched the ball. Brand took eight shots during the game. For all the talk about Duke's dominance inside, UConn outrebounded the Blue Devils, 41–31. Duke scored close to 20 points below its season average.

The Huskies were not shocked that they won. Calhoun had convinced them that they were the best team in the country. The 1997–1998 season, foreign competition, and a rigorous regular season schedule prepared UConn to win the national championship. For the players, the result was a foregone conclusion.

This game was no upset. UConn was the best team in the nation in 1999 and one of the best college basketball teams over the last 25 years. It beat every team it played at least once and its schedule was loaded with the nation's top-ranked teams.

As UConn's fight song played in the background, Calhoun hugged Tim Tolokan; the coach's face remained placid during the public part of the postgame celebration. The win revealed the coach's public and private sides. He did not smile when he cut down the net. The picture on the cover of *Dare to Dream*, Calhoun's account of the 1998–1999 championship season, shows the coach with the net in his hand and a blank expression on his face.

Calhoun's favorite picture features the family — the 1999 team, coaches,

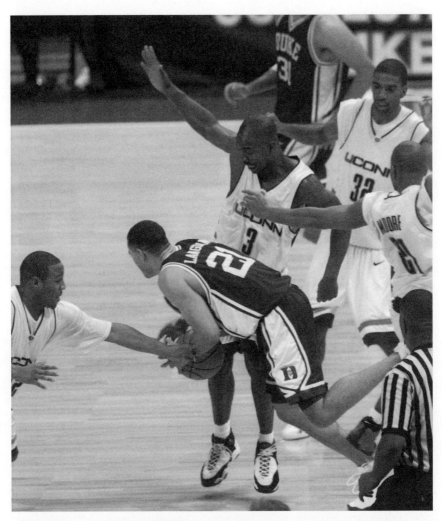

Defense wins championship. Khalid El-Amin (*left*), Rashamel Jones (no. 3), Richard Hamilton (no. 32), and Ricky Moore (no. 21) weren't going to allow Duke's Trajan Langdon to tie the national championship game on the Blue Devils' last possession. UConn 77–Duke 74. National championship game, March 29, 1999, Tropicana Field, St. Petersburg, Florida.

AP Photo/Chris O'Meara

trainers, managers, the athletic director, academic counselor, and the head coach—in the locker room after the national championship game. Everyone in that photograph is in ecstasy.

Coaches and players compete for that feeling, the one that comes with winning. The people in that photograph showed what that feeling looks like.

The champions bring the trophy home to Gampel. With his team around him and the scoreboard showing the final of the previous night's game, Jim Calhoun holds the 1999 national championship trophy. March 31, 1999, Gampel Pavilion, Storrs, Connecticut.

University Photograph Collection, Archives & Special Collections at the Thomas J. Dodd Research Center, University of Connecticut Libraries. Photo published with permission.

They still have it; the feeling may subside, but it never goes away. "You share winning with a great group of guys," Hamilton would say more than 10 years after the championship.

The family made the game: Donny Marshall, Oliver Macklin, John Gwynn, and Lyman DePriest went to St. Petersburg. Ray Allen spent $20,000 to charter a plane to UConn's first national title game. Allen stood next to Calhoun and Moore as the coach and player talked to CBS's Nantz and Packer. The former players reserved a spot outside the team's hotel for themselves and the current players; the family celebrated the championship together.

Calhoun left one strand of the net on the rim. That piece was for Joe McGinn.

As expected, Hamilton turned pro. His draft stock was as high as it was going to get. The number-seven selection by the Washington Wizards, Hamilton became the third Husky in six years to be among the top seven draft picks.

"It was the best." That's how Hamilton characterized his time playing for

UConn. "If I never got an opportunity in the NBA, playing for UConn is just like being in the NBA," he said of the experience in Storrs. "It was the only game in town." After the 1997 National Hockey League season, the Hartford Whalers moved to North Carolina and became the Carolina Hurricanes. When the Big East started and the Hartford Whalers began to play in the NHL, the Hartford Civic Center often hosted doubleheaders on Saturdays. UConn would play in the afternoon and the Whalers were featured at night. When UConn became really good and the Whalers began to tank, the roles reversed. It was not a coincidence that UConn's success coincided with diminished interest in the Whalers. At that time, the Connecticut dollar didn't stretch as far as it had, and the people reserved their entertainment dollars for the Huskies. UConn became the state's major sports team after Rip's freshman year.

As president of basketball operations and part owner of the Washington Wizards, Michael Jordan traded Hamilton to the Pistons, and ended up reviving the wrong franchise. Hamilton helped lead the Pistons to the Eastern Conference finals in his first season with the team. A year later, he averaged 17.6 points per game and exacted some revenge against Kobe Bryant, whose team had defeated Hamilton's for the championship in the players' senior year in high school. Rip's Pistons swept Bryant's Lakers in the 2004 Finals. Hamilton is a three-time all-star who has earned second-team All-NBA honors on three different occasions. In 2011, Hamilton was waived by Detroit and signed a three-year, $13 million contract with the Chicago Bulls.

Two weeks after winning the championship, El-Amin attended a ceremony at North High School, where his jersey was retired. The following day, he was arrested in the North End of Hartford for possession of less than four ounces of marijuana. Hamilton was with him, but didn't get arrested. El-Amin received six hours of community service, a standard punishment for first-time offenders of this kind of misdemeanor. For his community service, El-Amin spoke at three Hartford schools to warn students about the dangers of drugs.

On Saturday April 15, 1999, El-Amin and the rest of the Huskies participated in the one-and-a-half-mile parade through downtown Hartford. Between 200,000 and 300,000 spectators showed up to see the players, who wore shirts that read, "Mission Accomplished."

In the 1999 draft, Duke became the first college team to have four players selected in the first round. Four of the first 14 picks played for Duke. Brand went number one overall to the Bulls, followed by Langdon (number 11 to the Cavaliers), Maggette (number 13 to the Clippers), and William Avery (number 14 to the Timberwolves).

El-Amin returned to defend the national championship and mentor the next generation of Huskies. Even with three of five starters back, the first post-championship season felt like a hangover. UConn beat Arizona in the Great Eight Classic in Chicago and won games over Texas and Syracuse in Hartford. The Huskies became the first team in Big East tournament history to win three games to make it to the finals. There, they couldn't catch Erick Barkley and St. John's.

The record shows that the season ended on March 19, 2000, when Tennessee beat the Huskies in the second round of the NCAA tournament. In reality, the season was over two days before when El-Amin suffered a high-ankle sprain late in the game against Utah State. He tried to play against Tennessee but couldn't. Instead, El-Amin's three-year college career ended as he opted to enter the NBA draft. The careers of Voskuhl and Freeman also concluded that day in Birmingham, Alabama. Those players were the last of UConn's first national championship core.

The 1999 national title didn't satisfy Calhoun. He wanted another. In the first post-El-Amin season, he landed another legend.

17

I Wanted to Play for a Tough Coach, and He's One of the Toughest

Caron Butler grew up fatherless, the son of a mother who worked two jobs. He spent his youth in gangs in Racine, Wisconsin. Butler sold drugs, handled thousands of dollars in cash, and carried weapons to defend himself. On the streets, Butler lived by Scarface's rule, "Never get high off your own supply." Years later, Butler would insist he wasn't a bad kid. "I just made some very, very bad decisions," he said.

In his mother's presence, Butler worked a paper route. When he left the house, Butler switched into designer sneakers and worked for a gang. By the time he was 15, he had appeared in court one time for each year he was on the earth.

Also at age 15, Butler was arrested for possession of an unloaded weapon and crack cocaine. At the time of the arrest, he was carrying $20,000. Butler spent 15 months in jail and a juvenile correctional facility. When he went from jail to the Ethan Allen House in Wales, Wisconsin, his mother—Mattie Paden—followed the Wisconsin Department of Corrections van in her car. She slept in the parking lot on Butler's first night in the facility. Watching his mother follow him to prison saddened and mortified Butler, but it didn't cause him to change his behavior.

At the Ethan Allen House, Butler fought another kid from Racine and went to solitary confinement. Butler reevaluated his life in that cell. The future held two possibilities: change or die. "I'd had enough," Butler said to himself. "It's time to grow up." When most prisoners go to the hole, they think about ways to become a better criminal. Not Butler. Solitary confinement changed him.

After a return to the general population of Ethan Allen, Butler worked as a cook in the kitchen for 27 cents an hour and played lots of basketball. The inmates played for Twinkies, Little Debbie cakes, and cases of Mountain Dew. "It's big time," Butler said about basketball games in prison. "We were starving. We had to eat."

The players tackled each other in prison basketball. No fouls. Prison rules forbid fouls. If he could make layups while getting hit as hard as a wide receiver going over the middle, then he could finish a basket under most any circumstance. "You don't see anyone get fast-break layups or dunks in [prison]," Butler said. One of his future coaches would describe Butler "as having a penitentiary game. He is so tough. And I mean that in the most complimentary way. He remembers where he came from."

Butler avoided trouble for the rest of his sentence. Inmates told him to never look back at the facility when he exited prison. Those who look back, come back. Butler kept his eyes forward and never ran into trouble with the law again.

Racine's public schools shunned Butler. They didn't want someone they perceived as a gangster. Butler assumed his birth name, James Butler, and worked at Burger King while he took courses at a technical college, where he received straight Bs on his report card. Some old friends showed up at BK and ridiculed Butler: "Quit this damn job," they said. "We about to hit the block." Not with me, Butler said, and the so-called friends came around less and less often until they didn't visit again. Caron wasn't going back to prison.

Racine Park High School accepted Butler when its administration received his grades and saw that he had stayed out of trouble. His parole officer searched him in the halls on a regular basis. "It was embarrassing. I knew they were doing the right thing. I just wanted the opportunity," Butler said.

During his only full season in high school, Butler averaged 24.3 points and 11.1 rebounds. He made the Associated Press's all-state team and Racine Park went from a four-win team in the previous season to a 19-3 mark and a share of the division title.

Arizona, Butler (no relation), DePaul, Georgetown, Marquette, Maryland, Pitt, Purdue, UNLV, and Wisconsin recruited Butler, a top-30 prospect at the time. Butler appealed to play another season in Wisconsin because his eligibility had expired. The state rejected the appeal, and Butler, short on credits to graduate, enrolled in Maine Central Institute (MCI), a prep school with a rich basketball tradition. Located in Pittsfield, Maine, MCI makes Storrs look like Gotham City.

Butler needed $5,800 to pay MCI's tuition. He made one last trip to the street to get it. According to Butler, he told "a street hustler" that he had a plane ticket but was short on money. "Man, don't come back," the drug dealer said, and he gave the cash to Butler. Not forgetting what had been done for him, Butler kept in touch with the drug dealer, who ended up with a 10-year prison sentence for doing what Butler described as "street stuff." He said he wanted to repay the street hustler for his act of kindness.

MCI's coach, Max Good, had experience with players with troubled backgrounds. Good realized that Butler needed a male figure in his life, one who provided discipline and structure. He became that man. On the ride to Pittsfield, Butler started casual conversation: "Boy, there's not much to do around here." Good said, "If you want to go back to the airport, we can. It'll make things a lot easier on the both of us."

Good had no tolerance for Butler's act, which included high-fiving fans in the stands after a basket. "I checked last year's roster," Good told Butler. "We were 35-0 and you weren't here. You need us a lot more than we need you."

In his first year at MCI, Butler averaged 18.9 points and 12.1 rebounds. His maturation continued too. Butler ran from the offensive end to the other basket to try to stop a layup . . . in a pickup game. He got in the face of teammates who did not play as hard as they could.

In basketball terms, a "slasher" scores by moving diagonally toward the basket. Most experts refer to Butler as a slasher, but Butler doesn't move from one spot to another, he gnashes the defense and whoever is in his way. No matter how big or strong the defenders are, they don't want to get in the way of this kind of movement.

On a visit to see DerMarr Johnson, Butler's teammate at MCI, Karl Hobbs saw Butler play and put him on UConn's wish list. Butler's past concerned the UConn staff, but Good assured Calhoun of the player's loyalty and progress. Calhoun knew that Butler was committed to basketball and changing his life because the star player left Racine and spent two years in Maine.

Butler made a verbal commitment to UConn in the first week of August 1999. Then his recruiting odyssey began. Good left MCI after Butler's first year and became an assistant coach at UNLV. Many speculated that Good went to UNLV to get Butler to come to Vegas. A few weeks after committing to UConn, Butler made an unofficial visit to UNLV to see Good.

Media sources in Las Vegas reported that Butler had changed his mind and would enroll at UNLV. Butler denied it. In November, Butler and his mother signed a binding letter of intent to attend UConn. Butler said the decision was close, but he had chosen his head — UConn — over his heart — Good and UNLV.

"I wanted to play for a tough coach, and he's one of the toughest," Butler said about Calhoun and his decision to play for UConn. Butler could not take advantage of Calhoun. No one can. Butler wouldn't be tougher than Calhoun. No one is.

Calhoun's ability to produce top-quality NBA players at his position attracted Butler to UConn. And, of course, UConn's popularity appealed to Butler. When asked later what it was like to play for UConn, Butler said, "Are you kidding? It's like being a rock star."

Butler helped convince a guy who would become a key piece of UConn's next championship run to join him. In 2000, the nation's best basketball point guards played for New York City high schools. The Big Three or the Holy

Trinity, as the media and others called them, were Andre Barrett from Rice High School in Harlem, Taliek Brown of St. John's Prep in Astoria, Queens, and Omar Cook from Christ the King in Middle Village, Queens. This crop of point guards was the best produced by New York City since at least 1983, when Mark Jackson, Kenny Smith, and Dwayne "Pearl" Washington played in the city.

UConn recruited all three; according to Cook, the first to accept UConn's scholarship offer would be a Husky. To some, Brown, six foot one and 185 pounds, resembled former Pistons guard Vinnie Johnson. Both players were guards out of the city; they looked a bit like each other; they had muscular builds; and they could score in an instant. Brown's body made him look more like a running back than a basketball player. He used his strength to harass opposing point guards.

Brown had averaged 22.7 points and six assists per game as a junior in high school. Recruiting experts lauded his ability to explode to the basket but criticized him for the lack of an outside shot. Syracuse, St. John's, UMass, Miami, USC, and Kentucky, among others, pursued Brown, who was considered one of the top 10 or 15 players in the class of 2000.

In September, Calhoun and Hobbs visited Brown's home in Queens. They played video clips of UConn's national championship. As he watched the tape, Brown saw himself playing for a national championship in a UConn uniform. He liked UConn's style of play, the current roster, and the team's recruits, especially Butler.

"If you come here," Calhoun said to Brown during the in-home visit, "you will learn a lot and win a national championship." When Caron Butler told Brown that he would sign with UConn, Brown committed to the Huskies too.

During a trip to New Haven to play Weaver High School of Hartford, Brown was greeted by UConn fans who showed their support. The point guard appreciated the love and felt right at home in Connecticut. During his career, Brown would also experience the negative side of Huskymania.

By the standards set by Calhoun, the 2000–2001 season wasn't all that great, but the team did finish 20–12 overall, .500 in the Big East, and 16–2 at home. Its 1–8 road record, one-and-done performance in the Big East tournament, inability to qualify for the NCAA tournament, and loss in the second round of the NIT did not satisfy fans who were two years removed from a national championship.

Weeks after UConn defeated South Carolina in the first round of the NIT, Gamecocks athletic director Mike McGee offered the men's basketball head coaching position to Jim Calhoun. McGee knew that Calhoun owned property in Hilton Head, South Carolina, and had plans to retire there.

And he knew that Calhoun craved a challenge. The Gamecocks hadn't won an NCAA tournament game in 28 years. Calhoun rejected McGee's first offer, but South Carolina came back with a contract worth $1.9 million a year. In turning down the counteroffer, Calhoun reiterated his feelings for UConn and his desire to stay there.

Calhoun wanted to win another national championship at UConn. At the time, he was heavily interested in a player from the Houston area.

18

If Maryland Is Number One in the Country, Connecticut Is Right Beside Them

Calhoun needed an inside player and depth at guard. Never again did he want to be as low on guards as he was after El-Amin suffered an injury. To fill the gap inside, he turned to Texas. To add depth on the outside, he went to Mount Vernon, New York.

Chukwuemeka "Emeka" Ndubuisi Okafor's family, immigrants from Nigeria, emphasized academics. Emeka had to be a solid student. When Okafor was eight, his father registered him to play basketball at a YMCA in the Houston area. The elder Okafor knew nothing about basketball, but figured that his son needed extracurricular activities to occupy his attention.

"Dad, why did you do that?" asked Emeka about his father's decision to enroll him in a youth league. "I don't feel like playing. I don't want to do this." Despite his lack of knowledge about the game, Pius Okafor realized that his son had talent. In high school, Emeka was an honors student and excelled in basketball and football. He gave up football to avoid injury and concentrate on basketball.

As a senior at Bellaire High School outside Houston, Okafor was the MVP of his district. Okafor's high school coach said that his star player had "God-given" ability to block shots. His offensive moves were raw. In late April 2001, Bob Gibbons rated Okafor as the 106th best player in the country and the 17th best center in the senior class.

The elite programs in the country—Duke, Kentucky, North Carolina—don't pay much attention to recruits outside the top 25. UNC coach Matt Doherty made an obligatory call to Okafor late in the recruiting process. Okafor ignored it.

Karl Hobbs saw Okafor play in July of 2000. He wasn't impressed. Hobbs recruited four or five players who chose other schools. Okafor's name was still on his list, so he went to see him play again in December. "Wow," was all Hobbs could say when he saw Okafor this time. He told Calhoun, "Whatever you're doing, we need to stop it and go after this guy right now. If he gets even bigger and stronger—man!" Hard work and dedication combined with talent allowed Okafor to improve in the months between Hobbs's visits. He would continue to use that recipe in the future.

Okafor wanted playing time, a good coach, and a style that fit his strengths.

His university of choice needed a strong academic profile and basketball tradition. In the fall, he made official visits to Rice and Vanderbilt, universities with better academic profiles than basketball programs. He visited Georgia Tech, which excels in both basketball and academics. To increase his value, Okafor waited to commit until the spring signing period. Most elite players sign their letters of intent in the fall.

By spring 2001, Okafor had drawn interest from Texas Tech, Arkansas, and UConn. The day after he was hired by Texas Tech, Bobby Knight went to Houston to recruit Okafor. Emeka was impressed by Knight, but he thought there wasn't much to the university or its basketball program besides Knight. If Knight left, then Okafor would be stuck at a university and in a program without much appeal to him. His decision came down to UConn and Arkansas.

Calhoun saw Okafor play in the Pittsburgh Hoops Classic on April 14, 2001. The game featured Division I-caliber high school players against similar talent from Pennsylvania. Top coaches like Nolan Richardson of Arkansas, Knight, Pitino, and Doherty joined Calhoun at the game to watch Okafor and a handful of others who had yet to sign. Richardson said he "drooled" as he watched Okafor score 26 points, block 10 shots, and get 12 rebounds.

As he analyzed Okafor's performance against players who had committed to schools in the SEC, Atlantic 10, and Big East, Calhoun drew one conclusion: Okafor was the best player on the court. Others agreed: Okafor garnered the game's MVP award.

Calhoun likes players whose style of basketball resembles that of a construction worker—hard hat, lunch pail, lots of work, never afraid to get dirty—and Okafor fit that profile. Calhoun loved him for it, and Hobbs knew it. Okafor was a typical Calhoun recruit. He was hungry, would do what the coach wanted to improve, and, as a three- or four-star recruit, was no prima donna.

Okafor selected UConn because the university was a "championship school with a championship coach." Okafor thought he could be more successful in Storrs than in Fayetteville, Arkansas. His high school coach told Emeka that "Coach Calhoun's record of turning out quality players is second to none."

Before Okafor took a class or blocked a shot at UConn, he consulted with Ted Taigen, the team's academic advisor. "Most good players leave for the pros after their junior year," Okafor said to Taigen. "Can we devise a course of study that will allow me to graduate in three years? I want to earn my degree before I leave for the NBA." These didn't seem like questions that should be asked by the 106th best player in his class, but Okafor knew that his hard work and Calhoun's magic would make the NBA an option for him in three years. Taigen laid out how Okafor could finish in that time.

When Ben Gordon was in the fifth grade, Bob Cimmino, his future high school coach, invited him to a basketball camp. As Cimmino watched him play in a scrimmage, Gordon streaked to the right of the basket and made a left-handed shot. Impressed with the play, Cimmino asked Gordon if he could try to take the shot right-handed the next time. "Coach, I am right-handed," Gordon said. Seven years later, Gordon averaged 24.6 points a game as a junior and led Cimmino's Mount Vernon team to a 28-0 record and New York State's Class A and Federation titles.

Gordon was raised by his mother, Yvonne, and his grandmother Avis, who migrated from Jamaica, then spent a brief time in London, where Ben was born, before coming to Mount Vernon. Gordon was less than a year old at the time he came to the U.S. He grew up in a religious household. He was laid-back and quiet; as a kid, he dug for worms in the backyard. When he grew up, he wanted to be an ecologist. According to Gordon's mother, Ben "doesn't have an aggressive nature. He's just a very gentle person." Gordon received the nickname Gentle Ben, because of his laid-back style.

At age 10, Gordon took up basketball at the Mount Vernon Boys Club, and he developed his game from there. In high school, he preferred shooting the ball for hours alone in the gym to organized games in the summer. On more than one occasion, the police kicked him out of the high school gym for practicing late. After his sophomore season in high school, major college programs took note of Gordon. Duke and Seton Hall were at the top of the list. Mike Krzyzewski called Gordon twice during the summer of 2000.

Coach K tends to get whomever he wants. Gordon was not going to reject Duke if he received an offer from Krzyzewski. The Blue Devils played on television all the time; Gordon wanted to be a part of that. He regarded Duke as the Chicago Bulls of college basketball.

At the ABCD camp on the campus of Fairleigh Dickinson University in Teaneck, New Jersey, Daniel Ewing from Willowridge High School in Missouri City, Texas, impressed Duke's coaching staff. Gordon did not. Ewing became a Blue Devil. Gordon did not.

But while Duke chilled, UConn warmed up. Gordon, his mother, and Cimmino took a trip to Storrs in August 2000. They visited with Calhoun and Leitao. Hours after returning from the trip, Gordon decided to commit to UConn. Cimmino wanted his star to spend more time on the decision. He quizzed Gordon: What if we had visited Villanova first? What about UConn's loaded backcourt, which included Brown, who would be a sophomore, and junior-to-be Tony Robertson? No matter. UConn was the best program. Gordon announced his intentions to be a Husky shortly thereafter.

UConn's previous championship and the program's ability to win another impressed Gordon, who liked the Big East and claimed to have been a UConn fan for years. "It was all about winning for me. I wanted to win right way, and UConn was at the top of that list," Gordon said.

Calhoun did not want UConn to be a shooting star, another good program that happened to win a national championship and then disappeared. Despite others' claims of his mellowing, Calhoun made sure to keep his intensity high, even after he had achieved the ultimate success. He saw the negative effects of losing one's edge. "You know, they say Rollie Massimino won a championship and maybe just took his foot off the pedal a little bit, just a little bit," he said. "Once you let the pedal up, even just a little, it can all come to an end."

Big East supremacy and national prominence were Calhoun's goals for the 2001–2002 team. He had watched Butler score between 11 and 18 points in UConn's final 12 games of the 2000–2001 season and concluded that Butler needed to raise that total to 20 per game and 30 in critical ones. He told Butler that great players and great leaders dominate. The coach needed Butler to dominate.

Gordon and Okafor roomed together in their freshman year. They needed to adjust to each other. As Gordon tells it, he kept the room neat, pristine, and in order while Okafor cluttered it up. But another difference between the two caused Gordon to complain to Calhoun. As Calhoun tells it, Gordon said that Okafor would wake up in the middle of the night, turn on a small light, and study. This routine bothered Gordon as he tried to sleep. "You know you're in college, right?" Calhoun said to Gordon. He then told Gordon to go and work out this situation with Okafor, and they did. As Okafor tells it, his study habits weren't a big deal.

UConn entered a late-December home game against St. Bonaventure with a 6–1 record and a national ranking in the mid-30s. The Bonnies beat UConn by 18, and the game wasn't even as close as that score indicated. The loss also ended a 21-game UConn winning streak against non–Big East teams at the Civic Center and a 75-game home winning streak in November and December, the latter of which had started after the boo-bird game against Villanova in December of 1989.

The players held a meeting after the St. Bonaventure game. For a month, they didn't tell the coaches about what was said in the session. Behind closed doors, senior forward Johnny Selvie apologized to his teammates for selfish play against St. Bonaventure. He said it wouldn't happen again; it didn't.

UConn started 5–0 in the conference and was in first place in the league's East Division as it prepared for a game at Gampel against Carolina. This version of the Tar Heels was the worst in program history. UNC's streaks of 27 consecutive NCAA tournament appearances and 37 straight top-three finishes in the ACC were to end in 2002. The Tar Heels came into the game on a five-game losing streak. A Carolina team hadn't lost that many games in a row in 50 years.

"Everyone, to a degree, needs to be convinced of his self-worth," said Calhoun. "When I chastise a player, many times I'll talk very simply. 'You're too good a player to do that,' for example. In that small way, I'm chastising and praising at the same time." If he didn't know about chastising before the Carolina game, Caron Butler knew it afterward.

Calhoun benched Butler less than two minutes into the game. He wanted his team to attack Carolina from the start. When Calhoun watched Carolina score the game's first seven points and 11 of the contest's initial 13, he pulled Butler and yelled, "You set the tone for our team. Why don't you just sit here, and if we get a big lead, you can go back in." "You singled me out," Butler said. "You're darn right," Calhoun responded. "You're our best player."

Butler received the star treatment. Calhoun had benched stars like Donyell Marshall and Ray Allen to send a message. That day, Butler got his.

Calhoun said that Butler didn't have much street left in him, save for his game. The coach wanted to see that kind of play against Carolina. He got it. After a brief stay on the bench, Butler scored 29 points on 12 for 18 shooting to help UConn destroy Carolina, 86–54. Get benched. Get mad. Get even. Toward season's end, Calhoun said that Butler was "as good as anyone I've ever had as a leader."

The loss was Carolina's worst against a nonconference team since a 42-point defeat to Kentucky in 1950. Based on five straight wins, victories in six of seven, an undefeated record in the Big East, and its dominance of UNC, UConn made the top 25 for the first time in close to a year.

After a five-point win over St. John's at Gampel, UConn traveled to number-10 Arizona. With 19 seconds to go and his team down by two, Butler tied the game at 91. Okafor blocked point guard Jason Gardner's shot as time expired in regulation. Near the end of overtime, with the score 100–98, Arizona guard Will Bynum attempted an uncontested three-pointer for the win. He missed; the Huskies danced and celebrated following the victory.

Usually more mild-mannered than Clark Kent, Gordon turned into Superman and flew into Calhoun's arms after UConn's win. Calhoun waited 10 minutes to enter the locker room after the game because his "players were off the wall."

Okafor scored 19 points, snared 15 rebounds, and rejected nine shots. Calhoun and the CBS announcers argued that Okafor swatted at least 12 shots, but, according to the UConn coach, official scorers are "reluctant to give guys blocked shots." Okafor was the third Husky to reject nine or more shots in a game—Donyell Marshall (10 versus Hartford on January 17, 1994) and Cliff Robinson (nine versus Georgetown on February 6, 1988) were the other two.

After the Arizona game, UConn suffered defeats at Rutgers (61–53), Miami (68–66), and St. John's (85–83, in overtime). Ray Allen attended the first loss. He spoke to the team for an hour after the game. The team needed a leader; Butler needed to take on that role.

After a 46–40 win over Villanova at the Hartford Civic Center, the Huskies seemed to be on their way to a fourth loss in six games. With 2:37 remaining, BC led by 10 and many fans began to leave the Civic Center. BC star Troy Bell held his index finger to his lips to tell UConn fans to be quiet.

During a time-out, Butler screamed at his teammates; they had been in this position before, the star said. He and the Huskies were going to have to will their way to another win. Calhoun felt that BC "relaxed because they thought the game [was] over." He said that BC didn't factor in "how hungry we were. We said this had to be our game."

Following the time-out, UConn went on a 14–4 run to send the game to overtime, where the Huskies won by two. The win was UConn's 13th straight on its home court over BC and its 25th in the last 26 games against the Eagles. The UConn fans who stayed mocked Bell with fingers to their lips as the BC player went to the locker room. This wouldn't be the last time UConn fans embarrassed Bell.

UConn entered the Big East tournament with a 13–3 record in the league and an overall mark of 21–6. Caron Butler, the lone unanimous choice for first team All-Big East, shared conference MVP honors with Pitt's Brandin Knight. Okafor and Gordon made the all-rookie team and Okafor was third-team all-conference. Notre Dame's Chris Thomas captured the conference's rookie of the year award. Chris Thomas.

In UConn's first game in the Big East tournament, against Villanova, it trailed by a point with 34 seconds to go. Calhoun drew up a play for Gordon to take the shot. With a little less than 12 seconds remaining in the game, Gordon's three-pointer moved UConn from a one-point loss to a two-point win.

Gordon's 23 points tied a career high, which he had set in Arizona and at Madison Square Garden in an overtime loss to St. John's. Gordon had signed with UConn to make these kinds of shots and win these types of games.

The Huskies beat Notre Dame by five to advance to the tournament finals, where they faced Pitt, the top team in the west division and the seventh-ranked team in the nation. The Big East championship game was close throughout.

Pitt tied the game at 52 with 30 seconds remaining in regulation. Brandin Knight twisted his knee on the ensuing play and went to the bench. The teams went to overtime.

With the game tied at 60 and less than two seconds left in overtime, Pitt coach Ben Howland reinserted Knight to take the Panthers' final shot. "I don't know if that's a good idea—look at him limp—unless he's playing possum," said ESPN's Len Elmore. Knight didn't walk. He hopped. Gimp aside, Knight's bomb from just inside the half-court line almost went in as the star collapsed to the floor in pain. "But I am telling you this, I think that's somewhat irresponsible," Elmore said as ESPN showed the replay. "I love Ben Howland, but you can't take a chance with this guy's health. You can't do it." Knight didn't return.

In the second OT, with just under two minutes to go, the game was tied at 64 when Butler made a fade-away shot to give a 66–64 lead to UConn. Butler made the shot despite Pitt's flypaper defense. Howland called this basket the toughest one for him to swallow.

After two Pitt misses and UConn's attempt to kill some of the clock, Gordon was tied up. With the possession arrow in their favor, the Huskies kept the ball but only two seconds remained on the shot clock. Taliek Brown received the inbounds pass and took a 30-footer, which looked like it would hit the spires at the top of MSG. It went in. The shot sealed UConn's fifth conference tournament title.

Caron Butler scored 23 points in the tournament final and was named the MVP. Now the leader, Butler went into the MSG stands to celebrate with UConn's fans. His teammates followed.

In two weeks, UConn went from being unranked and having the likes of Xavier and Western Kentucky ahead of it in the polls to finishing first in the Big East's East Division, capturing the conference tournament title, and moving to 10th in the nation. Some of Calhoun's power teams hadn't been as prolific as this group. Calhoun liked this team as much as any other he had coached. During games, he rotated between coaching and cheering.

In the round of 32, second-seeded UConn led North Carolina State, the seventh seed, by 10 with 4:27 remaining, but the Wolfpack cut that margin to one with 47 seconds left in regulation. Calhoun wanted to kill time and set up UConn's final shot. The ball was in Butler's hands. With the shot clock running down, Butler took a three-pointer with 11 seconds left on the game clock. He missed. The teams began to run to the other end of the court.

Then, referee Scott Thornley stopped play and signaled that he had called a foul on N.C. State's Julius Hodge. Almost no one had heard the whistle. Butler

Caron Butler returned UConn to elite status. Now he refers to Calhoun as Dad.
UConn 74–Pitt 65 (two overtimes). March 9, 2002, Big East tournament finals,
Madison Square Garden.

Ezra Shaw/Getty Images

made the free throws to extend UConn's lead to four with a little more than 10 seconds remaining.

N.C. State's Ilian Evtimov hit a three-pointer with 4.3 seconds remaining and it appeared Okafor ran into him after the shot. No call was made. With 3.6 second left, Butler was fouled again and he made two free throws. Hodge missed a long three-pointer as the clock expired and he tumbled to the floor in anguish: UConn 77–N.C. State 74.

Perhaps Calhoun's Huskies were bailed out by the kinds of favorable whistles and noncalls reserved for the most elite of programs. Wolfpack players and coaches thought so.

The referees didn't beat N.C. State. Caron Butler did. During the game, chants of "jailbird" cascaded toward Butler, but he didn't care. He had heard much worse. Butler scored a career-high 34 points, 20 of which came in the final 10:44. He had 16 of UConn's final 20 points, and made all of his 10 free throws. After his experience in prison, Butler said, "Playing basketball is not pressure." He lived these words against N.C. State.

Calhoun wondered how Butler didn't even make third-team All-American. "There has to be room for him somewhere in the first twenty, first fifteen," Calhoun said. "He's the real deal—and I've had some pretty good kids at UConn." Toward the end of the season, Calhoun regarded Butler as "one of the five or ten top players in America." Truth is, at the time of the NCAA tournament, Butler was the best player in the country.

In the Sweet 16, the Huskies beat 11th-seeded Southern Illinois by 12. Early in the season, Maryland had beaten UConn by 12 in Washington, DC. After the game, Butler predicted a rematch—and a UConn win—in the NCAA tournament. After the win over Southern Illinois, UConn played top-seeded Maryland for the right to advance to the Final Four in Atlanta. In the first half, the lead changed 12 times and the score was tied 13 times, but Maryland pulled away with Okafor and Butler on the bench in foul trouble. It went into the locker room at the half with a seven-point advantage and momentum on its side. Maryland had lost once in the previous 27 times that it led at halftime. Things looked bleak for UConn, and Calhoun knew it.

Basketball strategy wasn't on Calhoun's mind. He needed to get his team fired up. He had to devise a way to get momentum on UConn's side. Calhoun doesn't coddle his team and he often saves his wrath for the best players. One player could take the kind of special attention Calhoun was about to administer. One player could carry UConn to the Final Four. Calhoun knew it.

Calhoun screamed at Butler, "Are you going to let them take what you've worked so hard for?" As Butler says, those weren't the specific words used by his coach, but that's the G-rated version. "Hell yeah," Butler yelled back. "I'm fucking ready. I'll show you."

Butler wanted to be considered along with Donyell Marshall, Ray Allen, and Rip Hamilton as one of the greats to play for the program. Heading into the Elite Eight game, Butler had scored in double figures in all but one of the 62 games he had played as a Husky. His double-figure streak stood at 48 games, which is pretty legendary. If Butler wasn't already a legend before the Maryland game, he became one during the second half.

As soon as the game resumed, Butler made three three-pointers and started an 11-4 UConn run. He scored 15 points in the first nine minutes of the second half. UConn led by three with less than four minutes to go. It doesn't look good, thought Maryland coach Gary Williams. Destination Atlanta looked like Mission: Possible for UConn.

Okafor had picked up his third foul about a minute into the half and didn't return until 12:19 remained. Maryland's Lonny Baxter dominated in Okafor's absence; he finished with 29 points and nine rebounds. With 3:53 left, Terrapins' guard Juan Dixon made a three-pointer to tie the game at 77. He and Baxter combined for 62 percent of Maryland's offense in the game. With 55 seconds to go, the Huskies trailed 83–80; they needed to stop Maryland one more time to keep it a one-possession game.

Maryland called time-out with 34 seconds left in the game and 14 on the shot clock. Calhoun thought his team was going back to the Final Four. Taliek Brown nearly asphyxiated Dixon, who couldn't get open. Point guard Steve Blake, who had been held scoreless in the game, dribbled the ball with about 30 seconds remaining. Calhoun liked that Maryland fumbled through this play with the shot clock expiring. Blake took the ball toward Okafor, who had a choice to make: defend Blake on the perimeter or drop back to guard Baxter, who was open on the wing. He chose the latter.

Blake stopped his dribble and Tony Robertson flew past him. With his feet aimed toward his bench, Blake took a three-pointer with seven seconds left on the shot clock. The ball went in. "That ends the basketball game because now we've got to get six points in twenty-five seconds," Calhoun said. Mission: Impossible: Maryland 90–UConn 82.

Baxter was named the MVP of the East regional; the award should have gone to Caron Butler. In the second half, Butler scored 26 of his game-high 32 points. He finished the game shooting 69 percent (nine for 13) from the field and 60 percent (three for five) from three-point range.

The *Journal Inquirer*'s Phil Chardis regards Butler's performance as the best half played by any Husky during the three decades he's covered the team. As the team boarded the bus after the game, Chardis congratulated Butler on his play. Butler appreciated the compliment, but he wanted to head to Atlanta, not Storrs.

Butler continued to lead the team, even after a devastating defeat. He concealed his emotions. "I'm really affected by the loss," he said, "but my team looks to me and has followed my lead all season. So I've got to hide my feelings. I'm keeping my head up and keeping them right."

Calhoun knows a championship team when he sees one. The 2001–2002 Maryland squad was such a team. "They're more than capable of winning the national championship. They're a great team. And that's no BS," he said. No, it wasn't. Butler thought that the winner of this game would win the national championship, and he was right. Eight days after Calhoun and Butler made these statements, the Terps cut down the nets in Atlanta. Of Maryland's six opponents in the NCAAs, the Huskies had given them the hardest time; no other team came close.

"If Maryland is number one in the country, Connecticut is right beside them," Calhoun concluded after the game. Taliek Brown still believes that UConn would have been national champions had it defeated Maryland. The 2002 Huskies joined their 1990, 1994, 1995, 1996, and 1998 predecessors as a national-championship-caliber team.

The 2002 team returned UConn to national prominence. It won the Big East regular and postseason title and came close to making the Final Four. The emergence of Caron Butler as the team leader and best player in the country along with the development of Okafor and Gordon made this team special.

Butler loved playing for Calhoun and UConn, but his choice to turn pro was easy. He was 22 and needed to provide for his two kids. After an outstanding performance in international competition in the summer before his sophomore year, MVP honors in the Big East regular season and postseason, and his play in the NCAA tournament, Butler's stock wouldn't go much higher than it was in the spring of 2002. At Butler's press conference, Calhoun thanked the Connecticut media for treating Butler fairly and telling Caron's "story so well."

When asked about his favorite Husky to cover and be around, Dave Solomon, former UConn beat writer for the *New Haven Register*, responded without hesitation: Caron Butler. Caron was a man, Solomon said. Butler showed maturity and treated everyone with respect. To a person, all who were around Butler during his UConn days praise Caron for his leadership, maturity, and personality.

Butler was selected 10th in the 2002 NBA draft by the Miami Heat. On draft night, Charles Barkley commented that Butler would be the best pro in the bunch. In his first season, Butler played more minutes than any other rookie. Butler was traded to the Lakers as part of the deal that sent Shaq to Miami. Butler played one year for the Lakers, which traded him to Washington. After playing parts of six seasons for the Wizards, Butler was traded to the Dallas Mavericks in 2010. At the start of the strike-shortened 2011–2012 season, he signed with the Los Angeles Clippers. Of the 57 players taken in that draft, only Yao Ming (first pick), Amar'e Stoudemire (ninth pick), Butler, and Carlos Boozer (34th pick) have made at least one NBA All-Star team.

Ernie Grunfeld, general manager of the Washington Wizards, found that Butler made his team stronger and tougher. When Butler arrived in DC, he noticed that his teammates lacked toughness. Some of you need to drink tough juice, Butler said. Because of this comment, the Wizards referred to Butler as Tough Juice.

Butler regards Calhoun as "the closest thing to a father I ever had." He doesn't have a relationship with his biological father. Of all his former players, Calhoun maintains the closest contact with Butler. The two speak regularly on the phone. Sometimes they talk about the weather and most often Butler tells Calhoun how he's doing.

Butler calls Calhoun on Father's Day.

When Butler went to the pros, he stopped using the word "Coach" to address Calhoun.

Instead, Butler calls Calhoun "Dad."

We're Connecticut. We're Not Some Rinky-Dink Team

When people visited the university in the fall of 2002, as they turned onto North Eagleville Road off Route 195 they saw the 200,000-square-foot, five-story Chemistry Building. The red bricks, glass atriums, and smokestacks that rose from the roof let everyone know that UConn was state of the art. This $53 million centerpiece of UConn 2000 set the university apart from other schools.

The plastic sheets that wrapped the library were removed in time for President Clinton's visit to dedicate the new Thomas J. Dodd Research Center on October 15, 1995. UConn 2000 paid for the library's renovation.

Also, as part of UConn 2000, Fairfield Way, the main strip alongside Babbidge Library, was torn up and repaved in red brick, complete with the university's new acorn logo. The business school's new $27 million, 100,000-square-foot building replaced the mall area between the library and Gampel Pavilion.

In March 2002, Governor John Rowland said, "It would be an understatement to say that the plan [UConn 2000] has succeeded." At the time, UConn 2000 had provided more than a hundred new and renovated facilities to UConn's various campuses. From 1995 to 2002, enrollment went up by 56 percent, joined by a 62 percent increase in minority students. The average SAT score of UConn students improved by 30 points. The endowment went from $50 million in 1995 to $220 million in 2000.

In 2002, about 74 percent—or $712 million—of the UConn 2000 money had been spent. Based upon the success of UConn 2000, Rowland asked the State Legislature for $1.3 billion to continue the program for 11 years. The Connecticut General Assembly passed the measure. As a result of the plan—named UConn 21st Century—the Storrs campus would see more renovations, new buildings to replace rotted old ones, another parking garage, and a new student health center. UConn 21st Century planned to replace the Torry Life Sciences Building, Monteith Hall, and Arjona Hall, among others. Its funding allowed for the renovation of Jorgensen auditorium and the Connecticut State Museum of Natural History.

The men's and women's basketball teams spurred executive and legislative action on UConn 2000 and UConn 21st Century. Those legislative programs made the university resemble the basketball teams in its excellence. The basketball programs helped build a world-class university.

Calhoun needed Emeka Okafor to continue to develop an offensive game. Okafor's 7.9 points per game as a freshman would need to increase if UConn wanted to meet or exceed preseason expectations. In his freshman season, Okafor had averaged 4.1 blocks per game, fourth most in the nation. He asked teammates about opposing players' tendencies to shoot or pass so that he could get into proper position for a rejection. Okafor worked to keep blocked shots in play because his father told him that blocked shots did little good if the other team maintained possession.

Ben Gordon, the other part of the new dynamic duo, played too gently for Calhoun's taste. Calhoun thought Gordon could take over any game he played. He believed that Gordon could put up as many as 40 points a game if he were more aggressive. If UConn wanted another Big East title and national championship, Gordon needed to be more assertive.

In the first half of a game against UMass at the Civic Center on December 10, 2002, UConn scored nine first-half points, which broke the program record for lowest-scoring half by four. Okafor spent most of the first half on the bench because of foul trouble. Throughout the season, UConn's fate would be tied to whether Okafor was on the court. "We really aren't the same without Emeka," Calhoun said later in the season.

Fans booed the UConn players at halftime. The year before, the crowd jeered the Huskies during the St. Bonaventure game. UConn fans treat the players like they are rock stars but they voice their displeasure when the team loses. This hostility is most intense at the Civic Center. No one can remember booing of UConn at Gampel.

After the booing started in the second half, the coach waved his arms up and down to mockingly encourage louder jeers. The crowd obliged. UMass's lead grew to 25. The boos grew louder. Then, in a span of eight-minutes, 25-seconds, UConn went on a 22-0 run. This time, UConn's full-court press held UMass to nine points in the second half. UConn won, 59-43. Based on this performance, the 2002-2003 UConn team learned that it was never out of a game.

This game marked the second time a Calhoun-coached team rallied from 25 points behind to win a game. In 1995, the Huskies overcame a 40-15 deficit in the first half to win at Pitt. Calhoun's teams don't give up because they fear Calhoun's wrath. Calhoun's teams don't give up because they want to prove their coach wrong. Calhoun's teams don't give up because a comeback is nothing compared to the practices that they've been through.

After the comeback win over UMass, Calhoun acknowledged that the will to win existed. "The best thing we did was we learned hopefully who we are, that we can win a game under almost any circumstance. If you believe that, you can will yourself," Calhoun said.

In its next three games, a home win over Virginia Tech was sandwiched between losses at Oklahoma and Carolina. At Miami in its next contest, UConn fell behind by double-digits for the sixth straight game, but Gordon's 32 points helped the Huskies gain a four-point advantage over the Hurricanes with 8.9 seconds left. Miami made an uncontested basket to cut UConn's lead to two. Calhoun had his best free throw shooters in the game because Miami was going to foul with little time remaining. Taliek Brown was supposed to inbound the ball, but junior Shamon Tooles, a cousin of Richard Hamilton, did so instead. Miami's Darius Rice intercepted the ball and stroked a three-pointer to hand UConn one of the worst regular season losses in program history.

When the reporters walked toward UConn's locker room to conduct postgame interviews, one player awaited them. It was Tooles. The reporters had grown accustomed to such behavior from the Huskies, who had learned from Coach Calhoun to be accountable for their actions. On this night, Tooles told the reporters, "I did the wrong thing and it cost us the game." Calhoun called the loss one of the toughest he could remember. This defeat affected the team for an extended period.

UConn's plan in its next game, versus Boston College at Gampel, was to dominate the Eagles as usual. The Huskies had won all but one of their previous 10,000 games against BC. Actually, UConn had only won 26 of the previous 27 games between the two teams. Domination took place, but not as the Huskies planned. According to Gordon, the game "was out of our grasp" after BC scored 11 of the game's first 12 points. The Eagles extended their first-half lead to 23. In the second half, BC led by 30 on its way to the largest win by a visitor at Gampel: BC 95-UConn 71.

To Okafor, this game was the worst defeat in his career at UConn. To lose like that to Boston College in what he called the "house that Coach built" was unacceptable to Okafor. Calhoun felt that the team lost its will to win early in the game. The ability to compete and overcome challenges is at the core of Calhoun's coaching philosophy, and this team had violated that principle.

A day before the BC game, Calhoun learned that he suffered from an early stage of colon cancer. The diagnosis knocked the wind out of the coach, who took a seat when he received the news. Calhoun was frightened at the moment. He told no one connected with the team until after the BC game. The news stunned the players. Okafor thought the whole thing was a joke. Brown said that his jaw hit the ground when he heard the announcement.

Doctors expected Calhoun to be out three to four weeks. They thought Calhoun would return in time for the Big East tournament. Calhoun put Assistant Coach George Blaney in charge of the team. Blaney had an established career as a head coach at Dartmouth, Holy Cross, and Seton Hall. He and Tom Moore ran practices in Calhoun's absence.

Calhoun approached cancer as if it were a Big East basketball season: work as hard as you can, overcome obstacles, win in the end. After the diagnosis, Calhoun called Jim Boeheim, who had received treatment for an enlarged prostate in the winter of 2002 and lost both parents to cancer. Calhoun said that Boeheim "was great."

The players talked to Calhoun before they left for a February game at Virginia Tech. For the first time since 1986, the Huskies left Storrs without Calhoun, who felt lonely to be the only one back at Gampel.

In UConn's first game without Calhoun, Taliek Brown broke his finger, which required surgery. He would not return for two weeks. The Hokies beat the Huskies by 21. In the Calhoun era, back-to-back losses were rare, but consecutive defeats by 20 or more happened about as often as Hanson brothers turned down a fight. The other time that a Calhoun-coached, UConn team lost consecutive games by at least 20 occurred in his first season, the 9–19 one: on January 31, 1987, UConn lost by 21 at Pitt and three days later St. Peter's beat the visiting Huskies by 25. As a result of the loss at Virginia Tech, UConn had lost four of six.

Blaney used UConn's tradition to get the players to respond. "We're Connecticut. We're not some rinky-dink team," Blaney said to the team. The Huskies won by 18 at Providence and came home to drill number-17 Syracuse by 14 at the Civic Center. Okafor scored 15 points and pulled down 12 rebounds for his 13th double-double in 20 games. Orangemen star Carmelo Anthony scored a game-high 29 points; he reminded Blaney and Gordon of Caron Butler. By season's end, Anthony would be regarded by most as the better of these two players.

Calhoun was restless at home during his recovery. He talked to Blaney on the phone, exercised on treadmills and Stairmasters, and looked for ways to escape to Storrs. During a snowstorm less than a week after the surgery, Calhoun needed to visit his team. He searched for the keys to his Ford Expedition, but Pat had hid them. Calhoun found the keys to his Jaguar, an unreliable car in wintry weather, and headed outside to take the sports car to Gampel. The coach no longer drove a Dodge Shitbox. As Calhoun started the Jag, Pat yelled, "Here you fool," and threw the keys to the Expedition to her husband, who was off to Gampel.

On the eve of Valentine's Day 2003, Ben Gordon and a female student slapped each other and were arrested. The police charged Gordon with third-degree assault and disorderly conduct. Gordon posted the $1,000 bond and started at Villanova in UConn's next game amid "convict" taunts from Wildcat fans. Gordon scored 25 in the nine-point loss. He performed 30 hours of community service and missed no playing time. More than four years after the incident, Gordon said, "It's something that I learned from. I'm not embarrassed that it happened. It was kind of a blessing in disguise because it was serious. But I learned from it and moved on."

As a result of the loss to Villanova, UConn fell to 2-2 under Blaney and dropped out of the top 25 for the first time in close to a year. Gordon lamented the absence of Calhoun: "We're just stronger as a team when he's here. That's our captain, and when he's not here, things aren't the same."

Blaney could have used Brown's defense against Villanova's Gary Buchanan, who scored 28 to lead the Wildcats against the Huskies. In UConn's win over Villanova earlier in the season, Brown held Buchanan to 14 points.

UConn came home after the Villanova loss and beat Rutgers, 87-70. Calhoun ran the team's two practices before the Huskies' next game, and the university announced that the coach might be back on the sidelines for the next contest—at Gampel against St. John's on February 22. And then, the sheriff returned.

Before the St. John's game, the Gampel crowd gave a standing ovation to Calhoun for two minutes and Mike Jarvis and some opposing players congratulated their adversary's leader on a quick return. In the game, a nine-point UConn win, Okafor passed Donyell Marshall for the most blocked shots by a UConn player.

In the days leading up to the game at Boston College, Calhoun questioned his team's desire. Coming into this game, the regular season finale for both teams, the Huskies trailed BC by one game in the conference's East Division. UConn scored the first 14 points and handed BC the Eagles' worst loss at Conte Forum: UConn 91-BC 54. This game avenged BC's 24-point victory at Gampel. The result was so bad that senior Troy Bell, one of the best to play for BC, was booed at home on senior day. Husky Nation travels well and it often found plenty of seats at Conte Forum games. With a small BC crowd already gone, the UConn fans let Bell have it. When the NCAA tournament selection committee saw the 17–9 Eagles on the bubble and then looked at this game, it concluded that BC was NIT material.

This UConn team overcame the loss of its coach during the season, an off-the-court distraction, a monumental defeat, and a streak of losing four of six to capture a share of the East Division championship.

UConn beat Seton Hall by 13 in the quarterfinals of the Big East tournament to set up a return match against Syracuse. The Orangemen came into the game on an eight-game winning streak. The Huskies led by 21 with about 10 minutes remaining and won by 13. The game wasn't that close. UConn regular Rashad Anderson and others sat on the bench as the Huskies prepared for the next night's championship rematch against Pitt. Calhoun made a brief statement after the game before heading back to his hotel room to rest. Blaney answered the media's questions about the game. The loss was the last of the season for Syracuse and the final one in the collegiate career of Carmelo Anthony, who went 0-for-UConn in his one season with the Orangemen.

In the championship game against Pitt, UConn trailed by four with 5:58 remaining but scored five points for the rest of the game and lost by 18.

Duke receives preferential treatment from the NCAA's tournament selection committee. UConn does not. In its 24 NCAA tournament appearances from 1987 to 2011, Duke played in the East region eight times; from 1988 to 1990, Duke stayed in the East even though it was twice a second seed and once a third seed. It stayed in the South region six times and in the Southeast bracket three times. It played 26 (26!) tournament games in its home state.

UConn, the most dominant team in the Big East since 1990, played in Hartford in 1990, on Long Island in 1994, and in Washington, DC, in 1998, 2002, and 2006. For the most part, the Huskies were NCAA tournament vagabonds forced to travel from one coast to another.

In 1996, did UConn play in Providence, a site of first and second games? Not a chance. The East's number-one seed, UMass, received that honor. Instead, the Huskies were the top seed in the Southeast. That season, UConn played in Indianapolis and then Lexington, Kentucky.

The NCAA tournament selection committee is not consistent in its desire to keep teams in their regions. In 1998 and 2002, the committee placed UConn in the East so that the Huskies could play UNC in Greensboro and eventual champion Maryland in the Elite Eight in Syracuse. In 1999, UConn, with all two of its regular season losses, was shipped to Denver and Phoenix.

In 2003, the tournament selection committee did not allow the Huskies to play their first two games in Boston. It sent UConn, the fifth seed in the South, to Spokane, Washington, for the first two rounds. It kept UConn's first two opponents, 12th-seeded Brigham Young and Stanford, the fourth seed, in the West.

At this point, Calhoun was convinced that his squad could beat anyone in the country. And he meant *anybody*. He wasn't sure his team could win six straight but the Huskies' recent play made the coach feel that a trip to the Final Four was realistic.

In UConn's five-point win over BYU in the first round, Okafor blocked seven shots. At one point, BYU's Travis Hansen, who Calhoun characterized as a terrific player, shot the ball over the basket to avoid Okafor. BYU center Rafael Araujo, a 57 percent shooter, made two of his 11 attempts. "He looked nervous and unsettled," his coach said.

BYU players complained about the lack of fouls called on the UConn center. "Okafor is so big-time that they don't call those fouls — but I don't think he's that big-time," said BYU's Hansen after the game. Calhoun disagreed. "He's the best defensive player in the country. He alters games. He alters everything," the coach said of Okafor, who scored a team-high 20 points.

In its next game, UConn trailed Stanford 44–40 at the break. In the locker room, Calhoun attacked Gordon and Okafor for their timidity on the floor. He hated that these two players carried their off-the-court politeness into games with them. Late in the first half, he pulled Gordon from the game for coming weakly off a screen, and, according to Paul Schwartz of the *New York Post*, gave his star guard "a subtle nudge to help him find a seat." At halftime, Calhoun said to Gordon, "You need to take this game over offensively." Gordon's 11 first-half points weren't enough for his coach.

"They're not taking the ball to you so you need to do something else, like rebound and score," Calhoun said to Okafor, who scored six in the first half. The assistant coaches complained to Okafor that he was too tentative and not his usual bouncy self. You have zero offensive rebounds, the coaches said. If we are going to win, you have to be a major part of it.

Julius Barnes, Stanford's leading scorer for the season, averaged 15.8 points per game. In the first half, he made four of six from three-point range and six of nine overall for a half high of 16 points. In the second half, Calhoun deployed Taliek Brown, his defensive weapon, and Tony Robertson to face-guard Barnes and prevent the game's hottest shooter from getting the ball.

Down by two about five minutes into the second half, UConn went on a 14–4 run to take an eight-point lead with less than nine minutes left. It won by 11.

As demanded by Calhoun, Gordon took over on offense. He scored 12 of his 18 second-half points with less than 8:16 remaining. Okafor took over. He scored 12 points in the first eight minutes of the second half and finished with 18 points and 15 rebounds, six of which came off the offensive glass. Okafor spent about 4:30 of the game's last six minutes on the bench in foul trouble. The preferential treatment he supposedly received from officials in the BYU game was a limited-time offer.

Barnes scored seven points in the second half; he went one for five from the field. "Whenever I passed the ball, they denied the turn-back," he said.

As Calhoun and Gordon walked toward the postgame press conference, the coach told his player, "You're one of the best guards in America. You could have forty-one of these nights." "He's really laid-back," Calhoun said of Gordon. "I'd be letting up on him if I didn't push him to be his best." Gordon understood Calhoun's motivation. "Coach wants the best for me. . . . He's helping all of us realize how good we really can be," Gordon said when asked about his coach's tendency to ride him at practice and during games.

Jim Calhoun is not one to stop and appreciate a win or an accomplishment, but after cancer, the UConn coach reflected on the significance of making the Sweet 16: "As we were walking off the floor in Spokane after beating Stanford, I remember thinking there is something a little more special to this. It does have a better taste to it this time." In a month's time, Calhoun and his team had turned what looked like a trip to the NIT (at best) to the program's ninth Sweet 16 appearance in the last 14 years.

UConn's defense was championship caliber; it included two elite defenders—Taliek Brown on the outside and Okafor on the inside. UConn's offense approached championship caliber. It included two prominent scorers—Gordon on the outside and Okafor on the inside—with guest appearances from Rashad Anderson, among others. The team had depth too. Against Stanford, six Huskies played 20 minutes or more and eight were in the game for at least 10 minutes.

Even before UConn arrived in San Antonio, the national media started to talk about the Huskies as the favorite to win the next year's Final Four, which would also be held in the Alamodome. Each of UConn's core players would return for the next season. Calhoun continued to tell his team and everyone else that the Huskies were good enough to make the Final Four in 2003.

Playing the University of Texas less than 90 miles from its Austin campus had no effect on whether the Huskies would beat the Longhorns. Calhoun said so. He insisted that the Alamodome was a neutral site. Calhoun had convinced his team of the insignificance of the game site. Taliek Brown wanted the Longhorns to beat Purdue in the round of 32 because he wanted to play the top seed in its home state.

With 12 minutes left in the game against Texas, the Longhorns led by 14, and they hadn't relinquished a lead that large all season long. Then, Calhoun switched to zone on defense and ordered his team to feed the ball to Okafor on offense. After these changes, UConn turned its deficit into a three-point advantage. Naismith Award winner T.J. Ford picked up his fourth foul with 10:30 left in the game and was relegated to the bench for the next five minutes. He may have been glad to spend a few minutes away from Taliek Brown. Under pressure from Brown, Ford missed all but three of the 15 shots he took for the game.

Calhoun credited Brown and the UConn defense for preventing Ford from going down the lane, the move that made the player of the year so successful during the season. Calhoun isolated Ford in film sessions and told his players how to defend him. It worked.

Despite all of Brown's strengths, Husky fans complained that he didn't score enough or that he turned the ball over too much. They wanted him to be Khalid El-Amin. No one could do that. Critics logged on to the fan blog Boneyard.com or other chat rooms and blogged about how Calhoun should bench Brown. When questioned about Brown's play, Calhoun said that the critics didn't understand that the point guard defended the opponent's best player and provided leadership, toughness, and energy.

The criticism bothered Brown. Family helped him get through it. Calhoun told him to ignore what others said and concentrate upon what he has done and will accomplish at UConn. Calhoun defended Brown to the world, but he was tough on Taliek too. "Playing point guard for Coach was a very demanding job," he said. "I had to try to play perfectly every time I touched the floor, and also make my teammates play perfectly because all the blame went on me. He made me a strong person mentally." Brown was as much a part of the core of the team as Okafor and Gordon were, and his performance against Ford and other elite players showed his value.

With 47 seconds remaining and UConn down by two, Rashad Anderson missed a jumper that was more of a layup for a scorer of his caliber. UConn got the rebound and Taliek Brown hit an open Marcus White near the basket. Texas's Brian Boddicker deflected White's shot, and the ball lodged between the backboard and the rim with 35 seconds left. The possession arrow, which dictates which team receives the ball under this circumstance, pointed to Texas.

Texas's Royal Ivey made two free throws to give an 80–76 lead to the Longhorns with 20 seconds to play. An Okafor dunk off Taliek Brown's missed layup put UConn down by one possession with 11.8 seconds left, but two T.J. Ford free throws ended UConn's season.

"A game played with that intensity is decided by an arrow rather than a basketball play?" Calhoun asked after the game. "Because of the genius of officiating, they don't want to throw the ball up. . . . Tossing the ball up is difficult. It can't be that difficult," he said.

Possession arrow aside, Calhoun understood that his team created its fate. The Huskies missed two open, foul line jumpers and a layup in the game's final two minutes. They made 14 of their 25 free throws. "We were a heartbeat away from winning the game," Calhoun said. "We got a real sniff that, without question, we could have been in the Final Four. I think that's really important for this team because it was really a season of joy in many ways. We were really good in the end."

Against Texas, Okafor took on an enormous and deep front line by himself at times and scored 21 points, gathered 17 rebounds, and blocked six shots. In 2003–2004, any discussions about a national player of the year would include the name Emeka Okafor. Only foul trouble or injury could stop him.

"I've never seen a player improve in a two-year span as quickly as Emeka," Calhoun said. Hobbs was surprised by Okafor's development but admits that he shouldn't have been. He said that very intelligent players work hard and improve. When Okafor reached the Storrs campus and found out that all he had to do to become a star was work hard, he said, "That's all? No problem."

As heartbreaking defeats go, this one came with advantages. It convinced the Huskies that they were as good as any team in the country, and with the core of Okafor, Brown, Gordon, Anderson, Denham Brown, and Hilton Armstrong returning, the players believed they could return to the Alamodome in 2004 and win the program's second national championship. After the final game of the season, Brown said, "We're going to be back next year."

20

Emeka Okafor Comes along Once in a Lifetime

Calhoun and his staff added Josh Boone to help Okafor and Marcus Williams to give Brown some rest. Boone chose UConn over Kansas and Georgetown because of the university's relative proximity to his family in Baltimore, the school's academic reputation, and Coach Calhoun's record of producing NBA players. The opportunity to play with Okafor also attracted Boone to Storrs. Georgetown no longer had the advantage of a Hall of Fame coach, a slew of former players in the pros, and a dominant center on its side. UConn did.

Rivals.com rated Williams as the seventh best guard and 61st best player in the senior class. Georgia Tech, Maryland, N.C. State, and North Carolina had showed interest in Williams, but the feeling wasn't mutual. Williams cancelled a trip to Georgia Tech and committed to UConn during a visit to Storrs in late August 2002. He respected Calhoun's ability to produce NBA players. Getting to "the league," as players refer to the NBA, is a big attraction for recruits and by this time, no one did it better than Calhoun. Williams and his parents also liked UConn's computer science program, which would be a bit ironic considering Williams' future connection with laptops.

By late spring, Charlie Villanueva, a six foot ten power forward from Brooklyn who played at Blair Academy in Blairstown, New Jersey, was the highest-rated unsigned player in the country. Rivals.com ranked him as the nation's fifth best. Villanueva is bald and has no eyebrows because he suffers from alopecia areata, a disease that causes hair loss on the scalp and other spots on the body.

In the fall of 2002, Villanueva made a nonbinding commitment to play for Bill Self at Illinois. When Self went to Kansas at the end of April, Villanueva looked elsewhere. In May of 2003, he declared for the NBA draft, but maintained his college eligibility because he hadn't hired an agent. Villanueva wanted to be the first New York City player to jump from high school to the pros.

Villanueva's game was flashier than that of most UConn recruits. Those who watched him play marveled at his step-back three-pointers, behind the head dunks, fancy passing, and lots of dribbling. Calhoun considers El-Amin, Donny Marshall, and Villanueva to be the most flamboyant players he coached at UConn.

Because he was projected to be a borderline first-round pick at best, Villanueva signed with the Huskies. Calhoun's ability to churn out blue-chip pro players drove his decision. He wanted to win a national championship and felt that Okafor, Gordon, and Calhoun gave him the best opportunity to accomplish that goal.

Steve Pikiell, then an assistant to Karl Hobbs at George Washington University, watched Villanueva play many times on recruiting trips to Blair Academy. When he heard that Villanueva had picked UConn, Pikiell said this was the smartest decision the star made in his life. Pikiell knew that Villanueva had NBA talent, but also saw that the player needed to address criticisms about his work ethic, attitude, and toughness. For Pikiell, Camp Calhoun in Storrs was the best place to develop these attributes.

At UConn, Villanueva would run at full fucking speed, bang underneath, and do what Calhoun wanted—or he wouldn't play. Many of the nation's top five high school players couldn't handle Calhoun or these expectations. This explains in part why UConn doesn't sign many five-star players.

In the fall of 2003, experts predicted that UConn would win the national championship in men's and women's basketball. Diana Taurasi returned for the two-time defending champion Huskies. *ESPN the Magazine*'s basketball preview issue featured Taurasi pretending to surf and her board was Okafor in push-up position. The cover asked, "Will UConn Be the Ones?" Inside the magazine, Dick Vitale ranked the UConn men number one followed by Michigan State, Duke, and Kansas. He chose the UConn women as his preseason number one too.

At Midnight Madness, the symbolic start of the college basketball season across the country, Calhoun pointed at the 1999 championship banner and told the large crowd at Gampel, "What we want to do is try to put another one right next to it." For UConn fans, the season would be a disappointment if it ended without victory in San Antonio.

In the semifinals of the preseason NIT against Georgia Tech at MSG, Okafor experienced back spasms that made him run like an old man, according to Calhoun. The doctors allowed Okafor to play because they said that the center couldn't further injure himself in game action. The Yellow Jackets held a 42–35 advantage at halftime and won by 15. The Huskies made 10 of 30 free throws. UConn shot a higher percentage from the floor than from the line against Tech. Calhoun said that the missed free throws deflated him and the team.

The team played an un-UConn game. "I was deflated myself and I rarely get deflated," Calhoun said in the postgame press conference. "We were getting dunked on. We were getting beat down the floor, sometimes four-on-

one. Those effort kind of things scare me," he said. The Huskies received the wrath of Calhoun; the turkey couldn't have tasted too good for the Huskies on Thanksgiving Day 2003. UConn spent more than an hour that day shooting free throws at the Garden and the players got an earful of Calhoun unpleasantness throughout the day as well.

In the consolation game of the preseason NIT, Utah faced a 51–15 deficit with 13 minutes left in the game. UConn held the Utes scoreless for periods of 6:48, 4:04, and 5:40. No chance: UConn 76–Utah 44. Okafor scored 21 on 10 of 13 shooting and abused Andrew Bogut, a freshman for Utah who would go on to be the first overall pick in the 2005 NBA draft.

In this game, Rick Majerus, who brought Utah to national prominence and the brink of an NCAA title in 1998, suffered his worst defeat as coach of the Utes. He predicted that UConn would win the 2004 national championship.

Based on the loss to Georgia Tech, UConn fell out of the nation's top spot, which it regained in mid-December. After the first 13 games, the Huskies had 12 wins but no quality victories on its resume. That situation had the potential to change, as number-six and undefeated Oklahoma visited Gampel in UConn's 14th game.

Upon seeing the students camp out for the Oklahoma game in single-digit weather, Okafor said, "It's crazy, man. I always said Connecticut has a special breed of fans."

This game ended after UConn held Oklahoma scoreless for 7:46 in the first half. After this stretch, UConn led 28–10 and won by 27. Okafor's line said it all: 21 points, 10 rebounds, and nine blocks. The win moved the Huskies to 6–1 against top-10 opponents at Gampel. OU coach Kelvin Sampson called Okafor "a difference maker." He said, "There's nobody else like him. They might be the same height, but there's a difference. Okafor's just a different breed of cat."

UConn went 2–1 in its next three and returned to the Civic Center and beat undefeated and ninth-ranked team Pitt by three.

Then, Ryan Gomes returned to Connecticut.

A Waterbury native and Wilby High School star, Gomes averaged 18.4 points and made second-team all-Big East as a sophomore for Providence. In 2003-2004, he was playing like one of the best players in the country. Reporters and fans wanted to know why Gomes wasn't a Husky. They asked endless questions about how Calhoun could miss this one.

Calhoun wasn't impressed by Gomes's six foot six, 260-pound, build and neither were the coaches at St. John's, Villanova, Seton Hall, and even URI, each of whom passed on Gomes. Calhoun signed Butler instead. The next time

Gomes entered the picture, after he had attended Notre Dame Prep School in Fitchburg, Massachusetts, to improve his SAT score, UConn signed Okafor. Calhoun and other college coaches questioned how hard Gomes played. Gomes didn't slip across the borders; Calhoun had said no thank you.

Against UConn in Hartford on this day, Gomes scored 26 points and had 12 rebounds as PC beat UConn by 10. Okafor put in 19 points and grabbed 13 rebounds. The only UConn player to reach double figures in points, Okafor finished with his 12th double-double in 18 games.

After the game, Dave Solomon of the *New Haven Register* asked the first question about Gomes. "Jim, recruiting's hardly an exact science," Solomon said. With those words, the blood rushed out of Calhoun's face. With both of his eyebrows raised, Calhoun sucked in his lower lip and moved his tongue to the side of his mouth. "But what does Gomes do that just blows you away now that maybe no one saw . . ." And with those words, Calhoun winced, turned his head away from Solomon, and let out a "Whew." Then he started . . .

"You want me to go throughout the country at the guys that came and didn't go?" Translation: many teams don't sign players who star at other schools. "I'm a genius," Calhoun said, "I took Emeka Okafor at a hundred." That statement is accurate. Then he said, "It's the dumbest fucking question I have ever heard," which wasn't so true.

"I've explained it a thousand times," which may have been a low number. "I fucked up, I didn't take Ryan Gomes. Does that make you happy?" Calhoun said as he pressed his hand against his chest. He didn't raise his voice that much, but his tone indicated urgency and frustration.

"But I'm tired of talking about it." He reiterated that Gomes looked like one of the best players in the league and perhaps the country. With arms outstretched to his side, Calhoun said, "I don't know what else I can say."

"And if you want me to say I fucked up, I fucked up." Again, no yelling. Then Calhoun shook his head and said, "Write it. I answered the question, I don't know how else I can answer it and you want to go deeper into . . . you want me to say I fucked up . . . for the fifth time . . . I fucked up. Alright. So put it five times."

Calhoun wanted to stop the never-ending story. Two days later, he apologized to Solomon during a conference call with reporters. Calhoun also called Solomon, who appreciated the apology but said it was "not necessary."

Because of this explosion and others like it, people compare Calhoun to Bobby Knight, and some similarities do exist between them. They are passionate; they yell at their players; they have maniacal looks on their faces at times during games.

Coach Calhoun is never out of control like Knight frequently was. Knight punched a police officer in Puerto Rico after he couldn't get the gym open for a Team USA practice for the Pan-American Games. Among other outbursts, Knight flung a chair across the court in one game and after getting ejected in another, he walked to the opposite end of the court, circled referee Ted Valentine, and walked to his locker room at the other end of the court.

YouTube features some of Bobby Knight's worst moments. It has a clip of a calm Knight, who turns angry, says he's "disappointed in the fucking progress" of his team, kicks something in front of him, and ends the show when he says, "Goddamn it! Fuck this show. Take this fucking show and forget fucking basketball." In other videos, Knight ridicules and yells at reporters, curses missed golf shots for an instructional video, and storms out of postgame press conferences.

Isiah Thomas received an award at a Bloomington country club in 1982. With Knight over his right shoulder and in camera shot, Thomas said that "Fuck you," "Asshole," and "Son of a bitch" were the three things he learned from Knight at Indiana. When Thomas started this list, those in attendance bent over in laughter. The people behind the podium wiped tears from their eyes as they laughed at Thomas's words. Thomas was not done.

"But the most important word that he [Knight] ever taught me in the whole English language that I'll never forget and I think he created it hisself, it's called a sunt. It originated from the word cunt. . . ."

The laughter stopped.

The men behind the podium now stood with arms folded almost as if they had been ordered to do so. Knight stared at Thomas as the condemnation continued. It became clear that Isiah was not kidding.

As far as these examples are concerned, Calhoun differs from Knight. For the most part, Calhoun tries to be amenable to the media. When he is interviewed on television, Calhoun tries to be witty, friendly, and accommodating. Calhoun may use inappropriate language with his players, but his profanity-laced tirades with the media pale in frequency and depth compared to Knight's.

Calhoun's former players, especially the superstars, fall over themselves to praise their college coach. Donyell Marshall's wife teases her husband about wearing only UConn gear. Calhoun has said that he sends more UConn stuff to former players than he gives to those on the current team. Former players credit Calhoun for their successes and regard their coach as a second father or a dad they never had. It is hard to imagine one of Calhoun's players vilifying him in public in the same way in which Thomas, the best player to play for Knight, condemned his coach in a public setting in the university's backyard.

Play hard. Run fast. Calhoun believed that if UConn did those things, his team would be unbeatable. After road wins against Virginia Tech (96–60) and BC (63–58), the fifth-ranked Huskies suffocated and outran number-18 Syracuse, 84–56, on *Big Monday* at the Civic Center.

The Huskies then lost at Notre Dame and Pittsburgh. Prior to the Pitt game, Calhoun questioned his team's toughness. According to Calhoun, Pitt had bravado, UConn didn't. "We had that [bravado] with Caron and Khalid . . . ," he said. "This team is quiet. You can take everyone home with you. As a coach, you always wish you had a few tough guys you can't take home." After these losses, some in the national media regarded UConn as the most disappointing team in the country. Coach Calhoun hears everything, reads everything, and remembers everything.

Emeka Okafor would end his UConn career with 441 blocks, close to 200 more than Donyell Marshall (245), who held the previous mark. Okafor's two most important blocks came on February 28, 2004, at Villanova. Rashad Anderson's three-pointer tied the game with seven seconds left in regulation. Anderson, who would become the best clutch shooter to play for Calhoun, regards this shot as his favorite.

Villanova's Randy Foye tried to win the game with a layup as time expired but UConn's Superman rejected Foye's shot and sent the game into overtime.

With UConn up one with 5.5 seconds left in overtime, Villanova's Foye lost Brown when the UConn defender ran into a screen. Foye had his eyes on a game-winning dunk as time expired. Okafor saw Brown's collision and knew he had to get in position to redirect or swat Foye's shot, but he slipped. As Foye went hard to the basket, the ball went in the other direction. Okafor had regained his balance, fired straight up, and rejected the shot as the red lights that signal the end of the game illuminated the glass. "I couldn't calm them down in the locker room," Calhoun said of his team's reaction to the victory.

"Nobody in the country can change a game like that," Calhoun said of Okafor's final block. "We were saved by the best player in the nation. . . . He showed why he's the best defensive player in the country. Emeka Okafor comes along once in a lifetime." That was good news for Foye and Villanova, which wouldn't have to play against him again. Years after this block happened, Calhoun called it one of the best plays by a Husky during his time at UConn.

After the loss to Pitt, Calhoun said he wanted to win the regular season's final six games, head into the Big East tournament with momentum, and face Pitt in the championship game of the tournament. His wishes almost came true.

After five consecutive wins, UConn lost by 11 to Syracuse in front of 32,944, the second largest crowd to watch a basketball game at the Carrier Dome.

Okafor had reaggravated his back during a practice at LeMoyne College before the game. Against the Orange, he scored two points on 1–2 shooting. At the Carrier Dome following the game, Calhoun said, "By the time we hit the ground in Hartford I want somebody there to look at him, and I want to know what the hell is going on. We certainly haven't discovered whatever is bothering him, because he could barely walk."

No Okafor, No Big East tournament title. No Okafor, No NCAA title. Or so everyone thought.

The days after the regular season ended were all about Okafor. The center earned many awards and honors that week: academic All-American of the year, Big East player of the year, Big East defensive player of the year, and Big East scholar-athlete of the year. He became the first player in the history of the conference to win three postseason honors in the same season. He joined Donyell Marshall and Patrick Ewing as the only players to win player of the year and defensive player of the year in the same season.

When Commissioner Tranghese presented the player of the year award trophy, he said that Okafor was in the same company as Patrick Ewing. In response, Okafor said, "I don't think I've done anything yet to be compared to him. That caught me off guard a little bit." For once, Okafor was wrong. His dominance on offense and defense put him in the same company as Ewing. In his last year at Georgetown, Ewing averaged 14.6 points, 9.2 rebounds, and 3.6 blocks per game. In his final year at UConn, Okafor outperformed Ewing in each category: 17.6 points, 11.5 rebounds, and 4.1 blocks per contest. Okafor broke Ewing's conference record of 3.98 blocked shots per game.

Okafor earned many postseason honors in 2004: National Association of Basketball Coaches (NABC) player of the year, *Sports Illustrated* player of the year, and a consensus All-American. St. Joseph's Jameer Nelson, who led the Hawks to an undefeated regular season, beat Okafor for the Naismith Award.

Calhoun screamed at Okafor once in three years. "I yell at my dog every night when I come home," he said about the frequency of his tone to man and canine alike. "I've been in Division I for thirty-two years, and I've seen very few guys who can dominate a game. I've never seen anyone like him, and I've faced very, very few players who can change a game like he can," Calhoun said.

Okafor was questionable for the Big East tournament because of muscle spasms caused by a small stress fracture of the fifth lumbar vertebra. Four doctors examined the UConn center's back. The day after the Big East awards, Okafor and a UConn doctor traveled to a spine specialist in Dallas to get an independent evaluation. All doctors reached the same conclusion: the injury would be temporary but painful; Okafor could play if he could stand the pain.

Husky Nation knew that Okafor was the centerpiece of a championship run. Many emailed prescriptions for Okafor's back to Calhoun. "I have been given all kinds of advice and even have people who want to put their hands on his back and cure him. . . . I've received emails suggesting different lotions to use on his back. Everyone has a remedy."

"Others have written us off. One Connecticut columnist said, 'We're all done,'" Calhoun told his team. "Are you ready to prove them wrong?" Throughout the Calhoun era, the UConn coach used this whole-world-is-against-us strategy to motivate his team. He employed it again. The *Connecticut Post*'s Chris Elsberry surveyed all the state's columnists and concluded that no one had written anything close to a column on UConn's end. No matter.

Calhoun challenged Ben Gordon to carry UConn in Okafor's absence. Gordon knew he had to play much better than he had in his previous five or six games.

Emeka Okafor missed the first two games of the Big East tournament, but Ben Gordon did not. He scored 29 points in each game as UConn beat Notre Dame and Villanova.

Against Villanova, Brown moved past Sheffer and Ollie for the single-season mark for assists and ahead of Tate George for the most in a career at UConn.

Of his team's point guard, Okafor said, "He's the engine that keeps us going. Basically, he sets the pace of the game. The question is, 'Alright, can we keep up with Taliek today?' When you have a player like that, you're bound to be successful."

Okafor couldn't understand why Brown drew such intense criticism. "Don't people see the same player we see?" the star center asked. "He leaves it all out on the court and is capable of driving this team with his will." Brown was also Pat Calhoun's favorite player because he had helped her do the dishes when he visited her house during his recruiting trip.

Despite Okafor's return against Pitt in the championship game, UConn trailed by 11 with 8:23 remaining. Gordon wanted UConn to keep the score close; he knew that he would have to take over late in the game. The Panthers laughed and smiled on their bench. Gordon noticed. Pitt, a cocky group according to Gordon, must have thought the game was over. It wasn't.

UConn trailed 55–51 with less than four minutes to play when Pitt's Julius Page, one of the best defensive guards in the Big East, blocked Gordon's three-point attempt. Gordon got the ball right back and made a top-of-the-key three to cut the deficit to one.

Page nodded at Gordon, as if to say, "Damn, that was a good shot." After the gesture, Gordon "knew it was over."

Ben Gordon wins the 2004 Big East tournament. Gordon scores over Pitt's Mark McCarroll (in front of Gordon), Julius Page (no. 1), and Chevon Troutman (no. 2) to win the game with 30 seconds left. Gordon set the record for most points scored in a Big East tournament. UConn 61–Pitt 58. March 13, 2004, Big East tournament finals, Madison Square Garden. AP Photo/Julie Jacobson

After a free throw increased the Panther lead to two, 56–54, Taliek Brown shot an air ball, but Anderson got the ball and made a three-pointer to give the Huskies their first lead since midway through the opening half. Pitt responded with a basket and one point separated UConn from its record-tying sixth Big East tournament championship.

On UConn's next possession, its most critical one of the season, Gordon got his shot blocked again, but once more, he got the ball back. Then, he came off a pick-and-roll and dodged the one man he had to beat. Gordon penetrated the lane and made a short shot to give a one-point lead to UConn with half a minute to go.

As a result of free throws after a Pitt miss, Gordon scored 81 points for the Big East tournament, two more than Allen Iverson's 79-point record set in 1996. Gordon scored 13 of UConn's final 25 points and the Huskies won by three. After several years in the pros, Gordon continues to see that the Pitt win was a big game for his career. Calhoun agreed. He said that the Big East tournament put Gordon "in that category of the great players we've had here before."

The Big East tournament championship smoothed UConn's road to the Final Four. UConn received a number-two seed in the NCAA tournament in a weak Phoenix bracket.

In Buffalo, UConn beat Vermont and Dave Leitao's DePaul Blue Demons by 17. UConn advanced to its eighth Sweet 16 in the previous 10 years. Duke, Kentucky, and Kansas were the only other teams that could make this claim.

In the Sweet 16, UConn bombed sixth-seeded Vanderbilt by 20. In the Elite Eight, it drilled Alabama by 16. At halftime of that game, Anderson and Gordon had outscored Alabama 40–29. Later in the game, the score was Alabama 62 and Anderson and Gordon 60. Gordon, the regional's most valuable player, finished with 36 points, the same amount Ray Allen had against UCLA nine years earlier.

In 1999, Phoenix's America West Arena was filled with emotion as UConn made its first Final Four. The 2004 Huskies congratulated one another and cut down the nets in a tame fashion. They expected to win the Final Four.

And then, there was Duke.

21

Mike, Over the Years When We've Seen Teams Collapse . . . Maybe That's a Bad Word

Many of the national stories about the UConn-Duke national semifinal game focused upon the relative talent of the two teams. As it had in every year in which Calhoun coached the Huskies, Duke possessed more talent than UConn. Six Blue Devils were McDonald's All-Americans; UConn had two. Gordon and Okafor weren't good enough in high school to get Duke scholarships. UConn was in the Final Four because of three- and four-star talent, coaching, and great player development.

Duke sophomore J.J. Redick, who would end his career as the ACC's all-time leading scorer, described his team as "blue collar" because of its scrappy play. "What gets us wins is doing tough things," Redick said. Blue chip, yes. Blue blooded, yes. Blue collar, no. The game would show which team was tougher.

In San Antonio, Coach Krzyzewski bristled at questions about the effect of the 1999 championship game on this contest. He insisted that 1999 was irrelevant to 2004, but it wasn't. If the Huskies could beat the best team in the Coach K era, it could also defeat this one. That meant a lot to Calhoun and company.

For Calhoun, the 2004 Final Four was all about Duke. Beat Duke, win the national championship. He told his team that Duke would not be easy to defeat; Calhoun said that UConn would have to take Duke's last breath away.

Coming into the Final Four, Calhoun was a finalist for the Naismith Hall of Fame. That decision would be announced on Monday, the day of the national championship, but Calhoun wanted the news sooner so he could focus on the game. He should have been a lock for the Hall, regardless of the weekend's outcomes. Calhoun had won 680 games in his career and turned the worst program in the Big East into the league's most dominant power and an elite national program. No other coach could make such a claim.

The Hall of Fame called Calhoun on the Thursday before Final Four weekend and delivered bad news: no Hall of Fame this year. Win two national championships and we'll talk. "He was devastated," Tim Tolokan said. The executive director of the Hall of Fame explained that some voters never elect a college coach on the first ballot. Lute Olson, Bobby Knight, and John Thompson weren't first-ballot Hall of Famers and now Calhoun wasn't one either.

Four minutes into the first half in Calhoun's 41st NCAA tournament game at UConn, Duke's Luol Deng dribbled the ball and banged into Okafor, who guarded his opponent near the baseline and the basket. Referee Ted Hillary called a blocking foul on Okafor, the center's second foul of the game. Even after the call was made, Okafor statued himself to show Hillary that he didn't initiate the contact and that he held his position. No matter.

"You have to be kidding me. You have to be kidding me," Okafor said. Hillary wasn't kidding. Calhoun yelled, cursed, and pretended to kick the scorers' table in reaction to the call.

Calhoun Rules: two fouls in the first half equal a seat on the bench for the remainder of the half, and Okafor knew it. Calhoun had made exceptions to his two-foul rule in the past depending upon the score, the style of play, and the individual player's tendency to avoid fouls. With the frequency with which the referees blew their whistles in this game, Calhoun knew that Okafor, or any other post player for that matter, wouldn't avoid fouls. Because he wanted his star in the game at the end, the coach sat his center and hoped that his team could stay close to Duke.

Okafor whacked his seat with his back as he slammed himself onto the bench. "You can't make the conditions," Calhoun told his star, "you can only react to them." If UConn could stay within 10 points or so, a manageable deficit for Calhoun, Okafor would remain on the bench. If the lead ballooned, Calhoun might have put Okafor back in the game.

Sitting on the bench against Duke was one of the hardest things that Okafor had ever done. For the first two or three minutes, the situation ate him up. Then, he turned his attention to the game and encouraged the Huskies. His teammates, Calhoun, and Assistant Coach Tom Moore helped relax Okafor. "Keep your head in the game, you will be a factor in this game before it's over," Moore said to Okafor time and again during the first half.

Two fouls on Okafor in the first four minutes of the national semifinal . . . if Christian Laettner took out a gun and shot an opposing player in a national semifinal, the referees would call a blocking foul on the player who got shot. Not yet Duke's star, Laettner did foul out of his first Final Four in 1989. That was an exception to what became the rule. In the national semifinal against UNLV in 1991, Laettner committed two fouls and shot 11 free throws, four fewer than the Runnin' Rebels' team. The critical play of this game came when Vegas's Greg Anthony was called for a charge with UNLV up three and 3:51 left in regulation. The charge negated Anthony's basket, which would have put UNLV up 76–71 with Anthony at the line shooting one. Instead, Anthony fouled out of the game as a result of the play, Vegas lost its floor leader, and Duke outscored UNLV 8–3 to win the game.

In the 1991 championship game, Laettner committed three fouls and made all of his 12 free throws. That's four more free throw attempts than the Kansas team took. Laettner scored six points from the field in that game.

Duke took 11 more free throws than Kentucky in the 1992 East Region final. Two Wildcats fouled out, including UK's best player, Jamal Mashburn. Laettner committed four fouls in 43 minutes.

In the 1992 national semifinal against Indiana, Duke shot 42 free throws to 16 by the Hoosiers. Duke outscored Indiana by 16 at the free throw line in a game it won by three. In the 1992 finals, Duke shot 10 more free throws than Michigan.

No wonder Laettner—and most other Duke players—didn't have prolific professional careers. They didn't have the Duke advantage of favorable calls from the referees. No wonder why the term Duke Rules has been coined by college basketball experts. When it comes to favorable calls, especially in big games, Duke Rules. Coach K built a dynasty on such calls.

UConn had come a long way and received the benefit of the doubt from the referees under many circumstances. In this instance, the refs gave an advantage to Duke by putting the most dominant player in college basketball on the bench less than four minutes into the national semifinal.

Without Okafor, UConn's 15-4 lead at the 15:04 mark turned into a 10-point Duke advantage with 3:54 left in the half. In the midst of that run, Calhoun called time-out and stomped on the floor to criticize Anderson's one-handed and halfhearted attempt to stop a Deng layup. Anderson was used to such tirades. When asked about his coach's reaction, Rashad said, "Nothing is good enough. He is going to push you to your limits to get the max out of you."

UConn cut the deficit to seven, 41-34, at the break. Deng scored 12 first-half points, each of which came with Okafor on the bench. Backup center Shavlik Randolph scored nine points in the first half and was Duke's second-leading scorer.

Shavlik Randolph.

Redick struggled with human glue stuck to him. He didn't score when Brown guarded him. Then, Brown picked up his second foul with 3:54 remaining in the half and went to the bench. Calhoun Rules. Redick made his first three-pointer one minute later and scored five points in the half. Duke Rules.

Some Duke players experienced foul trouble in the first half, but the team's three best players—Deng, Redick, and Chris Duhon—were not among them. After centers Shelden Williams and Randolph picked up two fouls in the first half, Coach K kept them in the game. Each picked up his third foul before the end of the half.

In one stretch in the second half, Okafor scored eight of UConn's 12 points and grabbed three rebounds, two of which came on offense. He helped cut UConn's deficit to one with more than nine minutes left.

One of the key plays during this comeback took place when Okafor blocked Deng's windmill dunk attempt at one end and scored at the other. UConn could not take the lead, however, and when Shelden Williams fouled out with 5:04 left, Duke held an eight-point advantage, 70-62, with Okafor at the line shooting two.

At the final TV time-out with 3:28 to go, Duke led 75-67. During the break, Calhoun told the Huskies to play "shell defense. . . . If we can get three or four stops we will score. . . . Attack. Attack. Attack. And then stop them."

With 2:41 remaining, Rashad Anderson hit a three-pointer to cut the Duke lead to 75-70. Anderson's shot ranks in the top five biggest UConn shots ever along with Tate George's shot against Clemson, Allen's game-winner in the 1996 Big East championship game, and Hamilton's three toward the end of the 1999 NCAA finals. It was that important.

In the final three minutes, Okafor and UConn's defense forced Duke to take bad shots from the outside. UConn cut the deficit to one with 1:18 left. A Deng three-point attempt hit the rim, hurdled the backboard, and bounced out of bounds with 44.5 seconds remaining. Deng scored four of his 16 points with Okafor on the floor. He was one of the most hyped college players in the last 25 years, but Okafor dominated him.

UConn had an opportunity to take its first lead since the score was 16-15. As Brown dribbled the ball up court, "Let's go, Huskies" chants echoed through-out the Alamodome. Brown beat Duke guard Daniel Ewing off the dribble, penetrated the lane, drew Nick Horvath toward him, and passed to Okafor on the left side of the lane. With 32 seconds left, Okafor took one dribble and shot the ball over Horvath.

He missed.

Boone got a hand on the ball as it bounced off the rim and a scrum resulted. As he battled with Deng for the ball, Okafor thought, "I better grab this ball or the referees are going to call a foul." Grab it, he did. Okafor spun and laid the ball in to give a 76-75 lead to the Huskies with 25 seconds left.

Duke called time-out. In the huddle, Krzyzewski relied on an old ally to win the game for the Blue Devils—the officials. He diagrammed a play in which Redick would drive toward the basket—not his strong suit—and either score or get fouled. Krzyzewski hadn't learned from the 1999 national champion-ship game, in which his slower shooter—in that instance Trajan Langdon— couldn't beat UConn's superior defender, Ricky Moore, to the basket.

Emeka Okafor led UConn to a comeback win over Duke and the 2004 national championship over Georgia Tech two days later. Here, he scores the game-winning basket against the Blue Devils. UConn 79–Duke 78. April 3, 2004, national semifinal, Alamodome, San Antonio, Texas.

Stephen Dunn/Getty Images

Redick executed the play as designed by his coach. He caught the ball on the far left wing and made a semicircle cut to the basket. Okafor, Boone, and Anderson converged as Redick drove into the lane with 15 seconds remaining. Anderson stripped the ball and Okafor knocked it away from Redick, who flailed his arms and stumbled to the court.

Coach K jumped off his seat and screamed, "Foul!" "Foul!" He stomped toward the scorers' table, argued for a foul so hard that his plastic-like hair became disheveled, like his team. "That's a foul. That's a foul," Krzyzewski told the referees as his eyebrows pointed upward to give him a demonic look. "You killed us," Krzyzewski screamed once and again at referee Olandis Poole.

"That was the game right there," Coach K said of this play after the game. He whined so much about this particular play that the *Boston Herald*'s headline read, "Coach K: Defeat Boiled Down to Redick No-Call."

Anderson was fouled and made two free throws to put UConn up by three (77-74) with 11.6 seconds left. Redick's three-point attempt scraped the front of the rim. Okafor rebounded the ball and was fouled. He had the opportunity to take Duke's breath away with 3.2 seconds left. Coach K, still upset about the fouls, could be seen saying "Bullshit" in the direction of the referees.

Okafor strutted to the line and with index finger extended said, "One" — the number of free throws he needed to end Duke's season. He missed his first shot. As the second free throw took flight, Calhoun followed the ball down his sideline and into the basket. As soon as the shot went through the net, Calhoun told his team to get away from the ball and avoid fouls at all costs. Okafor pumped his fist and jumped up and down. He knew Duke had gasped its last breath in the 2003-2004 season.

Without a UConn player in sight, Duke's Chris Duhon made a 38-footer at the buzzer: UConn 79-Duke 78. That shot made winners of those who bet on Duke, a two-point underdog heading into the game. Duhon's basket caused between $30 million and $100 million to change hands.

As the two coaches shook hands, Krzyzewski couldn't even look Calhoun in the eyes. "He was as devastated as I've ever seen him," Calhoun said of Coach K's demeanor at the game's conclusion. UConn stopped Duke six consecutive times in the final minutes of the game. The Huskies went on a 12-0 run to win the game.

"The tougher team pulled it out that year," Taliek Brown said in 2010.

In the postgame press conference, Krzyzewski whined about the officials. "Our centers played forty minutes and had fifteen fouls," he said. Later, a reporter began a question to Coach K with the following premise, "Mike, over the years when we've seen teams collapse . . . maybe that's a bad word. . . ." Krzyzewski raised his right eyebrow, his face crinkled, and he said, "Obviously, you didn't see the game tonight." The reporter had seen the game. Duke had collapsed under UConn's pressure.

Calhoun Rules worked. The coach put Okafor on the bench in the first half to have his star in the game at winning time.

In regard to Duke's decision to not offer a scholarship to him, Gordon said everything worked out for the best. Duke won no championships during Gordon's time at UConn. The Huskies now had to beat one team—Georgia Tech—to win the NCAA title.

Krzyzewski became more annoyed when a reporter asked Duhon and Ewing to handicap the national championship game between UConn and Georgia Tech. "That's alright. Let's just ask about tonight's game," Coach K said. "You can ask me as soon as they leave."

"Very even. It will be a very even game." That's how Krzyzewski saw the finals.

Very even.

Thoughts of the high expectations placed on his team and UConn's back-to-back losses to Notre Dame and Pitt in the middle of the season disturbed Calhoun's sleep the night before the finals. He knew that UConn stunk against Georgia Tech in November and that Okafor's injury was no excuse, but physical pain had limited his star center. "They were talking about how they handled him before," Calhoun said of the Yellow Jackets' attitude toward a rematch with Okafor. "I was thinking, you haven't seen Emeka before."

If Calhoun was concerned about a letdown, he expressed it to no one. He acted like someone who figured that the leadership provided by Brown and Okafor—and the team's more than yearlong quest for the national title—negated overconfidence and the ultimate disappointment.

For Brown, the national championship was a "revenge game" against Georgia Tech. The year before, he had tossed his gear in frustration after UConn's near upset of Texas. Now, one year later in the same locker room, he saw one focused player after another.

To begin the game, the Yellow Jackets missed 16 of 21 shots and all but one of their first eight three-pointers. In the middle of the first half, UConn went on a 10-point run from which Georgia Tech never recovered.

UConn led by 25 on three separate occasions in the second half, the last of which came with 12:22 left and the Huskies ahead 60–35. From that point, UConn went into what Calhoun called "conservative mode." Georgia Tech made four three-pointers to cut the Huskies' lead to seven with 11 seconds left in the season. UConn won by nine, 82–73. In reality, Tech had been clobbered like Alabama, Vanderbilt, DePaul, and Vermont.

Okafor scored 24 points and grabbed 15 rebounds against the Yellow Jackets; he was named the tournament's most outstanding player. The second part of the dynamic duo, Ben Gordon, scored 21 and would have been the MVP if it weren't for Okafor's championship-saving performance against Duke.

UConn overcame the officials and won the national championship for the second time in six seasons. The program had already arrived; now it put itself into the elite category. Calhoun joined Krzyzewski as the only coach to win multiple championships since the NCAA tournament expanded to 64 teams in 1985.

Students and fans overturned two cars and burned various and sundry things around the Storrs campus. "It was the worst up here in recent memory," said UConn's police major, but only two people were arrested. The campus partied again the next night. Diana Taurasi and the UConn women's team beat Tennessee for the team's third straight national championship. The University of Connecticut became the first school to produce the men's and women's national champion in the same season. Storrs, of all places, was the basketball capital of the United States. The next weekend, Hartford, and not Storrs, hosted a parade for the men's and women's teams.

The 2004 national championship ended the Okafor-Gordon era. True to his plan, Okafor graduated in three years and turned pro. Gordon gave up his last year of eligibility because of the likelihood that he would be taken in the first 10 picks in the NBA draft.

Tim Tolokan, who has seen more UConn games than Jim Calhoun, said that Gordon emerged as a player when Okafor suffered his back injury. For Tolokan, Gordon, who didn't make any All-American teams, became a great player when Okafor went down. In the season's final 12 games, Gordon averaged 21.9 points, more than three points higher than his season average. He averaged 27 points per game in the Big East tournament and 21.2 points per contest in the NCAAs. This streak of play put Gordon in a position to become a projected lottery pick in that spring's NBA draft.

No college had produced the first and second picks in the same NBA draft. In 2004, Okafor and Gordon joined Duke's Jason Williams and Mike Dunleavy, Jr., as the only college teammates to go second and third. With the number-one pick in the 2004 NBA draft, Orlando gambled on high schooler Dwight Howard, who turned into one of the best players in the NBA. Okafor went second to the Charlotte Bobcats and the Chicago Bulls took Gordon with the next pick. Okafor won the rookie of the year in the 2004–2005 NBA season and, in the same season, Gordon became the first rookie to win the league's best sixth man award.

Emeka Okafor was the quintessential student athlete. He studied, received good grades, excelled at sports, stayed out of trouble, and was a model citizen. With his departure, some Huskies had a difficult time living up to that standard.

4

ANTIHEROES

Winning may be the only thing, but sometimes it's not enough. The longer Calhoun stayed at UConn, the more fans became agitated by his behavior and the tolerance for the coach and his players decreased. After all the winning, many people deified UConn and its coach, but others demonized them. For the latter group, the Huskies and their coach became antiheroes after an incident in the summer of 2005.

Calhoun had flare-ups with the media in the past. These incidents were brushfires. Calhoun and his players were Teflon. After the laptop incident, they became Velcro.

Fans and the media are less patient with edgy coaches, even if they are legends, than they are with warmer coaches, like Florida State football coach Bobby Bowden. The UConn men's team and Calhoun also paled in comparison to the women's team and Geno Auriemma. After both teams won national titles in 2004, the women won 90 straight games and championships in 2009 and 2010. The women stayed out of trouble and served as role models for student athletes. The UConn men's team won no national titles during this period and some of their players got into trouble. These comparisons illustrate why, for many, the women's teams were heroes and the men's teams were antiheroes from 2005 to 2010.

22

I'm Just a Very Blessed Individual, Lucky to Be Here in Front of You Alive

In July of 2002, UConn assistant coach Tom Moore traveled to Orlando to watch Josh Boone play for the Cecil-Kirk, a 17-and-under AAU team from Baltimore, but another player jumped out. Moore fell in love with a "gangly," "coltish," and "young" player on the Cecil-Kirk team. His name was Rudy Gay.

Gay wouldn't get national attention until the following summer when he scored 30 points per game at the Nike camp in Indianapolis. At that point, Syracuse, Arizona, and Kentucky caught Rudy Gay fever, but the summer before, UConn and Tom Moore were the first with its symptoms. Gay reminded Moore of Tracy McGrady. Indiana, Villanova, Virginia, Florida, and Florida State came to see Gay play during his junior season, but the battle for Gay came down to UConn and Maryland.

Gay took an unofficial trip to UConn, his second visit to Storrs, when he accompanied his best friend and teammate Jesse Brooks, who was on his official visit to the Connecticut campus. Many questioned this move because Brooks, who signed at Towson, wasn't good enough to play for the Huskies and UConn hadn't recruited him until that point.

If Brooks's visit didn't raise eyebrows, UConn's decision to pay $22,000 to the Beltway Ballers, a team in the Cecil-Kirk Athletic Council, for an exhibition game, did. Speculation was that UConn paid Gay's AAU organization for this game against UConn—a legal maneuver, by the way—and, in exchange, Gay signed with the Huskies. On November 3, 2003, about six weeks after UConn signed the agreement with the Beltway Ballers, Gay committed to UConn.

In April of 2004, the NCAA outlawed exhibition games against noncollegiate teams. Instead, teams like UConn could now play exhibitions against Division II or Division III teams or hold closed scrimmages against Division I opponents.

The program's ability to produce NBA All-Star caliber players at Gay's position impressed the high school senior. On the day he announced his decision to become a Husky, Gay said, "When I went to UConn, I fell in love with their system and how they play. They don't run a lot of sets; they run NBA sets. In the future, I hope to play in the NBA. . . . I actually like Maryland a lot, but I just don't think it was a good fit for me." Gay liked how Calhoun showcased his forwards.

Not long after Gay committed to UConn, Maryland coach Gary Williams said that he "could have scheduled an AAU team and given them $25,000 like some schools I know." "If (playing the Ballers) is how we got a kid, that's a sad commentary. We got Rudy Gay because we recruited him for two years," Calhoun said. Gay's high school coach agreed with Calhoun.

In the spring of 2004, Gay played in a high school all-star game at the Comcast Center, Maryland's home court. When Gay, the Gatorade player of the year from Maryland, was introduced before the game, some fans booed. They jeered every time Gay touched the ball. Gay tossed his headband toward the booers after a monstrous dunk. When asked about the incident, he said, "I was about to take it off anyway. Why not take it off then?"

The 2004–2005 UConn team included talented newcomers and returnees. Marcus Williams, who missed the second half of the previous season to concentrate on his grades, started at point guard.

Calhoun and company recruited Anthony Jordon "A.J." Price of Amityville, New York, to relieve Williams at point as well as to play shooting guard. Price, a six foot two point guard and one of the top 40 seniors in the country, is the son of Anthony "Tony" Price, the leading scorer on the University of Pennsylvania team that advanced to the Final Four in 1979. A.J. is named after the two best basketball players his mother, Inga, knew: Anthony Price and Michael Jordan. Price's mother was a four-year starter at Morgan State. Price chose UConn over Kansas, St. John's, and Syracuse.

Price didn't make the McDonald's All-American team, but Mike DeCourcy of the *Sporting News* insisted he should have. Price increased his stature when he earned co-MVP honors at the Roundball Classic high school all-star game at the United Center in Chicago with 15 assists, a record for this game, and eight points.

The game featured six players who would be selected among the top 19 picks in the first round of the 2004 NBA draft: Dwight Howard (first), Shaun Livingston (fourth, and the game's co-MVP), Robert Swift (12th), Sebastian Telfair (13th), Josh Smith (18th), and J.R. Smith (19th). Arron Afflalo (UCLA), Joakim Noah (Florida), Marvin Williams (UNC), and Cedric Simmons (N.C. State) also played in the game and became first-round draft choices in subsequent years.

On October 4, 2004, a brain hemorrhage caused Price to fall into a coma and remain in critical condition for almost two weeks. Price lost between 15 and 25 pounds during that time. Calhoun visited Price in the hospital for 17 straight days.

This was not the first time—nor the last—that Calhoun would visit a member of his basketball family in the hospital. Phil Gamble, the second best player on Calhoun's first few teams at UConn, suffered from skin cancer, which required surgery. When Gamble awakened from his operation on Christmas Day, Coach Calhoun and his wife were in the waiting room.

During Midnight Madness, Calhoun asked fans to remember Price and predicted that the guard would be one of the greatest players in UConn history. Price stayed out for the entire year and his status for the following season wasn't clear either.

In the 2004–2005 season itself, following UConn's eight-point win at number-eight Syracuse, the Huskies were 15-5 overall, 7-3 in the conference, and ranked 19th in the nation. After that game, Calhoun said, "This is just the beginning for us. I have to believe we can get a lot better." Calhoun had Carolina on his mind. The Tar Heels, the second-ranked team in the nation, were the Huskies' next opponent.

A six-and-a-half-point underdog, the Huskies led by three at the half. The game was tied with a little more than 12 minutes to go, but UNC won by seven, 77-70. "I don't believe in, well, you played pretty well. That's not good enough for me and it's not good enough for any of my kids," Calhoun said.

Coming into the UNC game, Rashad Anderson was UConn's leading scorer at 13.8 points per game. He thought he was invincible. He was wrong.

Anderson missed the UNC game because of a skin abscess. After doctors removed the abscess, a bacterial infection in Anderson's leg spread to the player's pulmonary system and kidneys. Anderson experienced breathing troubles, something that caused his father to leave the room in grief. His mother, a nurse, said it "would take [Rashad] several minutes just to get a sentence out." He spent time in a hyperbaric oxygen chamber and stayed in the hospital for 13 days. Anderson didn't care if he played basketball again; he wanted to live first and walk outside second. On more than one occasion, he didn't think he was going to make it.

Calhoun claimed that the players rallied around Price and Anderson and grew closer because of these near fatal illnesses. The evening he returned to UConn's bench to watch a game, Anderson told reporters, "I just feel like I'm just a very blessed individual, lucky to be here in front of you alive." The fans at the Civic Center gave a standing ovation to Anderson when he walked to the bench.

After the loss to Carolina, UConn won its final five games of the regular season by an average of 16.4 points. Calhoun earned his 700th career win in

UConn's second-to-last game of the regular season. In the final game, the 15th-ranked Huskies beat number-13 Syracuse by 18 points at Gampel to earn a share of the Big East regular season title. The following week, Syracuse beat UConn by four in the Big East tournament quarterfinals. In that game, UConn scored 19 points in the first half and trailed by as many as 21 in the second.

The Huskies were the second seed in the East. In the first round, UConn beat 15th-seeded Central Florida by six and moved to 13-0 in first-round games under Calhoun. In the round of 32, UConn overcame an 11-point deficit with five minutes to go, but lost when N.C. State's Julius Hodge converted a three-point play with 4.3 seconds left. Calhoun attributed the loss to a lack of "bullets and energy. . . . It's one of the few times in my coaching career that we ran out of gas and players. A lot of things caught up with us." The illnesses of two players and a knee injury to Denham Brown led to the Huskies' demise in 2004-2005. "These are not excuses," Calhoun said. "They are just facts."

At the close of the 2004-2005 season, Charlie Villanueva declared his eligibility for the NBA draft. Calhoun wanted Villanueva to stay, but didn't think his player was making a mistake by turning pro. Villanueva changed as a result of his time under Calhoun. He had to earn everything, including playing time, while he was at UConn. "If you can play for Coach Calhoun, I believe that you can play for anyone," Villanueva said.

The Toronto Raptors used the seventh pick to take Villanueva, who finished second to Chris Paul in the rookie of the year voting in 2006. Through 428 NBA games, Villanueva has averaged 12.7 points, 5.6 rebounds, and 25.2 minutes per game for Toronto, the Milwaukee Bucks, and the Detroit Pistons. For UConn, however, the loss of Villanueva wouldn't dampen national championship expectations.

Calhoun Is Feared, but He Is Not Respected

Two days after North Carolina won the 2005 NCAA tournament, John Rowe of the *Bergen Record* of northern New Jersey handicapped the top five contenders for the 2006 title. He put UConn ahead of Kentucky, Duke, Villanova, and Gonzaga. Rowe believed that the expected addition of a New Jersey giant would help UConn make another Final Four.

Andrew Bynum, a six foot eleven, 280-pound, center from Metuchen, New Jersey, came into the 2004 Nike All-American camp as one of the 50 best rising seniors in the country. Based on his performance at that camp, he rocketed to become the sixth-rated prep star in the 2005 class. In mid-July 2004, the *Sporting News* reported that Calhoun was "smitten" with Bynum.

In late August 2004, Bynum, along with his mother and brother, drove three hours to visit UConn. Calhoun's ability to develop Okafor impressed Bynum, who saw this as a sign that the coach knew how to teach big men. In late October 2004, Bynum chose UConn because the Huskies gave him an opportunity to win a national championship in each of the next two seasons. He mentioned Calhoun's early interest in him as a reason he picked UConn.

Bynum's NBA stock increased after he scored nine points, grabbed five rebounds, and blocked a shot in 11 minutes at the McDonald's All-American game. In mid-May 2005, he entered the NBA draft. "You're doing *what!?*" Calhoun said when Bynum informed him of the decision. Calhoun told Bynum—and everyone else—that Bynum wasn't ready for the NBA. He resented the player's decision because he helped get his recruit into the McDonald's All-American game, through which Bynum increased his exposure and draft status. The Lakers used the 10th pick in 2005 to make him the youngest player ever selected.

Six years into his NBA career, Bynum has been at the core of a Lakers team that won back-to-back championships in 2009 and 2010. Calhoun acknowledges Bynum's success, but still believes that Bynum made a mistake by entering the NBA early. During the 2009 playoffs, Lakers coach Phil Jackson benched Bynum because the Lakers center didn't work hard or play defense. He would not have needed to level these criticisms had Bynum participated in Camp Calhoun.

In the 2011 NBA playoffs, Bynum clotheslined Dallas's Jose Barea and the referees ejected him. As he headed to the locker room, Bynum took off his jersey and was bare-chested on the court. He may well have learned to accept defeat and keep his jersey on if he had played for Jim Calhoun. In 2012, fans voted Bynum as the Western Conference's starting center for the NBA All-Star game.

Even though Jeff Adrien averaged 27 points and 14 rebounds as a senior at Brookline High School outside of Boston, only Wright State and Nebraska showed interest in him. To improve his academics and game, Adrien prepped for a year at Brewster Academy in Wolfeboro, New Hampshire.

Calhoun and Assistant Coach Tom Moore watched Adrien outrebound and outscore larger players with more prominent reputations at the 2004 Peach Jam AAU tournament in Augusta, Georgia. In the first game of the tournament, Adrien's Boston Area Basketball Club (BABC) faced Team Texas, loaded with future college and pro players. Calhoun saw Adrien dominate for a few minutes, then turned to Moore and said, "I'm convinced; sign him." BABC won the game, 83-75, and Adrien was its leading scorer with 21 points. This game was Team Texas's only loss in the tournament.

In the two weeks after the tournament, Pitt, Miami, Virginia, Virginia Tech, Providence, and Villanova offered scholarships to Adrien. Growing up, Adrien had dreamed of going to one of two schools: UConn or UNC. He began to follow UConn after the 1999 national championship. Adrien visited Pitt to confirm his instinct to choose UConn, and the trip did just that. The epitome of a Calhoun player, Adrien was a bit undersized for a power forward at six foot six, 220 pounds, but he used toughness and determination to make up for physical limitations.

Four laptop computers, worth about $11,000, haunted UConn for an entire season and beyond. They clouded people's opinions of Calhoun, the university, and the program. In August 2005, police arrested Marcus Williams and A.J. Price on larceny charges. From June 9 to June 14, 2005, the two were involved in the theft of laptop computers, which they attempted to sell at pawnshops in Manchester, Connecticut. Incoming women's basketball players Renee Montgomery and Kalana Greene and a member of the women's track team had owned three of them.

Price denied that he had two of the computers but confessed when police presented him with text messages that showed he had tried to hide the laptops in his room. Upon the players' arrest, Calhoun suspended Williams and Price from basketball activities.

Some programs — like the old UNLV basketball team or the Florida State football team — commit a greater share of illegal activities and these programs have problems that need to be fixed. During his time at UConn, however, Calhoun punted potentially valuable players, like Phil Dixon, Doug Wren, and Antonio Kellogg, for breaking the law or committing unethical or criminal acts. The UConn team was not notorious for problems, but when its players got into trouble, the media covered every facet of the story. This kind of exposure is typical for programs in the spotlight. The players receive the glory when they win and the agony when they make mistakes.

In mid-September and mid-November, a judge ordered Williams and then Price to serve 18 months of probation and 400 hours of non-basketball-related community service. Upon completion of the probation, the incident would disappear from each player's criminal record.

In late October 2005, the university suspended Williams for an academic year, during which time he could continue to take classes. He could neither live on campus nor eat in the university's dining halls until the start of the next academic year in August 2006. He had to perform 25 hours of community service. Williams would not be able to play in a game until the start of the second semester in January of 2006; he could resume practices on December 17, 2005. Because he had lied to the police, Price could not resume basketball-related activities with the team until April 29, 2006.

Critics argued that Price got the longer punishment because he wasn't going to play in 2006 anyway; he was still recovering from his brain hemorrhage. In response to calls for harsher punishments, Calhoun said that neither the basketball program nor the university should abandon young men who make mistakes.

In September of 2005, Calhoun was inducted into the Naismith Hall of Fame. This wasn't just an induction ceremony for the coach; it was a family reunion. At the end of his speech, Calhoun asked his 97 guests to stand. Some were literal family members, but more than 50 were part of his other family—including players from the coach's 1971-1972 Dedham High School team that went 23-1 as well as his Northeastern and UConn teams. Most of these attendees acknowledge that they wouldn't have been where they got without their coach. On this night, Calhoun acknowledged that they were the reason for his successes.

Calhoun-bashing intensified after the laptop incident. CBS Sportsline.com's Gregg Doyel, a former ACC reporter for the *Charlotte Observer*, wrote, "UConn coach Jim Calhoun is a Hall of Famer and a champion, but when it comes to coaching, he is not a moral beacon of light. This is not a news flash." AAU teams connected to Rudy Gay, Denham Brown, and Brandon Bass, a Huskies recruit who signed with LSU, received money in exchange for playing against

UConn. Doyel used the different punishments received by Williams and Price in the laptop incident to support his claim that "Calhoun honors nothing but his own program." He implied that Calhoun—not the university—decided the players' punishments. "Calhoun is feared, but he is not respected. Not by coaching colleagues who have grown tired of his cutthroat negative recruiting tactics and by his exploitation of NCAA loopholes like the one that landed him Brown and Gay," Doyel wrote.

In the 2004–2005 season, UNC had won the Maui Invitational and the national championship. Many thought UConn could do the same in 2005–2006. Without Marcus Williams, UConn beat Arkansas, Arizona, and Gonzaga to win the Maui Invitational. The Huskies stayed a few extra days in Hawaii in order to bond.

When UConn returned to the mainland, it beat its next seven opponents by an average of 39 points. Then, the Big East season started and Marcus Williams returned.

When Williams saw his first action of the season, Marquette fans chanted, "Where's my laptop? Where's my laptop?" Williams even smiled when one fan yelled, "Can we get a printer, too?" Calhoun did not. In 23 minutes, Williams scored four points and had seven assists. Marquette beat UConn by 15 in its first game as a member of the Big East.

The team that looked like a national championship favorite in Maui without Williams resembled the worst team in the Big East when the so-called star came back. Williams's presence seemed to create a new team, one that played without rhythm on offense and passion or toughness on defense. Whether these observations were correct was less important than the reality that people blamed Williams for UConn's failures.

In its next game, UConn trailed by 14 with less than six minutes to play against LSU. Calhoun called time-out and several flocks of boo-birds returned to the Hartford Civic Center. As he did in the UMass game in 2002, Calhoun waved his arms in an upward motion to indicate his disgust with the booing. The fans intensified their jeers.

After the game, Calhoun said, "Very simply, it's unacceptable for fans, who I love very much here in Connecticut, to boo us when we fall down." Howie Dickenman used to say that 16,924 assistant coaches attended UConn games at the Civic Center. The 2005–2006 team received the wrath of the fans after it had played its first three and a half bad halves of the season. Led by Hilton Armstrong, UConn erased the 14-point deficit against LSU in less than three minutes and won, 67–66.

Rudy Gay starred on the dominant, but not quite great enough, 2006 team.

Melissa Arbo/ *The Daily Campus*

The victory over LSU started an 11-game winning streak. During that stretch, UConn beat four teams ranked in the top 25: Syracuse (20th), Louisville (17th), Pittsburgh (ninth), and Indiana (22nd). When the January 23 poll came out, the AP ranked UConn as the top team in the nation.

On the day of the Pitt game at Gampel, a newspaper column refocused attention on Calhoun as a self-centered ogre and UConn as a school and program that would do anything to win. "From Now on, Jim, I Give No Quarter" was the title of a January 31, 2006, column in which Jeff Jacobs of the *Hartford Courant* explained how he would no longer be bullied by Calhoun.

In an earlier column, Jacobs had reported that Jerry Tarkanian accused a UConn assistant coach of telling future-Husky Souleymane Wane that Tarkanian was dying of cancer in order to steer the recruit away from Fresno State. "This malignant recruiting trick can't be true, can it?" Jacobs wrote in response to Tarkanian's claim.

Calhoun thought Jacobs's use of malignant referred to *his* cancer. In front of the UConn beat writers, Calhoun said, "Jerry Tarkanian. Malignant cancer . . . I really think that for a cancer survivor, that's a real nice thing to say. Don't worry. You don't have to print that because I'll tell him when I see him tomorrow. If he has enough balls to come up, he better come up with a couple of armed guards, talking about malignant cancer." In response, Jacobs wrote,

Antiheroes | 197

"Shame on me for allowing myself to be pushed around like the kid who has to give the bully a quarter every day at school."

The "no quarter" debate distracted neither Calhoun nor UConn. The Huskies beat number-nine Pitt behind 22 points from Rudy Gay. They won the next three games by an average of 24. Then came Villanova.

UConn (21-1, 9-1) and Villanova (19-2, 9-1) entered their February 13 game tied for first place in the conference. With 15 seconds to go in the game and UConn down by three, Williams lost the ball and after two Villanova free throws, UConn lost, 69-64. The largest crowd (20,859) to watch a college basketball game in Pennsylvania erupted and the Villanova students stormed the court to celebrate the upset. UConn circled February 26, the date of the rematch at Gampel.

Before the second meeting between UConn and Villanova, Wildcat Randy Foye said, "We're being the bullies in the Big East now." Calhoun let his team know about Foye's remark. The Huskies responded. UConn won, 89-75, in a Gampel game that was over with six minutes to play. It moved to 25-2 and 12-2 in the conference with the win.

UConn won its next two to capture a share of the Big East regular season championship, the 10th in school history. It now had two more regular season titles than Syracuse, three more than Georgetown, five more than St. John's, and six more than Villanova, the team that shared the 2005-2006 regular season championship with UConn.

Seniors Denham Brown, Rashad Anderson, and Hilton Armstrong played for the Big East regular season champions in three of their four years in Storrs. The season during which they didn't win the regular season championship, the Huskies won the Big East and NCAA tournament titles. But the 2006 team didn't get excited after it won the Big East regular season title; it had bigger goals in mind.

That Team Should Have Won
the National Championship

Syracuse lost three straight to finish the regular season at 19-11 and 7-9 in the league. In one of those defeats, DePaul—which finished with a 5-11 record in the conference—beat the Orange by 25. Syracuse trailed by two to Cincinnati with time expiring in the pre-quarterfinals of the Big East tournament. Gerry McNamara's running three-pointer with one second left allowed the Orange to advance to play UConn.

One month earlier, the sports editor of Syracuse University's student newspaper wrote, "Gerry McNamara is overrated." Following the Cincinnati win and with McNamara at his side, Boeheim said, "Without Gerry McNamara, we wouldn't have won ten fucking games this year. Okay? Not ten." The coach called the claim that McNamara was overrated "the most bullshit thing" he had seen in 30 years. McNamara had been double-teamed all season, Boeheim said, and the league's coaches still named him to the all–Big East first team. "The head coaches, they don't know shit I guess," he said.

All of this Syracuse drama was bad news for Calhoun, who warned the Huskies that this Orange team wasn't the same team that UConn beat twice by an average of 15.5 points.

Syracuse took an 11-point lead (39-28) into the locker room at the half. Calhoun was right: this team wasn't the same one that UConn led by 20 (45-25) and 18 (37-19) at halftime of the first two games. Syracuse was up nine (65-56) with 6:36 remaining in the game. In about a minute and a half, the Huskies tied the game at 65.

With 30 seconds left, Anderson made a three-pointer to put UConn up for the first time. After a Syracuse miss and two free throws by Denham Brown, the Huskies led 74-71 with 11.2 seconds left. Calhoun called time-out and told his team to stop McNamara from catching the inbounds pass. He didn't want to let McNamara beat the Huskies.

In the Syracuse huddle, Boeheim told McNamara to pass the ball to one of three players. McNamara asked Boeheim if he could shoot the ball. The coach said yes, but he was convinced that UConn wouldn't let his star take a shot. "But if they do," Boeheim said, "shoot it!"

As the teams returned to the floor, Calhoun was there too. He pointed at McNamara, stomped his feet, and said, "There he is, there he is." Eric Devendorf caught the ball and passed to McNamara. Against Calhoun's orders, the Huskies played off of McNamara, who received the pass without much resistance. McNamara caught the ball in front of Calhoun, who was still standing on the court, looking like he wanted to guard McNamara.

As McNamara dribbled up the court, the coach turned to his bench to ask how that happened. Calhoun knew. McNamara made a straightaway three from behind the NBA three-point line to tie the game with 5.5 seconds to go. Syracuse won by two in overtime.

Calhoun couldn't remember the last time his team lost a game in which it led by three with 11 seconds left. (Answer: UConn relinquished a four-point lead with 8.9 seconds left at Miami in 2003.) Boeheim called the win one of the best, if not the best, in program history. Calhoun didn't watch the rest of the Big East tournament; he said it would be too painful. Had he tuned in, he would have seen Syracuse beat Georgetown and Pittsburgh to win the tournament championship.

The NCAA tournament selection committee seeded the Huskies as the top team in the Washington, DC, region. Before this game, number-one seeds were 87-0 against 16th-seeded teams. UConn trailed number-16 Albany 50-38 with 11:33 left. In a little more than five minutes, the Huskies tied the game; from there, they went on a 20-7 run to win, 72-59. Calhoun hugged Albany's coach and told him that his team was special. The Huskies beat Kentucky, 84-80, to advance to the Washington, DC, regional semifinal.

In the Sweet 16, a cat would have marveled at how many lives the UConn basketball team had. The Huskies should have lost to Washington, but a technical foul that put Brandon Roy on the bench for seven minutes and three-pointers by Rashad Anderson with 35 and 1.8 seconds left allowed UConn to tie the game in regulation and win it in overtime. These kinds of shots led Calhoun to regard Anderson as one of the three best clutch shooters he ever coached. Richard Hamilton and Khalid El-Amin were the other two. Next to his shot at Villanova in 2004, this basket is Anderson's favorite at UConn.

The crowd booed when the game ended.

"Well, we're not a pretty twenty-nine and three," Calhoun said in response to the plethora of questions raised about his team, one of two to hold the top position in the AP poll. "Now we're thirty and three, and everybody wants to see a smooth-running machine."

Eleventh-seed George Mason, UConn's next opponent, had beaten half of the previous year's Final Four—Michigan State and UNC—and seventh-seeded Wichita State to reach the Elite Eight. George Mason's campus is located about 22 miles from where the game was played, the Verizon Center.

The day before the game, Calhoun said, "It's going to be nice playing an away game. I'm really looking forward to that. That pod system is really working out to protect the ones, right?"

Proximity was not the only factor that attracted fans to George Mason. After the NCAA announced its 65-team tournament bracket, CBS's Billy Packer criticized the tournament committee for giving an at-large bid to George Mason, the first team from the Colonial Athletic Conference to receive that distinction. That began the march to the Mason bandwagon. After Coach Jim Larranaga suspended one of his best players before the team's first NCAA tournament game for fighting in the previous game, more people started to root for George Mason. After each win in the NCAA tournament, the bandwagon expanded. The classic David versus Goliath matchup meant that all so-called neutral fans in attendance would pull for George Mason and give more than a home-court advantage to the Patriots.

During the game, whenever UConn double-teamed down low, Mason's Lamar Butler or some other Patriot made a three-pointer. Whenever the Huskies went man-to-man in the post, GMU's Jai Lewis hit another clutch shot. The smaller Mason team outrebounded UConn, 37–34. George Mason's front line outscored Gay, Armstrong, and Boone by 20 (54–34).

Calhoun prodded, cajoled, encouraged, and yelled to get his team to overcome its struggles. After Mason missed three of five free throws in the final minute, Denham Brown made a reverse layup to tie the game as the horn sounded. After Lewis missed two free throws with 6.1 seconds remaining in overtime and the score 86–84, Brown missed an open three and the season ended. In the locker room after the game, Calhoun told the players that they only have so many opportunities to go back to the Final Four. The team didn't take advantage of a perfect chance to win the national championship. Each player on the team had to digest and handle that reality, he said.

On ESPN Radio that night, Doug Gottlieb likened UConn to the Dark Side and said that Jim Calhoun was its Darth Vader. He suggested that Calhoun should wear Vader's cape and helmet on the sidelines. In the antiheroes era, Gottlieb wasn't the only one to think, say, or write that UConn was evil.

Friend and associate director of athletics Tim Tolokan described Calhoun as "unbelievably disappointed," calling the loss easily the worst defeat in the Calhoun era. "Look at that roster," said Tolokan, who goes to every UConn game and is often within camera view of Calhoun. Each starter was picked by an NBA team in that summer's draft. Two players were among the top 12 taken and two others were first-round selections. "That team should have won the national championship," Tolokan said.

One of the worst losses in the Calhoun era. George Mason 86–UConn 84 (overtime). March 26, 2006, Elite Eight, NCAA tournament, Verizon Center, Washington, DC.
Melissa Arbo/ *The Daily Campus*

In the fall of 2009, Mike Anthony of the *Hartford Courant* compiled lists of the most memorable wins and losses in UConn men's basketball history. The George Mason defeat sat atop the list of worst defeats. In his first line about this game, Anthony wrote, "If Jim Calhoun could change the result of any game, this would be it."

The 2005–2006 team created its fate. For Calhoun, the individuals cared more about themselves than the team. For these reasons, the GMU loss is the worst for Calhoun.

In retrospect, the Mason loss wasn't as bad as the defeats to end the 1990, 1994, and 1996 seasons. The Dream Season should have ended in the Final Four. The missed free throws against Florida and Ray Allen's last game were painful because UConn hadn't made a Final Four. UConn fans had a choice after the Mason game—they could watch the 1999 championship game or the one from 2004.

People judge the 2006 team as a disappointment, but keep these statistics in mind: that team won 30 of the 34 games it played. Half of its losses came in overtime and UConn had a chance to win three of the four games at the end. That team was dominant but will forever be judged as a failure because it didn't reach the new bar, an NCAA title.

Steve Pikiell referred to the 2006 NBA Draft as a two-hour infomercial for UConn basketball. The 2006 Huskies joined the 1999 Duke Blue Devils and the 2005 Carolina Tar Heels as the third team to produce four first-round picks. On June 24, 2010, Kentucky would become the first program to have five players selected in the first round. The difference among these teams is that the Duke, Carolina, and Kentucky players came to Durham, Chapel Hill, and Lexington as diamond-studded recruits and probable high-first-round draft picks.

Rudy Gay, the fifth-rated player in his class, and Rashad Anderson, who earned a five-star rating from Rivals.com, were UConn's most accomplished recruits. Rivals.com rated Boone and Williams as the 54th and 61st best players in the recruiting class of 2003. Denham Brown was a three-star recruit and Armstrong had zero stars; he was unranked.

On draft night, the Houston Rockets selected Gay at number eight, but traded his rights to the Memphis Grizzlies. In five seasons in the NBA, Gay continued Calhoun's legacy as one of the best developers of NBA talent. Through the 2010–2011 season, Gay had scored 17.8 points per game.

The Nets took Marcus Williams at number 22 and Boone at number 23. Williams played two seasons in New Jersey, where he was supposed to back up and then replace Jason Kidd. He averaged about six points and three assists in a little more than 16 minutes per game for the Nets. The Nets traded Williams to Golden State before the 2008–2009 season. After Williams averaged 1.3 points and 1.4 assists in nine games and got benched for more than a month, Golden State cut him in March of 2009. Williams returned to NBA's Memphis Grizzles in the 2009–2010 season and he played in Russia the next season. In his first five years in the NBA, Boone averaged 5.2 points and 4.9 rebounds per game.

The New Orleans Hornets used the 12th pick to take Hilton Armstrong. In four years, Calhoun and the UConn coaching staff helped develop Armstrong into a lottery pick. With the Seattle SuperSonics' selection of Denham Brown as the 40th pick overall, UConn became the first program to have five players taken in the same draft since 1989, the year the draft was consolidated to two rounds. Brown was waived in the preseason, but has played in the NBA's minor league, also known as the Developmental League or the D-League, and in Turkey and Italy. Rashad Anderson went undrafted and played in Greece, Italy, Latvia, and the D-League.

It Won't Happen Again

Five of UConn's eight recruits for the class of 2006 were ranked among the top 100 seniors, according to Rivals.com, which graded two of those players — Stanley Robinson and Curtis Kelly — as five-star talent and three others — Jerome Dyson, Hasheem Thabeet, and Dougie Wiggins — as four-star players. Rivals.com ranked UConn's recruiting class as the fourth best in the country.

In the summer of 2004, Hasheem Thabeet, then 17 years old, used an internet café in his hometown of Dar es Salaam, Tanzania, to contact college basketball programs in the United States. Thabeet learned English from Sunday school and reruns of *The Cosby Show*. Most college programs ignored the emails. Northern Iowa wanted to know the part of "Tasmania" where Thabeet resided.

With little hope of receiving a scholarship, Thabeet stopped playing basketball for Makongo High School. Then, his high school teammates begged him to travel with them to a tournament in Nairobi, Kenya. At that tournament, French businessman Oliver Noah realized that this player with giant-like height but limited playing experience was worth taking to the United States.

Noah tried to convince Thabeet to play basketball in the United States, but Thabeet didn't trust him. Talk to my mother, Thabeet said. His mother saw basketball in the United States as a good opportunity for her son, and off to the U.S. he went.

Thabeet's father died when Hasheem was 14. Like Calhoun, Thabeet took over the caregiver role after his father's death. He saw basketball as a way to care for his mother, who had lost her job in the wake of the family tragedy.

Ineligible to play as a high school junior in the United States, Thabeet bounced from Stonebridge Prep in Los Angeles to Picayune High School in Mississippi. In L.A., Thabeet didn't like that he stayed at the coach's house instead of a dorm and the school couldn't figure out Thabeet's grade level. The athletic director at Picayune didn't know how Thabeet had arrived in Mississippi. "He was being maneuvered," the athletic director told *USA Today* in January of 2007. "I'm not on the ground floor of knowing how he came here."

Thabeet then reunited with a coach and family he met in Houston while playing in a showcase tournament. He moved in with the Jurney family and attended Cypress Community Christian School. The living arrangements in the Jurney home made Thabeet look like Buddy the Elf. Thabeet slept in the fetal position in the bed of a 14-year-old.

In his first season of intense, organized basketball, Thabeet averaged 16 points, 10 rebounds, and four blocks per game. His Cypress Community team won the Texas 4A state championship, and Thabeet earned second-team all-Houston honors.

In April, Thabeet's AAU coach claimed that Thabeet's basketball skills had improved from a three to an eight-point-five or nine on a scale of one to 10. At the end of the high school basketball season, Rivals.com speculated that Thabeet "could develop into a very good high-major post player."

Thabeet texted his mother, who still lived in Tanzania. He wanted to make enough money to take care of his mother and family.

On a tip from someone with whom he had played professional basketball in Australia, UConn assistant coach Andre LaFleur asked around about Thabeet, but no one knew him or his game. His size and athleticism intrigued LaFleur, but the UConn assistant coach regarded Thabeet as a "really raw" prospect. Tom Moore saw him block 15 shots, but he thought the center should have rejected even more than that. "Do you realize what you just said?" LaFleur asked Moore when he heard this.

Thabeet picked UConn because of the program's history of producing top-of-the-line NBA players. He wanted to play right away and the center position was open after Boone left for the NBA. He felt that Storrs's small-town atmosphere would allow him to concentrate upon basketball with few distractions. Storrs wasn't sure whether that was a compliment or criticism. Thabeet finished the year as the 63rd-rated player in his senior class.

Two questions confronted the UConn program as it entered the 2006–2007 season: Could UConn win even though the team lost its top six scorers from the year before, returned two players with experience, and needed contributions from nine players who never logged a minute of college basketball? Could A.J. Price run a top 25 team after he missed two seasons?

At the Big East's annual media day in late October, Calhoun warned reporters with front-row seats that the ball would be coming their way this season. "Keep your hands up," Calhoun said. UConn had committed 32 turnovers at a recent practice session. "If things go right," Calhoun concluded, "we can compete with anyone." "Our goal is to be great, sneaky, or otherwise," he said. "Our goal is to win the Big East."

On *Big Monday*, February 5, 2007, UConn inducted its inaugural class of

"Huskies of Honor" at halftime of the Syracuse game at Gampel. Individual panels with each player's picture, uniform number, and accomplishments hung on the wall at the west end of Gampel, and the Huskies of Honor for the women's team appeared on the east wall. Three coaches—Calhoun, Hugh Greer, and Dee Rowe—received this distinction that night. Six of the 13 Huskies honored played for Calhoun: Ray Allen, Richard Hamilton, Donyell Marshall, Emeka Okafor, Cliff Robinson, and Chris Smith. Wes Bialosuknia, Walt Dropo, Tony Hanson, Toby Kimball, Art Quimby, Corny Thompson, and Vin Yokabaskas also received this honor. A panel for John Toner was added during the 2009 season. The next player would join this group on April 5, 2011.

When Calhoun got his plaque at halftime with his team up by one, he told the crowd, "We're going to play better in the second half." The Huskies scored 12 of the game's last 15 points to beat Syracuse. The win was Calhoun's 500th victory at UConn and the best one of the season.

UConn lost five of its final seven regular season games in the conference and its only game in Big East tournament. It finished at 17–13 overall and 6–11 in the Big East. The team suffered prolonged scoring droughts in the second half of games. For the year, it shot 62.8 percent from the free throw line while its opponents made 72.6 percent of their free throws. In a four-point loss to Villanova, UConn missed 20 of 44 from the line, including the front end of five one-and-one opportunities. After the game, Calhoun said, "Thank God those glass backboards are pretty sturdy. Otherwise we would have broken them."

In the 2006–2007 season, UConn fell out of the top 25 for the first time in 67 weeks, and it lost three straight for the first time in six seasons. UConn lost consecutive home games for the first time in 10 years. It missed postseason play for the first time in 20 years and the second time in the Calhoun era.

UConn had few players who could teach the new ones how to play Huskies basketball. "We got caught in a situation where we didn't expect everyone to go," Calhoun said in mid-January. "We got caught without linkage. Maybe Rip Hamilton's freshman year was the last time I thought we didn't have any linkage." This team had lost too much talent, too fast.

The antihero phase continued in the 2007 season. After UConn lost its first conference game of the year at West Virginia, Brett Orzechowski, the beat writer for the *New Haven Register*, started a question about the team's leadership with the premise that Price and Adrien disappeared during the game.

After a brief answer to the question, Calhoun said, "You must think you know them very well. I read some of your columns. Some are good. Some you must have disappeared." Orzechowski responded that he wrote news stories, not columns. Calhoun said, "No, you don't write columns, you write shit."

The UConn coach then threatened to cut off Orzechowski's access. He said he was upset because Orzechowski was a smart-ass.

Boon and Otter of *Animal House* said that others couldn't ridicule their pledges. Only they could do that. Calhoun coaches in much the same way. Reporters can't criticize his players, only he can.

The incident made the local papers and lasted a little longer than previous flare-ups. Jeff Pearlman of ESPN.com used Calhoun as the example of why he wouldn't want his three-month-old son to become a prominent college athlete. In the online column, Pearlman wrote that Calhoun is "a vile ogre who has as much business molding young men as I do breeding llamas." Other than a summary of the exchange between the UConn coach and Orzechowski, Pearlman never told the reader why Calhoun was so bad for college athletes.

Calhoun's response showed that the coach cared about what others said about his players. Nevertheless, this was the post-laptop era, one in which many people other than Pearlman saw Calhoun as a monster.

During the season, Calhoun complained that his team lacked leadership. A.J. Price wasn't the superstar that UConn, Calhoun, and fans hoped he would be—and for good reason. He had missed two full seasons of games and practices. Throughout the season Price said, "My shot is getting there. I'm getting there, but it's going to be some time before I'm the same player I was a few years ago." He needed to adjust to the speed of the college game and strengthen his legs to improve his shot.

Thabeet started every game and averaged 6.3 points, 6.4 rebounds, and 3.9 blocks. He rejected 119 shots, good for third in the nation and second behind Emeka Okafor's single-season record for a UConn player of 138 in 2002–2003. But at times during the year, his offense was so bad that the guards wouldn't throw the ball to him. By mid-February, Calhoun saw that Thabeet's offense had developed and that the guards gave the big man more touches. His game improved during the season because of extra work given to him by Calhoun and the UConn coaching staff.

According to Calhoun, Thabeet was not happy with the extra practices, which he viewed as punishment. "All we're trying to do, and it's selfish because we want you to be good here, is make you hundreds of millions of dollars," the coach said. Complaints were a rarity for Thabeet, who was the team's court jester. Jerome Dyson described him as a people person who never had anything negative to say to his teammates.

After the season's last game, Calhoun said, "This will never happen again as long as I'm the coach at UConn. It won't happen again." After Calhoun first made such a promise, UConn started a streak of 20 consecutive appearances in postseason play after the 1986–1987 season. Following Calhoun's second pledge in 1993, UConn made two trips to the Sweet 16 and one to the Elite Eight.

After he watched UConn beat St. John's at Madison Square Garden in mid-January, the *New York Post*'s Lenn Robbins wrote, "If this group stays together, the Huskies will contend for a third national title in two years."

26

That's Why He's in the Hall of Fame

The Price-Thabeet-Dyson Huskies lost all seven games to ranked opponents over a two-year span. UConn hadn't dropped that many games against top 25 teams since Calhoun's first two seasons at Storrs, when the Huskies fell in 10 straight to ranked teams.

The streak stopped on January 20, 2008, when Thabeet scored 15 points, grabbed seven rebounds, and had six of UConn's 10 blocks to beat number-13 Marquette by 16 at Gampel. After a come-from-behind one-point win at Cincinnati, Calhoun called Price "the best point guard in this league," and said that Price improved the play of everyone on the team. He characterized Price as the "most vocal person" during the Cincinnati comeback and regarded Price as "absolutely our leader."

The two straight wins and the manner in which UConn won those games set up the Huskies for a trip to one of college basketball's sacred places—Bloomington, Indiana. Seventh-ranked Indiana entered the game with a 17-1 record, having won 13 straight overall and 29 in a row at Assembly Hall. UConn needed an A game to beat Indiana . . . provided it brought all of its players to Bloomington.

The Friday before the Indiana game, the beat reporters gathered in UConn's hotel in Bloomington and awaited the Huskies. They would ask a few questions and file a story. No big deal. Right?

As the Huskies filed into the lobby of their hotel, Dyson and Wiggins weren't with them. Calhoun informed the press that the two had broken an unspecified team rule. Based on the information he had, the coach decided to leave the players at home. He provided no specifics and said none would be forthcoming in the near future.

Beat reporters scrambled in the Texas Roadhouse, located in the parking lot of their Courtyard by Marriott hotel in Bloomington. The *Hartford Courant* was in panic mode. If any paper was going to get the story, it had to be the one, thought the *Courant*'s editor. Kyle Muncy, sports information director for the UConn basketball team, provided no details. Neither did Calhoun. The players didn't know anything so checks of their MySpace pages were futile.

During the initial part of the game, Calhoun punched the chair next to him on the bench. He wanted this one extra-bad. With 16:23 left in the first half,

UConn trailed 9–0. After Calhoun's early time-out, UConn outscored Indiana 29–18 and went to the locker room with a five-point lead.

Calhoun never takes a play off during a game, but focused doesn't begin to describe his state on this day in Indiana. At one point in the second half, the Indiana student section started to count down the shot clock as if it were about to expire . . . ten, nine, eight . . . except UConn had the ball. The shot clock had plenty of time left. The IU students wanted a UConn player to take a desperate shot because he thought the shot clock was about to hit double zero. The ploy worked. Thabeet heard the crowd, forgot he wasn't in Storrs, and banged a jumper off the backboard. The Indiana students roared in laughter. They got the ball back for their team.

Calhoun didn't laugh. He didn't hear the crowd. When Thabeet took this shot, Calhoun extended his arms, wrenched his shoulders, and turned to his bench and said, "What was that?" When the coaches explained that the IU students had tricked Thabeet, Calhoun's shoulders slumped and the coach tilted his head to the side. Then, Calhoun got on with watching his team play defense.

Despite this gaffe, Thabeet blocked two shots and put up 20 detour signs. The Indiana players came into the middle with the ball but left without shooting. The UConn center made an abyss out of the area around the basket.

To increase his stamina, after practice Price ran on a machine cranked to the maximum level of resistance for 15 minutes every day for five weeks running. He needed all that conditioning in this game. He puked twice on the court during the game, but fatigue didn't stop him. In 36 minutes, Price scored 14 points and had six assists and eight rebounds, four of which came off the offensive boards. UConn won by five.

As Tim Tolokan waited for Calhoun to leave the court, he said, "That's why he's in the Hall of Fame."

After the game, Calhoun sat at a table draped in red cloth with a red backdrop dotted by the IU logo and the name of a local energy company. When Calhoun started his remarks, he opened his suit jacket to reveal a sweat-stained shirt. He explained that the sweat wasn't his, but instead came from hugging each UConn player following the game.

Calhoun tilted and nodded his head and guessed that this win was the best for the program—or at least in the discussion for the best win—since the championship game in 2004. Given the circumstances, it might have been better than the game against Georgia Tech and was as special as the comeback against Duke in the 2004 national semifinal. He said he would remember this win for an "awful, awful, awful, awful long time."

The Indiana drama showed that this UConn team could beat anyone in the country, but it didn't answer another important question: What did the bad boys do?

At 11:51 p.m. on the Thursday night before the Indiana game, UConn police had spotted Wiggins and Dyson in a car near X lot on the UConn campus. They found a bottle of vodka and cognac inside the car and a small amount of marijuana outside it. They cited Wiggins and Dyson for possession of alcohol by a minor. Wiggins received a summons for driving with a suspended license.

Under provisions of UConn's student-athlete handbook, the university had the right to drug-test Wiggins and Dyson because it had probable cause to believe that the players may have taken drugs. Dyson flunked the drug test and received a 30-day suspension, which amounted to nine games. Wiggins did not test positive for drugs and he sat out two games.

In the absence of Dyson and Wiggins, Price turned into UConn's top scorer and playmaker. Two days after the Indiana game, he scored 20 points and turned the ball over twice in a two-point win over Louisville at the Civic Center. Against number-18 Pitt at the Civic Center, Price scored 21 and made a layup and two free throws as part of a 9-2 game-ending run to beat the Panthers, 60-53. He scored 26 in a win over Notre Dame and 23 at South Florida.

UConn moved into the top 25 and made it as high as number 13. The Huskies won 10 games in a row during the season and three of its last four and finished at 13-5 in the Big East, good for fourth in the conference and a first-round bye in the league tournament.

Under first-year coach Bob Huggins, West Virginia handed UConn its fourth consecutive loss in the Big East tournament: Mountaineers 78–Huskies 72. "They came out and kicked our butts," Calhoun said.

"I've been waiting one year for this," Calhoun said in reference to Selection Sunday. "I did not want to ever be here when we're not going to the NCAAs. This program and a whole bunch of kids and coaches before us, working with us, have really established something here and the NCAA tournament is where we think we should end up every single year."

In the first round of the NCAA tournament, 13th-seeded San Diego, which had never won an NCAA tournament game, ended UConn's season when De'Jon Jackson made a shot with 1.2 seconds remaining in overtime to give his team a 70-69 victory. Some would argue that the Huskies' season ended when A.J. Price tore his anterior cruciate ligament (ACL) with 9:39 left in the first half, but Calhoun wasn't one of them. He saw his team play without passion and complained about a lack of defense. The loss was UConn's first in the opening round of the NCAA tournament during the Calhoun era.

Despite the team's 10-game winning streak during the season and UConn's return to national prominence, the Huskies lost four of their last seven games. The team had no momentum heading into the next season, but that wouldn't diminish Final Four expectations for 2009.

A trip to Detroit, the site of the 2009 Final Four, hinged upon whether Thabeet would return for a third year. In 2007–2008, the Big East and the NABC named Thabeet as their defensive player of the year. He had averaged more than 10 points and close to eight rebounds per game, and blocked 147 shots, good for second in the nation, and UConn led the country in blocks for a seventh straight year.

In late April, Thabeet decided to return. He wanted to win a Big East title and challenge for a national championship. Calhoun reiterated that the big man had made as much progress as any player he coached in his 36-year career.

From the start, Dougie Wiggins was more trouble to UConn and Calhoun than he was worth. The media had accused Calhoun of stealing Wiggins from St. John's, the team to which the East Hartford guard had made a verbal commitment in the spring of 2005. Wiggins transferred to UMass, where he was suspended in November of 2008 for breaking and entering. He sat out the season, as required of Division I transfers, but left UMass at the end of the season.

The addition of Kemba Walker more than offset the loss of Wiggins. After the 2006 season, three players on his Rice High School (Harlem) team signed with high-level Division I programs. Point guard Edgar Sosa went to Louisville, Kashif Pratt chose Seton Hall, and Curtis Kelly committed to UConn. Expectations were low for the 2007 Rice High School team, which would be led by junior Kemba Walker. During his sophomore year, Walker sat on the bench and took notes. "I didn't play a lot last year," Walker said at the beginning of the 2007 season, "but I learned a lot. I learned a lot about leadership and being a leader."

Walker, at six foot one and 172 pounds, looks like his bones are made out of steel. He considered himself a defensive specialist, so he worked on his offense throughout the summer and in AAU tournaments. "You could see that he was ready when he came back to school in September," said Rice coach Mo Hicks. "He was anxious about starting our preseason program and when we were in the gym, he was always in there working on his shot." Walker and the team he led were most dangerous when experts lowered their expectations of them.

In his last two years in high school, Walker led and Rice won. It went undefeated in the city's Catholic High School Athletic Association (CHSAA) in his junior year. In his senior year, Walker was asked if he was disappointed that the player of the year award went to Sylven Landesberg. He said no because he cared more about winning the CHSAA tournament. "That's what I want," said Walker. "That's what matters."

In his junior year, Walker showed that he could make shots when his team needed him the most. With time about to expire and the score tied in the state Catholic AA title game against Christ the King at Fordham, "Walker heaved an off-balance three-pointer and landed on his rear end." The shot went in. Rice won, 44–41.

Kristie Ackert of New York's *Daily News* referred to Walker as a "defensive bulldog, assigned to stopping some of the nation's best guards." Those point guards included Derrick Rose. When asked about playing one-on-one against Rose, Walker said, "I was very excited. I heard he is the top player in the country and I wanted a chance to prove myself against him. I think I did." Rice upset Rose's Simeon Academy, the 14th-ranked team in the nation, by two at MSG.

By the time Walker's high school career was over, most recruiting services listed him as the second best point guard in the class of 2008. Brandon Jennings, the top-rated point guard, played one year of professional basketball in Europe and then was the 10th overall pick in the 2009 NBA draft. In its final rankings on the class of 2008, Scout.com moved Walker up to sixth overall.

Paul Gilvary, the CHSAA coach of the year in 2008 from Holy Cross High School in Flushing, Queens, said of Walker, "He was the one guy you knew you had to try to stop and you couldn't really do that, anyway. And on that team, to stand out like that is saying something."

Walker played on the New York Gauchos AAU team, whose prominent alumni include Kenny Anderson and Stephon Marbury. After the Gauchos won the Peach Jam tournament for the 18th time in the summer of 2007, Walker said, "Personally, I think I'm as good as those guards were." Wherever Walker played, his coaches commended his work ethic, leadership ability, toughness, quickness, defense, and scoring. And his teams won. After Walker's junior year, Hicks characterized him as someone with the will to win, and this sounded like Calhoun's type of player.

Several schools, including Cincinnati, St. John's, and Providence, offered a scholarship to Walker, but the game ended when UConn came into the picture. Walker called UConn his dream school. He wanted to play in a pro-style offense, which moves the ball quickly up the floor. He wanted to play for a

Hall of Fame coach. Most of all, he wanted to play in the NBA. Few programs offered these three things. UConn did.

Of Uconn's recruiting pitch to him, Walker said, "They didn't sell me the dream."

Coaches heap praise upon the players they have just signed. Sometimes these assessments prove to be right; many times, they are not. Calhoun used platitudes to describe Walker: "Kemba has great character, charisma, and leadership qualities to go along with an infectious personality that will be of outstanding benefit to our program and to the entire university." In this case, the coach's assessment was correct.

In the summer before he arrived in Storrs, Walker played for the Under 18 USA Basketball Team in the FIBA Americas U18 Championship in Argentina, leading his team to a silver medal. In the championship game, Walker scored a game-high 21 points; in 36 minutes, he also had seven rebounds, three assists, two blocks, and a steal. He was named MVP of the tournament even though his team finished second. Davidson head coach Bob McKillop, the head coach of the U18 team, referred to Walker as his team's catalyst and "a superb leader."

After the 2008 season, Calhoun revoked Stanley Robinson's scholarship and told the player to get a job. Alabama and UAB wanted Robinson to return home and play for them. Robinson chose Willimantic, Connecticut, and work instead. Starting in July of 2008, he took a three-day-a-week job sorting scrap metal into boxes and stacking aluminum wheels for $17 an hour at Prime Materials Incorporated. Ruslan Inyatkin, a former Husky, was his plant manager. If Robinson matured, he could rejoin the team in December, but he would have to pay for classes and books until a scholarship opened the following season.

Robinson's father had died when Stanley was 15, and Rosa Robinson wanted a coach who wouldn't let her son get away with much. She wanted a coach who would discipline her son, if necessary. Calhoun found it necessary.

Thabeet was never the most valuable or best player on the UConn teams for which he played. A.J. Price was. UConn relied on Price to lead the team, score in double-figures, and make the biggest shots. Thabeet never faced those kinds of expectations. He was the most dominant player in the country, but he played inconsistently. If Price played like that, UConn wouldn't have been in the top 25.

With Price at the helm and Adrien in the hold, UConn could afford to have some inconsistent games from its center. Price and Adrien made UConn a top 25 team. Thabeet turned the Huskies into a national contender. Over the summer, he played with Okafor in New York, other elite college players at LeBron James's camp in Akron, and trainers in Los Angeles and Houston. When Thabeet returned for practice, the team began to run offensive plays through Thabeet, who, according to his coach, passed the ball better than ever.

Calhoun wanted to turn Thabeet's game from finesse to power. He ordered Thabeet to punish the rim. The center listened. He had to wear a brace to protect his wrist from injuries when he dunked. Thabeet's defensive prowess was unquestionable. Price described him as a "one-man zone."

In a preseason interview with *ESPN the Magazine*, Thabeet said, "Tyler Hansbrough? I don't see nothing." Notre Dame's Luke Harangody, the 2008 Big East player of the year and a second-team All-American, was "not tough." These quotes appeared along with Thabeet on the cover of the magazine. The blogs blew up.

Thabeet claimed the quotes were a joke. Elena Bergeron, who conducted the interview, said she felt like UConn's coaches and sports information department informed Thabeet "about the weight of the quotes."

The AP and college basketball ranked Carolina and UConn as the top two teams in their preseason polls. Thabeet's return gave Calhoun and UConn basketball a familiar goal—make the Final Four or else.

27

Not a Dime Back

The Huskies won their first nine games in the 2008–2009 season and faced their biggest challenge to date at the "Battle in Seattle" against Gonzaga. UConn cut an 11-point second-half deficit to three and had the ball with 24.7 seconds left. Craig Austrie missed a three-pointer with 16 seconds left, but Dyson grabbed the rebound.

Price had the ball for the final possession. Jeremy Pargo, the star of the previous year's UConn-Gonzaga game, played him so closely he could count the number of fillings in Price's teeth. No matter. Price made a three-pointer with 7.8 seconds left. Tie game.

Price clenched his fist to tell the partisan crowd, Gonzaga, and all his detractors to "Take that!" The celebration didn't prevent Price from knocking the ball away from Pargo on the ensuing play. UConn outscored Gonzaga by five in overtime.

The win and the manner in which UConn took the game reminded Calhoun of the way previous UConn teams played. "Somewhere, Ray Allen is smiling. Somewhere, Caron Butler is smiling," he said. By late 2008, Calhoun had built a tradition that he could reference. Everyone associated with basketball knew Ray Allen and Caron Butler.

This UConn team showed that it could beat a good team, anywhere, and under any circumstance. At this time, a trip to the Final Four was more than realistic; it was expected.

Nine days after UConn fans had purchased their trips to the Final Four, they wanted a refund. Georgetown, the nation's 12th-rated team with a 9-1 record, demolished UConn in the teams' first conference game of the season: Georgetown 74–UConn 63. Thabeet didn't score in the first half and finished with four points. Afterward, Calhoun apologized for the way his team played against the Hoyas. In the past, opposing coaches had been the ones to say they were sorry for their teams' play against UConn. Not on this night.

The Huskies won 13 straight after that loss. After number-one Duke lost to Wake Forest in early February, UConn became the fourth team to be ranked number one in as many weeks. After UConn pummeled number-five Louisville by 17 at Freedom Hall, Cardinals coach Rick Pitino said that UConn was "truly the number-one team in the country." According to Pitino, the Huskies "were totally out of our league."

The Georgetown game was an aberration.

In UConn's eight-point win over Michigan at Gampel, Adrien became the fifth Husky to grab 1,000 rebounds and score 1,000 points in his career. UConn had inducted the four other members of the 1,000-1,000 club—Okafor, Quimby, Thompson, and Kimball—into its first Huskies of Honor class. Adrien should make that wall some day as well.

Anchored by the one-man zone, UConn held Syracuse to 49 points in a February game, the third lowest output in Jim Boeheim's 33 years as head coach of the Orange. But the victory came with a price: Jerome Dyson, UConn's best one-on-one defender, tore his lateral meniscus and would miss the rest of the season. As a result of this injury, UConn lost defense, a shooter, and depth.

Against Seton Hall, Thabeet played 39 minutes, scored 25 points on 10 of 13 shooting from the field, and inhaled 20 rebounds, seven of which came off the offensive glass. He blocked nine shots. Based on these kinds of games, Boeheim called Thabeet the best inside force in the history of the Big East.

Pitt stopped UConn's winning streak in Hartford, outscoring UConn 15-7 in the final 3:26 to win the game. At six foot six, 277 pounds, Pitt's DeJuan Blair had the body of a tight end. With a seven-foot, two-inch, wingspan, he had the length of a starting center in the NBA. Blair could neither outjump nor outreach Thabeet, but he could move the UConn center.

Blair scored 22 points and punished 23 rebounds against Thabeet. Blair flipped Thabeet in the first half and the UConn center was out of the game for about four minutes. Overall, Pitt outrebounded UConn, 48 to 31. In a not-so-veiled reference to his dissatisfaction with the style of play and the referees, Calhoun said, "We'll get back to playing basketball in our next game." The physical play didn't favor Thabeet, who scored five points, had four rebounds, and had as many steals as blocks (two) in 23 minutes.

UConn's next game provided even more excitement than the Pitt contest, but not for anything that happened on the court.

On May 6, 2008, doctors removed a tumor and lymph nodes from Calhoun, leaving a substantial scar on the right side of the coach's neck. Calhoun received six weeks of radiation treatment after the surgery. At times during the season, he appeared tired and emaciated. Whether the radiation treatments, the season, or both had caught up to him wasn't clear. As he readied for his first question after a 14-point win over South Florida at the Civic Center, Calhoun swallowed hard on his right side, an apparent effect of the cancer surgery and treatment. He looked tired.

"Coach, considering you are the highest paid state employee, and there's a two-billion-dollar budget deficit . . . ," a voice asked.

Calhoun said, "Yup," and nodded his head. The reporter continued, "Do you think . . ." Calhoun interrupted: "Not a dime back." One person chuckled uncomfortably.

"Not a dime back?" the reporter asked. "Not a dime back," Calhoun said as he shook his head from side to side in front of a blue plastic sign imprinted with the UConn Huskies and Dunkin' Donuts logos. "I'd like to be able to retire some day," Calhoun said. He wasn't going to take a pay cut in response to the state's financial situation. "I'm getting tired," he said.

Back and forth they went until Calhoun blinked a couple of times, looked away for a second or two, and then asked, "You're not really that stupid, are you?" Then he said, "My best advice to you. Shut up."

Calhoun said that the press conference was about basketball, but the questioner said, "If these guys covered this stuff, I wouldn't have to do it." The room groaned.

Calhoun said, "Will you please?" And then he went off. "Quite frankly, we bring in twelve million dollars to the university, nothing to do with state funds," Calhoun yelled.

"We make twelve million dollars a year for this university."

Loud.

"Get some facts and come back and see me."

Louder.

"Get some facts and come back and see me."

Even louder.

"Don't throw out salaries and other things."

Even louder.

"Get some facts and come back and see me."

Ludicrous loud.

"We turn over twelve million dollars to the University of Connecticut, which is state-run. Next question."

Conversation over.

The person who asked the question was a political activist, best known for getting arrested during Governor Jodi Rell's inauguration on January 3, 2007. At halftime of the South Florida game, he told his friend John Murray, publisher of the *Waterbury Observer*, "Make sure you stick around because I'm going to drop a bomb on Calhoun." He did.

When Calhoun began at UConn, his total annual compensation from the university was estimated to be $125,000. In 2009, Calhoun made $1.6 million from UConn alone. That figure included a base salary of $200,000, an extra $1.2 million per year for public speaking and other appearances on behalf of the university, along with an automatic $25,000 increase each year.

This 1:13 conversation restarted debates about Calhoun's value to the university, the importance of collegiate athletics to the state, and the coach himself. When asked for her opinion on the incident, Governor Rell said, "I think if Coach Calhoun had the opportunity right now, he would welcome a do-over and not have that embarrassing display." Calhoun did not appreciate that comment.

According to a Quinnipiac University poll, 80 percent of 1,335 respondents agreed that the university should not discipline Calhoun for the incident. Calhoun enjoyed a favorability rating of 68 percent, and 60 percent of the respondents thought that Calhoun should keep his entire salary. More than half of the respondents approved of the way he handled the situation, 48 percent did not.

After this incident, Murray used his *Waterbury Observer* to fillet Calhoun: "Forget the press conference meltdown, the real issue with Jim Calhoun is not his salary, it's his courtside behavior. He swears at his players, kicks chairs, abuses referees and curses at fans. Is this the price of victory?"

Murray included the standard examples of Calhoun's behavior: Calhoun calls time-out, walks onto the court, and commands Hasheem Thabeet to "dunk the fucking ball"; Calhoun twice instructed fans behind the bench at a home game to "shut the fuck up"; he "grabbed Stanley Robinson's jersey and physically pulled him towards the bench."

Former governor John Rowland once brought a priest to a game and the two needed to move because of Calhoun's language. According to Murray, Calhoun's game-time manners bothered Governor Rowland so much that he told Lew Perkins, UConn's athletic director, to manage the coach's behavior. Perkins sat near the UConn bench to monitor Calhoun until he left for Kansas.

State legislators asked the General Assembly's Office of Legislative Research to determine how much money UConn's men's basketball generated and the team's graduation rate. A research analyst for the state found that the program took in more than $14 million and spent a little less than $8 million. The basketball team's graduation rate was 33 percent for the players who entered school in the fall of 2002 (Rashad Anderson and Denham Brown's cohort). The university's graduation rate for that class was 74 percent, but only 49 percent of Division I basketball players in that class had received their degree. Calhoun said that players like Donyell Marshall, Ray Allen, Rip Hamilton, Caron Butler, Ben Gordon, and others did not graduate but fulfilled their financial and personal goals with lucrative NBA contracts.

The controversy over Calhoun's comments obscured important business on the court. A.J. Price scored a career-high 36 points against Marquette and gave Calhoun his 800th career victory, putting him in an exclusive club with

Bobby Knight (902), Dean Smith (879), Adolf Rupp (876), Jim Phelan (830), Mike Krzyzewski (825), and Eddie Sutton (804).

A 10-point loss in their final regular season game at Pitt cost the Huskies the Big East regular season championship and knocked them to third in the league.

UConn's game against Syracuse in the 2009 Big East tournament began at 9:36 p.m. on Thursday March 12, 2009.

Kemba Walker tied the game at 71 with 1.1 seconds to go. Syracuse's Paul Harris underthrew the ensuing inbounds pass, which was deflected to his teammate Eric Devendorf, who made a 28-foot jumper as the buzzer sounded. He ripped his jersey out of his shorts, jumped on one of the media tables that lined the court, and posed for a few seconds.

Calhoun started to walk over to Boeheim but stopped. Do I go over and shake his hand? Would that concede the game? The referees watched replays to determine if Devendorf had released the ball before the clock struck zero. The naked eye suggested he had. Standard replays indicated the same, but when ESPN slowed the play, the ball left Devendorf's hand after the clock showed all zeros. No basket. UConn lived.

Syracuse tied the game with 4.7 seconds left in the first overtime. Both teams missed several shots to try to win it in the second overtime. The game now became the second in conference tournament history to go to three overtimes. In the 1981 Big East tournament finals, Syracuse beat Villanova by three points in three overtimes. Leo Rautins, father of current Orange player Andy, played for Syracuse in that game. That year was Jim Boeheim's fifth as coach of the Orangemen.

In the final minute of the third overtime, UConn missed three of four free throws and Rautins made a three-pointer to tie the game with 11.7 seconds left. Then, Price shorted a shot from well beyond the NBA three-point line. Then Adrien missed a 10-foot jumper off the glass. Price's shot selection angered Calhoun, who pointed to the spot of the 27-footer, looked to his bench and Price, and asked, "What was he thinking?" The game was now the longest in Big East history.

Thabeet fouled out with a little less than four minutes left in the fourth overtime. As Thabeet headed to the bench, Calhoun avoided eye contact with his star center. Adrien blocked two layup attempts by Paul Harris with less than four seconds remaining to keep the game tied at 104 after 60 minutes of basketball.

Syracuse's Jonny Flynn made two free throws to tie the game at 110 with 20 seconds remaining in overtime number five. He scored all six of Syracuse's points in the fifth overtime and finished the game with 34 points and 11 assists in 67 minutes. In the fifth overtime, Flynn thought, "Lord, just get this game over with. Whoever wins the game, let's just get it over with."

Price missed another NBA three-pointer with four seconds left. The rebound bounced to Adrien, who turned and had a nice look at a 10-footer to win it at the buzzer. Off the rim, but not by much. Overtime number six was on the way.

Rautins made a three-pointer four seconds into the sixth extra period, which marked the first time that UConn trailed since regulation. Syracuse scored the first eight points in the sixth overtime and won, 127–117.

The game ended at 1:22 a.m. on Friday March 12, 2009.

The *Sporting News* voted this contest as the game of the decade in college basketball. The Big East conference created SixOvertimes.com to commemorate the game and sell DVDs of the telecast. The game ended later than any one played at the current Madison Square Garden, which opened in 1968, and was the longest game in the history of both the UConn and Syracuse basketball programs. It was also the longest game in the shot clock era of college basketball. The teams broke the scoring record for a conference tournament game by 55 points.

More than 40 minutes after the game, Thabeet was still in his uniform. Adrien could barely answer reporters' questions. Walker held himself upright and Austrie said his body felt like it had been hit all over. It had been eight hours since the players ate the team meal of chicken and pasta.

According to Jerome Dyson, Calhoun wasn't mad at his team after the game because "he knew that everyone gave everything he had." This was the only time Dyson could recall that a loss didn't anger Calhoun.

Calhoun had enough energy to run a practice right then. The players would have shot free throws. The Huskies made 24 of 42 free throws (57.1 percent) for the game and 13 of 20 (65 percent) in the extra sessions.

In the press conference afterward, the Jims disagreed over what the game meant. Boeheim referred to the contest as "the greatest game ever played." Calhoun wanted his team to regain its confidence and dominance; he didn't care about the place of this game in NCAA basketball lore. His team lost.

Adrien, Thabeet, Price, and Austrie ended their UConn careers without a win in the conference tournament. When asked to reflect upon four straight losses in the Big East tournament, Price said, "That's something I'm going to have to live with for the rest of my life."

Josh Nochimson, the Team's Manager and Rip's Friend, Became the Unofficial Go-Between

Despite the loss to Syracuse, the NCAA tournament selection committee made UConn the number-one seed in the West region. The team became Calhoun's fifth to earn a number-one seed. Pitt and Louisville also received number-one seeds and the Big East became the first conference to produce three number-one seeds in the same NCAA tournament. North Carolina, the top seed in the South, was the favorite to win the national championship.

Calhoun missed all or parts of games because of sickness in the early rounds of play during both of UConn's trips to the Final Four. He was hospitalized before UConn's first-round game against the University of Tennessee at Chattanooga at the Wachovia Center in Philadelphia. Doctors treated him for dehydration. The Huskies didn't need him in their 56-point win. Calhoun returned and UConn beat Texas A&M by 26 in its next game. "I don't think I've played a team that good since I've been at A&M," said second-year head coach Mark Turgeon. The Huskies were on to the Sweet 16 for the first time since 2006 and the 12th time under Jim Calhoun.

Then, the shit hit the fan.

Adrian Wojnarowski and Dan Wetzel wrote a story for Yahoo.com that accused Calhoun and the UConn coaching staff of major recruiting violations. According to the story, Josh Nochimson, a former UConn team manager and a former business manager and personal assistant for Rip Hamilton, was now a professional agent who acted as an intermediary between the UConn coaching staff and recruit Nate Miles, a six foot seven high school guard who some compared to George Gervin. Miles signed with UConn, but never played a game because the university's judicial board expelled him for violating a restraining order.

When asked about the hardest players to guard, Dyson said that Price and Wiggins were the first two names that came to his mind. Nate Miles was the third. This was based on the player's limited practices with the young guard.

Because of Nochimson's previous relationship with UConn, the NCAA considered him to be a "representative of UConn's athletic interests." NCAA rules restrict contact between a recruit and any representative of the program.

They also prohibit the representative from giving anything of value to the recruit. Reports indicated that Nochimson provided lodging, transportation, meals, and representation to Miles.

The Yahoo! reporters used the Freedom of Information Act to obtain cell phone records of the UConn coaching staff. Five members of the UConn staff had text-messaged or called Nochimson a total of 1,556 times. Calhoun talked to Nochimson for close to four minutes in August of 2007 and the two exchanged 15 calls or text messages.

Former Oklahoma and Indiana coach Kelvin Sampson had just lost his job for improperly calling recruits at IU. Oklahoma volunteered to cut scholarships and recruiting visits to campus because Sampson and his staff made five hundred calls that broke the rules.

When asked about Nochimson, Calhoun said, "He was with our program for six years, got his master's degree, but beyond that while he was within our program, he was a good kid, worked hard, et cetera. That was my relationship with him during that particular point in time."

In 1998, Calhoun used Nochimson to find out what Hamilton thought about turning pro and to convey the coach's feelings to the star player. In *Dare to Dream*, Calhoun wrote, "Josh Nochimson, the team's manager and Rip's friend, became the unofficial go-between. He would tell me what Rip was thinking, then go back upstairs and tell Rip what I was thinking. It was like diplomatic negotiations, Washington and Belgrade."

Wojnarowski and Wetzel claimed that Calhoun reappointed Nochimson as an emissary, this time in a mission to sign a high school player.

Hamilton fired Nochimson as his personal assistant and business manager and, in August of 2009, accused him of stealing $1 million. Following this incident, Nochimson filed to decertify as an NBA agent. Hamilton said Nochimson "was pretty much running his business as an agent off of me." "He admitted to stealing," Hamilton added. "He cried. . . . I always remember my agent saying, 'Rip, don't put your hands on him because he'll sue you.'"

When asked about the incident as his team prepared for Purdue in the Sweet 16, Calhoun said, "The university is taking good care of it. They will look into it." In response to the story, UConn claimed that the "NCAA's Eligibility Center reviewed all information that it had concerning [Miles's] eligibility status and determined that he was eligible for his freshman year." Calhoun also said, "I want to talk about Purdue."

Wojnarowski, Wetzel, and Yahoo! wanted as much exposure and buzz as they could get. They didn't know whether UConn would make the Final Four, so the best time to run the story was then. The timing inflicted the maximum damage on Calhoun, the 2008–2009 team, and the UConn men's basketball program.

In addition to text messages, graduation rates dented Calhoun's reputation as the Huskies moved toward the Final Four. The University of Central Florida's Institute for Diversity and Ethics in Sport reported that UConn graduated 33 percent of its players—the lowest proportion for any of the top seeds. Four of UConn's 12 freshmen who enrolled between 1998–1999 and 2001–2002 earned their college degrees within six years. They were Okafor, Tooles, Justin Brown, and Ryan Thompson. As for the other top seeds, UNC graduated 86 percent, followed by Pitt (69 percent) and Louisville (42 percent). Derrick Jackson of the *Boston Globe* condemned UConn for its 22 percent graduation rate for African-American players.

The basketball program and university noted that the institute's graduation rate included players who went to the NBA and those who transferred. The players who left for the NBA were millionaires and UConn had no influence over whether transfer students received a college diploma.

The reality is that 80 percent of players who exhausted their eligibility at the university (i.e., didn't leave early for the NBA) received degrees during the Calhoun era. Rod Sellers, Kevin Freeman, Ruslan Inyatkin, and Rashamel Jones received their degrees after the six-year window and did not count toward UConn's graduation rate based on the institute's formula. Scott Burrell graduated more than 21 years after he entered UConn in the fall of 1988.

The Huskies beat Purdue by 12 to advance to the Elite Eight, but the Yahoo! allegations remained the story.

The day before its Elite Eight game against Missouri, Calhoun admitted that a mistake might have been made, but, regardless of the contents of the 508-page NCAA rules manual, "It's not my job to know what every human being who's ever graduated from UConn is doing—every single moment, twenty-four hours a day." He said that NCAA rules weren't clear and were open to interpretation. The NCAA didn't limit text messages until September 2008, long after Calhoun and his staff recruited Miles.

UConn's athletic director and president publicly supported Calhoun and told the coach to concentrate on winning the next game.

With 2:34 to go against Missouri, UConn's lead was three—68–65—and Calhoun called time-out to set up the next possession. After the break, Kemba Walker controlled the ball the entire possession. He pierced the lane with five seconds left on the shot clock, spun, dipped his shoulder into the defender, and took a one-handed shot, which banked off the glass and in with two seconds left on the shot clock and 2:11 on the game clock. UConn led by five at

Hasheem Thabeet takes on Missouri in the Elite Eight. UConn 82– Missouri 75. March 28, 2009, NCAA tournament, University of Phoenix Stadium, Glendale, Arizona.

Dan Gindraux / *The Daily Campus*

that time and won by seven. Walker scored 23 points, which tied his career high. This performance gave hope to UConn fans that the 2009–2010 team would be strong with Walker as its leader.

This trip to the Final Four differed from the other two. In 1999 and 2004, excitement surrounded the Huskies and its stars. In 2009, the state, the media, and even the fans didn't seem to feel the same way about the Huskies. Perhaps everyone had grown accustomed to success. The allegations against the program may have dropped some people off the bandwagon. It's also likely that the women's team, then on its way to an undefeated season and the national championship, took some of the steam away as well.

The 2008–2009 team had no beloved figure. Thabeet was a fan favorite but he didn't have the popularity that El-Amin, Hamilton, Okafor, or Gordon commanded. The fans may have chilled on Price because of his involvement with the laptops in the summer of 2005.

Antiheroes | 225

People may have also grown weary of Jim Calhoun. More than one person came to criticize how the coach handled the media and his players. Some probably became tired of what they saw as an act. The various and sundry problems that plagued the program—from laptops, arrests, suspensions, claims of unethical recruiting, to allegations of cheating—fatigued people. Whatever it was, the excitement, passion, and enthusiasm about UConn basketball waned. Sure, the state still followed the team, but Huskymania wasn't quite what it was in 2009 compared to the 1990s, 1999, and 2004.

The Yahoo! story dogged Calhoun and the Huskies as they traveled to Detroit to face Michigan State. At the Final Four, Calhoun said that an NCAA gag order prevented him from commenting on the allegations. He took Dean Smith's advice and would not make a decision about his future right after a good season or a disappointing one. Calhoun asked Smith why he had retired. "I can still coach basketball," the Carolina legend said. Smith left to escape "the other stuff." At this point, Calhoun understood what Smith meant.

According to Michael Rosenberg of the *Detroit Free Press*, Rip Hamilton was angry because Calhoun didn't distance himself from Nochimson. In the middle of December 2009, however, with a smile on his face, Hamilton said, "Calhoun's my guy." He also said that he kept in touch with Calhoun.

The Final Four was a party to which UConn was not welcome. Michigan State's fans occupied about two thirds of the 72,456 seats at Detroit's Ford Field. The Spartans played for the entire state of Michigan and the city of Detroit, both of which had been devastated by the national recession. Michigan State was the feel-good story of the Final Four; UConn was not.

The Huskies led by two with 14:35 left in regulation, but the Spartans scored 17 of the game's next 22 points and UConn faced a 10-point deficit with about seven minutes to play. Ford Field vibrated. UConn cut the deficit to three with about a minute to play but lost by nine.

The critics panned Thabeet, who scored 17 points and had six rebounds. Calhoun said that Michigan State slowed UConn's big man by triple-teaming him in the second half. He said that not all of his center's passes out of the post were good ones but Thabeet still had an effect on the game.

People who have been around Calhoun for years said the coach looked as distracted as they had ever seen him during the Detroit Final Four. Calhoun was gracious in defeat and his tone lacked any hint of bitterness about the game's result. He admitted that his team had difficulty staying focused over the previous two weeks, but he didn't use the distraction as a reason for defeat. He credited Tom Izzo for a job well done and referred to the Michigan State coach as one of his best friends and a future Hall of Famer.

Five days after the season ended, UConn announced Calhoun would return.

In the 2009 NBA draft, the Memphis Grizzlies took Thabeet with the second overall pick. In late February of 2010, Thabeet became the highest draft pick to be demoted to the D-League, the minors of the NBA. In his first year in the NBA, Thabeet scored 3.1 points, grabbed 3.6 rebounds, and blocked 1.3 shots in 13 minutes a game. The next season, he was traded to the Houston Rockets, for which he played two games, and finished the season with the Rio Grande Valley Vipers, the Rockets' D-League team.

Indiana used the 52nd overall pick to take A.J. Price, who played in 106 games in his first two seasons and averaged 6.9 points, two assists, and one turnover in 15.7 minutes a game.

At the time, no one knew that UConn already had a legend in its midst. It would take almost two years to find out that perhaps the greatest Husky ever was already in Storrs.

29

I Don't Get Defeated

In mid-June 2009, a little more than a month after he turned 67, Jim Calhoun participated in his annual bike ride to fight cancer. About 12 miles into the 50-mile race, Calhoun hit a pothole and flipped over the handlebars. Many people would have given up, but not Jim Calhoun. He waited for an hour to get a replacement helmet and wheel, received a bandage for a cut on his knee, and pedaled the final 38 miles and finished. When he crossed the finish line, he said that this was the "best I've ever felt."

Shortly thereafter, he passed out from a combination of dehydration and trauma.

His son Jeff and daughter-in-law Amy took off his shoes and socks and poured water on his head. Calhoun was conscious by the time the ambulance arrived five minutes later. He wanted to drive himself to the hospital, but Ray Allen—who participated in the race—Scott Burrell, and others talked him out of that idea.

When he arrived at the hospital, Calhoun learned that he had broken five ribs as a result of the fall. He stayed overnight and was released the next day. For the 2010 ride, Calhoun promised to bike 75 miles. Calhoun is a finisher. He won't quit. He will come back. Those are three things that people relearned in the summer of 2009, the basketball season of 2009-2010, and beyond.

UConn failed two early tests to see if it was among the best teams in the country. It lost by nine to eventual-national-champion Duke in the championship game of the preseason NIT at Madison Square Garden. Less than two weeks later, John Calipari, John Wall, and number-four Kentucky beat UConn by three in an SEC-Big East invitational game, also at MSG.

Two days after a game against Michigan, the Huskies' sixth loss of the season, Calhoun had a regular visit with his physician, Dr. Peter Schulman of the UConn Health Center. The doctor recommended that Calhoun take an immediate medical leave "to address some temporary medical issues." Calhoun listened. He put George Blaney in charge of his team.

Calhoun, the doctor, and UConn said that the medical issue was not related to previous illnesses such as cancer nor was it career threatening. Reports suggested that high blood pressure and stress caused the hiatus, but no one confirmed these speculations.

The medical leave called into question whether Calhoun would return at all and, if so, how long he would continue to coach. His contract was set to expire at the end of the season, but over and again, Calhoun said that he and UConn had agreed on a five-year extension.

The Huskies went 3–4 during Calhoun's absence. Its biggest win came at Gampel against Texas, the nation's outgoing number-one team that lost to Kansas State earlier in the week. In the first game that UConn had ever played on campus against a number-one team, Walker, Dyson, and UConn outran Texas in the second half. Walker finished with 19 points and 10 assists. "Kemba was the fastest guard we've played against," Texas's Avery Bradley said. Dyson scored a career-high 32 and Robinson had 17. UConn outscored Texas by 22 in the second half and won by 14. When the Huskies' version of the Big Three played well, UConn could beat anyone. That didn't happen often enough during the season.

The students stormed the court after the game. People pay hundreds of thousands of dollars to sit behind the UConn bench. Calhoun doesn't acknowledge them, ever, beyond occasionally telling some who sit there to "shut the fuck up." The UConn coach has such dominance over this area of the arena that fans who sit there often whisper so that the coach can't hear them. After the win over Texas, Blaney went into the crowd and shook the hands of those behind the bench. The players called Calhoun after the game. The coach said he was proud of his team and the players' toughness. They told him to get well and hurry back.

Calhoun's medical leave lasted 23 days. At the time of the coach's return, UConn was 14–10 overall and 4–7 in the Big East. When he rejoined his team after cancer surgery in 2003, the Huskies played with new energy; the 2010 team did not.

"I'm embarrassed by it." That's how Jim Calhoun described his feelings about his team's 60–48 loss to Cincinnati at the Civic Center. He called the performance one of the worst he remembered during his 24-year career at UConn.

Calhoun looked refreshed and like he had lost weight. It would have been easy to slip a finger or two between the coach's shirt collar and neck. In the postgame press conference, he cut short a question from the *Connecticut Post*'s Chris Elsberry, who wanted to know whether the coach should have returned. Calhoun wanted to talk about the game.

Later in the press conference, Calhoun referenced Elsberry by saying, "I came back because I had a job that I feel I needed to finish. I came back because I want to coach. And I was as befuddled—I guess one gentleman thinks [players] quit on me, which is fine. That's his terminology, a twist. But he's been known to do that on occasions, or set up a question that way." The gentleman—Elsberry—said he never used the word quit.

Calhoun offered some advice to all those who would doubt him: go see a therapist. The boss was back; his team wasn't . . . yet.

On ESPN's *Big Monday* at number-three Villanova, Kemba Walker scored a career-high 29 points, 20 of which came in the second half, to lead UConn to an 84-75 win. This game fit the "us versus them," "they don't think we can win, but I do" kind that Calhoun loves and tends to win.

UConn won at Rutgers by 18 and beat number-eight West Virginia by four at the Civic Center. Walker, who scored 21 in the WVU game, emerged as the leader of the Huskies, who were 3-1 since their coach returned. At 17-11 overall, 7-8 in the Big East, and with three wins over top 10 teams in the previous month, the Huskies moved inside the NCAA tournament bubble. As it headed into its final three games, the team must have felt like Captain Chaos at the end of the *Cannonball Run*. As he drove the final miles of the cross-country race, the Captain (Dom DeLuise) said, "It's only ten blocks to the finish; I feel very confident that we will be—triumphant."

Then, like Captain Chaos, the Huskies couldn't finish. They lost at the end of the game to Louisville at Gampel. After Notre Dame beat UConn, 58-50, in South Bend, an at-large bid to the NCAA tournament was out of the question.

After a 75-68 loss at South Florida, the Huskies finished in 12th place in the Big East, and earned the right to play on the Tuesday of the Big East tournament. Tuesday.

Against St. John's, which finished in 13th place, UConn committed 19 turnovers and lost by 22. The performance made it look like some of the Huskies had given up.

UConn didn't play like a Calhoun-coached team during the season. At times, the Huskies didn't run back on defense. A lack of fundamentals against Notre Dame embarrassed Calhoun. "For a team with its back to the wall, I'm not used to them coming out that way," the coach said. "When you get down to eighty minutes (left in the regular season), you'd like to see an awful lot more than what we got."

UConn beat Northeastern in the first round of the NIT and lost by two at the end of the next game at Virginia Tech. The only good news for the Huskies was that Kemba Walker led the team and played his best basketball of the season after Calhoun returned.

A disappointing season ended and an interesting off-season began. Calhoun's contract, or lack thereof, became an issue. Rumors circulated that UConn may not offer an extension because of Calhoun's age and health in addition to the ongoing NCAA investigation. The Huskies pursued several prominent recruits in the spring and many reporters speculated that Calhoun's uncertain future with UConn caused the players to sign elsewhere.

Then, on May 7, 2010, Calhoun and UConn announced the coach's five-year, $13 million extension. The contract took effect retroactively, beginning with the 2009–2010 season, so the deal meant that Calhoun would coach the team for at least four more years. The $2.3 million salary for the 2010–2011 season made Calhoun the highest paid coach in the conference, surpassing Rick Pitino's $2.25 million. According to the contract, if Calhoun retired during the life of the deal, the university would pay $1 million to him or the coach could take a $300,000-per-year position within the athletic department for no longer than five years. If Calhoun was found guilty of NCAA violations, the new contract allowed the university to suspend him without pay or terminate him. That provision didn't get much attention at the time, but it would become more prominent by the end of the month.

The night before the athletic department and basketball program were to reveal the violations alleged against them by the NCAA, reports surfaced that assistant coaches Patrick Sellers and Beau Archibald had resigned. The next day, Athletic Director Jeff Hathaway, Calhoun, and legal counsel retained by the university announced that the NCAA had concluded that UConn committed eight major violations, which ranged from impermissible phone calls, benefits, and gifts to Calhoun's inability to "promote an atmosphere of compliance." The NCAA claimed that Sellers and Archibald lied to it. UConn had 90 days to address the charges.

This day wasn't anywhere near the high point of his career, Calhoun said. "As a matter of fact, it's certainly one of the lowest points at any time that you are accused of doing something. It's a very serious matter." The coach said that he hadn't lost. "I don't get defeated by things," he said.

Calhoun continued to hold out the possibility that the program had done nothing wrong. He responded to one question with the caveat "if in fact we did make mistakes," an answer that bothered Jeff Jacobs of the *Hartford Courant*. In his column titled "'If' Not the Answer We Need from Calhoun," Jacobs wrote, "Oh, mistakes were made, Jim. Some serious ones, too."

If Jim Calhoun-bashing were a sport, the Olympics began on May 28, 2010. Columnists throughout the country criticized Calhoun for allowing Archibald and Sellers to serve as scapegoats. This was Calhoun's program and he was to blame for violations, they argued. Filip Bondy of the New York *Daily News* began his column on the incident writing, "One thing we learned long ago about UConn: The state university doesn't care much what people think of its ethical or academic standards, as long as the men's basketball team wins games and produces giant revenue streams." Most columnists portrayed the UConn coach as a master schemer in the cesspool of college basketball.

The NCAA investigations followed Calhoun more closely than his shadow during the summer. At the coach's semiannual reunion game, Calhoun answered questions about his former players and what they meant to him. When the *New Haven Register*'s David Borges asked about the NCAA investigations, Calhoun lost his smile and squinted as if he were about to vaporize Borges with his heat vision. "It's the farthest thing from my mind," Calhoun said.

A little more than a week before it was set to address the charges in person to the NCAA in Indianapolis, UConn submitted its response to the NCAA allegations. The university's 700-page report admitted that Calhoun gave complimentary tickets to high school and AAU coaches and that the staff made impermissible recruiting calls. The university denied that its coach failed to promote an atmosphere of compliance, a charge, if shown to be true, that would come with the greatest penalties. The university recommended that the NCAA place its men's basketball program on probation for two years, reduce its scholarships from 13 to 12, and restrict the number of coaches who call recruits.

Most people concluded that these proposed punishments were too lenient. In many instances, UConn didn't use 13 scholarships and Associate Head Coach George Blaney tended to stay in Storrs anyway. No big deal.

In *Casino*, three slot machines hit the jackpot within minutes of one another and Ace Rothstein, played by Robert De Niro, realizes that the casino he runs is the victim of a scam. Rothstein asks Ward, the manager of the slots, "Do you have any idea what the odds are?" After dim-witted Ward explains that people win in casinos, Rothstein says, "If you didn't know, you're too fuckin' dumb. If you did know, you were in on it. Either way, you're out."

That's the predicament in which Calhoun found himself with the Miles situation. If Calhoun didn't know what his assistants were doing and how they interacted with Miles, then he was to blame for a lack of control over his program. If he knew, then he was in on it. Either way, Calhoun loses.

After UConn responded to the allegations, most commentators found it hard to believe that Calhoun didn't know what his assistants were doing with Miles. Dana O'Neil of ESPN.com wrote that Calhoun and all other coaches who get investigated for wrongdoing in their programs turn into Sergeant Shultz when the NCAA comes calling. Like the fictional character from *Hogan's Heroes*, Calhoun said, "I know nothing."

Calhoun said he had warned his athletic director, the university's NCAA compliance officer, Miles, and Assistant Coach Beau Archibald about Nochimson. For these reasons, the UConn coach thought that the NCAA should not have singled him out. Jeff Jacobs had a hard time believing Calhoun. He claimed that Calhoun was so smitten with Miles that he tried to keep the player in school after his arrest for violating a restraining order and following his departure at Southern Idaho.

The Miles incident led many to consider how corrupt Calhoun's program was. Charles Pierce, who covered Calhoun when the coach was at Northeastern, wrote that the "program at UConn has been wildly out of control for too long now—dating back in my mind, to an assistant's having been involved with king-sleazoid street-agent Rob Johnson back in the early 1990s."

Calhoun's UConn program has never been out of control. For the most part, his players have been solid citizens at UConn and in life. Players and the media who cover UConn will confirm that the Huskies don't have free reign in Storrs and they can't do whatever they want.

At this time, the fall of the Calhoun empire seemed to have commenced. Writers like the *Sporting News*'s Mike DeCourcy and *Sports Illustrated*'s Seth Davis echoed what many thought: the Calhoun era was over. Over? Was it over when the Germans bombed Pearl Harbor?

5

RESILIENCE

30

From Maui . . .

In the summer of 2010, Calhoun's return was in doubt and an NCAA investigation and penalties loomed. Even if Calhoun came back and the NCAA cleared UConn, the 2011 team had Kemba Walker and not much else. Alex Oriakhi and Jamal Coombs-McDaniel turned in average freshmen years; they didn't scare the rest of the Big East or give people a sense of confidence that they would help UConn win games.

The recruiting class included Jeremy Lamb, son of the same Rolando Lamb whose buzzer-beater eliminated Calhoun's Northeastern Huskies from the 1984 NCAA tournament. Jeremy didn't start on his Norcross (Georgia) high school team during his junior year. Calhoun was quick to point out that Reggie Lewis didn't start on his high school team either. Lamb had impressed Calhoun during the summer of 2009 at the Georgia Peach Jam. At six foot four, 175 pounds, and with the wingspan of someone a foot taller, Lamb fit Howie Dickenman's description of the ideal or prototypical Calhoun player. He was long, lean, and athletic.

ESPN rated Lamb as the 43rd best shooting guard in his class. UConn, Texas, and Georgia offered a scholarship to Lamb, who picked UConn because of its tradition and his opportunity to play right away because of the loss of Dyson and Robinson. Calhoun didn't think Lamb could guard a chair, but he had cured other players who suffered from that ailment.

Before the start of the season, Calhoun said that Lamb was "at least as talented as Richard Hamilton coming in, and more athletic." He said, Lamb "will be our best shooter. If he doesn't make it, here and beyond, I'll be very surprised." That was a bold assessment of the 43rd best shooting guard in the high school class of 2010.

Roscoe Smith was UConn's lone recruit in the ESPN-U top 100. ESPN ranked Smith as the 34th best player in the class of 2010 and the seventh best small forward. A native of Baltimore, Smith played his senior year at Oak Hill Academy. Duke, Georgetown, Kansas, and Florida expressed interest in Smith, who was Duke's number-two option at small forward; the Blue Devils preferred Harrison Barnes, who signed with Carolina. Coach K called Smith immediately after Barnes chose Carolina and told Smith how effective he could be in Duke's offense.

Calhoun compared Smith to another Baltimore product—Rudy Gay. He said that Smith was a better shooter and stronger than Gay but not as athletic. Calhoun referred to Smith as "an incredibly talented kid, [who's] going to be terrific in time."

Smith chose UConn because of Calhoun's ability to develop players at the wing and the program's pro-style offense. Despite predictions of the program's demise, Smith was the first recruit in the Calhoun era to choose UConn over Duke. Few players pick another school when they have a chance to play for Duke.

Calhoun took his leave of absence less than two weeks after Smith signed. Smith said he would play at UConn as long as Calhoun was still coach. Once the staff told him that Calhoun would return, Smith honored his commitment.

Calhoun said that Shabazz Napier was "probably the best player in the class." Napier, a five foot eleven (at best) point guard from Randolph, Massachusetts, played for Charlestown (Massachusetts) High School and then Lawrence Academy in Groton, Massachusetts. A member of the Boston Amateur Basketball Club (AAU) team, Napier drew comparisons to Dana Barros, but with the exception of UConn, the nation's elite programs were not after Napier, whose other options included UMass, Miami, Providence, Arizona State, and St. John's.

Napier's Lawrence team went 29-0 and captured the New England Class C prep school championship. In the title game, Napier scored 29 points and earned tournament MVP. His coach at Lawrence described Napier as "a good kid and an exciting player . . . probably one of the more dynamic point guards around." Originally slated to begin at UConn in the fall of 2011, Napier was reclassified and joined the team for the 2010-2011 season. Calhoun admired the seven players in the recruiting class because they trusted him.

The Big East coaches predicted that UConn would finish 10th in the Big East in 2010-2011. Pitt was the preseason number-one team in the conference, and Georgetown's Austin Freeman was the preseason selection for player of the year. Kemba Walker made the Big East's first team in the preseason after he had earned third-term all-conference honors as a sophomore.

In response to the rankings, Calhoun said, "First time in a long time I've got a chance to be coach of the year. That's the way you've got to do it. You've got to be number eight or below, otherwise it's not going to happen." He said that UConn was probably picked where it belonged, but could have been picked 11th or 12th as well.

At the league's preseason meeting at MSG, Calhoun said, "You're saying that maybe we can qualify for the NIT. I think we can do more than that." He made similar statements about his team in 1990.

CALHOUN RULES
Set the Tone on Day One

On October 15, 2010, Calhoun, Hathaway, and interim university president Philip E. Austin testified for more than 12 hours before the NCAA's committee on infractions in Indianapolis. Calhoun returned to Storrs the next day for the first practice and annual Guyer Gym torture chamber session. He didn't comment on the NCAA hearing and would wait more than four months to hear the NCAA's decision.

In the 2010–2011 season, UConn played in the Maui Invitational, but unlike the trip five years earlier, most people didn't expect UConn to win two games in Hawaii, let alone three. The team entered the season unranked and didn't receive a vote in the AP's top 25 preseason poll. The Huskies were not thought to be championship material.

Before it went to Hawaii, UConn trailed Vermont by three at the half in the Civic Center, but Kemba Walker led a comeback and tied a Calhoun-era record for points in a game (42) with Cliff Robinson and Donyell Marshall. UConn won by 16.

In UConn's first game in Maui, it faced a 60–51 deficit with less than 10 minutes left. At this point, fans on Twitter condemned UConn and predicted a disastrous season for the Huskies. With 3:54 to go, Wichita State was still up, 76–71. Then, Walker made two free throws and a three-pointer and in the blink of an eye—or about a minute of game time—the score was tied. After two more free throws and two more baskets by Walker, UConn led 82–79 and won the game, 83–79. Walker scored 13 of UConn's final 14 points.

In the next game, with UConn trailing second-ranked Michigan State 61–56 with 7:17 left, Walker scored four quick points to cut the deficit to one. Still down one with less than a minute left, Walker made a fade-away jumper to give a one-point lead to the Huskies.

Calhoun had a tough time watching the end of this game. Oriakhi missed three of four free throws in the final 39 seconds and UConn went two for six from the line in this stretch, but when State's Draymond Green missed a three at the end, UConn had a 70–67 win.

"We had Kemba Walker and Tom [Izzo] didn't." That's how Calhoun explained the win. Walker scored 30 points; Oriakhi had 15 points and 17 rebounds.

For Walker, this victory made a statement: "We just showed the world we can play."

In the final game of the tournament, UConn crushed Kentucky, 84–67. It used a 21-2 run to close the first half and take a 50-29 lead at the break. The Wildcats never threatened the Huskies again. During UConn's game-changing spurt, Walker hit back-to-back threes and when he got into position to make number three, the entire commonwealth of Kentucky, including Colonel Sanders, converged on him. Walker fired a pass to Coombs-McDaniel for an uncontested layup. Calhoun loved that play. Walker scored 29 points, which left him three points short of the record for most points in a single Maui Invitational.

This UConn team had fire. Calhoun gave it a mission: get us back to where we belong. Kemba Walker got the message: "We wanted to show the world, we're still UConn."

This UConn team was fun. Shabazz Napier played the game with excitement and light blue sneakers. It was apparent he loved the game. The team's youth and boyish looks endeared fans to them. Kemba Walker—by all accounts a nice person and mature adult—was a great new face for the program.

When the AP's next poll came out, UConn went from unranked to number seven in the nation. This jump marked the second largest in the history of the AP poll. (In 1989, Kansas beat the first- and 25th-ranked teams in the same week and went from unranked to number four.)

After Maui, UConn won five nonconference games but got clobbered at Pitt, 78-63. After a blasé New Year's Eve win over South Florida at the Civic Center, UConn lost by three at Notre Dame. Ben Hansbrough, brother of Tyler, scored 21; Walker had 19. It was the first time in 12 games that Walker scored fewer than 20 points.

With the score tied at 73 and about 12 seconds left in regulation at number-12 Texas, Oriakhi pinned Gary Johnson's layup attempt against the glass and the ball came to Roscoe Smith, who turned and launched a full-court shot into the Texas pep band. Eleven seconds remained.

At some point in every game, it seems, Calhoun outstretches his arms, looks at Associate Athletic Director Kyle Muncy, Tim Tolokan, the assistant coaches, or anyone near the bench and asks, "Why did he do that?" Through his facial expressions and body language, Calhoun appears to be stunned at least five times per game. But he had never seen anything like Smith's shot. He laughed about the play after the game. He wouldn't have had UConn lost.

With 2:15 to go in overtime, the game tied at 77, and the shot clock about to hit zero, Walker swished a one-handed 30-footer from Fort Worth on the State of Texas logo at midcourt. "I guess God was on my side," he said of the shot. When asked about the heave, Texas's Jordan Hamilton said, "I guess God was on his side."

With UConn down 81-80, Walker received the ball at midcourt with 15 seconds to go in overtime. He sprinted to the left of the free throw line, stepped back, and made a fall-away shot with 5.1 seconds left. The Longhorns failed to score on the next possession. Walker scored UConn's final seven points.

The victory at Texas started a six-game winning streak. Walker won a Gampel game against number-eight Villanova when he made a 10-foot floater with 2.5 seconds left. The next two games turned the regular season.

to Mediocrity . . .

Against number-23 Louisville at Gampel, UConn lost by one after it relinquished a nine-point second-half advantage and a four-point lead with 37 seconds remaining in overtime. In the next game, Syracuse beat the Huskies, 66-58, in Hartford. The Orange held the lead the entire second half. The Louisville and Syracuse games started a streak in which UConn lost seven of its final 11 to finish in ninth place in the conference. During this stretch, UConn lost by blowouts—89-72 at St. John's and 71-58 at Louisville—and in close games—70-67 to Notre Dame at Gampel and 74-67 in overtime to Marquette in Hartford.

In UConn's first loss to Louisville, Walker finished with 20 points on seven for 23 shooting overall and two for 10 from three-point range. After the game, Calhoun said, "I don't want to talk about Kemba. Next question." He didn't talk about Walker after the Syracuse game, in which his star scored a season-low eight points.

When Calhoun finally explained the reasons for Walker's troubles, he said, "He's playing thirty-six minutes a game, getting a lot of attention, getting banged around an awful lot. . . . And, very simply, I haven't had a great player [without] a lot of help. And remember, his help is predominantly five freshmen and a sophomore. He's trying to lead them."

The rest of the team struggled too. Oriakhi grabbed 10 rebounds against Tennessee on January 22 but didn't reach double digits in rebounds for another month. He had one double-digit rebounding game in the team's final 12 regular season contests. Starting with the Texas game, he scored double digits in five straight, but after Tennessee, he went four games without doing so. Oriakhi had started every game for UConn until the regular season finale against Notre Dame. Calhoun called the benching a nonpunitive measure designed to increase Oriakhi's comfort.

Jeremy Lamb showed signs he would be the program's next elite wing player. He scored 21 against Louisville and 22 against Syracuse but reached double figures in only three of the Huskies' final nine games. He scored no points at Louisville and five at West Virginia. Napier scored 23 points against Louisville but didn't reach double figures in the next seven games. He went scoreless in two games during that span. Smith averaged less than five points in an eight-game stretch that started with the Louisville game.

After UConn lost two of three and got shellacked at St. John's, *Hartford Courant* beat writer Mike Anthony summarized why the season had turned: "Walker's efficiency has regressed. Winnable games against Louisville and Syracuse got away. Free throws aren't falling like they were. Playmaking against zone defenses has been stagnant. Defense has been spotty at key times. The post play of Alex Oriakhi and his supporting cast has not been consistent."

After a win over Georgetown, the UConn coach said, "[Walker] is fifth in the Big East, a pretty good conference, in defensive rebounding. He is second in assists. Third in steals. And he averages twenty-two points a game while leading a lot of young people to some awfully good places and right now we are twenty and five. You hear he can't be Big East player of the year. They're right. He should be national player of the year."

By this time, Calhoun was about the only person to mention Walker and this prize in the same sentence. By season's end, Walker wouldn't win conference player of the year—that honor went to Notre Dame's Ben Hansbrough—nor would he be a unanimous selection for first team all–Big East. BYU's Jimmer Fredette won the Naismith Award and was the AP's player of the year.

The NCAA announced its ruling on the UConn investigation four days after Louisville pummeled UConn, 71–58. On February 22, 2011, it reduced the number of basketball scholarships by one per year from 2012 to 2014, decreased the number of contact hours UConn's coaches could have with recruits, and placed the program on probation for three years. The committee exonerated Sellers but Archibald received a two-year show-cause penalty, which meant that any university needed permission from the committee on infractions if it wanted to hire him over that two-year period.

The NCAA suspended Calhoun for the first three Big East games of the 2011–2012 season. Through his attorney, Calhoun said that the decision disappointed him and that he would evaluate how he should proceed.

UConn's regular season ended with a three-point loss to Notre Dame at Gampel. Walker participated in senior day activities even though a year of eligibility remained for him. He would graduate in May and believed that his draft status was high enough to go pro. The game ended when Walker sprinted the ball up the floor but skipped a pass to Donnell Beverly, who couldn't corral the ball and shoot it before time expired. The loss cost the Huskies a first-round bye in the Big East tournament. For the second consecutive year, they would begin the tournament on Tuesday.

Tuesday, again.

The Huskies finished the regular season with a 21–9 record overall and a 9–9 mark in the conference. They fell to 19th in the AP poll. Most everyone gave UConn no chance to win the Big East tournament.

None.

Not Kemba Walker.

In the time between the final regular season game and the Big East tournament, Walker called a players only meeting. His message was simple: "We can win the Big East tournament."

to Manhattan . . .

In its first victory in the Big East tournament since 2005, UConn beat DePaul, the league's worst team, 97–71. In its next game, UConn went on a 22–7 run in the first half and the 22nd-ranked Hoyas never recovered. Walker scored 26 in the first game and 28 in the second.

When asked how a coach could leave Walker out of his first-team all-Big East ballot, Calhoun said, "I think someone took a vacation and didn't tell us and has been gone five months. . . . I think he's the best player in the country, and that should be more important." The best player in the country, Coach, really?

Following the game, Calhoun told reporters that he would not challenge the NCAA's ruling on the investigation into the program. That was that.

Pitt, the top seed in the Big East tournament and the nation's third-ranked team, had a bye for the first two rounds but had lost twice in previous years when it had double byes. UConn overcame a 12-point first-half deficit and a seven-point gap in the second half to lead by three with a little more than a minute left. Pitt's Ashton Gibbs tied the game with a three and 49 seconds remained.

Everyone knew Kemba Walker would shoot the ball. The fans knew. The security guards knew. The peanut vendors knew. Walker shot and missed. Coombs-McDaniel got the rebound and called time-out in the same motion as the Panthers clawed at the ball and 18 seconds remained. In the UConn huddle, his teammates told Walker to stay aggressive, take the last shot, and win the game for them.

Pitt switches its defenders on every ball screen. In the 1999 title game, Calhoun used these switches to create mismatches against Duke to win the national title. Calhoun knew Pitt would change defenders, so he called for Coombs-McDaniel to set a screen for Walker. After the switch, a bigger Pitt player would guard Walker.

With 14.2 seconds left, Walker dribbled on the Reese's Peanut Butter Cups logo on the MSG court. He was on UConn's sideline about 40 feet from the basket. With 12 seconds left, Calhoun flicked his wrist and pointed to a spot near the top of the key where Coombs-McDaniel raced to set a screen. He sealed Walker's defender and left six foot eleven, 250-pound, Gary McGhee, Pitt's center, on Walker. Poor Gary.

The ankle breaker: Kemba Walker's move on Pitt's Gary McGhee to set up the game-winning shot against the Panthers. UConn 76–Pitt 74. March 10, 2011, Madison Square Garden.

Stephen Dunn/*Hartford Courant*/MCT via Getty Images

Walker backed up for three seconds and surveyed the scene. He was one-on-one with McGhee. Walker exploded forward with five seconds left and McGhee tried to cut him off. Walker stopped and stepped back then lunged forward, a move that sent McGhee stumbling to the floor. In basketball terms, Walker had performed an ankle breaker.

Walker stepped back one last time and let it fly with about 1.5 seconds left in regulation. His movements created space to take an open shot. The ball felt great coming out of his hands. He released the ball early and got what he described as "good legs" into the shot.

In.

Calhoun hopped as the ball went into the basket. He pumped his fist for a moment. His actions resembled those he had taken after Tate George's buzzer-beater in 1990. Afterward, Calhoun said he felt as good inside about this shot as he did after George's 21 years earlier.

"I think [Walker is] the most important guy for a single college basketball team in the country," Calhoun said after the game. He was right. Now, people with normal basketball intelligence could see what Calhoun saw throughout the season.

Walker learned the kinds of moves he performed on McGhee during the summer when he played for the USA Select Team against Kevin Durant, Derrick Rose, Rudy Gay, and Team USA. Throughout Walker's career, Calhoun wanted him to play in many gears instead of just one. When Walker saw how the pros played and realized that he needed to change speeds to deceive them, he understood what Calhoun meant. UConn benefited from the five-speed Walker. McGhee and Pittsburgh did not.

Walker was not the only story. Lamb scored 17 points and Oriakhi had 13 points and seven rebounds. UConn scored 18 second-chance points and outrebounded Pitt, 32–25. During the regular season, Pitt grabbed a league-leading 11 more rebounds per game than its opponents. "It was one of those games where Pittsburgh asks you, 'How tough are you? If you're tough enough, you can beat us.' And we were tough enough today," said Calhoun.

The Huskies were in the Big East semifinals for the first time since 2005. Syracuse had beaten UConn four times (2005, 2006, 2007, 2009) during the Huskies' six-game losing streak in the conference tournament. UConn would have its chance for revenge against the 11th-ranked team in the nation.

UConn led by six with 25 seconds left, but Syracuse's Scoop Jardine made three-pointers with 21 and 4.8 seconds left to tie the score. Walker was mad that the game didn't end in regulation. He wanted no part of another six-overtime game. Lamb and Walker outscored Syracuse 8–3 in overtime. Walker finished with 33 points, 12 rebounds, and six steals. He broke Eric Devendorf's record for most points in a Big East tournament. After four games, including the six-overtime contest, Devendorf had scored 86 points. In four games and one overtime, Walker scored 111. Lamb scored double-digit points for the fourth consecutive game, and Oriakhi contributed 15 points and 11 rebounds.

"Tell me any other guard who is getting twelve rebounds, six steals, five assists. I've never seen a guard dominate a game inside and out," Calhoun said. "I think he is the most valuable player on any college team in America."

Calhoun was right.

Bill Clinton attended the game and took a picture with Walker and Kemba's mother afterward. Andrea Walker wore her son's 2009 Final Four jersey and a lei. Maui to Manhattan was the mission. After the Syracuse win, UConn was 7–0 in tournament games for the season. Walker and the Huskies had recaptured the excellence they displayed in Maui.

Rick Pitino's 14th-ranked Louisville Cardinals stood in UConn's way of completing the five-for-five. Calhoun and Pitino coached against each other in the late 1970s and early 1980s when Calhoun was at Northeastern and Pitino coached Boston University. Calhoun said the rivalry was too intense.

"We had a great relationship when he was at BU and I was at Northeastern; we didn't speak for five years," Calhoun said. "That was convenient. That way you never get in a fight."

They jogged similar routes along the Charles River in Boston and only nodded when they ran past each other. According to Calhoun, the relationship warmed over the years because the two men matured and overcame personal struggles with cancer and the loss of relatives. The two coaches, formerly the most bitter of rivals, faced each other again.

"We're going to shock the world," El-Amin had said in 1999; Walker repeated it in 2011. He told the media during UConn's run toward the Big East championship game that the Huskies would win and "shock the world."

The Huskies almost knocked out Louisville at the beginning of the game. Walker stole the ball from Peyton Siva, thunder-dunked it, and then roared. With eight minutes left in the first half, UConn led by 12.

The game changed less than a minute later when Walker picked up his second foul. UConn never regained its momentum after this call. Louisville cut its 12-point deficit in half as it went to the locker room. In the second half, it had outscored UConn 25-11 since Walker picked up his second foul.

The score remained close for the rest of the game; UConn had the ball and a chance to take the lead with 53 seconds remaining. Calhoun called time-out and waved his players to take a seat on the bench. One minute earlier, Walker couldn't feel his legs. "That's usually a sign that you're tired," Calhoun said.

Again, everyone thought that Walker would shoot the ball. When action resumed, Walker beat two Louisville defenders, got to the basket, and passed to a wide-open Lamb for a layup. UConn led by one and was 33.4 seconds away from its record-tying seventh Big East tournament title. A Napier steal and two Walker free throws put UConn ahead by three with 16 seconds left.

A debate resumed: should UConn foul to prevent Louisville from tying the game with a three. The ESPN announcers had asked Calhoun what he would do in this situation, but the response was the same: no foul. The night before, the announcers talked about whether UConn should foul Syracuse to prevent the Orange from hitting a game-tying three-pointer. As it turned out, Calhoun chose not to foul and Scoop Jardine made a three-point basket to tie the game. UConn won anyway.

Calhoun would take the same approach in the championship game. Louisville's Preston Knowles missed a three, but the Cardinals' Kyle Kuric swatted the ball beyond the three-point line to teammate Mark Marra, who was fouled by Walker after a pump fake. With 3.9 seconds left, Marra had the opportunity to tie the game at the line, but he doinked the second free throw.

After Marra made the third free throw, Napier sank both of his free throws to put UConn up by three with three seconds left. Preston Knowles got an open view of the basket for a game-tying three-pointer at the buzzer.

Jeremy Lamb became UConn's next star during the team's 2011 postseason run. Here, he dunks home two of his 17 points against Pittsburgh in the Big East tournament quarterfinal. March 10, 2011.

Ed Ryan/ *The Daily Campus*

He missed.

UConn won, 69–66.

When the horn sounded, Calhoun threw a hug at Donnell Beverly reminiscent of the one he unleashed on Tim Tolokan after Tate George's shot in 1990. Calhoun referenced his sons in a postgame interview with ESPN's Doris Burke. When the camera pulled back, Calhoun wasn't talking about Jim Jr. and Jeff. He meant his players.

ESPN's Bill Raftery had seen all the greats play in the Big East tournament: Ray Allen, Allen Iverson, Chris Mullin, Patrick Ewing, Pearl Washington, Derrick Coleman, and Luther Wright. "I have never seen a performance like this in the Big East tournament," he said in reference to Walker and UConn's five wins in five days; a feat never accomplished in the history of college basketball.

In five days in New York, Kemba Walker moved onto the all-Calhoun-era first team — sorry Khalid El-Amin — and entered the conversation about the best player in the Calhoun era. "He is as special as any player I've ever coached," Calhoun said of Walker. "No one's going to surpass him. They may equal him but no one is going to surpass him. . . . Five games in five days. He's amazing."

Walker, the tournament MVP, scored 19 points against Louisville, averaged 26 for the five games, and set a new record for most points in the Big East tournament—130. When the outcome was in doubt, Walker either scored to win the game or got the ball to a teammate for an easy basket. He rebounded, stole the ball, and defended well. Walker led. The team understood that it had to help Walker win the games.

Lamb and Oriakhi answered this call. Lamb reached double-figure points in each game. He made baskets during important game-changing stretches, in overtime to beat Syracuse, and at the end of the Louisville game. Lamb and Walker were the only two Huskies to make the all-tournament team. Oriakhi should have been on it too. In the Big East tournament, he averaged 10 points and 10 rebounds per game. He grabbed close to five offensive rebounds per game for the tournament.

Coaching also allowed UConn to win. Calhoun wouldn't let the team use fatigue as an excuse. Many coaches would have given up on their team. Not Calhoun. When it came time for Calhoun to call time-out at the right moment or design the correct play, he did it. The win over Louisville was Calhoun's 600th victory at UConn.

In his postgame remarks, ESPN's Sean McDonough said that it would be easier for UConn to win the national championship than the Big East tournament because it wouldn't have to beat four top 25 teams to do so.

. . . to Monday

UConn's run in NYC earned the team the number-three seed in the West, the region from which the program advanced to its three Final Fours. In Washington, DC, UConn beat Bucknell and then Cincinnati to advance to the Sweet 16 in Anaheim, California. There, it would face second-seeded San Diego State (34-2), which entered the NCAA tournament as the number-six team in the country. Jimmer Fredette's BYU Cougars were the only team to beat SDSU during the season.

For the seventh time in the Calhoun era, UConn would play an NCAA tournament game in its opponent's home state. The Huskies had played Ohio State in Cincinnati, Florida in Miami, UCLA in Oakland, North Carolina in Greensboro, Texas in San Antonio, and Michigan State in Detroit. These examples do not include the home game George Mason played against UConn in Washington, DC, in the 2006 tournament. UConn lost all of these so-called neutral-site games.

Calhoun remembered.

"We played UCLA in Oakland and they went on to win a national championship that year. We played George Mason on their campus—oh, it was the Verizon Center, my bad. . . . We played North Carolina in the Final Eight in Greensboro. That was the year they gave out stats at halftime with just North Carolina on it. We've seemed to have an awful lot of that."

Reporters referred to the Honda Center, the site of the game, as Montezuma Mesa (a nickname for SDSU's campus) North. Jeremy Lamb had never experienced a crowd like this one. The UConn players didn't use location or fatigue as excuses. Calhoun wouldn't allow them to do that. That this game was UConn's eighth in 17 days was irrelevant. Walker said that the team's mental toughness—read, Calhoun—would get them over the hump.

The game turned with 9:19 to go and the Aztecs up 53-49. SDSU's Jamaal Franklin and Walker were talking trash to each other when Franklin banged into Walker, who fell to the court. The referees assessed a technical foul and Walker scored 14 of UConn's next 16 points. He scored 22 of his 36 points in the second half. After the technical foul, UConn outscored San Diego State by 11. Lamb's three-pointer with 1:39 left extended UConn's lead to four and put SDSU into panic mode. His two dunks in the final 21 seconds put the Aztecs away, 74-67.

And then, there was Duke, right?

Not quite.

Top-seeded Duke and number-five Arizona played in the second game of the regional and most people expected the Blue Devils to win. A 19–2 second-half run and 32 points by Derrick Williams, however, allowed Arizona to pummel Duke, the defending national champion, 93–77.

This Arizona team, coached by former Pitt star Sean Miller, loved to shoot the three-pointer. Williams, a six foot eight forward, finished the season shooting 56.8 percent from three-point range, which put him second behind Steve Kerr, who held the school record at 57.3 percent.

For the second straight game, UConn played a road game in the NCAA tournament. Red-clad Arizona fans made up at least 85 percent of the fans in attendance. Throughout the game, Williams and his teammates encouraged the Arizona fans to get louder. They did. The Honda Center echoed with chants of "U-of-A . . . U-of-A." "It felt like a home game," Miller said.

The game came down to the final possession. Arizona had the ball and trailed by two. Williams clanged a three-pointer from the top of the key with 7.8 seconds but Kyle Fogg got the rebound and passed to an open Jamelle Horne, who launched a three with 3.2 seconds left.

Jeremy Lamb was late in getting to Horne. After he attempted to block the shot, Lamb turned and watched the ball on its flight toward the basket. He was convinced it was going in.

Napier thought, "Oh man, I hope they don't do it to us."

If the shot goes in, UConn loses; season over.

If the shot goes out, UConn wins; Final Four.

When Horne's shot went up, Walker said, "Game time." He thought the ball was going in.

It didn't.

When Horne's shot bounced off the rim, Lamb said, "Whooooo!!!!" and experienced the best feeling of his life. It is hard to tell with Lamb, who plays the game in an expressionless manner. His face doesn't even flinch when he tomahawks a dunk.

Lamb finished with 19 points. His jumper with 5:52 left gave the lead to UConn for good. Walker told Calhoun to run plays for Lamb in the second half; when the coach did, Walker said to Lamb, you'll make these. He did.

Arizona shot a season-low 19 percent from beyond the three-point line. Williams made one of six from three-point range.

His team's run flabbergasted Calhoun, who said, "Never did I imagine a team winning nine games in tournament play in nineteen days. These brothers, these young guys, have just given me a thrill beyond compare. Our march in the past nine games, I haven't experienced anything like this." Again, his family got Calhoun there.

UConn fans hadn't experienced a trip like this either. After the Notre Dame game at Gampel, the season seemed lost. The unranked team that played so well to start the season finished with a whimper. Then the magic returned.

Kemba Walker was a great lead man; he played every game with a smile. The players on the team came with no baggage. They were likable. Shabazz Napier played the game with so much enthusiasm and fun that it was hard not to root for him. This group of Huskies, led by Walker, moved the program beyond the antihero phase. Walker was every bit the hero, probably more so than any of his predecessors.

At the Final Four, UConn would meet John Calipari's Kentucky Wildcats. Leading up to the game, the media asked Calhoun and Calipari about their relationship with each other. Calhoun described it as nonexistent; Calipari said it was fine. When pressed on his answer, Calipari said the two don't exchange Christmas cards.

UConn went hard after elite recruits from the class of 2010. Many sources, including the *Wall Street Journal*, speculated that a combination of Calhoun's health, the unsigned contract, and NCAA allegations caused Josh Selby (number one, according to Rivals.com) to sign with Kansas, Corey Joseph (number nine) to choose Texas, and C.J. Leslie (number 14) to pick N.C. State over UConn.

Brandon Knight (number six) from Fort Lauderdale and Oak Hill's Doron Lamb (number 21) from Queens impressed UConn's staff. Knight was named the Gatorade national player of the year in 2009 and 2010. He liked UConn because of the program's tradition and ability to produce NBA stars and Calhoun's tendency to get "straight to the point."

In April of 2010, Knight chose Kentucky. According to Knight's coach, the murder of UConn football player Jasper Howard on the Storrs campus, Calhoun's uncertain contract, and the NCAA investigation bothered Knight, who liked Calipari's ability to produce lottery picks like Derrick Rose, Tyreke Evans, and John Wall, each of whom played one year of college basketball. Lamb committed to Kentucky for the same reasons.

At the Final Four, Calhoun said he wouldn't trade his Lamb and Napier for the other Lamb and Knight. And why not? Jeremy Lamb had turned into Richard Hamilton; he scored in double figures in each of UConn's nine tournament victories. Napier provided leadership, scoring, and energy off the bench. He finished the games on the court.

The 2010 recruiting classes show the difference between typical Calhoun and Calipari teams. Calhoun signed one top 100 player. Calipari signed four players within the top 28. According to UConn assistant coach Andre La-Fleur, "We don't recruit by the numbers. Coach always has had success his whole career finding guys that weren't rated as high. . . . Rankings don't mean anything."

Actually, they do. Eight of the 10 starters in the 2011 NBA All-Star game were McDonald's All-Americans. Only Yao Ming and Dwyane Wade were not. A roster full of players outside the top 100 doesn't allow a program to compete for and win national championships.

UConn had at least one McDonald's All-American on each of its Final Four teams. In the national championship seasons of 1999 and 2004, it had two on each team. In 2011, its leader and best player, Kemba Walker, played in the McDonald's All-American game. Oriakhi made that distinction in 2009.

Houston's Reliant Stadium held a record 75,421 people for the Final Four, well more than half of whom wore Kentucky blue. They took up every seat in three sections and the entire student section. Kentucky fans were also smattered throughout the rest of the building. UConn fans took up one section and its student body sat in one quarter of the seats allocated for it. The rest of the students were probably studying back at the Babbidge Library.

UConn held Kentucky to 21 points in the first half and took a 10-point lead into the locker room. Amidst chants of "Go Big Blue, Go Big Blue," Kentucky evaporated UConn's lead within five minutes of the start of the second half, after which UConn held Kentucky scoreless for more than three minutes and reestablished a four-point lead with 8:41 left. After Knight and Doron Lamb tied the score with 7:19 left, Oriakhi dunked UConn into the lead with 6:39 remaining. It was the kind of dunk that makes one wonder how the basket remained connected to the backboard.

Walker and Napier gave a six-point lead to UConn with 2:28 remaining. Kentucky didn't score a point between 7:19 and 1:41 left in the game. These Huskies could now stake a claim as Calhoun's best defensive team.

A Kentucky three-pointer cut UConn's six-point lead in half with 1:41 left. After DeAndre Liggins made one of two free throws—Kentucky went four for 12 from the line for the game—Napier attempted to take time off the clock. Instead, he dribbled the ball off a Kentucky player's leg and Knight took the ball the other way with 18 seconds left.

With nine seconds to go, Liggins lined up for a three-pointer to give his team a one-point lead.

He missed.

Napier got the rebound and was fouled. Two seconds remained. This was the same amount of time Calhoun used to practice the Scott Burrell Home Run play, so enough time remained for Kentucky to tie or win if Napier missed one or both free throws. Calipari was convinced that his team would hit a three-pointer at the buzzer. Napier made the first. Now, Calipari thought the game would go to overtime. Napier made the second. Now, Calipari knew his season was over. So did the Kentucky fans, who stopped chanting and walked out of the building. They said nothing.

Calipari was right. Knight hit a three at the buzzer, but that left Kentucky one point short. During practice the week before, Calipari told his team it would win if it held UConn to 56 points. He mentioned that number specifically. Calipari was wrong; his team lost 56–55.

As the UConn players ran back to their locker room, they yelled, "We gonna shock the world."

In the finals, UConn played Butler, which was making its second straight appearance in the national championship game. Butler won in the last seconds in three of its five victories in the tournament, and it would have about 74,000 people cheering for it on Championship Monday. As he left Reliant Stadium on Saturday night, former UCLA and national championship coach Jim Harrick said that UConn would be in a tough position in the final game because neutral observers always pull for underdogs like Butler.

On Championship Monday, Calhoun and Walker started the morning by attending the Bob Cousy Award ceremony, which Walker won. The Cousy Award goes to the top collegiate point guard in the country. When Calhoun returned to the J.W. Marriott, which is located across from the Galleria in Houston, he did not have the look of someone who was about to coach in a national championship game. He signed a few autographs for fans in the lobby and walked around relatively unbothered in khaki pants, a blue UConn polo shirt, and loafers.

The players strolled around the Galleria; some ate at Taco Bell for lunch. Oriakhi, Coombs-McDaniel, and Lamb talked to Oriakhi's mom, Angela, in the Galleria. A few fans recognized them and asked for pictures and autographs. The whole scene was low key and low pressure.

In the Final Four game against VCU, Butler's Shelvin Mack scored 24 points on eight of 11 shooting from the floor and five for six from three-point range. His offense could sink UConn. At six foot eight, 240 pounds, Matt Howard, Butler's other star, didn't have the strength to score consistently on the inside against UConn's bigger players, who could also make it difficult for Howard, who shot nearly 40 percent from three-point range during the season, to make shots from there.

The first half of the national championship game was fugly—that's the combination of two words. Mack made a three-pointer at the buzzer and Butler took a three-point lead (22–19) into the locker room at halftime.

Calhoun said it was a good thing that CBS's cameras weren't in the locker room. If they were, he speculated, he would have created a video similar to the "Not a dime back" exchange that runs on YouTube. When asked what Calhoun said, Walker said "it was not nice."

Calhoun cursed out his team at halftime. If we're going to lose, that's one thing, he said, but let's not go out like this. We're better than that. We're better than they are. Think about what you're doing, Calhoun told his team.

He did not allow the team to make excuses. The triumvirate—Walker, Lamb, and Oriakhi—sat on the bench at the end of the first half because each had picked up two fouls. No matter. Go out there and win the game. Calhoun was particularly hard on Lamb, who went scoreless in the first half. Get it going, he said.

In the first 2:10 of the second half, Lamb scored five points. Thirty-eight seconds later, he stole the ball and dunked it and then he made a jumper. That spurt put UConn up 33–26.

As the second half progressed, UConn's long players prevented Butler from shooting over them. Mack couldn't see the basket with Lamb's seven foot, four inch, wingspan in the way. Mack made four of 13 shots overall and four for 11 from three-point range. Howard struggled with longer defenders on him as well. He went just one for 13 from the field.

UConn's defenders didn't let Butler near offensive rebounds and they set a national championship game record with 10 blocks.

Butler made two free throws and no field goals from the 19:40 mark of the second half to 12:32 remaining. Its next points came with 6:13 left. After that basket, the 70,000-plus people in attendance gave a Bronx cheer. Butler trailed by 11 and the game was over. UConn won, 53–41.

CBS's Jim Nantz told Jim Calhoun that Butler shot 18 percent from the floor for the game—a record low for an NCAA championship game. That announcement made the coach snap his head, smile, and quake with happiness. That number was a compliment to him and his team. Calhoun said that his team won the game by using two ingredients that made UConn a top program—will and work.

At the rally at Gampel to welcome the national champions, UConn inducted Walker into the Huskies of Honor on the west-end wall of the arena. Walker,

Calhoun celebrates a national championship with his grandchildren and close friend
Tim Tolokan (background). UConn 53–Butler 41. April 4, 2011, Reliant Stadium, Houston,
Texas.

the first men's player to earn this distinction since the inaugural class, trembled when the black drape was pulled off his plaque. He had no idea it was coming. The fans chanted, "One more year." Despite an impending work stoppage in the NBA, Walker's departure was a foregone conclusion. He would graduate on May 8 and his draft stock was as high as it could get. A week after the celebration, Walker announced he would enter the NBA draft. The Charlotte Bobcats drafted Walker with the ninth pick overall.

As soon as UConn won the NCAA tournament, speculation began about Calhoun's future. At 68, Calhoun was the oldest coach to win the Final Four. Phog Allen, who was 66 when Kansas won the 1952 NCAA tournament, held the previous mark. Calhoun was twice as old as Butler coach Brad Stevens and a year older than the combined age of Stevens and VCU coach Shaka Smart.

The coach gave his standard response: I'll wait and see. He hadn't made future plans immediately after the season in the past and he wasn't going to start now. On the court during the celebration in Houston, Pat Calhoun said, "If it is the end, what a beautiful way to finish."

Whenever Calhoun retires, his accomplishments aren't likely to be matched, but will they ever be appreciated?

Best Program Builder of All Time and Best Coach of His Generation

Jim Calhoun is one of the best coaches ever to coach in college basketball. People don't mention him that much when they talk about great coaches. He's done more—taking a program from the Yankee Conference to the top of college basketball—than anybody else has ever done, at any school. If you look at the other great programs, they were great before their coaches got there.

Jim Boeheim

When Rick Pitino took the Kentucky job in 1989, he walked into a tough situation. "Kentucky's Shame," the phrase *Sports Illustrated* used to describe the 17 NCAA violations committed by the program and then coach Eddie Sutton, was now Pitino's mess to clean up. As a result of the scandal, the NCAA banned Kentucky from postseason tournaments for two years, prohibited the team from playing games on television for one season, and cut the number of basketball scholarships to three per season for two years. The NCAA prohibited two players, including Chris Mills, who would go on to star at the University of Arizona and play 10 seasons in the NBA, from playing for Kentucky.

Even under these extreme conditions, Pitino walked into a program loaded with assets that he could use to build a college basketball juggernaut in a few years. Kentucky had won five NCAA Final Fours before Pitino arrived; this number of championships is second to UCLA. It had Rupp Arena, a state-of-the-art basketball facility that hosted the 1985 Final Four. Kentucky had a university president, athletic director, and fan base that craved a return to greatness. Pitino's 'Cats made it to the Elite Eight in 1992, the Final Four the next season, and won the NCAA tournament in 1996.

Roy Williams took over two programs down on their luck. Not long after Williams arrived, the NCAA had placed Kansas on probation for recruiting violations. As part of the sanctions, Kansas could not appear in the NCAA tournament in Williams's first year. By Williams's third season, Kansas played in the national championship game against Duke. After Carolina went 10-22 in the ACC in Matt Doherty's last two seasons as coach, it hired Williams, who won a national championship in his second year back in Chapel Hill.

When Calhoun arrived at UConn, the program had no culture of winning. Its facilities were hardly second to none and compared unfavorably to some high school gyms. The university's administration didn't know how to run a top-flight program. Unlike Pitino and Williams, Calhoun had to create his resources.

The league, the coach, the players, and the support create a national powerhouse. In UConn's case, Calhoun developed these resources and employed them in ways not thought of by others. He turned the University of Connecticut into a basketball paradise. Calhoun used the Big East's media exposure to recruit players; he taught UConn how to operate a big-time college basketball program; he energized the fan base and used the accomplishments of his previous teams and former players to bring talented high school basketball players to Storrs, a location he turned into an asset.

Calhoun Changed College Basketball

Before Calhoun arrived, the Connecticut Huskies lived at the bottom of the Big East. A few years later, the Huskies replaced Georgetown as the Big East's most dominant team. Duke would have six national championships if Calhoun weren't around to outmaneuver Coach K in two Final Fours. During the Calhoun era, the road to the Final Four went through UConn: the Huskies lost in the NCAA tournament to a team that made it to the Final Four on nine different occasions—1990 (Duke), 1991 (Duke), 1994 (Florida), 1995 (UCLA), 1996 (Mississippi State), 1998 (UNC), 2002 (Maryland), 2003 (Texas), and 2006 (George Mason). In 1991, 1995, and 2002, the eventual national champion knocked UConn from the NCAA tournament.

During Calhoun's time as coach at UConn, the Huskies won more national championships than Kansas, Kentucky, Indiana, and UCLA. Only Coach K won more Final Fours than Calhoun since 1987.

Calhoun Changed a State

The UConn men's basketball team launched Huskymania. The 1990 team introduced UConn basketball to the state. In turn, Connecticut became obsessed with UConn basketball. Since the Dream Season of 1990, residents spend their winters watching, cheering for, and stressing about UConn basketball. Over time, some changed their focus from Calhoun's team to Auriemma's, but the point still remains—Calhoun introduced them to UConn basketball.

Calhoun Changed UConn

When Calhoun came to Storrs, the University of Connecticut wasn't highly regarded by the state, the nation, or the Connecticut General Assembly, which is the chief financier of the university. UConn was a safety school, one that students attended for financial reasons or because they wanted to stay near home. It wasn't the preferred choice for many who went there.

State legislators joined the Husky Nation as they watched Calhoun's UConn teams. Once they found the bandwagon, these legislators decided to allocate billions of dollars in upgrades for the university. On the day the State Legislature passed the billon-dollar rebuilding program for the university, Rebecca Lobo may have been the best lobbyist for the school, but Calhoun and his teams made this law a possibility in the first place. They had introduced the state and the nation to UConn.

Calhoun brought public and private dollars to UConn. Around the country, professors tend to complain about the effect of big-time athletics on their institutions. College athletics moves the focus from academics to money, they say. Universities compromise their academic mission when they allow students onto campus who don't belong there and pay millions for sports and not chemistry departments. The president's committee that studied athletics at UConn in 1986 concluded that the university community distrusted and disliked intercollegiate athletics at UConn. Calhoun changed that.

UConn's faculty has seen how Calhoun's team improved their libraries, colleges, departments, facilities, equipment, and salaries. They acknowledge Calhoun's contribution to the university and understand that increased pay and better facilities for them followed the success of the men's and women's teams.

Once the basketball team reached national dominance, more and more students from Connecticut and the rest of the country began to make UConn their top choice. The SAT score and rank of UConn's incoming classes increased after Calhoun's teams won in basketball, and as the state invested in the university.

Calhoun's journey serves as a metaphor for the transformation undertaken by UConn and the basketball program during the coach's tenure. Calhoun started as a blue-collar person and coach. When he achieved success, the money increased, the clothes changed, and the cars improved. The blue-collar person was still there. The blue-collar attitude remained.

UConn changed. Majestic buildings replaced the blue-collar ones that resembled housing projects and military barracks. The university increased in stature and the students who attended were more elite than those from previous generations. Despite these changes, the blue-collar student still attends UConn. Contrary to stereotypes, Connecticut has more than its share of blue-collar towns and cities. Students from Ansonia, Naugatuck, New Britain, Torrington, Waterbury, and Willimantic continue to attend UConn. The working class continues to make up the core and essence of UConn. Calhoun serves as its representative.

Calhoun Is the Best Program Builder of All Time

Calhoun overcame more obstacles than anyone who built a program. Coach K did not build Duke's basketball program. Vic Bubbas did. In 10 seasons at Duke (1960–1969), Bubbas took the Blue Devils to three Final Fours (1963, 1964, and 1966) and one Elite Eight (1960). In six seasons at Duke (1975–1980), Bill Foster took the Blue Devils to the final game in 1978 and the Elite Eight in 1980. The Blue Devils won the ACC championship in 1978 and 1980.

Duke had a tradition of winning long before Coach K arrived. Krzyzewski improved upon what was already there. He took his teams to 11 Final Fours, including five in a row from 1988 to 1992 and seven out of nine from 1986 to 1994. Duke won the national championship in 1991, 1992, 2001, and 2010 (and counting).

Is Coach K a legend? Yes. But did Coach K build Duke's basketball program? No. Coach K took a strong program and made it better.

Branch McCracken coached Indiana University to national championships in 1940 and 1953. The Hoosiers advanced to the Sweet 16 under Coach Lou Watson in 1967, four years before Bobby Knight took over as coach in Bloomington. Indiana basketball was successful before Knight arrived.

Is Bobby Knight a legend? Yes. He won three national championships and his 1976 team went 32–0. But did Bobby Knight build Indiana's basketball program? No.

Frank McGuire coached North Carolina in the first eight years of the ACC. During that time, the Tar Heels captured five conference titles. In the 1956–1957 season, UNC won all 32 games it played and beat Wilt Chamberlain's Kansas Jayhawks in triple-overtime in the NCAA championship game. McGuire resigned in 1961 after the NCAA sanctioned him for "improper recruiting entertainment." The school chancellor picked Dean Smith, a McGuire assistant, to take over the team. From 1961 until 1997, Smith won two national championships and his Tar Heels appeared in 11 Final Fours. He led North Carolina to 17 regular season titles and 13 tournament championships in the ACC. Smith went 879–254 (.776) overall and 364–136 (.728) in the ACC as Carolina's coach.

Is Dean Smith a legend? Yes. But did Dean Smith build North Carolina's basketball program? No.

Denny Crum, who began coaching Louisville in 1971, is in the running for best program builder of all time. He won two national championships at Louisville and took the Cardinals to 15 Sweet 16s and six Final Fours, but Crum also built upon a foundation created by others. The Cardinals played in the 1959 Final Four and advanced to the Sweet 16 in 1961. Wes Unseld led Louisville to the Sweet 16 in 1967 and 1968.

Is Denny Crum a legend? Yes. But did Denny Crum build Louisville's basketball program? No.

Before his reign at Arizona, Robert Luther "Lute" Olson won 65 percent (168-90) of his games as head coach at Iowa. His tenure at Iowa included a trip to the Final Four in 1980. The Arizona Wildcats made the NCAA tournament three times before Olson was hired in 1983. They advanced to the Sweet 16 on two occasions and the Elite Eight once before Olson arrived in Tucson. After an 8-10 season in 1983-1984, Olson's Arizona teams made 23 consecutive appearances in the NCAA tournament. During that stretch, Olson took the Wildcats to four Final Fours and 11 Elite Eights. In 1997, Arizona became the only team to defeat three number-one seeds in a single NCAA tournament. Olson won 598 and lost 188 in his 23 years at Arizona, a 76 percent winning percentage.

For these reasons, Olson is an elite program-builder, but is he better than Calhoun?

The University of Arizona provided advantages to Olson that UConn didn't give to Calhoun. The Big East is a better basketball conference than the PAC-10. Olson had an easier time than Calhoun in moving his team up the conference ladder. Calhoun thought long and hard about how to sell Storrs to recruits. Olson didn't have as difficult a time pitching the beauty of Tucson, Arizona, and the U of A campus to 18-year-olds. Calhoun won two more NCAA tournaments than Olson and he needed to overcome greater obstacles than his Arizona counterpart to build the UConn program.

Rick Pitino says that the three best coaching jobs he has seen in his career are Calipari bringing UMass to national prominence, Calhoun's work at UConn, and Jerry Tarkanian's career at UNLV. Calipari's accomplishments at UMass were legendary. He took that second-rate program to the Final Four in 1996. That achievement has nothing on what Calhoun did at UConn.

The UNLV Runnin' Rebels made their first NCAA tournament in 1975, Jerry Tarkanian's second year in the desert and five years after that program joined Division I. Two years later, it made the first of its four Final Fours. Tarkanian coached the Rebels in each of these Final Fours. In 1990, UNLV annihilated Duke to win the national championship. The next year, its only loss came to Duke in the national semifinal. At UNLV, Tark's teams went 509-105, an 82 percent winning margin. Calhoun won three times as many national titles as Tarkanian and appeared in the same number of Final Fours.

The Best Coach of His Generation

The focus on Calhoun as the best program builder ignores a more important fact about the coach. He has done more with less than any other coach in his generation. He never—ever—had the talent that Dean Smith, Roy Williams, Mike Krzyzewski, or Rick Pitino's Kentucky teams possessed. Not even close. Calhoun has developed his players while other coaches trotted out the best high school talent in the country.

Michael Jordan won Smith's first national title; Christian Laettner won half of Coach K's. Five-star talent helped both of these coaches win championships. Roy Williams's teams were overloaded with the nation's elite high school recruits.

Carolina, Duke, Louisville, Kansas, Kentucky, and Indiana have a national recruiting base, a legacy, and programs and universities geared toward basketball. Calhoun produced all those things for Connecticut; the resources available once he created a tradition at UConn continued to lag behind these elite programs. In 2010, Ray Allen worried that the lack of a basketball practice facility would cost both the men's and women's teams recruits in the future.

Calhoun's legacy also includes his ability to develop unranked players like Hilton Armstrong into lottery picks in the NBA draft. Big-time recruits at other programs have tanked in the pros, but most of Calhoun's players excel in the NBA or, in El-Amin's case, overseas.

Rocky, Rocky, Rocky

The media will write Jim Calhoun's basketball epitaph; it's their job to do so. They will include the national championships, the hundreds of wins, and the development of pro players like Allen, Butler, and Hamilton. Calhoun's behavior, rather than the coach's accomplishments, will no doubt also shape the body of his resume.

The Nate Miles incident, Calhoun's reaction to it, and the resultant penalties from it provide an opportunity for media members and others who have been Calhouned—or know someone who has—to exact revenge on the UConn coach.

The NCAA violations are part of Calhoun's record now, but they don't define him or his program. UConn basketball kept clean for most of the Calhoun era; it wasn't out of control and didn't break every rule to get any recruit. The NCAA infractions shouldn't be the lead on Calhoun's career. Neither should his personality.

So what's the big deal about Jim Calhoun? He's not revered in Connecticut like Geno Auriemma is. Calhoun is not revered in college basketball like coaches who have accomplished far less than he has. Why not?

One longtime writer described the difference between Calhoun and Auriemma in this way: "Geno is hot shit; Jim is Jim." If you polled UConn women's fans, Geno would probably have a 100 percent approval rating—certainly in the 90s. Men's basketball fans (and, of course, many people follow both teams) also probably have a favorable perception of Auriemma. But Calhoun would not have a 100 percent approval rating even among men's basketball fans. Fans of the UConn women's team would rate him even lower. On a bad day, spectators jeer Calhoun at home games. Geno has several advantages over Calhoun. He's won more than twice as many national championships and counting; all of his players graduate; his players stay out of trouble.

Calhoun is guarded and hard to get to know. Geno isn't. Geno drinks wine with his friends during Final Fours in which his team is participating. Calhoun would never do that.

Connecticut basketball fans and residents of the state have been in a 26-year marriage with Jim Calhoun. In that time, they have seen, heard, and read about everything that Calhoun has done on the court and most of the things he has done off it. In a relationship of this length, people get tired of the person to whom they are married. The negative aspects grow more prominent; the positives diminish. This is what has happened to Calhoun in Connecticut. Some people revere him, but others are sick of the yelling, confrontations with the media, snide remarks to reporters, and cold personality.

Calhoun is tough, gruff, and guarded. Those traits don't make one a bad basketball coach. They prevent love from outsiders but his players love him.

Calhoun doesn't have John Wooden's personality, which is no sin. He's grandfatherly to his grandchildren; that's it. Wooden was grandfatherly to everyone. Calhoun isn't playful with the media. Most basketball coaches behave differently in front of a camera than they do behind it. Ask their players.

Calhoun doesn't do anything different from hundreds of coaches in all kinds of sports. Does that make what Calhoun does right? No. It makes it common. If obnoxious behavior and yelling were banned from coaching, the profession would cease to exist.

The players who lived with Calhoun for multiple years appreciated what their coach's style did for them as basketball players and people. The media speculated that Toraino Walker quit the team in December of 1992 because he had enough of Calhoun's verbal abuse. In 1999, Walker, then an inmate at the Hernando Correctional Institution in Brooksville, Florida, told Jeff Jacobs of the *Hartford Courant* that he left UConn in 1992 because he didn't like basketball anymore. He even wrote a letter to his old coach to ask if Calhoun could help him complete his degree.

Aside from rumors that Walker quit because Calhoun wore him out, other former players praise the UConn coach. After UConn won the national championship in 2011, a parade of Calhoun's former players joined the coach on the Reliant Stadium court. They acknowledge how tough he was, but love the personal and professional results. Calhoun's former players speak as highly of him as old UCLA Bruins and Carolina Tar Heels do about John Wooden and Dean Smith.

It's a Cinderella Story

UConn basketball, not Sylvester Stallone, is the real *Rocky*. Its accomplishments in the Yankee Conference mirror Rocky's fight with Spider Rico at the beginning of the first movie. The scene was dark, gruesome, and not all that important to people who weren't there.

In *Rocky*, the hero gets lucky and fights, and nearly beats, world champion Apollo Creed, the stronger, faster, and better fighter. In UConn's version of *Rocky*, the hero gets lucky and makes it into an elite basketball conference, but then the two stories diverge. When UConn takes on its Apollo Creed, it loses, and loses, and loses. The Huskies couldn't even beat Spider Rico for the right to get pummeled by Apollo Creed.

Then Jim Calhoun arrived, and, at first, the knockouts came hard, fast, and often but they subsided. UConn hit back and knocked out many contenders until it beat its Apollo Creed to win three national championships.

So why no *Rocky: The UConn Version?* In *Rocky*, the protagonist is a lovable character. UConn's protagonist . . . not so much.

Jim Calhoun represents the public face of UConn's *Rocky* story. He is responsible for the program's success. Unlike Rocky Balboa, this protagonist isn't lovable. He is brash and self-confident. What kind of Rocky is that? Calhoun has blown his cool at reporters and fans, which is something that Rocky doesn't do. Calhoun provides an earful of curse words to his players, the coaches, the fans, and the referees. Rocky is supposed to be polite.

If a film director looked for the hero of a feel-good story, Calhoun would not arrive on set. He is fiery and, to some, obnoxious. The manner in which

Calhoun treats the media from time to time and his game-day tirades aimed at his players, the referees, and others do not make his story and the amazing accomplishments at UConn a likely subject for a book or reverence.

Calhoun's behavior clouds people's opinion of his work. It shouldn't.

In a perfect world, Calhoun wouldn't tell one of his assistants to shut the fuck up or refer to one of his players as the dumb guy. All things taken together, however, Calhoun's positives far outweigh his negatives.

Because of Jim Calhoun, UConn has a chance to win every game it plays. Calhoun increased the value of a UConn degree — even one earned before he got there. His basketball team gave an identity to the university and it provided a rallying point for alumni, students, and residents of Connecticut. Calhoun changed how people felt about UConn. He also helped many players and coaches make millions of dollars. And he did what once seemed impossible: he made it cool to go to UConn.

During his time in Storrs, Calhoun changed a basketball program, the state, the university, and college basketball. That's the lead. A very select group of coaches can make this claim and Calhoun's name rarely gets mentioned among them.

What Jim Calhoun did at the University of Connecticut is one of the most remarkable feats in modern sports. Soon, all UConn fans will miss him when he's gone. It is doubtful that UConn will dominate in the post-Calhoun era like it did with the Hall of Fame coach in charge. Calhoun made UConn basketball what it is, and, in some senses, what it will be.

The University of Connecticut should build a statue of Calhoun and place it in front of the library. The location would symbolize Calhoun's importance to the university. The plaque should read: "Jim Calhoun: Coach, Teacher, Father," the attributes that Calhoun's players ascribe to him, and not necessarily in that order.

Few appreciate what Calhoun accomplished.

Some of that is his fault. Some of that is the media's fault. Some of it, however, is ours.

2012 and Beyond

May 2012: This time, the Calhoun era had to be over. The NCAA denied the university's appeal of UConn's suspension for failure to meet the requirements of its Academic Progress Report (APR). As a consequence, the Huskies could appear in neither the Big East nor NCAA tournaments in 2013. Before the denial of the appeal, rising senior Alex Oriakhi decided to transfer, and he eventually chose the University of Missouri. After the confirmation of the suspension, rising junior Jeremy Lamb and rising sophomore Andre Drummond announced they would forego their remaining years of eligibility and enter the NBA draft. In early April 2012, Roscoe Smith's father announced that his son would transfer as well.

The suspension, transfers, and early exits weren't the program's only problems. Coach Jim Calhoun, the father of UConn basketball, missed eight games in the 2011–2012 season because of spinal stenosis. During his 40-year coaching career, Calhoun had missed 29 games and left another 11 early. Clearly, the loss of the team's best players and the uncertain future of the coach spelled the end to the Calhoun dynasty.

Right?

Not so fast.

Calhoun faced similar obstacles in the past and overcame them each time. After Calhoun's first season, the Huskies were the worst program in the history of the Big East. The next season, UConn won the NIT. Two seasons later, it captured the Big East's regular- and postseason titles. After the Ray Allen era ended in 1996, critics thought Calhoun could never win the so-called big one. Three seasons after Allen left for the NBA, UConn won the national championship. When it appeared that UConn would never awaken from its championship slumber, Caron Butler led the team to the Big East tournament title and the Elite Eight. In 2007, the year after UConn's disastrous 30–4 season, the Huskies missed the postseason for the first time since Calhoun's first year. Two years later, they made the Final Four.

In many ways, the 2009–2010 and 2011–2012 off-seasons mirror each other. After the 2010 season, basketball writers implored Calhoun to quit and wrote that the program had hit bottom. A major NCAA violation loomed, and Calhoun had missed seven games that season because of an undisclosed medical issue. Other coaches used the NCAA investigation and Calhoun's health issues to lure top recruits away from Storrs. In the 2011 season, the one most people told Calhoun to avoid, UConn captured the program's third national championship.

Yes, the situations are different. UConn does not have a Kemba Walker-like player on its team, unless incoming freshman Omar Calhoun or rising sophomore Ryan Boatright turns into one. And the 2011 team was eligible for postseason play, an advantage not afforded the 2013 squad. One common denominator remains: Calhoun.

Calhoun exemplifies the lyrics to Tom Petty's song "I Won't Back Down." "You can stand me up at the gates of hell, but I won't back down. No I won't back down." As the pages of this book indicate, Calhoun is no quitter, and he has dominated every challenge in his way.

Is this the big one? Perhaps. All signs seem to indicate that the Calhoun era has seen its best days, but these indicators were present two years ago as well. In response to the D-Day predictions about his program, Calhoun said that UConn would be a good team in the Big East in 2013 and he wished the best to those who bolted Storrs.

Throughout this book, I have used the coach's actions and attitudes to develop "Calhoun Rules." Two of those rules apply here: "It's Not Over" and "It's Us Against Them." Calhoun and his program thrived when games, seasons, and even the era appeared to be over. UConn is now back in that position. Calhoun loves to tell his players that everyone except him believes they can't win. UConn is back in that position, too.

Will Calhoun and his Huskies persevere? The past 26 years say yes.

If they don't, *Shock the World* provides a history of the times when they did.

Appendix 1
Standout Games and Players of the Calhoun Era

First Team for the First 25 Seasons of the Calhoun Era (1987–2011)

Emeka Okafor (C)
2001–2004

Ray Allen (G)
1993–1996

Kemba Walker (G)
2008–2011

Donyell Marshall (F)
1991–1994

Rip Hamilton (G)
1997–1999

Second Team for the First 25 Seasons of the Calhoun Era (1987–2011)

Cliff Robinson (F)
1985–1989

Ben Gordon (G)
2001–2004

Khalid El-Amin (G)
1997–2000

Caron Butler (F)
2000–2002

Chris Smith (G)
1988–1992

All–Calhoun Era, Most Underrated Team

John Gwynn
1988–1991

Travis Knight
1992–1996

Jeff Adrien
2005–2009

Donny Marshall
1991–1995

Ricky Moore
1995–1999

All–Calhoun Era, Best Defenders

Lyman DePriest
1987–1991

Ricky Moore
1995–1999

Emeka Okafor
2001–2004

Nadav Henefeld
1989–1990

Taliek Brown
2000–2004

All–Calhoun Era, Best Wins

1. UConn 77–Duke 74
    March 29, 1999
    Finals, NCAA Tournament
    Tropicana Field, St. Petersburg, Florida

2. UConn 79–Duke 78
    April 3, 2004
    National Semifinal
    Alamodome, San Antonio, Texas

All–Calhoun Era, Best Wins *(continued)*

3. UConn 71-Clemson 70
   March 22, 1990
   NCAA East Region Semifinal
   Brendan Byrne Arena, East Rutherford,
      New Jersey

4. UConn 75-Georgetown 74
   March 9, 1996
   Big East Tournament Finals

5. UConn 76-Pitt 74
   March 10, 2011
   Big East Tournament Quarterfinals
   Madison Square Garden

6. UConn 56-Kentucky 55
   April 2, 2011
   National Semifinal
   Reliant Stadium, Houston, Texas

7. UConn 67-Gonzaga 62
   March 20, 1999
   NCAA West Region Final
   America West Arena, Phoenix Arizona

8. UConn 75-Washington 74
   March 19, 1998
   NCAA East Region Semifinal
   Greensboro Coliseum, Greensboro,
      North Carolina

9. UConn 74-Pitt 65 (double-overtime)
   March 9, 2002
   Big East Tournament Finals
   Madison Square Garden

10. UConn 78-Syracuse 75
    March 11, 1990
    Big East Tournament Finals
    Madison Square Garden

All–Calhoun Era, Best Regular Season Wins

1. UConn 70-Georgetown 65
   January 20, 1990
   Hartford Civic Center

2. UConn 86-Syracuse 75
   February 12, 1995
   Gampel Pavilion

3. UConn 70-Pittsburgh 69
   December 12, 1998
   Fitzgerald Field House, Pittsburgh,
   Pennsylvania

4. UConn 70-Stanford 59
   February 6, 1999
   Maples Pavilion, Palo Alto, California

5. UConn 94-BC 91 (double-overtime)
   February 9, 1994
   Conte Forum, Chestnut Hill,
   Massachusetts

6. UConn 82-Texas 81
   January 8, 2011
   Frank Erwin Center, Austin, Texas

7. UConn 100-Arizona 98 (overtime)
   January 26, 2002
   McHale Center, Tucson Arizona

8. UConn 84-Kentucky 67
   November 24, 2010
   Lahaina Civic Center, Lahaina, Maui,
   Hawaii

9. UConn 75-Villanova 74 (overtime)
   February 28, 2004
   First Union Center, Philadelphia,
   Pennsylvania

10. UConn 89-Villanova 75
    February 26, 2006
    Gampel Pavilion

All–Calhoun Era, Most Underrated Wins

1. UConn 56-Seton Hall 54
   February 28, 1987
   Hartford Civic Center

2. UConn 57-Seton Hall 56
   March 4, 1999
   Big East Tournament Quarterfinals
   Madison Square Garden

3. UConn 61-Pitt 58
   March 13, 2004
   Big East Tournament Finals
   Madison Square Garden

4. UConn 79-LSU 62
   March 14, 1991
   First Round, NCAA Tournament
   Hubert H. Humphrey Metrodome,
      Minneapolis, Minnesota

5. UConn 90-Duke 86
   November 29, 1994
   Great Eight
   The Palace of Auburn Hills,
      Auburn Hills, Michigan

6. UConn 78-St. John's 74
   January 30, 1999
   Madison Square Garden

7. UConn 77-N.C. State 74
   March 17, 2002
   Second Round, NCAA Tournament
   Verizon Center, Washington, DC

8. UConn 68-Indiana 63
   January 26, 2008
   Assembly Hall, Bloomington, Indiana

9. UConn 72-VCU 61
   March 25, 1988
   Quarterfinals, NIT
   Storrs, Connecticut

10. UConn 70-Michigan State 67
    November 23, 2010
    Lahaina Civic Center
    Lahaina, Maui, Hawaii

All–Calhoun Era, Worst Defeats

1. Mississippi State 60-UConn 55
   March 22, 1996
   Elite Eight, NCAA Tournament
   Rupp Arena, Lexington, Kentucky

2. Duke 79-UConn 78
   March 24, 1990
   Elite Eight, NCAA Tournament
   Brendan Byrne Arena, East Rutherford,
      New Jersey

3. Florida 69-UConn 60 (overtime)
   March 25, 1994
   Sweet 16, NCAA Tournament
   Miami Arena

4. George Mason 86-UConn 84
   (overtime)
   March 26, 2006
   Elite Eight, NCAA Tournament
   Verizon Center, Washington, DC

Year-to-Year Team Records and Game Results of the Calhoun Era

Year One of the Calhoun Era, 1986–1987

Big East Record: 3–13 | Overall Record: 9–19

Date		Opponent	Result	
November 29, 1986	vs.	Massachusetts	Win	58-54
December 2, 1986	at	Yale	Loss*	75-77
December 4, 1986	vs.	Central Connecticut State	Win	62-52
December 6, 1986	vs.	Purdue	Loss	70-88
December 9, 1986	vs.	Boston University	Loss	71-80
December 11, 1986	vs.	Rhode Island	Win*	96-94
December 13, 1986	vs.	Villanova	Loss	51-66
December 23, 1986	vs.	Fairfield	Win	54-51
December 29, 1986	vs.	Hartford	Loss	48-49
December 30, 1986	vs.	Lehigh	Win	71-57
January 3, 1987	vs.	Syracuse	Loss	71-88
January 6, 1987	at	Seton Hall	Win	77-68
January 14, 1987	at	Providence	Loss	89-103
January 17, 1987	vs.	St. John's	Loss	54-89
January 21, 1987	at	Georgetown	Loss	51-65
January 24, 1987	vs.	Providence	Loss	53-61
January 27, 1987	at	Boston College	Win	66-60
January 31, 1987	at	Pittsburgh	Loss	52-73
February 3, 1987	at	St. Peter's	Loss	50-75
February 5, 1987	vs.	Holy Cross	Win	64-54
February 7, 1987	at	Syracuse	Loss	53-59
February 11, 1987	vs.	Georgetown	Loss	50-78
February 14, 1987	at	Villanova	Loss	57-68
February 18, 1987	at	St. John's	Loss	55-76
February 21, 1987	vs.	Pittsburgh	Loss	66-76
February 26, 1987	vs.	Boston College	Loss	60-66
February 28, 1987	vs.	Seton Hall	Win	56-54
March 5, 1987	vs.	Boston College†	Loss	59-61

*Overtime
†Big East Tournament
Source: Information throughout this appendix comes from Fanbase.com, Uconnhuskies.com, Espn.com, and the author.

UConn Starters and Key Contributors, 1986–1987

No.	Name	Position	Year	Points per game
00*	Cliff Robinson	F	So.	18.1
21*	Steve Pikiell	G	Fr.	8.2
23*	Greg Economou	G	Jr.	3.5
25*	Phil Gamble	G	So.	11.1
31*	Robert Ursery	G	Jr.	3.9
32*	Tate George	G	Fr.	9.9
33	Gerry Besselink	C	Sr.	10.3
40*	Jeff King	F/C	Jr.	11.8

*Denotes starter

Year Two of the Calhoun Era, 1987–1988
Big East Record: 4–12 | Overall Record: 20–14 | NIT Champions

Date		Opponent	Result	
November 28, 1987	vs.	Maryland–Eastern Shore	Win	102–63
December 2, 1987	vs.	Yale	Win	69–59
December 6, 1987	vs.	Virginia	Loss	59–72
December 8, 1987	at	Villanova	Loss	61–63
December 12, 1987	vs.	Morgan State	Win	103–80
December 22, 1987	vs.	Central Connecticut State	Win	99–70
December 28, 1987	at	Hartford	Win	96–94
December 29, 1987	vs.	Princeton	Win	49–46
January 2, 1988	at	Pepperdine	Win	63–60
January 5, 1988	at	Seton Hall	Loss	58–71
January 9, 1988	vs.	Providence	Win	79–72
January 13, 1988	at	Pittsburgh	Loss	58–61
January 16, 1988	at	Syracuse	Win	51–50
January 20, 1988	vs.	Villanova	Loss	58–69
January 23, 1988	at	St. John's	Loss*	72–79
January 30, 1988	at	Georgetown	Loss	59–60
February 2, 1988	vs.	Seton Hall	Loss	59–61
February 4, 1988	at	Holy Cross	Win	82–81
February 6, 1988	vs.	Georgetown	Win	66–59
February 8, 1988	at	Providence	Loss	79–85
February 15, 1988	vs.	Boston College	Win	53–49
February 18, 1988	at	Fairfield	Win	74–48
February 20, 1988	vs.	Syracuse	Loss	71–73
February 23, 1988	at	Boston College	Loss	56–64
February 27, 1988	vs.	Pittsburgh	Loss	69–74
February 29, 1988	vs.	St. John's	Loss	62–77
March 5, 1988	vs.	Brooklyn	Win	90–51

Year Two of the Calhoun Era, 1987–1988 *(continued)*

March 10, 1988	vs.	Providence†	Win	75-62
March 11, 1988	vs.	Pittsburgh†	Loss	58-75
March 17, 1988	at	West Virginia△	Win*	62-57
March 21, 1988	vs.	Louisiana Tech△	Win	65-59
March 25, 1988	vs.	VCU‡	Win	72-61
March 29, 1988	vs.	Boston College△∞	Win	73-67
March 30, 1988	vs.	Ohio State△∞	Win	72-67

*Overtime   ∞Madison Square Garden
†Big East Tournament
△NIT

UConn Starters and Key Contributors, 1987–1988

No.	Name	Position	Year	Points per game
00*	Cliff Robinson	F	Jr.	17.6
20*	Murray Williams	F	Fr.	5.0
21	Steve Pikiell	G	So.	2.5
22	Greg Economou	G	Sr.	3.1
23*	Lyman DePriest	F	Fr.	3.9
25*	Phil Gamble	G	Jr.	15.0
31	Robert Ursery	G	Sr.	3.2
32*	Tate George	G	So.	10.0
33	Willie McCloud	F	Jr.	5.1
40	Jeff King	F/C	Sr.	6.1

Year Three of the Calhoun Era, 1988–1989
Big East Record: 6–10 | Overall Record: 18–13 | NIT Quarterfinals

Date		Opponent	Result	
November 26, 1988	vs.	Hartford	Win	67-55
November 30, 1988	at	Yale	Win	75-44
December 5, 1988	vs.	Marist	Win	93-71
December 8, 1988	at	Purdue	Loss	73-88
December 10, 1988	at	Virginia	Win	68-61
December 13, 1988	vs.	Fairfield	Win	71-48
December 23, 1988	vs.	Pepperdine	Win	76-70
December 28, 1988	vs.	Harvard	Win	84-43
December 29, 1988	vs.	Air Force	Win	68-55
January 4, 1989	vs.	Villanova	Win	57-55
January 7, 1989	vs.	Providence	Loss	78-80
January 10, 1989	at	St. John's	Loss	63-71
January 14, 1989	at	Seton Hall	Loss	62-76
January 16, 1989	vs.	Syracuse	Win	68-62

January 21, 1989	at	Georgetown	Loss	55-59
January 28, 1989	vs.	St. John's	Win	80-52
January 30, 1989	vs.	Massachusetts	Win	104-75
February 4, 1989	at	Providence	Loss	61-65
February 8, 1989	vs.	Georgetown	Loss	58-70
February 11, 1989	vs.	Boston College	Win	86-49
February 15, 1989	vs.	Seton Hall	Loss	69-72
February 18, 1989	at	Villanova	Loss*	67-76
February 22, 1989	at	Boston College	Win	77-75
February 25, 1989	vs.	Pittsburgh	Win	64-62
February 28, 1989	at	Syracuse	Loss	72-88
March 4, 1989	at	Pittsburgh	Loss	80-88
March 6, 1989	vs.	Central Connecticut State	Win	94-55
March 10, 1989	vs.	Seton Hall[†]	Loss	66-74
March 15, 1989	at	UNC Charlotte[Δ]	Win	67-62
March 20, 1989	vs.	California[Δ]	Win	73-72
March 22, 1989	at	UAB[Δ]	Loss	79-85

*Overtime
[†]Big East Tournament
[Δ]NIT

UConn Starters and Key Contributors, 1988–1989

No.	Name	Position	Year	Points per game
00*	Cliff Robinson	F	Jr.	20.0
13*	Chris Smith	G	Fr.	9.9
15	John Gwynn	G	So.	5.6
20*	Murray Williams	F	So.	6.1
22	Rod Sellers	C	Fr.	3.8
23*	Lyman DePriest	F	So.	2.3
25*	Phil Gamble	G	Sr.	12.5
32	Tate George	G	Jr.	7.3
33	Willie McCloud	F	Sr.	4.6
55	Dan Cyrulik	C	Fr.	2.5

Year Four of the Calhoun Era, 1989–1990

Big East Record: 12–4 | Overall Record: 31–6 | NCAA Elite Eight

Date		Opponent	Result	
November 24, 1989	vs.	Texas A&M[◊]	Loss	81-92
November 25, 1989	vs.	Auburn[◊]	Win	95-91
November 26, 1989	vs.	Florida State[◊]	Win	63-60
November 30, 1989	vs.	Yale	Win	76-50
December 2, 1989	vs.	Howard	Win	78-59

Year Four of the Calhoun Era, 1989–1990 *(continued)*

December 4, 1989	vs.	Maryland	Win	87-65
December 7, 1989	vs.	Hartford	Win	79-54
December 9, 1989	vs.	Maine	Win	95-55
December 12, 1989	vs.	Villanova	Loss	57-64
December 29, 1989	vs.	St. Joseph's (Pa.)	Win	83-58
December 30, 1989	vs.	Mississippi State	Win	84-68
January 2, 1990	at	St. John's	Loss	62-93
January 6, 1990	vs.	Pittsburgh	Win	79-61
January 9, 1990	at	Villanova	Win	71-54
January 13, 1990	at	Seton Hall	Win	79-76
January 15, 1990	vs.	Syracuse	Win	70-59
January 20, 1990	vs.	Georgetown	Win	70-65
January 25, 1990	vs.	Central Connecticut State	Win	99-77
January 27, 1990	vs.	St. John's	Win	72-58
January 30, 1990	at	Massachusetts	Win	94-75
February 3, 1990	at	Providence	Win	92-77
February 6, 1990	vs.	Fairfield	Win	74-39
February 10, 1990	at	Syracuse	Loss	86-90
February 13, 1990	at	Pittsburgh	Win	80-77
February 17, 1990	vs.	Boston College	Win	89-67
February 19, 1990	vs.	Providence	Win*	75-72
February 24, 1990	vs.	Seton Hall	Win	79-57
February 28, 1990	at	Georgetown	Loss	64-84
March 3, 1990	at	Boston College	Win	95-74
March 9, 1990	vs.	Seton Hall[†]	Win	76-58
March 10, 1990	vs.	Georgetown[†]	Win	65-60
March 11, 1990	vs.	Syracuse[†]	Win	78-75
March 15, 1990	vs.	Boston University[†]	Win	76-52
March 17, 1990	vs.	California[‡]	Win	74-54
March 22, 1990	vs.	Clemson[‡]	Win	71-70
March 24, 1990	vs.	Duke[‡]	Loss*	78-79

[◊]Great Alaska Shootout
[†]Big East Tournament
[‡]NCAA Tournament

UConn Starters and Key Contributors, 1989–1990

No.	Name	Position	Year	Points per game
13*	Chris Smith	G	So.	17.2
15	John Gwynn	G	Jr.	10.6
20	Murray Williams	F	Jr.	3.3
22*	Rod Sellers	C	So.	8.2
23	Lyman DePriest	F	Jr.	3.2

24*	Scott Burrell	F	Fr.	8.2
32*	Tate George	G	Sr.	11.5
40*	Nadav Henefeld	G	Fr.	11.6
42	Toraino Walker	F	Fr.	2.7
55	Dan Cyrulik	C	So.	3.8

Year Five of the Calhoun Era, 1990–1991

Big East Record: 20–11 | Overall Record: 9–7 | NCAA Sweet 16

Date		Opponent	Result	
November 23, 1990	vs.	College of Charleston	Win	68–52
November 27, 1990	vs.	Hartford	Win	90–63
November 29, 1990	at	Yale	Win	49–48
December 6, 1990	at	North Carolina	Loss	64–79
December 9, 1990	at	Maine	Win	85–60
December 12, 1990	vs.	New Hampshire	Win	85–32
December 23, 1990	vs.	Fairfield	Win	94–70
December 28, 1990	vs.	Lafayette	Win	59–57
December 29, 1990	vs.	Rhode Island	Win	90–69
January 2, 1991	at	Boston College	Win	96–70
January 5, 1991	vs.	Pittsburgh	Win	81–76
January 8, 1991	at	Villanova	Win	74–71
January 10, 1991	vs.	Central Connecticut State	Win	115–47
January 12, 1991	vs.	St. John's	Loss	59–72
January 16, 1991	at	Syracuse	Loss*	79–81
January 19, 1991	vs.	Providence	Loss	102–108
January 22, 1991	at	St. John's	Loss	62–65
January 26, 1991	at	Seton Hall	Loss	62–76
January 28, 1991	vs.	Syracuse	Loss	66–68
February 2, 1991	vs.	Villanova	Win	67–59
February 5, 1991	vs.	Boston College	Win	76–59
February 11, 1991	vs.	Georgetown	Win	61–55
February 16, 1991	vs.	N.C. State	Loss	59–60
February 19, 1991	at	Providence	Win*	70–66
February 23, 1991	at	Georgetown	Loss	57–71
February 27, 1991	vs.	Seton Hall	Win*	62–60
March 2, 1991	at	Pittsburgh	Win	78–68
March 7, 1991	vs.	Georgetown†	Loss	49–68
March 14, 1991	vs.	LSU‡	Win	79–62
March 16, 1991	vs.	Xavier‡	Win	66–50
March 22, 1991	vs.	Duke‡	Loss	67–81

*Overtime
†Big East Tournament
‡NCAA Tournament

UConn Starters and Key Contributors, 1990–1991

No.	Name	Position	Year	Points per game
13*	Chris Smith	G	Jr.	18.9
15	John Gwynn	G	Sr.	12.5
20	Murray Williams	F	Sr.	4.5
21*	Steve Pikiell	G	Sr.	2.9
22*	Rod Sellers	C	Jr.	11.7
23	Lyman DePriest	F	Sr.	2.7
24*	Scott Burrell	F	So.	12.7
42*	Toraino Walker	F	So.	5.1
55	Dan Cyrulik	C	Jr.	3.0

Year Six of the Calhoun Era, 1991–1992

Big East Record: 10–8 | Overall Record: 20–10 | NCAA Second Round

Date		Opponent	Result	
November 22, 1991	vs.	Hartford	Win	76–46
November 29, 1991	vs.	Yale	Win	79–55
December 2, 1991	vs.	Wake Forest	Win	84–75
December 7, 1991	vs.	Maine	Win	85–71
December 14, 1991	at	Texas	Win	94–77
December 23, 1991	vs.	Fairfield	Win	89–59
December 27, 1991	vs.	Central Connecticut State	Win	112–58
December 28, 1991	vs.	Furman	Win	87–68
January 2, 1992	vs.	Miami	Win	85–62
January 4, 1992	at	Illinois	Win	70–66
January 7, 1992	vs.	St. John's	Win	85–76
January 11, 1992	at	Villanova	Loss	70–79
January 14, 1992	vs.	Pittsburgh	Win	87–77
January 18, 1992	at	Miami	Win	77–58
January 22, 1992	at	Providence	Win*	97–86
January 25, 1992	vs.	Boston College	Win*	83–77
January 27, 1992	vs.	Villanova	Win	72–58
February 1, 1992	at	St. John's	Loss	57–90
February 3, 1992	at	Syracuse	Loss	83–84
February 8, 1992	vs.	Seton Hall	Loss	69–81
February 12, 1992	vs.	Georgetown	Loss	63–70
February 19, 1992	at	Georgetown	Loss	58–60
February 22, 1992	vs.	Providence	Win	94–73
February 25, 1992	at	Pittsburgh	Loss	77–86
March 1, 1992	at	Seton Hall	Loss	64–77
March 4, 1992	vs.	Syracuse	Win	85–78
March 7, 1992	at	Boston College	Win	89–79

March 13, 1992	at	St. John's[†]	Loss*	59–64
March 19, 1992	vs.	Nebraska[‡]	Win	86–65
March 21, 1992	vs.	Ohio State[‡]	Loss	55–78

*Overtime
[†]Big East Tournament
[‡]NCAA Tournament

UConn Starters and Key Contributors, 1991–1992

No.	Name	Position	Year	Points per game
12	Kevin Ollie	G	Fr.	2.1
13*	Chris Smith	G	Sr.	21.2
21*	Toraino Walker	F	Jr.	6.7
22*	Rod Sellers	C	Sr.	12.3
24*	Scott Burrell	F	Jr.	16.3
34	Brian Fair	G	Fr.	6.3
42*	Donyell Marshall	F	Fr.	11.1
55	Dan Cyrulik	C	Sr.	1.5

Year Seven of the Calhoun Era, 1992–1993
Big East Record: 9–9 | Overall Record: 15–13 | NIT First Round

Date		Opponent	Result	
November 28, 1992	vs.	Purdue◇	Loss	69–73
December 5, 1992	at	N.C. State	Win	81–74
December 8, 1992	vs.	St. John's	Win*	74–72
December 10, 1992	vs.	Yale	Win	65–38
December 22, 1992	vs.	Fairfield	Win	90–66
December 28, 1992	vs.	Hartford	Win	91–66
December 29, 1992	vs.	Towson	Win	99–66
January 4, 1993	at	Seton Hall	Loss	69–72
January 9, 1993	at	Villanova	Win	87–80
January 12, 1993	vs.	Pittsburgh	Loss	78–80
January 16, 1993	at	Boston College	Win	66–64
January 18, 1993	vs.	Georgetown	Loss	69–86
January 23, 1993	vs.	Providence	Win	68–61
January 26, 1993	at	Miami	Loss	65–80
January 30, 1993	at	St. John's	Loss	59–72
February 2, 1993	vs.	Syracuse	Loss	57–60
February 6, 1993	vs.	Florida State	Loss	74–86
February 9, 1993	vs.	Villanova	Win	82–62
February 13, 1993	vs.	Miami	Win	88–72
February 15, 1993	at	Syracuse	Win	80–76
February 20, 1993	at	Pittsburgh	Win	81–80

Year Seven of the Calhoun Era, 1992–1993 *(continued)*

February 22, 1993	vs.	Maine	Win	108-72
February 24, 1993	vs.	Boston College	Win	69-64
February 27, 1993	vs.	Seton Hall	Loss	74-82
March 2, 1993	at	Providence	Loss	71-74
March 7, 1993	at	Georgetown	Loss	56-70
March 12, 1993	vs.	Providence†	Loss	55-73
March 19, 1993	vs.	Jackson State△	Loss*	88-90

◇Springfield, Massachusetts   △NIT
†Big East Tournament

UConn Starters and Key Contributors, 1992–1993

No.	Name	Position	Year	Points per game
12*	Kevin Ollie	G	So.	7.9
23*	Rudy Johnson	F	Fr.	2.7
24*	Scott Burrell	F	Sr.	16.1
31	Brian Fair	G	So.	13.7
33*	Donny Marshall	F	So.	7.8
40	Travis Knight	C	Fr.	2.9
42*	Donyell Marshall	F	So.	17.0
45	Eric Hayward	C	Fr.	3.7

Year Eight of the Calhoun Era, 1993–1994
Big East Record: 16–2 | Overall Record: 29–5 | NCAA Sweet 16

Date		Opponent	Result	
November 27, 1993	vs.	Towson△	Win	107-67
November 29, 1993	at	Virginia	Win	77-36
December 1, 1993	vs.	Yale	Win	81-64
December 8, 1993	at	Seton Hall	Win	82-66
December 11, 1993	vs.	Central Connecticut State	Win	117-63
December 15, 1993	vs.	Texas	Win	96-86
December 23, 1993	vs.	Fairfield	Win	75-57
December 28, 1993	vs.	Texas-Arlington◇	Win	112-72
December 29, 1993	vs.	Ohio◇	Loss	76-85
December 30, 1993	vs.	Tennessee Tech◇	Win	130-78
January 2, 1994	vs.	Winthrop	Win	113-59
January 4, 1994	vs.	Georgetown	Win	77-65
January 8, 1994	vs.	Boston College	Win	77-71
January 10, 1994	vs.	Syracuse	Win	75-67
January 15, 1994	at	St. John's	Win	85-81
January 17, 1994	vs.	Hartford	Win	88-62
January 19, 1994	at	Providence	Win	79-78

January 25, 1994	vs.	Villanova	Win	91-67
January 29, 1994	at	Pittsburgh	Win	88-67
February 1, 1994	at	Syracuse	Loss	95-108
February 5, 1994	vs.	Miami	Win	73-57
February 9, 1994	at	Boston College	Win**	94-91
February 12, 1994	vs.	Seton Hall	Win	80-68
February 15, 1994	at	Villanova	Loss	63-64
February 19, 1994	vs.	Providence	Win	81-73
February 22, 1994	at	Miami	Win	74-49
February 26, 1994	vs.	Pittsburgh	Win	78-66
February 28, 1994	at	Georgetown	Win	66-62
March 5, 1994	vs.	St. John's	Win	95-80
March 11, 1994	vs.	St. John's	Win	97-77
March 12, 1994	vs.	Providence[†]	Loss	67-69
March 17, 1994	vs.	Rider[‡]	Win	64-46
March 19, 1994	vs.	George Washington[‡]	Win	75-63
March 25, 1994	vs.	Florida[‡]	Loss*	60-69

*Overtime **Double-Overtime   [†]Big East Tournament
[△]Hershey, Pennsylvania   [‡]NCAA Tournament
[◇]Hilo, Hawaii

UConn Starters and Key Contributors, 1993–1994

No.	Name	Position	Year	Points per game
11*	Doron Sheffer	G	So.	11.9
12*	Kevin Ollie	G	Jr.	6.4
23	Rudy Johnson	F	So.	1.3
31	Brian Fair	G	Jr.	7.1
33*	Donny Marshall	F	Jr.	12.4
34	Ray Allen	G	Fr.	12.6
40	Travis Knight	C	So.	2.5
42*	Donyell Marshall	F	Jr.	25.1
45*	Eric Hayward	C	So.	3.4

Year Nine of the Calhoun Era, 1994–1995
Big East Record: 16–2 | Overall Record: 28–5 | NCAA Elite Eight

Date		Opponent	Result	
November 25, 1994	vs.	Lafayette	Win	110-48
November 29, 1994	vs.	Duke[◇]	Win	90-86
December 2, 1994	vs.	Yale	Win	105-53
December 6, 1994	at	Boston College	Win	74-70
December 23, 1994	vs.	Fairfield	Win	85-68
December 27, 1994	vs.	Illinois	Win	71-56
December 30, 1994	vs.	Northeastern	Win	88-70

Year Nine of the Calhoun Era, 1994–1995 *(continued)*

January 3, 1995	at	Villanova	Win	77-62
January 5, 1995	vs.	Hartford	Win	102-77
January 8, 1995	vs.	St. John's	Win	98-78
January 11, 1995	at	Pittsburgh	Win	85-76
January 14, 1995	vs.	Providence	Win	70-62
January 16, 1995	vs.	Georgetown	Win	93-73
January 21, 1995	at	Seton Hall	Win	86-81
January 23, 1995	vs.	Syracuse	Win	86-75
January 28, 1995	at	Kansas	Loss	59-88
January 31, 1995	vs.	Miami	Win	82-57
February 4, 1995	at	St. John's	Win	99-82
February 6, 1995	vs.	Pittsburgh	Win	90-61
February 12, 1995	at	Syracuse	Win	77-70
February 14, 1995	at	Georgetown	Win	91-85
February 18, 1995	vs.	Villanova	Loss	73-96
February 21, 1995	vs.	Boston College	Win	88-75
February 25, 1995	vs.	Seton Hall	Win	75-61
February 27, 1995	at	Providence	Loss	70-72
March 4, 1995	at	Miami	Win	75-67
March 10, 1995	vs.	Pittsburgh[†]	Win	81-78
March 11, 1995	vs.	Georgetown[†]	Win	88-81
March 12, 1995	vs.	Villanova[†]	Loss	78-94
March 16, 1995	vs.	Chattanooga[‡]	Win	100-71
March 18, 1995	vs.	Cincinnati[‡]	Win	96-91
March 23, 1995	vs.	Maryland[‡]	Win	99-89
March 25, 1995	vs.	UCLA[‡]	Loss	96-102

[◊]Great Eight, Auburn Hills, Michigan
[†]Big East Tournament
[‡]NCAA Tournament

UConn Starters and Key Contributors, 1994–1995

No.	Name	Position	Year	Points per game
11*	Doron Sheffer	G	Jr.	11.1
12*	Kevin Ollie	G	Sr.	9.8
23	Rudy Johnson	F	Jr.	2.6
31	Brian Fair	G	Sr.	9.6
32	Kirk King	F	So.	3.2
33*	Donny Marshall	F	Sr.	15.8
34*	Ray Allen	G	So.	21.1
40*	Travis Knight	C	Jr.	9.1
45	Eric Hayward	C	Jr.	3.0

Year 10 of the Calhoun Era, 1995–1996
Big East Record: 17–1 | Overall Record: 33–3 | NCAA Sweet 16

Date		Opponent	Result	
November 22, 1995	vs.	Texas Christian◇	Win	102–76
November 24, 1995	vs.	Iowa◇	Loss*	95–101
November 25, 1995	vs.	Indiana◇	Win	86–52
November 29, 1995	vs.	Northeastern	Win	86–39
December 3, 1995	vs.	Boston College	Win	63–62
December 6, 1995	at	Notre Dame	Win	85–65
December 8, 1995	vs.	Yale	Win	93–66
December 12, 1995	at	Florida State	Win	79–61
December 23, 1995	vs.	Fairfield	Win	86–52
December 27, 1995	at	College of Charleston	Win	77–60
December 30, 1995	vs.	Hartford	Win	102–63
January 3, 1996	at	West Virginia	Win	89–79
January 6, 1996	vs.	Miami	Win	73–52
January 9, 1996	vs.	Villanova	Win	81–73
January 13, 1996	at	Providence	Win	83–74
January 17, 1996	vs.	St. John's	Win	88–73
January 21, 1996	vs.	Syracuse	Win	79–70
January 23, 1996	vs.	Central Connecticut State	Win	116–46
January 25, 1996	at	Pittsburgh	Win	69–63
January 28, 1996	vs.	Virginia	Win	76–46
January 31, 1996	at	Rutgers	Win	77–59
February 3, 1996	at	St. John's	Win	77–63
February 6, 1996	vs.	Providence	Win	99–77
February 14, 1996	vs.	West Virginia	Win	87–69
February 17, 1996	vs.	Notre Dame	Win	85–65
February 19, 1996	at	Georgetown	Loss	65–77
February 25, 1996	at	Villanova	Win	70–59
February 28, 1996	vs.	Rutgers	Win	78–66
March 2, 1996	at	Seton Hall	Win	87–58
March 7, 1996	vs.	Seton Hall†	Win	79–58
March 8, 1996	vs.	Syracuse†	Win	85–67
March 9, 1996	vs.	Georgetown†	Win	75–74
March 14, 1996	vs.	Colgate‡	Win	68–59
March 16, 1996	vs.	Eastern Michigan‡	Win	95–81
March 22, 1996	vs.	Mississippi State‡	Loss	55–60

*Overtime
◇Great Alaska Shootout
†Big East Tournament
‡NCAA Tournament

UConn Starters and Key Contributors, 1995–1996

No.	Name	Position	Year	Points per game
3	Rashamel Jones	G	Fr.	5.6
11*	Doron Sheffer	G	Sr.	16.0
13*	Kirk King	F	Jr.	9.9
21	Ricky Moore	G	Fr.	4.7
23*	Rudy Johnson	F	Sr.	7.5
34*	Ray Allen	G	Jr.	23.4
40*	Travis Knight	C	Sr.	9.1
45	Eric Hayward	C	Sr.	3.3

Year 11 of the Calhoun Era, 1996–1997

Big East Record: 7–11 | Overall Record: 18–15 | NIT Third Place

Date		Opponent	Result	
November 15, 1996	at	Indiana◊	Loss	61–68
November 25, 1996	vs.	Northeastern	Win	89–37
November 29, 1996	vs.	Yale	Win	72–39
December 2, 1996	vs.	Texas State	Win	66–49
December 4, 1996	at	Pittsburgh	Loss	49–56
December 7, 1996	vs.	Boston College	Win	61–54
December 21, 1996	vs.	Fairfield	Win	68–58
December 23, 1996	vs.	Virginia	Win	64–61
December 27, 1996	vs.	Massachusetts	Win	64–61
December 29, 1996	vs.	Hartford	Win	104–62
January 2, 1997	at	Rutgers	Win	66–57
January 4, 1997	vs.	West Virginia	Win	79–62
January 8, 1997	vs.	St. John's	Loss*	67–71
January 11, 1997	at	Georgetown	Win	69–54
January 19, 1997	vs.	Kansas	Loss	65–73
January 22, 1997	at	Miami	Loss	46–69
January 26, 1997	vs.	Syracuse	Loss	53–65
January 29, 1997	vs.	Providence	Loss	47–62
February 1, 1997	at	Seton Hall	Win	62–55
February 3, 1997	vs.	Georgetown	Loss	51–52
February 8, 1997	at	Notre Dame	Loss*	65–71
February 12, 1997	at	Boston College	Win	61–56
February 15, 1997	vs.	Miami	Win	72–52
February 17, 1997	at	Syracuse	Loss*	66–71
February 23, 1997	at	Villanova	Loss	58–65
February 25, 1997	vs.	Pittsburgh	Loss	74–77
March 1, 1997	vs.	Seton Hall	Loss	60–73
March 5, 1997	vs.	Pittsburgh†	Loss	62–63

Date		Opponent		Result	
March 12, 1997	vs.	Iona△		Win	71-66
March 18, 1997	vs.	Bradley△		Win	63-47
March 21, 1997	vs.	Nebraska△		Win	76-67
March 25, 1997	vs.	Florida State△∞		Loss*	65-71
March 27, 1997	vs.	Arkansas△∞		Win	74-64

*Overtime △NIT
◇Indianapolis, Indiana ∞Madison Square Garden
†Big East Tournament

UConn Starters and Key Contributors, 1996–1997

No.	Name	Position	Year	Points per game
3*	Rashamel Jones	G	So.	13.0
13*	Kirk King	F	Sr.	11.8
15*	Kevin Freeman	F	Fr.	8.5
21*	Ricky Moore	G	So.	9.0
32*	Richard Hamilton	G	Fr.	15.9
43*	Jake Voskuhl	C	Fr.	4.0

Year 12 of the Calhoun Era, 1997–1998

Big East Record: 15–3 | Overall Record: 32–5 | NCAA Elite Eight

Date		Opponent	Result	
November 15, 1997	vs.	Yale	Win	88-57
November 17, 1997	vs.	Boston University△	Win	68-54
November 19, 1997	vs.	Rhode Island△	Win	80-67
November 24, 1997	vs.	Coppin State	Win	72-50
November 26, 1997	at	Florida State△∞	Loss	60-67
November 28, 1997	vs.	Arizona State△∞	Win	82-61
December 3, 1997	vs.	West Virginia	Win	88-75
December 7, 1997	at	Rutgers	Win	59-44
December 10, 1997	at	Virginia	Win	74-63
December 20, 1997	vs.	UNC-Wilmington	Win	93-55
December 23, 1997	vs.	Massachusetts	Win	72-55
December 28, 1997	vs.	Hartford	Win	100-69
December 30, 1997	vs.	Fairfield	Win	90-63
January 3, 1998	vs.	Notre Dame	Win	84-58
January 6, 1998	at	Miami	Loss	67-76
January 11, 1998	at	Boston College	Win	80-68
January 13, 1998	vs.	Seton Hall	Win	80-59
January 17, 1998	vs.	Georgetown	Win	86-72
January 19, 1998	at	St. John's	Loss	62-64
January 24, 1998	at	Syracuse	Win	63-54
January 27, 1998	at	Providence	Win	63-56

Year 12 of the Calhoun Era, 1997–1998 *(continued)*

January 31, 1998	vs.	Rutgers	Win	73–56
February 2, 1998	vs.	Villanova	Win	80–65
February 7, 1998	vs.	Stanford	Win	76–56
February 11, 1998	at	West Virginia	Loss	62–80
February 14, 1998	vs.	Pittsburgh	Win	92–67
February 17, 1998	at	Notre Dame	Win	88–79
February 21, 1998	at	Villanova	Win	83–76
February 23, 1998	vs.	Providence	Win	77–68
February 28, 1998	vs.	St. John's	Win	87–58
March 5, 1998	vs.	Providence[†]	Win	64–55
March 6, 1998	vs.	Rutgers[†]	Win	64–50
March 7, 1998	vs.	Syracuse[†]	Win	69–64
March 12, 1998	vs.	Fairleigh Dickinson[‡]	Win	93–85
March 14, 1998	vs.	Indiana[‡]	Win	78–68
March 19, 1998	vs.	Washington[‡]	Win	75–74
March 21, 1998	vs.	North Carolina[‡]	Loss	64–75

[△]Preseason NIT   [∞]Madison Square Garden
[†]Big East Tournament
[‡]NCAA Tournament

UConn Starters and Key Contributors, 1997–1998

No.	Name	Position	Year	Points per game
3	Rashamel Jones	G	Jr.	4.4
15*	Kevin Freeman	F	So.	10.3
21*	Ricky Moore	G	Jr.	7.5
32*	Richard Hamilton	G	So.	21.5
34	Souleymane Wane	C	Fr.	1.9
42*	Khalid El-Amin	G	Fr.	16.0
43*	Jake Voskuhl	C	So.	6.9

Year 13 of the Calhoun Era, 1998–1999

Big East Record: 16–2 | Overall Record: 34–2 | NCAA Champions

Date		Opponent	Result	
November 15, 1998	vs.	Quinnipiac	Win	102–60
November 19, 1998	vs.	Richmond	Win	77–57
November 24, 1998	vs.	Hartford	Win	95–58
November 27, 1998	vs.	Wagner	Win	111–46
December 1, 1998	vs.	Washington[◇]	Win	69–48
December 5, 1998	vs.	Michigan State	Win	82–68
December 9, 1998	at	Massachusetts	Win	59–54
December 12, 1998	at	Pittsburgh	Win	70–69

December 23, 1998	vs.	Fairfield	Win	102–67
December 30, 1998	vs.	Villanova	Win	100–76
January 2, 1999	vs.	Georgetown	Win	87–64
January 6, 1999	at	Boston College	Win	91–78
January 9, 1999	at	West Virginia	Win	80–45
January 12, 1999	vs.	Notre Dame	Win	101–70
January 16, 1999	vs.	Pittsburgh	Win	81–58
January 20, 1999	at	Miami	Win	70–68
January 23, 1999	vs.	Seton Hall	Win	62–47
January 25, 1999	at	Georgetown	Win	78–71
January 30, 1999	at	St. John's	Win	78–74
February 1, 1999	vs.	Syracuse	Loss	42–59
February 6, 1999	at	Stanford	Win	70–59
February 10, 1999	vs.	Boston College	Win	66–50
February 13, 1999	at	Seton Hall	Win	53–48
February 16, 1999	vs.	Rutgers	Win	77–64
February 20, 1999	vs.	Miami	Loss	71–73
February 22, 1999	at	Providence	Win	72–65
February 28, 1999	at	Syracuse	Win	70–58
March 4, 1999	vs.	Seton Hall[†]	Win	57–56
March 5, 1999	vs.	Syracuse[†]	Win	71–50
March 6, 1999	vs.	St. John's[†]	Win	82–63
March 11, 1999	vs.	Texas–San Antonio[‡]	Win	91–66
March 13, 1999	vs.	New Mexico[‡]	Win	78–56
March 18, 1999	vs.	Iowa[‡]	Win	78–68
March 20, 1999	vs.	Gonzaga[‡]	Win	67–62
March 27, 1999	vs.	Ohio State[‡]	Win	64–58
March 29, 1999	vs.	Duke[‡]	Win	77–74

[◇]Great Eight, Chicago
[†]Big East Tournament
[‡]NCAA Tournament

UConn Starters and Key Contributors, 1998–1999

No.	Name	Position	Year	Points per game
3	Rashamel Jones	G	Sr.	3.5
15*	Kevin Freeman	F	Jr.	12.2
21*	Ricky Moore	G	Sr.	6.8
23	Albert Mouring	G	So.	7.1
32*	Richard Hamilton	G	Jr.	21.5
34	Souleymane Wane	C	So.	2.0
42*	Khalid El-Amin	G	So.	13.8
43*	Jake Voskuhl	C	Jr.	5.5
51	Edmund Saunders	F	So.	6.0

Year 14 of the Calhoun Era, 1999–2000
Big East Record: 10–6 | Overall Record: 25–10 | NCAA Second Round

Date		Opponent	Result	
November 11, 1999	vs.	Iowa$^\infty$	Loss	68–70
November 12, 1999	vs.	Duke$^\infty$	Win	71–66
November 19, 1999	vs.	Vermont	Win	89–52
November 22, 1999	vs.	Massachusetts	Win	79–65
November 29, 1999	vs.	Coppin State	Win	89–44
December 4, 1999	vs.	UNC-Asheville	Win	98–68
December 7, 1999	vs.	Arizona$^\diamond$	Win	78–69
December 12, 1999	vs.	Fordham	Win	94–75
December 23, 1999	vs.	Fairfield	Win	84–60
December 30, 1999	at	Houston	Win	82–76
January 3, 2000	vs.	Sacred Heart	Win	83–56
January 5, 2000	vs.	Notre Dame	Loss	70–75
January 8, 2000	at	Pittsburgh	Win	73–51
January 10, 2000	vs.	Texas	Win	77–67
January 16, 2000	vs.	St. John's	Loss	77–82
January 22, 2000	at	Georgetown	Win	92–71
January 24, 2000	at	Syracuse	Loss	74–88
January 27, 2000	vs.	Providence	Win	64–50
January 30, 2000	vs.	Seton Hall	Win	66–56
February 2, 2000	at	Villanova	Win	74–60
February 5, 2000	at	Michigan State	Loss	66–85
February 9, 2000	vs.	Boston College	Win	87–58
February 12, 2000	at	Notre Dame	Loss	66–68
February 14, 2000	at	Seton Hall	Win	59–50
February 19, 2000	vs.	Miami	Loss	57–63
February 21, 2000	at	St. John's	Loss	64–79
February 26, 2000	vs.	West Virginia	Win	72–71
February 28, 2000	at	Rutgers	Win	74–69
March 4, 2000	vs.	Syracuse	Win	69–54
March 8, 2000	vs.	Boston College[†]	Win	70–55
March 9, 2000	vs.	Seton Hall[†]	Win	79–64
March 10, 2000	vs.	Georgetown[†]	Win	70–55
March 11, 2000	at	St. John's[†]	Loss	70–80
March 17, 2000	vs.	Utah State[‡]	Win	75–67
March 19, 2000	vs.	Tennessee[‡]	Loss	51–65

$^\infty$Madison Square Garden
$^\diamond$Great Eight, Chicago
[†]Big East Tournament
[‡]NCAA Tournament

UConn Starters and Key Contributors, 1999–2000

No.	Name	Position	Year	Points per game
4*	Ajou Deng	F	Fr.	4.5
23*	Albert Mouring	G	Jr.	13.5
32	Tony Robertson	G	Fr.	6.0
33*	Kevin Freeman	F	Sr.	11.0
34	Souleymane Wane	C	Jr.	4.3
42*	Khalid El-Amin	G	Jr.	16.0
43*	Jake Voskuhl	C	Sr.	8.5
51	Edmund Saunders	F	Jr.	7.6

Year 15 of the Calhoun Era, 2000–2001

Big East Record: 8–8 | Overall Record: 20–12 | NIT Second Round

Date		Opponent	Result	
November 17, 2000	vs.	Quinnipiac	Win	86–72
November 20, 2000	at	Dayton◇	Loss	66–80
November 21, 2000	at	Chaminade◇	Win	77–61
November 22, 2000	vs.	Louisville◇	Win	83–71
November 28, 2000	vs.	Brown	Win	88–78
November 30, 2000	vs.	Houston	Win	72–60
December 2, 2000	vs.	New Hampshire	Win	97–70
December 9, 2000	vs.	Arizona	Win	71–69
December 12, 2000	vs.	Massachusetts	Win	82–67
December 22, 2000	vs.	Fairfield	Win	100–66
December 26, 2000	vs.	Rhode Island	Win	87–76
December 28, 2000	vs.	Stony Brook	Win	67–58
January 3, 2001	at	Boston College	Loss	68–85
January 6, 2001	vs.	St. John's	Win	82–80
January 10, 2001	vs.	Pittsburgh	Win	73–53
January 13, 2001	at	Providence	Loss	68–81
January 15, 2001	at	Texas	Loss	56–60
January 20, 2001	at	Miami	Loss	74–77
January 24, 2001	vs.	Villanova	Loss	59–70
January 30, 2001	at	St. John's	Loss	55–60
January 31, 2001	at	Boston College	Loss	61–83
February 3, 2001	vs.	Virginia Tech	Win	85–72
February 6, 2001	vs.	Providence	Win	83–68
February 10, 2001	at	Villanova	Loss	60–74
February 13, 2001	vs.	Boston College	Win	82–71
February 17, 2001	at	Virginia Tech	Win	61–46
February 19, 2001	at	Syracuse	Loss	60–65
February 24, 2001	vs.	Miami	Win	60–53

Year 15 of the Calhoun Era, 2000–2001 *(continued)*

February 26, 2001	vs.	Notre Dame	Win	75-59
March 3, 2001	at	Seton Hall	Loss	63-65
March 7, 2001	vs.	Syracuse[†]	Loss	75-86
March 14, 2001	vs.	South Carolina[△]	Win	72-65
March 18, 2001	vs.	Detroit Mercy[△]	Loss	61-67

[◇]Maui Invitational   [△]NIT
[†]Big East Tournament

UConn Starters and Key Contributors, 2000–2001

No.	Name	Position	Year	Points per game
3*	Caron Butler	F	Fr.	15.3
12*	Taliek Brown	G	Fr.	8.1
23*	Albert Mouring	G	Sr.	15.1
32	Tony Robertson	G	So.	6.0
34*	Souleymane Wane	C	Sr.	4.6
44	Johnnie Selvie	F	Jr.	10.9
51*	Edmund Saunders	F	Sr.	9.9

Year 16 of the Calhoun Era, 2001–2002
Big East Record: 13–3 | Overall Record: 27–7 | NCAA Elite Eight

Date		Opponent	Result	
November 19, 2001	vs.	Vanderbilt	Win	84-71
November 26, 2001	vs.	New Hampshire	Win	110-58
December 2, 2001	vs.	George Washington[◇]	Win	84-76
December 3, 2001	at	Maryland[◇]	Loss	65-77
December 8, 2001	vs.	Northeastern	Win	80-44
December 11, 2001	at	Massachusetts	Win	69-59
December 21, 2001	vs.	Quinnipiac	Win	95-79
December 28, 2001	vs.	St. Bonaventure	Loss	70-88
January 2, 2002	at	Virginia Tech	Win	86-74
January 5, 2002	vs.	Miami	Win	76-75
January 7, 2002	vs.	Oklahoma	Loss	67-69
January 10, 2002	vs.	Virginia Tech	Win	95-60
January 13, 2002	at	Villanova	Win	70-65
January 16, 2002	at	Providence	Win	69-62
January 19, 2002	vs.	North Carolina	Win	86-54
January 23, 2002	vs.	St. John's	Win	75-70
January 26, 2002	at	Arizona	Win*	100-98
January 30, 2002	at	Rutgers	Loss	53-61
February 2, 2002	at	Miami	Loss	66-68
February 5, 2002	vs.	Providence	Win	67-56

February 9, 2002	at	St. John's	Loss*	83–85
February 11, 2002	vs.	Villanova	Win	46–40
February 16, 2002	vs.	Boston College	Win*	79–77
February 19, 2002	at	Georgetown	Win	75–74
February 23, 2002	vs.	West Virginia	Win	95–73
February 25, 2002	at	Boston College	Win	75–61
March 2, 2002	vs.	Seton Hall	Win	90–78
March 7, 2002	vs.	Villanova[†]	Win	72–70
March 8, 2002	vs.	Notre Dame[†]	Win	82–77
March 9, 2002	vs.	Pittsburgh[†]	Win	74–65
March 15, 2002	vs.	Hampton[‡]	Win	78–67
March 17, 2002	vs.	N.C. State[‡]	Win	77–74
March 22, 2002	vs.	Southern Illinois[‡]	Win	71–59
March 24, 2002	vs.	Maryland[‡]	Loss	82–90

*Overtime [†]Big East Tournament
°Washington, D.C. [‡]NCAA Tournament

UConn Starters and Key Contributors, 2001–2002

No.	Name	Position	Year	Points per game
3*	Caron Butler	F	So.	20.0
4	Ben Gordon	G	Fr.	12.6
12*	Taliek Brown	G	So.	9.2
32*	Tony Robertson	G	Jr.	11.3
44*	Johnnie Selvie	F	Sr.	11.4
50*	Emeka Okafor	C	Fr.	7.9

Year 17 of the Calhoun Era, 2002–2003

Big East Record: 10–6 | Overall Record: 23–10 | NCAA Sweet 16

Date		Opponent	Result	
November 23, 2002	vs.	Quinnipiac	Win	91–72
November 25, 2002	vs.	George Washington	Win	67–55
December 1, 2002	at	Vanderbilt	Win	76–70
December 3, 2002	vs.	Sacred Heart	Win	116–78
December 7, 2002	vs.	Wagner	Win	97–85
December 10, 2002	vs.	Massachusetts	Win	59–48
December 21, 2002	vs.	UNC–Asheville	Win	117–67
December 28, 2002	vs.	Central Connecticut State	Win	93–65
January 2, 2003	vs.	St. Bonaventure	Win	95–78
January 7, 2003	at	Oklahoma	Loss	63–73
January 11, 2003	vs.	Miami	Win*	83–80
January 14, 2003	vs.	Virginia Tech	Win	83–65
January 18, 2003	at	North Carolina	Loss	65–68

Year 17 of the Calhoun Era, 2002–2003 *(continued)*

January 20, 2003	at	Miami	Loss	76–77
January 25, 2003	vs.	Villanova	Win	74–65
January 27, 2003	at	St. John's	Win	74–68
February 1, 2003	vs.	Boston College	Loss	71–95
February 5, 2003	at	Virginia Tech	Loss	74–95
February 8, 2003	at	Providence	Win	84–68
February 10, 2003	vs.	Syracuse	Win	75–61
February 15, 2003	at	Villanova	Loss	70–79
February 19, 2003	vs.	Rutgers	Win	87–70
February 22, 2003	vs.	St. John's	Win	77–69
February 24, 2003	at	Notre Dame	Win	87–79
March 2, 2003	at	Pittsburgh	Loss	67–71
March 5, 2003	vs.	Providence	Loss	70–76
March 8, 2003	at	Boston College	Win	91–54
March 13, 2003	vs.	Seton Hall[†]	Win	83–70
March 14, 2003	vs.	Syracuse[†]	Win	80–67
March 15, 2003	vs.	Pittsburgh[†]	Loss	56–74
March 20, 2003	vs.	BYU[‡]	Win	58–53
March 22, 2003	vs.	Stanford[‡]	Win	85–74
March 28, 2003	vs.	Texas[‡]	Loss	78–82

*Overtime
[†]Big East Tournament
[‡]NCAA Tournament

UConn Starters and Key Contributors, 2002–2003

No.	Name	Position	Year	Points per game
4*	Ben Gordon	G	So.	19.5
11*	Hilton Armstrong	C	Fr.	2.8
12	Taliek Brown	G	Jr.	7.7
31*	Rashad Anderson	G	Fr.	8.2
32	Tony Robertson	G	Sr.	9.8
33*	Denham Brown	G	Fr.	7.7
50*	Emeka Okafor	C	So.	15.9

Year 18 of the Calhoun Era, 2003–2004

Big East Record: 12–4 | Overall Record: 33–6 | NCAA Champions

Date	Opponent		Result	
November 17, 2003	vs.	Yale[△]	Win	70–60
November 19, 2003	vs.	Nevada[△]	Win	93–79
November 22, 2003	vs.	Sacred Heart	Win	111–64
November 26, 2003	vs.	Georgia Tech[△∞]	Loss	61–77

November 28, 2003	vs.	Utah$^{\triangle\infty}$	Win	76-44
December 1, 2003	vs.	Lehigh	Win	75-55
December 6, 2003	vs.	Army	Win	74-46
December 13, 2003	vs.	Quinnipiac	Win	88-55
December 20, 2003	vs.	Iona	Win	104-54
December 28, 2003	vs.	Ball State	Win	101-62
December 30, 2003	vs.	Massachusetts	Win	91-67
January 2, 2004	at	Rice	Win	92-83
January 6, 2004	at	Rutgers	Win	75-74
January 11, 2004	vs.	Oklahoma	Win	86-59
January 14, 2004	vs.	Georgetown	Win	94-70
January 17, 2004	at	North Carolina	Loss	83-86
January 19, 2004	vs.	Pittsburgh	Win	68-65
January 24, 2004	vs.	Providence	Loss	56-66
January 28, 2004	at	Virginia Tech	Win	96-60
January 31, 2004	at	Boston College	Win	63-58
February 2, 2004	vs.	Syracuse	Win	84-56
February 7, 2004	vs.	West Virginia	Win	88-58
February 9, 2004	at	Notre Dame	Loss	74-80
February 15, 2004	at	Pittsburgh	Loss	68-75
February 18, 2004	vs.	Miami	Win	76-63
February 21, 2004	vs.	Notre Dame	Win	61-50
February 24, 2004	at	St. John's	Win	71-53
February 28, 2004	at	Villanova	Win*	75-74
March 1, 2004	vs.	Seton Hall	Win	89-67
March 7, 2004	at	Syracuse	Loss	56-67
March 11, 2004	vs.	Notre Dame†	Win	66-58
March 12, 2004	vs.	Villanova†	Win	84-67
March 13, 2004	vs.	Pittsburgh†	Win	61-58
March 18, 2004	vs.	Vermont‡	Win	70-53
March 20, 2004	vs.	DePaul‡	Win	72-55
March 25, 2004	vs.	Vanderbilt‡	Win	73-53
March 27, 2004	vs.	Alabama‡	Win	87-71
April 3, 2004	vs.	Duke‡	Win	79-78
April 5, 2004	vs.	Georgia Tech‡	Win	82-73

*Overtime
$^{\triangle}$Preseason NIT
$^{\infty}$Madison Square Garden
†Big East Tournament
‡NCAA Tournament

UConn Starters and Key Contributors, 2003–2004

No.	Name	Position	Year	Points per game
3	Charlie Villanueva	F	Fr.	8.9
4*	Ben Gordon	G	So.	18.5
11	Hilton Armstrong	C	So.	2.4
12*	Taliek Brown	G	Sr.	6.3
21*	Josh Boone	F	Fr.	5.9
31*	Rashad Anderson	G	So.	11.2
33	Denham Brown	G	So.	8.9
50*	Emeka Okafor	C	Jr.	17.6

Year 19 of the Calhoun Era, 2004–2005
Big East Record: 13–3 | Overall Record: 23–8 | NCAA Second Round

Date		Opponent	Result	
November 20, 2004	vs.	Buffalo	Win	90–68
November 30, 2004	vs.	Florida International	Win	99–48
December 4, 2004	vs.	Indiana	Win	74–69
December 6, 2004	vs.	Northeastern	Win	97–60
December 9, 2004	at	Massachusetts	Loss	59–61
December 19, 2004	vs.	Rice	Win	81–72
December 22, 2004	vs.	Central Connecticut State	Win	87–59
December 28, 2004	vs.	Sacred Heart	Win	73–55
December 30, 2004	vs.	Quinnipiac	Win	123–71
January 5, 2005	vs.	Boston College	Loss	70–75
January 8, 2005	at	Georgetown	Win	66–59
January 10, 2005	at	Oklahoma	Loss	65–77
January 15, 2005	vs.	Rutgers	Win	78–64
January 17, 2005	at	Seton Hall	Win	77–68
January 22, 2005	vs.	Pittsburgh	Loss	66–76
January 25, 2005	at	West Virginia	Win	68–58
January 30, 2005	at	Notre Dame	Loss	74–78
February 2, 2005	vs.	Villanova	Win	81–76
February 5, 2005	vs.	St. John's	Win	68–46
February 7, 2005	at	Syracuse	Win	74–66
February 13, 2005	vs.	North Carolina	Loss	70–77
February 15, 2005	at	Providence	Win**	94–89
February 19, 2005	at	Rutgers	Win	85–63
February 21, 2005	vs.	Notre Dame	Win	88–74
February 26, 2005	at	Pittsburgh	Win	73–64
March 2, 2005	vs.	Georgetown	Win	83–64
March 5, 2005	vs.	Syracuse	Win	88–70
March 10, 2005	vs.	Georgetown†	Win	66–62

March 11, 2005	vs.	Syracuse[†]	Loss	63-67
March 18, 2005	vs.	Central Florida[‡]	Win	77-71
March 20, 2005	vs.	N.C. State[‡]	Loss	62-65

**Double-Overtime
[†]Big East Tournament
[‡]NCAA Tournament

UConn Starters and Key Contributors, 2004–2005

No.	Name	Position	Year	Points per game
3*	Charlie Villanueva	F	So.	13.6
5*	Marcus Williams	G	So.	9.6
11	Hilton Armstrong	C	Jr.	3.8
21*	Josh Boone	F	So.	12.4
22*	Rudy Gay	F	Fr	11.8
31	Rashad Anderson	G	Jr.	11.9
32	Ed Nelson	F	Jr.	2.9
33*	Denham Brown	G	Jr.	10.4

Year 20 of the Calhoun Era, 2005–2006
Big East Record: 14–2 | Overall Record: 30–4 | NCAA Elite Eight

Date		Opponent	Result	
November 18, 2005	at	Pepperdine	Win	75-56
November 21, 2005	vs.	Arkansas◊	Win	77-68
November 22, 2005	vs.	Arizona◊	Win	79-70
November 23, 2005	vs.	Gonzaga◊	Win	65-63
November 29, 2005	vs.	Army	Win	68-54
December 2, 2005	vs.	Texas Southern	Win	113-49
December 8, 2005	vs.	Massachusetts	Win	78-60
December 18, 2005	vs.	New Hampshire	Win	86-44
December 23, 2005	vs.	Morehead State	Win	129-61
December 28, 2005	vs.	Stony Brook	Win	85-52
December 30, 2005	vs.	Quinnipiac	Win	111-75
January 3, 2006	at	Marquette	Loss	79-94
January 7, 2006	vs.	LSU	Win	67-66
January 9, 2006	vs.	Cincinnati	Win	70-59
January 14, 2006	vs.	Georgetown	Win	74-67
January 16, 2006	at	Syracuse	Win	88-80
January 21, 2006	at	Louisville	Win	71-58
January 25, 2006	vs.	St. John's	Win	66-50
January 28, 2006	at	Providence	Win	76-62
January 31, 2006	vs.	Pittsburgh	Win	80-76
February 4, 2006	at	Indiana	Win	88-80

Year 20 of the Calhoun Era, 2005–2006 *(continued)*

Date		Opponent		Result
February 8, 2006	vs.	Syracuse	Win	73–50
February 11, 2006	at	Seton Hall	Win	99–57
February 13, 2006	at	Villanova	Loss	64–69
February 18, 2006	at	West Virginia	Win	81–75
February 21, 2006	vs.	Notre Dame	Win*	75–74
February 26, 2006	vs.	Villanova	Win	89–75
March 1, 2006	at	South Florida	Win	66–53
March 4, 2006	vs.	Louisville	Win	84–80
March 9, 2006	vs.	Syracuse†	Loss*	84–86
March 17, 2006	vs.	Albany‡	Win	72–59
March 19, 2006	vs.	Kentucky‡	Win	87–83
March 24, 2006	vs.	Washington‡	Win*	98–92
March 26, 2006	vs.	George Mason‡	Loss*	84–86

*Overtime
◇Maui Invitational
†Big East Tournament
‡NCAA Tournament

UConn Starters and Key Contributors, 2005–2006

No.	Name	Position	Year	Points per game
4	Jeff Adrien	F	Fr.	6.5
5*	Marcus Williams	G	Jr.	12.3
11*	Hilton Armstrong	C	So.	9.7
21*	Josh Boone	F	So.	10.3
22*	Rudy Gay	F	So.	15.2
24	Craig Austrie	G	Fr.	3.3
31	Rashad Anderson	G	Sr.	12.8
32	Ed Nelson	F	Sr.	3.2
33*	Denham Brown	G	Sr.	10.7

Year 21 of the Calhoun Era, 2006–2007

Big East Record: 6–10 | Overall Record: 17–14

Date		Opponent	Result	
November 10, 2006	vs.	Quinnipiac	Win	53–46
November 17, 2006	vs.	Central Arkansas	Win	88–59
November 18, 2006	vs.	Fairfield	Win	74–49
November 19, 2006	vs.	Mississippi	Win	77–59
November 26, 2006	vs.	Albany	Win	86–55
November 29, 2006	vs.	Sacred Heart	Win	89–46
December 3, 2006	vs.	Texas Southern	Win	106–55

December 6, 2006	vs.	Northeastern	Win	81–53
December 17, 2006	vs.	St. Mary's (Calif.)	Win	89–73
December 20, 2006	vs.	Pepperdine	Win	88–66
December 27, 2006	vs.	Coppin State	Win	84–41
December 30, 2006	at	West Virginia	Loss	71–81
January 2, 2007	vs.	South Florida	Win	69–50
January 6, 2007	at	LSU	Loss	49–66
January 10, 2007	vs.	Marquette	Loss	69–73
January 13, 2007	at	St. John's	Win	68–59
January 16, 2007	at	Pittsburgh	Loss	54–63
January 20, 2007	vs.	Indiana	Loss	73–77
January 22, 2007	at	Louisville	Loss	54–68
January 27, 2007	vs.	Providence	Loss	72–84
January 31, 2007	at	DePaul	Loss	58–66
February 3, 2007	vs.	Rutgers	Win*	61–50
February 5, 2007	vs.	Syracuse	Win	67–60
February 11, 2007	at	Georgia Tech	Loss	52–65
February 14, 2007	vs.	Seton Hall	Win	67–55
February 17, 2007	at	Syracuse	Loss	63–73
February 21, 2007	at	Rutgers	Win	65–55
February 25, 2007	vs.	Louisville	Loss	69–76
February 28, 2007	vs.	Villanova	Loss	74–78
March 3, 2007	at	Georgetown	Loss	46–59
March 7, 2007	vs.	Syracuse†	Loss	65–78

*Overtime
†Big East Tournament

UConn Starters and Key Contributors, 2006–2007

No.	Name	Position	Year	Points per game
1*	Marcus Johnson	G	Fr.	5.5
3	Doug Wiggins	G	Fr.	6.8
4*	Jeff Adrien	F	So.	13.1
11*	Jerome Dyson	G	Fr.	13.8
12*	A.J. Price	G	So.	9.4
21	Stanley Robinson	F	Fr.	5.1
24	Craig Austrie	G	So.	5.8
33	Gavin Edwards	F/C	Fr.	2.0
34*	Hasheem Thabeet	C	Fr.	6.2

Year 22 of the Calhoun Era, 2007–2008

Big East Record: 13–5 | Overall Record: 24–9 | NCAA First Round

Date		Opponent	Result	
November 7, 2007	vs.	Morgan State	Win	69–65
November 8, 2007	vs.	Buffalo	Win	82–57
November 15, 2007	vs.	Gardner-Webb∞	Win	78–66
November 16, 2007	vs.	Memphis∞	Loss	70–81
November 20, 2007	vs.	Gardner-Webb	Win	89–72
November 26, 2007	vs.	Florida A&M	Win	93–54
December 1, 2007	vs.	Gonzaga◇	Loss	82–85
December 6, 2007	vs.	Northeastern	Win	69–60
December 16, 2007	vs.	Quinnipiac	Win	82–49
December 22, 2007	vs.	Maine	Win	105–60
December 28, 2007	at	Central Florida	Win	85–82
January 3, 2008	at	Seton Hall	Win	98–86
January 5, 2008	at	Notre Dame	Loss	67–73
January 8, 2008	vs.	St. John's	Win	81–65
January 12, 2008	at	Georgetown	Loss	69–72
January 17, 2008	vs.	Providence	Loss	65–77
January 20, 2008	vs.	Marquette	Win	89–73
January 23, 2008	at	Cincinnati	Win	84–83
January 26, 2008	at	Indiana	Win	68–63
January 28, 2008	vs.	Louisville	Win	69–67
February 2, 2008	vs.	Pittsburgh	Win	60–53
February 6, 2008	at	Syracuse	Win	63–61
February 9, 2008	vs.	Georgia Tech	Win	80–68
February 13, 2008	vs.	Notre Dame	Win	84–78
February 16, 2008	at	South Florida	Win*	74–73
February 19, 2008	vs.	DePaul	Win	65–60
February 23, 2008	at	Villanova	Loss	65–67
February 26, 2008	at	Rutgers	Win	79–61
March 1, 2008	vs.	West Virginia	Win	79–71
March 6, 2008	at	Providence	Loss	76–85
March 9, 2008	vs.	Cincinnati	Win	96–51
March 13, 2008	vs.	West Virginia†	Loss	72–78
March 21, 2008	vs.	San Diego‡	Loss*	69–70

*Overtime
∞Madison Square Garden
◇Boston
†Big East Tornament
‡NCAA Tournament

UConn Starters and Key Contributors, 2007–2008

No.	Name	Position	Year	Points per game
3	Doug Wiggins	G	So.	6.7
4*	Jeff Adrien	F	Jr.	14.8
11	Jerome Dyson	G	So.	12.5
12*	A.J. Price	G	Jr.	14.5
21*	Stanley Robinson	F	So.	10.4
24*	Craig Austrie	G	Jr.	7.5
33	Gavin Edwards	F/C	So.	2.9
34*	Hasheem Thabeet	C	So.	10.5

Year 23 of the Calhoun Era, 2008–2009
Big East Record: 15–3 | Overall Record: 31–5 | NCAA Final Four

Date		Opponent	Result	
November 14, 2008	vs.	Western Carolina	Win	81–55
November 17, 2008	vs.	Hartford	Win	99–56
November 21, 2008	vs.	La Salle◊	Win	89–81
November 23, 2008	vs.	Miami◊	Win	76–63
November 24, 2008	vs.	Wisconsin◊	Win	76–57
November 29, 2008	vs.	Bryant	Win	88–58
December 1, 2008	vs.	Delaware State	Win	79–49
December 4, 2008	at	Buffalo	Win	68–64
December 15, 2008	vs.	Stony Brook	Win	91–57
December 20, 2008	vs.	Gonzaga+	Win*	88–83
December 26, 2008	vs.	Fairfield	Win	75–55
December 29, 2008	vs.	Georgetown	Loss	63–74
January 3, 2009	vs.	Rutgers	Win	80–49
January 6, 2009	at	West Virginia	Win	61–55
January 10, 2009	at	Cincinnati	Win	81–72
January 15, 2009	at	St. John's	Win	67–55
January 18, 2009	vs.	Seton Hall	Win	76–61
January 21, 2009	vs.	Villanova	Win	89–83
January 24, 2009	at	Notre Dame	Win	69–61
January 28, 2009	at	DePaul	Win	71–49
January 31, 2009	vs.	Providence	Win	94–61
February 2, 2009	at	Louisville	Win	68–51
February 7, 2009	vs.	Michigan	Win	69–61
February 11, 2009	vs.	Syracuse	Win	63–49
February 14, 2009	at	Seton Hall	Win	62–54
February 16, 2009	vs.	Pittsburgh	Loss	68–76
February 21, 2009	vs.	South Florida	Win	64–50
February 25, 2009	at	Marquette	Win	93–82

Year 23 of the Calhoun Era, 2008–2009 *(continued)*

February 28, 2009	vs.	Notre Dame	Win	72–65
March 7, 2009	at	Pittsburgh	Loss	60–70
March 12, 2009	vs.	Syracuse†	Loss**	117–127
March 19, 2009	vs.	Chattanooga‡	Win	103–47
March 21, 2009	vs.	Texas A&M‡	Win	92–66
March 26, 2009	vs.	Purdue‡	Win	72–60
March 28, 2009	vs.	Missouri‡	Win	82–75
April 4, 2009	vs.	Michigan State‡	Loss	73–82

*Overtime   **Six Overtimes
◇St. Thomas   +Seattle
†Big East Tournament
‡NCAA Tournament

UConn Starters and Key Contributors, 2008–2009

No.	Name	Position	Year	Points per game
4*	Jeff Adrien	F	Sr.	13.6
11	Jerome Dyson	G	Jr.	13.2
12*	A.J. Price	G	Sr.	14.7
15	Kemba Walker	G	Fr.	8.9
21*	Stanley Robinson	F	Jr.	8.5
24*	Craig Austrie	G	Sr.	7.2
33	Gavin Edwards	F/C	Jr.	3.8
34*	Hasheem Thabeet	C	Jr.	13.6

Year 24 of the Calhoun Era, 2009–2010

Big East Record: 7–11 | Conference Record: 18–16 | NIT Second Round

Date		Opponent	Result	
November 13, 2009	vs.	William & Mary	Win	75–66
November 16, 2009	vs.	Colgate△	Win	77–63
November 17, 2009	vs.	Hofstra△	Win	76–67
November 25, 2009	vs.	LSU△∞	Win	81–55
November 27, 2009	vs.	Duke△∞	Loss	59–68
December 2, 2009	vs.	Boston University	Win	92–64
December 6, 2009	vs.	Harvard	Win	79–73
December 9, 2009	vs.	Kentucky∞	Loss	61–64
December 20, 2009	vs.	Central Florida	Win	60–51
December 22, 2009	vs.	Maine	Win	71–54
December 27, 2009	vs.	Iona	Win	93–74
December 30, 2009	at	Cincinnati	Loss	69–71
January 2, 2010	vs.	Notre Dame	Win	82–70
January 6, 2010	vs.	Seton Hall	Win	71–63

January 9, 2010	at	Georgetown	Loss	69–72
January 13, 2010	vs.	Pittsburgh	Loss	57–67
January 17, 2010	at	Michigan	Loss	63–68
January 20, 2010	vs.	St. John's	Win	75–59
January 23, 2010	vs.	Texas	Win	88–74
January 27, 2010	at	Providence	Loss	66–81
January 30, 2010	vs.	Marquette	Loss	68–70
February 1, 2010	at	Louisville	Loss	69–82
February 6, 2010	vs.	DePaul	Win	64–57
February 10, 2010	at	Syracuse	Loss	67–72
February 13, 2010	vs.	Cincinnati	Loss	48–60
February 15, 2010	vs.	Villanova	Win	84–75
February 20, 2010	at	Rutgers	Win	76–58
February 22, 2010	vs.	West Virginia	Win	73–62
February 28, 2010	vs.	Louisville	Loss	76–78
March 3, 2010	at	Notre Dame	Loss	50–58
March 6, 2010	at	South Florida	Loss	68–75
March 9, 2010	vs.	St. John's[†]	Loss	51–73
March 16, 2010	vs.	Northeastern[ΔΔ]	Win	59–57
March 22, 2010	at	Virginia Tech[ΔΔ]	Loss	63–65

[Δ]Preseason NIT
[ΔΔ]NIT
[∞]Madison Square Garden
[†]Big East Tournament

UConn Starters and Key Contributors, 2009–2010

No.	Name	Position	Year	Points per game
4	Jamal Coombs-McDaniel	F	Fr.	3.3
5	Ater Majok	F	So.	2.3
11*	Jerome Dyson	G	Sr.	17.2
15*	Kemba Walker	G	So.	14.6
21*	Stanley Robinson	F	Sr.	14.5
33*	Gavin Edwards	F/C	Sr.	10.6
34*	Alex Oriakhi	C	Fr.	5.0

Year 25 of the Calhoun Era, 2010–2011

Big East Record: 9–9 | Overall Record: 32–9 | NCAA Champions

Date	Opponent	Result	
November 12, 2010	vs.	Stony Brook	Win	79–52
November 17, 2010	vs.	Vermont	Win	89–73
November 22, 2010	vs.	Wichita State[◊]	Win	83–79
November 23, 2010	vs.	Michigan State[◊]	Win	70–67

November 24, 2010	vs.	Kentucky◇	Win	84-67
November 30, 2010	vs.	New Hampshire	Win	62-55
December 3, 2010	vs.	University of Maryland–Baltimore County	Win	94-61
December 8, 2010	vs.	Fairleigh Dickinson	Win	78-54
December 20, 2010	vs.	Coppin State	Win	76-64
December 22, 2010	vs.	Harvard	Win	81-52
December 27, 2010	at	Pittsburgh	Loss	63-78
December 31, 2010	vs.	South Florida	Win*	66-61
January 4, 2011	at	Notre Dame	Loss	70-73
January 8, 2011	at	Texas	Win*	82-81
January 11, 2011	vs.	Rutgers	Win	67-53
January 15, 2011	at	DePaul	Win	82-62
January 17, 2011	vs.	Villanova	Win	61-59
January 22, 2011	vs.	Tennessee	Win	72-61
January 25, 2011	at	Marquette	Win	76-68
January 29, 2011	vs.	Louisville	Loss**	78-79
February 2, 2011	vs.	Syracuse	Loss	58-66
February 5, 2011	at	Seton Hall	Win	61-59
February 10, 2011	vs.	St. John's	Loss	72-89
February 13, 2011	vs.	Providence	Win	75-57
February 16, 2011	vs.	Georgetown	Win	78-70
February 18, 2011	vs.	Louisville	Loss	58-71
February 24, 2011	vs.	Marquette	Loss*	67-74
February 27, 2011	at	Cincinnati	Win	67-59
March 2, 2011	at	West Virginia	Loss	56-65
March 5, 2011	vs.	Notre Dame	Loss	67-70
March 8, 2011	vs.	DePaul†	Win	97-71
March 9, 2011	vs.	Georgetown†	Win	79-62
March 10, 2011	vs.	Pittsburgh†	Win	76-74
March 11, 2011	vs.	Syracuse†	Win*	76-71
March 12, 2011	vs.	Louisville†	Win	69-66
March 17, 2011	vs.	Bucknell‡	Win	81-52
March 19, 2011	vs.	Cincinnati‡	Win	69-58
March 24, 2011	vs.	San Diego State‡	Win	74-67
March 26, 2011	vs.	Arizona‡	Win	65-63
April 2, 2011	vs.	Kentucky‡	Win	56-55
April 4, 2011	vs.	Butler‡	Win	53-41

*Overtime **Double-Overtime
◇Maui Invitational
†Big East Tournament
‡NCAA Tournament

UConn Starters and Key Contributors, 2010–2011

No.	Name	Position	Year	Points per game
2	Donnell Beverly	G	Sr.	1.7
3*	Jeremy Lamb	G	Fr.	11.1
4	Jamal Coombs-McDaniel	F	So.	5.6
5	Niels Giffey	G/F	Fr.	2.2
10*	Tyler Olander	F	Fr.	1.5
13	Shabazz Napier	G	Fr.	7.8
15*	Kemba Walker	G	Jr.	23.5
22*	Roscoe Smith	F	Fr.	6.3
34*	Alex Oriakhi	C	So.	9.6
35	Charles Okwandu	C	Sr.	2.9

Notes and Sources

General Notes

Interviews (players): Ray Allen, Rashad Anderson, Taliek Brown, Caron Butler, Lyman DePriest, Jerome Dyson, Greg Economou, Khalid El-Amin, Kevin Freeman, Rudy Gay, Tate George, Ben Gordon, John Gwynn, Rip Hamilton, Kirk King, Travis Knight, Donyell Marshall, Ricky Moore, Emeka Okafor, Kevin Ollie, Steve Pikiell, Rod Sellers, James Spradling, Charlie Villanueva, Kemba Walker, Souleymane Wane; (coaches) George Blaney, Jim Calhoun, Howie Dickenman, Karl Hobbs, Dave Leitao, Glen Miller, Tom Moore, Steve Pikiell; (reporters) Sean Barker, Phil Chardis, Dave Solomon; (others) Joe D'Ambrosio, Mike Gorman, Mike Tranghese, Tim Tolokan, John Tuite.

The following writers were cited several times in this book. Their full names are provided here and on the first reference to them. Mike Anthony, Michael Arace, Mark Blaudschun, David Borges, Bob Casey, Jack Cavanaugh, Phil Chardis, Jack Curry, Chris Dahl, Ken Davis, Pat Eaton-Robb, Chris Elsberry, Jeff Jacobs, Dick Jerardi, Kevin McNamara, Leigh Montville, Malcolm E. Moran, Jim O'Connell, Neill Ostrout, Dave Ramsey, William C. Rhoden, Lenn Robbins, Roger Rubin, Bob Ryan, Mike Shalin, Donna Tommelleo, Michael Vega, Mike Waters, Dick Weiss, and Tom Yantz.

Introduction

Wall Street Journal headline: Scott Cacciola, April 28, 2010.

DeCourcy and Davis's quotes: Mike DeCourcy, "NCAA Allegations . . . ," *Sporting News*, May 28, 2010; Seth Davis, "NCAA Allegations Could . . . ," May 29, 2010, and "Facing Another . . . ," January 20, 2010, http://sportsillustrated.cnn.com.

Dialogue from *Major League*: imdb.com.

Dick Weiss's top 50 Big East players: "The Best . . . ," *Daily News*, March 3, 1997, B1.

Details about task force: University of Connecticut, President's Task Force on Athletics, May 9 and 12, 1986. Jim Calhoun with Leigh Montville. 1999. *Dare to Dream*. New York: Broadway Books, 1999, 24–25; *New York Times*, "UConn Begins Search," January 23, 1987.

Details about Earl Kelley: Chris Dahl, Associated Press, April 30, 1985; May 31, 1985; June 5, 1985; September 17, 1985; September 30, 1985; October 1, 1985; November 20, 1985; December 20, 1985; December 23, 1985; December 24, 1985; December 26, 1985; UPI, December 25, 1985; December 26, 1985; AP, "Sports News," February 15, 1985; *New York Times*, December 27, 1985, A26; Uconnhuskies.com; Ken Davis, "Time for One . . . ," *Hartford Courant*, December 11, 2005, E8; Sam Smith, "Strange Bounces . . . ," *Chicago Tribune*, March 30, 1986.

Details about UConn's facilities: Jonathan Rabinovitz, "UConn to Get . . . ," *New York Times*, June 23, 1995, B1; Wayne Peacock, "Building a Better . . . ," *Bond Buyer*, April 4, 2002; Natalie Keith, "21st Century . . . ," *New York Construction*, March 1, 2005, vol.

52, no. 8, 63; Julie Stagis, "UConn Begins . . . ," *Connecticut Post*, December 26, 2009; *Mansfield Today* staff, "$95 Million . . . ," December 12, 2009.

Details about Calhoun's pre-UConn career and the coach's decision to take the UConn job: Davis, *Hartford Courant*, May 15, 1986, A1; May 16, 1986, E1, E8; Calhoun and Montville, *Dare to Dream*, chapter two; Jim Shea. 1995. *Huskymania*. New York: Villard Books, 1995, chapter four; Dahl, AP, May 16, 1986; AP, "New Basketball . . . ," June 10, 1986; Alan Greenberg, "He Seems . . . ," *Hartford Courant*, May 16, 1986, E1, E8; Owen Canfield, "History, New . . . ," *Hartford Courant*, May 16, 1986, E1, E8; Jackie MacMullan, "Calhoun to UConn," *Boston Globe*, May 16, 1986, 49, 61; Edward Lee, "McDuffie, Chasing . . . ," *Baltimore Sun*, August 6, 1994; Michael Gee, "Calhoun Sticks . . . ," *Boston Herald*, April 5, 2004, 84; Lukeman Literary Agency.

Information about UConn's media coverage: *Connecticut Basketball Illustrated*, "UConn Basketball: It's Always . . . ," 14, 1989–1990 season.

Information about Katha Quinn and the Horde: Bob Ryan, "No Question . . ." *Boston Globe*, April 2, 2004.

Quotes about arenas and plucky Northeastern: Calhoun and Montville, *Dare to Dream*, 28.

Dodge Shitbox: Calhoun and Montville, *Dare to Dream*, 22.

Information on Calhoun's initial contract: Bob Casey, *New Haven Register*, May 15, 1986, 25; May 16, 1986, 35.

1. I Don't Want My Managers to Have to Clean Up Puke

Stories about Herget and the death of Jim Calhoun's father: Fast Scripts, "An Interview . . . ," St. Petersburg, Florida, March 28, 1999; Calhoun and Montville, *Dare to Dream*, 46; Paul Harber, "Braintree Honors . . . ," *Boston Globe*, April 3, 2004.

Details about Herget and Calhoun's family style: *Meriden Record Journal*, September 4, 2005; Christopher Lawlor, "Jim Dandy," *Coach and Athletic Director*, April, 2000, 49; Dahl, AP, May 16, 1986.

Calhoun's quote about Herget: Malcolm E. Moran, "It Was . . . ," *New York Times*, March 26, 1995, 6.

The box on Calhoun's desk: Jack Curry, "Connecticut's Calhoun . . . ," *New York Times*, March 19, 1998, C1.

Calhoun discusses his father in *Dare to Dream*, 48.

Herget's regimen and infrastructure: Calhoun and Montville, *Dare to Dream*, 41; Ron Hobson, "Top Dog," *Patriot Ledger*, January 30, 1999, 39.

Details about Elliott Gordon: Brett Orzechowski, "Calhoun's Fire . . . ," *New Haven Register*, March 26, 2006.

Calhoun discusses the Tar Heels' program in Lawlor, "Jim Dandy," 49.

2. We Need a Couple of Guys to Get Us through the Rest of the Season

Karl Fogel's prediction: Davis, "The Honeymoon . . ."

"If it were up to me . . . all the reporters would stay home." Rick Bonnell, "Orange to Battle . . . ," *Post-Standard*, January 3, 1987, B1.

Calhoun discusses his patience with George in Davis, "Will Calhoun . . . ," *Hartford Courant*, November 21, 1986, E1.

"... insulting your intelligence" and details about Calhoun's first game at UConn: Davis, "Huskies Fall . . . ," *Hartford Courant*, November 14, 1986, C1; Owen Canfield, "Calhoun Working . . . ," *Hartford Courant*, November 15, 1986, C1.

"Get off your ass!" Michael O'Connor, "He's Still . . . ," *Boston Herald*, March 26, 1999.

Information about the BU game: Jeff Thoreson, "Calhoun Feels . . . ," *Post-Standard*, January 7, 1988, C1; AP, "Boston U. 80 . . . ," December, 10, 1986; Calhoun and Montville, *Dare to Dream*, 35; Casey, "Terriers May . . . ," *New Haven Register*, December 10, 1986, 39–40; Davis, "UConn Team . . . ,'" *Hartford Courant*, December 10, 1986, F1, F3; Joe Burris, "When Former . . . ," *Boston Globe*, March 15, 1990, 33.

Information about the University of Hartford game: Davis, "Hawks Top . . . ," *Hartford Courant*, December 30, 1986, B1.

Calhoun discusses Robinson and Gamble's eligibility problems in *Dare to Dream*, 36–37.

"... I need players" Davis, "Calhoun Searching . . . ," *Hartford Courant*, January 26, 1987, C11.

The 1987 regular season finale: Casey, *New Haven Register*, March 1, 1987, C1, C10; March 2, 1987, 37; Davis, *Hartford Courant*, March 1, 1987, E1, E7; March 1, 1987, E7.

UConn's 61–53 loss to PC: Davis, "Providence Deals . . . ," *Hartford Courant*. January 25, 1987, D1; Davis, "Calhoun Lands . . . ," *Hartford Courant*, November 19, 1986, B1, B3.

Details about Calhoun getting cut in the eighth grade: Lawlor, "Jim Dandy."

Details about Calhoun's marathon experience: Bob Snyder, "Former Marathon . . . ," *Post-Standard*, January 23, 1998, D4.

"Made a huge mistake . . ." Jim Calhoun and Richard Ernsberger. 2007. *A Passion to Lead*. New York: St. Martin's Press, 86.

3. You've Got to Learn How to Win

Recruiting in the early years of the Calhoun era: Solomon, "National Exposure . . . ," *New Haven Register*, November 11, 1992, 43; Davis, "Calhoun Lands . . ."

"This can be your stage" Montville, "Parallel Lives," *Sports Illustrated*, April 14, 2004, 56.

"We're at least two good recruiting years" Dahl, AP, December 5, 1986.

"I need players" Bonnell, "Orange to Battle . . ."

"As long as we're second" Davis, "Calhoun Lands . . ."

Quote about Lyman DePriest: Solomon, "With Classy . . . ," *New Haven Register*, April 11, 1991, 33.

The win at Syracuse: Davis, "UConn Nips . . . ," *Hartford Courant*, January 17, 1988, E1, E8.

The loss to Syracuse: Jeff Thoreson, "Sad Finish . . . ," *Post-Standard*, February 22, 1988, E1; Dave Ramsey, "Orange Steals . . . ," *Post-Standard*, February 21, 1988, D1.

VCU game: Davis, *Hartford Courant*, March 26, 1988, C1, C6; March 27, 1988, E1, E12; Wayne Norman and Robert S. Porter. 2008. *Hoop Tales: UConn Huskies Men's Basketball*. Guilford, CT, Globe Pequot, 90; *Huskymania*, 84–85; Tommy Hine, "But That . . . ," *Hartford Courant*, March 14, 2001, C1; AP, March 26, 1988.

Barros-DePriest game: UPI, "Sports News," March 29, 1988; Mike Weil, UPI, March 30, 1988; *New York Times*, "NIT: Ohio State . . . ," March 30, 1988; Bill Barnard, AP, March 30, 1988; *Hartford Courant*, "Coach's Calls," *Hartford Courant*, November 9, 2006, H8; Davis, "UConn Beats . . . ," *Hartford Courant*, March 30, 1988, B1.

NIT championship game: Bill Barnard, "Connecticut 72 . . . ," AP, March 30, 1988; Mike
Weil, UPI, March 30, 1988; Davis, "Huskies Hold . . . ," *Hartford Courant*, March 31,
1988, D1.

4. The Most Important Recruit in UConn Basketball History
Chris Smith's signing: Chris Elsberry, *Connecticut Post*, September 21, 2003; February 5,
2007; Steve Wilson, "Smith Chooses . . . ," *New Haven Register*, November 17, 1987,
55, 59; *Connecticut Basketball Illustrated*, "Chris Smith Poised . . . ," circa 1989–1990
season; Kevin Harmon, "Huskies' Top . . . ," *Post-Standard*, January 15, 2001, B1.
Details about Homer Babbidge Library: University of Connecticut, University Libraries,
Thomas J. Dodd Research Center.

5. We Weren't Just a Gnat Anymore
"We weren't just a gnat . . ." *Huskymania*, 99–100.
". . . you had to go through one of those seasons" *Huskymania*, 100.
Details about Burrell: Solomon, *New Haven Register*, May 7, 2010; May 9, 2010;
Uconnhooplegends.com, "Scott Burrell"; Steve Wilson, "Burrell . . . ," *New Haven
Register*, June 6, 1989, 49; Mike Anthony, "Coming Full . . . ," *Hartford Courant*, June
17, 2007, E9; Jim Shea, "Burrell Brings . . . ," *Hartford Courant*, February 3, 1991, D7;
Michael Vega, "Burrell Hit . . . ," *Boston Globe*, March 24, 1990, 33.
Calhoun's prediction: Curry, "A Five-Year . . . ," *New York Times*, January 26, 1990, B11.
Villanova boo-bird game: *Huskymania*, 116.
Game at Seton Hall: *New York Times*, "UConn Capitalizes . . . ," January 14, 1990, A3;
UPI, "Connecticut 79 . . . ," January 13, 1990; Tom Canavan, "Connecticut 79 . . . ,"
AP, January 13, 1990.
Details about Henefeld: *Huskymania*, 102–103; Calhoun and Montville, *Dare to Dream*,
chapter 4; Steve Berkowitz, "Henefeld Steals . . . ," *Washington Post*, February 28,
1990, D1; Jack Cavanaugh, "From Letter Writer . . . ," *New York Times*, December 13,
1989, D22; Dave Anderson, "I Feel . . . ," *New York Times*, March 18, 1990, A2.
Details about Gampel Pavilion: Owen Canfield, "New Arena . . . ," *Hartford Courant*,
January 30, 1987, D1; *Hartford Courant*, "Time Out . . . ," February 6, 1987; David
Fink, "Sports Center . . . ," *Hartford Courant*, January 28, 1987, B1; *Connecticut
Basketball Illustrated*, "A Case of Teamwork," 1990 season; *Connecticut Basketball
Illustrated*, "Welcome to Harry A. Gampel Pavilion," 1990 season.

6. I Know It Sounds Crazy, but I Never Thought We Were Going to Lose
UConn's rankings: Moran, "Soaring High . . . ," *New York Times*, March 5, 1990, C5.
Big East tournament quarterfinals: Bill Barnard, "No. 8 UConn 76 . . . ," AP, March 9,
1990.
Big East tournament semifinals: Moran, "UConn and Syracuse . . . ," *New York
Times*, March 11, 1990, section 8, 1; David Ramsey and Donna Ditota, "Thompson
Impressed . . . ," *Post-Standard*, March 11, 1990, E4; Vega, "UConn Downs . . . ,"
Boston Globe, March 11, 1990, 53; George Ferencz, Jr., and David P. Tosatti. 1990.
UConn's Dream Season, Chicago, IL: Bonus Books.
Big East tournament finals: Mike Waters, "Huskies Hound . . . ," *Post Standard*, March

12, 1990, D1; David Leon Moore, "UConn Prevails . . . ," *USA Today*, March 12, 1990, 3C; Vega, "UConn Rises . . . ," *Boston Globe*, March 12, 1990, 27; Moran, "UConn Beats . . . ," *New York Times*, March 12, 1990, C1; Ryan, "Gwynn Shows . . . ," *Boston Globe*, March 12, 1990, 31.

For Huskymania, see Kirk Johnson, "UConn Basketball . . . ," *New York Times*, March 13, 1990, B1; UPI, "Husky-mania . . . ," March 15, 1990.

California game: Vega, "UConn Rolls . . . ," *Boston Globe*, March 18, 1990, 43; Karen Allen, "UConn Blitzes . . . ," *USA Today*, March 19, 1990, B9; Vega. "UConn Getting . . . ," *Boston Globe*, March 19, 1990, 42.

Clemson game: Fred Lief, UPI, March 23, 1990; Bill Barnard, "No. 3 Connecticut 71 . . . ," AP, March 22, 1990; Vega, "Timeless Miracle . . . ," *Boston Globe*, March 23, 1990, 67; Moran, "Last-Second . . . ," *New York Times*, March 22, 1990, B7; Hubert Mizell, "UConn Bomb . . . ," *St. Petersburg Times*, March 23, 1990, 1C; Vega, "Burrell Hit . . ."

Duke game: Moran, "UConn Eliminated . . . ," *New York Times*, March 25, 1990, section 8, 1; Tom Withers, "UConn's Season . . . ," UPI, March 24, 1990; Anthony Cotton, "Duke Stuns . . . ," *Washington Post*, March 24, 1990, B1; Karen Allen, "Laettner's Last-Second . . . ," *USA Today*, March 26, 1990, 4C; Vega, "Duke Ends . . . ," *Boston Globe*, March 25, 1990, 45.

"The dirtiest player . . ." Calhoun and Montville, *Dare to Dream*, 84.

7. Oh, UConn, That's the Place Where They Made the Buzzer-Beater

Quote about Laettner's shot: Calhoun and Montville, *Dare to Dream*, 84.

Details about Calhoun's postseason awards: *UConn's Dream Season*, 131.

"Calhoun has done one of the most exceptional jobs . . ." Vega. "UConn Downs . . . ," *Boston Globe*, March 11, 1990, 53.

Details about 1991 recruiting class: Moran, "UConn Recruiting . . . ," *New York Times*, April 11, 1991, B20; Calhoun and Montville, *Dare to Dream*, 85; Solomon, "National Exposure . . ."; Weiss, "This Year's Connecticut . . . ," *Daily News*, March 9, 1995, 79; Blaine Newnham, "Marshall Key . . . ," *Seattle Times*, March 24, 1995, D1; Uconnhooplegends, "Brian Fair"; Peter Brewington, "Kansas Takes . . . ," *USA Today*, April 12, 1991, 14C.

Information about Donyell Marshall: Peter Brewington, "Top Pa. Boys . . . ," *USA Today*, April 12, 1991, C12; Vinnie Perrone, "Shadow of the . . . ," *Washington Post*, February 28, 1994, C10; David Ramsey, "Top Recruit . . . ," *Post-Standard*, April 8, 1991, D1; David Ramsey, "SU Probe . . . ," *Post-Standard*, March 16, 1991, C1; Solomon, "Marshall Says . . . ," *New Haven Register*, April 10, 1991, 40.

8. I Hope People Took Some Polaroids Tonight

Details about Henefeld: Cavanaugh, "The Israeli Connection . . . ," *New York Times*, December 23, 1994; *Jerusalem Post*, "No. 52 Nadav Henefeld," *Jerusalem Post*, March 10, 2008, 11.

Packer on Smith dribble: Davis, "Packer on . . . ," *Hartford Courant*, January 7, 1992, E3.

"I'm a proud father" Moran, "For Calhoun . . . ," *New York Times*. March 20, 1995, C6.

Calhoun's confrontation with Francesa: "Mike, Mad Dog . . . ," *Hartford Courant*, January 9, 1997.

Smith's last Gampel game: Mark Blaudschun, "Smith, UConn . . . ," *Boston Globe*, February 23, 1992, 38; Owen Canfield, "He Has the Mark . . . ," *Hartford Courant*, February 23, 1992, D1; Fast Scripts, "An Interview . . ."

Big East tournament quarterfinals: Davis, "One Quarter . . . ," *Hartford Courant*, March 10, 1991, E1, E12; Moran, "Mutombo and Hoyas . . . ," *New York Times*, March 9, 1991, section 1, 44.

LSU game: Davis, *Hartford Courant*, March 11, 1991, D1, D4; March 15, 1991, E1, E5; March 11, 1991, D1, D4; John Bannon, "O'Neal Set . . . ," *USA Today*, March 12, 1991, 12C; Jackie MacMullan, "He Has the Inside . . . ," *Boston Globe*, March 14, 1991, 85; Tom Yantz, "O'Neal Runs . . . ," *Hartford Courant*, March 15, 1991, E5; Vega, "Connecticut Shackles . . . ," *Boston Globe*, March 15, 1991, 29.

Pat Calhoun's quote about her husband as an underdog: Chardis, "The Calhouns Wish . . . ," *Connecticut Basketball Illustrated*, 1989–1990 season, 57.

Sellers and Laettner: Jarrett Bell, "NCAA Denies . . . ," *USA Today*, March 16, 1992, 4C; Blaudschun, "Tranghese Raps . . . ," *Boston Globe*, March 15, 1992, 58; Sean Kirst, "Black Hoops Coaches . . . ," *Post-Standard*, April 3, 1992, C1; *USA Today*, "Laettner Ruling . . . ," April 3, 1992, 9C; Michael Wilbon, "For Laettner . . . ," *Washington Post*, April 3, 1992, F1.

9. Calhoun Taught Me Everything

Dickenman relayed the story about his flights to the author on June 23, 2006. He told a similar version to Norman and Porter.

Candy Man nickname and Allen's statistics: Gary D'Amato, "Impressive Allen . . . ," *Milwaukee Journal-Sentinel*, October 31, 1996, 1.

Wooden's recruitment of Walton: David Halberstam. 2000. *The Breaks of the Game*. New York: Hyperion, 269; published by Alfred A. Knopf in 1981.

Ray Allen as a renaissance man: David Locke, "Allen's Embrace . . . ," *Seattle Post-Intelligencer*, July 6, 2005, D4; Gene Sapakoff, "Just Think . . . ," *Post and Courier*, June 4, 2008, C1; Mike Bergin, "Ray Allen," *Seattle Post-Intelligencer*, January 30, 2006, D3; Michael Hunt, "Depth Sets . . . ," *Milwaukee Journal-Sentinel*, June 27, 1996, 3; D'Amato, "Impressive Allen . . ."

Popeye quote: David Scott, "Beauty in the East," *Sport*, February 1999, 64.

Allen discusses his recruitment and Calhoun's approach in Montville, "A Style . . . ," *Sports Illustrated*, April 7, 1999, 18.

Dickenman on Storrs: Solomon, "National Exposure . . ."

Kentucky and Virginia's recruitment of Ray Allen: Al Featherston, "Recruiting Misses . . . ," *Herald-Sun*, December 27, 1995, D1; Doug Doughty, "Huskies' Allen . . . ," *Roanoke Times*, January 29, 1996, B1.

Blaney discusses Calhoun as a talent evaluator in Tom Kensler, "UConn Got . . . ," *NCAA Journal*, April 4, 2004, C12.

Details about Reggie Lewis: Northeastern University Men's Basketball 2010–2011 Media Guide and Yearbook; Mark Murphy, "Calhoun Still Lewis' . . ."; William Oscar Johnson, "Heart of the Matter," May 24, 1993, *Sports Illustrated*; Christine Hanley, AP, July 28, 1993; *Sporting News*, "Openers," June 20, 1994, 5; Kevin Mannix, "Marshall's So Good . . . ," *Boston Herald*, March 25, 1994, 98.

For the 1993 recruiting class rankings, see Gene Wojciechowski, "These 11 Programs . . . ,"
    Los Angeles Times, November 30, 1992, S12; "St. John's Basketball . . . ," *Post-Standard*,
    December 11, 1992, D6; Hoop Scoop Online, "Hoop Scoop's Final Ranking . . .";
    Solomon, "Marshall Responds . . . ," *New Haven Register*, November 30, 1992, A3.
Gibbons on King: Solomon, "Marshall Responds . . ."
Details about Sheffer: *Daily News*, "UConn Guards . . ."; Gary Nuhn, "Sheffer
    Knows . . . ," *Dayton Daily News*, March 17, 1996, D1; ULEP Cup, "Doron Sheffer
    Returns . . . ," ulebcup.com; "The Ice Man Goeth," *Jerusalem Post*, July 7, 2000, 6B;
    Kevin McNamara, "Friars Journal," *Providence Journal-Bulletin*, January 20, 1994, 4C.
Details about Maccabi Elite Tel Aviv: maccabi.co.il.
Game at Virginia: John Feinstein, "One November Game . . . ," *Washington Post*,
    December 4, 1993, B5.
Donyell Marshall's benching: Moran, "Double the Expectations . . . ," *New York Times*,
    March 7, 1994, C1.
Calhoun as a father figure: Barry Jacobs, "Tar Heels Stop UConn . . . ," *New York Times*,
    December 6, 1990, B10; Jeff Powalisz, "Calhoun Adds . . . ," April 6, 2005; Scott,
    "Beauty . . ."; Elsberry, "Calhoun Spreads . . . ," *Connecticut Post*, September 11, 2005.
Game at PC: McNamara, *Providence Journal-Bulletin*, January 20, 1994, 1C; January 20,
    1994, 4C; Davis, "UConn Answers . . . ," *Hartford Courant*, January 20, 1994, C1;
    Owen Canfield, "Friars Show . . . ," *Hartford Courant*, January 20, 1994, C1; Yantz,
    "Seconds Reflect . . . ," *Hartford Courant*, January 21, 1994, E1; Bill Reynolds, "Great
    Script . . . ," *Providence Journal-Bulletin*, January 20, 1994, 1C; Jim Donaldson, "Justice
    Rights . . . ," *Providence Journal-Bulletin*, January 20, 1994, 4C; William A. Wallace,
    "Ollie's Coast-to-Coast . . . ," *New York Times*, January 20, 1994, B11; Ray Formanek,
    Jr., AP, January 20, 1994.
Game at BC and Billy Curley's recruitment: *Hoop Tales*; Ryan, "BC Holds . . . ," *Boston
    Globe*, November 5, 1989, 58; Vega, "BC's O'Brien . . . ," *Boston Globe*, November 10,
    1989, 45; Vega, "UConn Escapes . . . ," *Boston Globe*, February 10, 1994, 69; William
    Wallace, "Only One Standout . . . ," *New York Times*, February 11, 1994, B15; Gerry
    Callahan, "Curley Warms . . . ," *Boston Herald*, February 10, 1994, 78; Mark Cofman,
    "BC Connquered," *Boston Herald*, February 10, 1994, 96.
Ollie's sense of responsibility: Moran, "For Calhoun, the Fires . . ."; Christopher Barrett,
    "UConn Basketball Coach . . . ," *The Good Five-Cent Cigar* via U-Wire, October 12,
    2005.
Ollie on Calhoun's demands: Moran, "UConn Cruises . . . ," *New York Times*, March 19,
    1995, section 8, 1.
Florida game: Moran, "Empty! UConn Shoots . . . ," *New York Times*, March 26, 1994, 29;
    Wayne Coffey, "UConn Job," *Daily News*, March 27, 1994, D4; Blaudschun, "UConn
    Was Dealt . . . ," *Boston Globe*, March 27, 1994, 61.

10. He's Going to Be a Special, Special Player

Calhoun on Allen as "the next guy . . ." Vega, "Now It's Show . . . ," *Boston Globe*,
    December 6, 1994, 66.
UConn's win at Seton Hall: George Willis, "Hall Nearly . . . ," *New York Times*, January
    22, 1995, section 8, 1.

UConn's defense against Georgetown: D. L. Cummings, *Daily News*, March 12, 1995, 48.

"Special, special player" UPI, "Connecticut 90 . . . ," UPI, November 30, 1994.

First Syracuse game: Waters, *Post-Standard*, January 24, 1995, D1; January 24, 1995, D4.

Second Syracuse game: Moran, "Opportunity Knocks . . . ," *New York Times*, February 12, 1995, C1; Blaudschun, "UConn Takes . . . ," *Boston Globe*, March 12, 1995, 47.

Thompson's quote about Ollie and Marshall: Blaudschun, "UConn Takes . . . ," *Boston Globe*, March 12, 1995, 47. Derogatory word is not in the original.

Kansas game: Jim O'Connell, AP, January 28, 1995; Bill Sullivan, "Kansas Gives . . . ," *Houston Chronicle*, January 29, 1995, 3.

Calhoun and the women's team: Greg Garber, "'Dynamic Tension' . . . ," *Hartford Courant*, February 26, 1996, A1; Montville, "Dynamic Tension," *Sports Illustrated*, March 8, 1999, 64; Frank Fitzpatrick and Joe Juliano, "No Sign . . . ," *Philadelphia Inquirer*, April 1, 2000, E7; Les Carpenter, "UConn Kings . . . ," *Seattle Times*, April 1, 2004; Calhoun and Montville, *Dare to Dream*, 136–138; Geno Auriemma and Jackie MacMullan. 2009. *Geno*. Grand Central Publishing, 146–149; Anthony, "Mailbag Question 12/31: Calhoun/Auriemma Relationship," *Hartford Courant*, December 31, 2009, blogs.courant.com/uconn_mens_basketball.

Donny Marshall profile: David Nakamura, *Washington Post*, March 19, 1995, D11; March 21, 1995, E5; Sandy Ringer, "Marshalling . . . ," *Seattle Times*, June 5, 1991, B5; David Leon Moore, "UConn Star . . . ," *USA Today*, March 23, 1995, 2C; Matt Michael, "Marshall Silences . . . ," *Post-Standard*, February 13, 1995, D4; Donna Ditota, "UConn Spoils . . . ," *Post-Standard*, February 13, 1995, D1; Anthony, "Garrison Sticking . . . ," *Hartford Courant*, May 3, 2006; Ken Goe, "Marshall's Final . . . ," *Oregonian*, March 25, 1995, C6; Steve Earley, "'Other Marshall' . . . ," *Seattle Times*, March 16, 1994, C1; Gary Dulac, "UConn Powers . . . ," *Pittsburgh Post-Gazette*, January 30, 1994, C1; Waters, "Moten Says . . . ," *Post-Standard*, January 24, 1995, D4; Ken Denlinger, "Hoyas Fall . . . ," *Washington Post*, March 1, 1993, E1.

Criticism of Marshall: Michael, "Marshall Silences . . ."; Ditota, "UConn Spoils . . ."; Bill Finley, *Daily News*, March 25, 1995, 40; Newnham, "Marshall Key . . . ," Bill Sullivan, "Whatever It Takes," *Houston Chronicle*, March 25, 1995, 4; D. L. Cummings, "Flashes," *Daily News*, March 12, 1995, 24.

UCLA game: Bill Finley, "Running Game . . . ," *Daily News*, March 26, 1995, 46; Ryan, "Runners Finally . . . ," *Boston Globe*, March 26, 1995, 49.

Ollie's career: John Branch, "NBA Career Full . . . ," *New York Times*, April 15, 2010; Anthony, "Road Back . . . ," *Hartford Courant*, June 15, 2010, C1; Branson Wright, "Recalling Those . . . ," *Plain Dealer*, January 4, 2004, 5.

11. Ray Allen, One of the Greatest

UConn 2000: Zonder, "Connecticut State . . ."; Rabinovitz, "UConn to Get . . ."; Peacock, "Building . . ."; Keith, "21st Century . . ."; Connecticut General Assembly, Senate session transcript for April 26, 1995.

Allen and Sheffer's decision to stay at UConn: Rick Stroud, "Allen: . . . ," *St. Petersburg Times*, December 12, 1995, 1C; Groner, "The Ice Man . . ."

"Our goal is to win a national championship . . ." Jeff Jacobs, "This Time . . . ," *Hartford Courant*, February 4, 1996, E1.

Perkins on a UMass-UConn game: Davis, "Garden Takes . . . ," *Hartford Courant*,
   February 6, 1996, C2.
Calhoun-Calipari rivalry: Ron Borges, "Clash . . . ," *Boston Herald*, April 2, 2011, 34;
   Patrick Reusse, "UConn's Family . . . ," *Star Tribune*, February 26, 1995, 12C; John
   Clay, "Revisiting the Calipari-Calhoun . . . ," *Lexington Herald-Leader*, November 24,
   2010; Art Stapleton, "Up Next . . . ," *St. Paul Pioneer Press*, March 28, 2011; Eddie
   Pells, "Calhoun, Calipari . . . ," AP, April 1, 2011.
Florida State apology: Davis, "Huskies Aren't . . . ," *Hartford Courant*. February 27, 1996,
   C1; Barry Meisel, "Seminoles to . . . ," *Daily News*, March 25, 1997, 53.
Villanova game at Gampel: Jere Longman, "Hot Start . . . ," *New York Times*, January 10,
   1996, B9; Mike Jensen, "Huskies Maul . . . ," *Philadelphia Inquirer*, January 10, 1996,
   E1; Dick Jerardi, "UConn, Nova . . . ," *Philadelphia Daily News*, January 10, 1996, 61.
Calhoun rates 1996 team as his best in Ed Graney, "Huskies Aren't . . . ," *San Diego
   Union-Tribune*. March 23, 1996, D1.
For Ray Allen as Big East player of the year, see Barker Davis, "Big East . . . ," *Washington
   Times*, March 6, 1996, B3; Steve Hirsch, "UConn's Allen . . . ," *Record*, March 16, 1996,
   S1; *Hartford Courant*, "Coach's Calls"; Bob Snyder, "Scary Element . . . ," *Post-Standard*,
   January 26, 1996, D6; Steve Hirsch. "Legend in . . . ," *Record*, January 31, 1996, S1.
"If we stop Ray Allen . . ." Weiss, "Attack Dogs," *Daily News*, March 8, 1996, 68.
Big East tournament championship game: D. L. Cummings, "Allen Makes . . . ," *Daily
   News*, March 10, 1996, 45; Weiss, "Allen Makes . . . ," *Daily News*, March 10, 1996, 44;
   Davis, "UConn's Moore . . . ," *Hartford Courant*, March 13, 1996, C1.
The loss to Mississippi State: Jim Mashek, "Southeast Upset," *Biloxi Sun Herald*, March
   22, 1996; Mike Shalin, "UConn Tumbles," *Boston Herald*, March 23, 1996, 39;
   Michael Kinsley, "Call of the Wild," *Sporting News*, March 18, 1996, 29.
Dickenman's ride from Bradley Airport to Storrs: Calhoun and Montville, *Dare to Dream*,
   211.
Calhoun on Dickenman's importance: *Dare to Dream*, 110.
For Locke's comments, see "Allen's Embrace . . ."
Details about Sheffer: Groner, "The Ice Man . . ."; AP, "Sheffer to Play . . . ," *New York
   Times*, August 1, 1996.
Details about Knight's pro career: Michael Owen Baker, "Knight Goes . . . ," *Los Angeles
   Daily News*, July 8, 1997.
Criticisms of UConn: Steve Campbell, "Again, UConn . . . ," *Times Union*, March 23,
   1996, C1; Rafael Hermoso, "UGone . . . ," *Record*, March 23, 1996, S1.

12. You Learn from Losses . . .

Details about Kevin Freeman: Davis, *Hartford Courant*, May 2, 1996, C1; May 17, 1996,
   C1; Kevin T. Czerwinski, "Taking Residence . . . ," *Record*, January 17, 1996, S10;
   Jon Reidel, "Day of Decision . . . ," *Post-Standard*, April 3, 1996, 17; Greg Mattura,
   "Freeman Picks . . . ," *Record*, May 2, 1996, S5; Anthony McCarron, "Freeman to
   UConn," *Daily News*, May 2, 1996, 98; *Hartford Courant*, "Building . . ."
Details about Jake Voskuhl: *Houston Chronicle* staff, "High Schools: Boys Basketball
   Preview . . . ," November 12, 1995, section 2, 22; Davis, "Calhoun Expects . . .";
   Michael Murphy, "Three Strake . . . ," *Houston Chronicle*, February 10, 1995, 1.

The recruitment of Rip Hamilton: E. J. Jacobs, "NCAA-Insider . . . ," *Sporting News*,
    January 26, 1996; Davis, "Following Huskies . . . ," *Hartford Courant*, February 13,
    1996, C1; *Tampa Tribune*, "How It . . . ," March 29, 1999, Special Sports, 6; Jacobs,
    "Hamilton Marked . . . ," *Hartford Courant*, November 21, 1996, C1; Waters, "The
    Big East: Connecticut," *Post-Standard*, November 20, 1996, D15; *Hartford Courant*,
    "Building the UConn Men," November 13, 1998, G4.
Rankings of the 1996 recruiting class: Waters, "Hart Is in . . . ," *Post-Standard*, C1;
    McNamara, "A Banner . . . ," *Providence Journal-Bulletin*, 1C.
Details about the suspensions: Davis, "UConn: Bigger Penalty," *Hartford Courant*,
    January 24, 1997, C1; Cavanaugh, "UMass and UConn . . . ," *New York Times*, May 9,
    1997; *Hartford Courant*, "Steps to NCAA's . . . ," January 25, 1997, C3; A. K. Ruffin,
    "Calhoun Has . . . ," *Star-Ledger*, March 25, 1997, 52.
King as a student coach: Waters and Ramsey, "Bad Time . . . ," *Post-Standard*, February
    18, 1997, C4.
Kansas game: Vega, "Still Tops," *Boston Globe*, January 20, 1997, F1; Weiss, "Jayhawks
    Mush . . . ," *Daily News*, January 20, 1997, 58; Jim Salisbury, "No. 1 Kansas
    Defeats . . . ," *Philadelphia Inquirer*, January 20, 1997, C1; Davis, "UConn Almost . . . ,"
    Hartford Courant, January 20, 1997, C1.
The midnight practice: Davis, "Calhoun Waits . . . ," *Hartford Courant*, March 5, 1997, C1.
"It's very difficult to grow as a team in losses" Yantz, "Huskies Pulling . . . ," *Hartford
    Courant*, March 25, 1997, C1.
"Rip went from a good young player . . ." Yantz, "Huskies Finish . . . ," *Hartford Courant*,
    March 28, 1997, C1.

13. The Kid Comes with a Bag of Tricks

Details about Davis and El-Amin's rankings: Brick Oettinger, "Recruiting Watch,"
    Sporting News, February 17, 1997, 36.
Details about Khalid El-Amin: Roman Augustoviz, *Star-Tribune*, March 23, 1995,
    4C; July 30, 1995, 15C; March 17, 1996, 15C; August 8, 1996, 8C; April 14, 1997,
    3C; Brian Wicker, *Star-Tribune*, March 19, 1996, 1C; November 13, 1996, 8C; Jerry
    Zgoda, "El-Amin Decides . . . ," *Star-Tribune*, August 11, 1995, 1C; Dennis Brackin,
    "Is El-Amin . . . ," *Star-Tribune*, January 24, 1996, 8C; *Sports News*, "Star Point . . . ,"
    February 14, 1996; Carolyn White, "Star Guard . . . ," *USA Today*, December 4, 1996,
    3C; Bill Minutaglio, "Making the Huskies . . . ," *Sporting News*, November 30, 1998,
    72–75; Sid Hartman, "El-Amin Still . . . ," *Star-Tribune*, March 26, 1996, 3C; Charley
    Walters, "El-Amin Puts . . . ," *St. Paul Pioneer Press*, July 25, 1996, 4D.
Details about El-Amin's performance at the ABCD camp: Augustoviz, "He's
    Making . . . ," *Star-Tribune*, July 30, 1995, 15C.
El-Amin's benching: Brian Wicker, "Parents Bench . . . ," *Star-Tribune*, January 15, 1997,
    1C; Wayne Washington, "El-Amin Benching . . . ," *Star-Tribune*, January 15, 1997, 6C;
    Carolyn White, "Parents Bench . . . ," *USA Today*, January 16, 1997, 13C.
El-Amin's senior year: Davis, "El-Amin Gives . . . ," *Hartford Courant*, April 20, 1997,
    E16; Richard Meryhew, "Basketball Boom," *Star-Tribune*, February 19, 1997, 1A;
    Augustoviz, "Amin, Millers . . . ," *Star-Tribune*, April 14, 1997, 3C.
UConn's recruitment of El-Amin: Roman Augustoviz, *Star-Tribune*, April 26, 1997,

1C; April 30, 1997, 4C; Michael Arace, "El-Amin's Play . . . ," *Hartford Courant*,
September 12, 1997, C1; Curt Brown, "FYI: El-Amin Passes . . . ," *Star-Tribune*, March
1, 1997, 1C; Jerry Zgoda, "Haskins Pursues . . . ," *Star-Tribune*, April 9, 1997, 1C;
Calhoun and Montville, *Dare to Dream*, 127–128; Davis, "El-Amin Gives . . ."; Dan
Barreiro, "Sore about . . . ," *Star-Tribune*, April 23, 1997, 1C; Gary Olson, "El-Amin
Chooses . . . ," *St. Paul Pioneer Press*, April 26, 1997, 1C; Solomon, "UConn Hits . . . ,"
New Haven Register, April 26, 1997, E1.

El-Amin pats Calhoun on the back, El-Amin's first-year statistics, and reaction to him:
Scott, "Beauty . . ."

El-Amin versus Florida State: Tara Sullivan, 'UConn Coach . . . ," *Record*, November 27,
1997, S2; Jere Longman, "Vindication . . . ," *New York Times*, November 27, 1997, C1.

Statistics about Hamilton's 1,000 points: Joe Juliano, "Hamilton Is Busy . . . ,"
Philadelphia Inquirer, F5.

Billet's quote: Jacobs, "Look at It . . . ," *Hartford Courant*, March 7, 1998, C1.

The Big East tournament championship game: Darren Everson, "Huskies Are . . . ," *Daily
News*, March 8, 1998, 68; Dave Hickman, "UConn Captures . . . ," *Charleston Gazette*,
March 8, 1998, 1D; Steve Serby, "Smokin' Khalid . . . ," *New York Post*, March 8, 1998,
96; Diane Pucin, "UConn Stymies . . . ," *Philadelphia Inquirer*, March 8, 1998, C10.

Washington game: Tony Barnhart, "Buzzer Beater!" *Atlanta Journal-Constitution*, March
20, 1998, 8E; Kirk Bohls, "UConn Survives . . . ," *Austin American-Statesman*, March
20, 1998, C6.

Elite Eight game: Josh Barr, "From Guthridge's . . . ," *Washington Post*, January 14,
1998, D1; Neil Amato, "For UConn . . . ," *Herald-Sun*, March 20, 1998, B6; Brian
Lewis, "UConn Knows . . . ," *New York Post*, March 23, 1998, 68; Curry, "Carolina
Snaps . . . ," *New York Times*, March 22, 1998, 8.1; Arace, "UConn Guards . . . ,"
Hartford Courant, August 28, 1998, C1; Jim Souhan, "North Carolina . . . ," *Star
Tribune*, March 22, 1998, 1C.

14. We're Having a Special Season

Details about Hamilton and the pros: Calhoun and Montville, *Dare to Dream*, 100, 103,
127–128; Weiss, "Jim, Geno . . . ," *Daily News*, May 19, 2004, 77; AP, "Hamilton
Staying . . . ," May 9, 1998; Peter Abraham, "UConn Star . . . ," *San Antonio Express
News*, May 10, 1998, C6.

Details about Joe McGinn: Bill Plaschke, "UConn Believed . . . ," *Los Angeles Times*,
March 24, 1999, 1; Martin Fennelly, "Guy Named . . . ," *Tampa Tribune*, March 27,
1999, 27; Yantz, "Martin Touches . . ."; Al Lara, "Joe McGinn . . . ," *Hartford Courant*,
March 11, 1999, B1; Calhoun and Montville, *Dare to Dream*, 135.

Details about the summer tour: Arace, *Hartford Courant*, August 30, 1998, E2; August
29, 1998, C4; August 28, 1998, C1; AP State & Local Wire, "Connecticut 82 . . . ,"
August 28, 1998; Calhoun and Montville, *Dare to Dream*, 35.

Previews of the 1999 season: Brian Landman, "College Basketball . . . ," *St. Petersburg
Times*, November 8, 1998, 8C; Mark Bradley, "College Basketball . . . ," *Atlanta
Journal-Constitution*, November 8, 1998, 2N.

Duke's ranking: Wire reports, "Cincinnati Drops . . . ," *Sunday Oregonian*, November 29,
1998; Tom Keegan, "UConn Likes . . . ," *New York Post*, December 3, 1998, 78.

Michigan State game: Ethan J. Antonucci, "UConn Beats . . . ," *Daily Campus*, December
7, 1998; O'Connell, "No. 1 Connecticut 82 . . . ," AP, December 5, 1998; Shira
Springer, "A Good . . . ," *Boston Globe*, December 6, 1998, C16; Ohm Youngmisuk,
"Cleaves Shut . . . ," *Daily News*, December 5, 1998.

The win at Pitt: Chuck Finder, "Pitt Fans . . . ," *Pittsburgh Post-Gazette*, December 13,
1998, D6; Newswire services, "Top-Ranked Huskies . . . ," *Buffalo News*, December 13,
1998; Alan Robinson, "No. 1 Connecticut 70 . . . ," AP State & Local Wire, December
12, 1998; Ron Cook, "Agony and Ecstasy . . . ," *Pittsburgh Post-Gazette*, December 13,
1998, D1; Ron Cook, "Pitt-UConn . . . ," *Pittsburgh Post-Gazette*, February 15, 2004,
D11; Gerry Dulac, "UConn Coach . . . ," *Pittsburgh Post-Gazette*, December 15, 1998, D1.

UConn's win at St. John's: Harvey Araton, "After Calhoun . . . ," *New York Times*, January
31, 1999, 8, 13; Blaudschun, "UConn Streak . . . ," *Boston Globe*, January 31, 1999,
E1; Judy Battista, "St. John's Emotions . . . ," *New York Times*, January 31, 1999, 8.1;
Davis, "Garden Great . . . ," *Hartford Courant*, January 31, 1999, E4; Anthony Gargano,
"UConn's Still . . . ," *New York Post*, March 1, 1999, 65; Bill Finley, "UConn Puts . . . ,"
Daily News, January 30, 1999; Darren Everson, "St. John's Gives . . . ," *Daily News*,
January 30, 1999; Tara Sullivan, "St. John's Comes . . . ," *Record*, January 31, 1999,
S14; O'Connell, "No. 1 Connecticut 78 . . . ," AP, January 31, 1999; Matthew Doyle,
"UConn, St. John's . . . ," *Daily Campus*, February 1, 1999; Mark Kriegel, "Ronnie on
the . . . ," *Daily News*, January 31, 1999, 88.

The loss to Syracuse: Joe Burris, "Loss No. 1," *Boston Globe*, February 2, 1999, C1.

Stanford game: Weiss, "Khalid El-Amin . . . ," *Daily News*, February 6, 1999; William
C. Rhoden, "Yes, This Rivalry . . . ," *New York Times*, March 7, 1999, 7; Calhoun and
Montville, *Dare to Dream*, 161.

UConn's 70–58 win over Syracuse: Ethan Antonucci, "UConn Beats . . . ," *Daily Campus*,
March 1, 1999; Gargano, "UConn's Still . . . ," *New York Post*, March 1, 1999, 65.

"We've already proven we're the best . . ." Arace, "Holding Fire . . . ," *Hartford Courant*,
March 4, 1999.

The Big East tournament quarterfinals: Brian Lewis, "UConn's Great . . . ," *New York
Post*, March 5, 1999, 119; Weiss, "Huskies Survive . . . ," March 5, 1999, *Daily News*,
85; Joe Drape, "Hit or Miss . . . ," March 5, 1999, *New York Times*, D4; Joe Juliano,
"Stars Have . . . ," *Philadelphia Inquirer*, March 5, 1999, D6.

"Wrecking machine" CBS Sportsline, "No. 1 Duke Demolishes . . . ," March 5, 1999.

Details about Emily Calhoun: Waters and Matt Michael, "Freeman Makes . . . ,"
Post-Standard, March 6, 1999, D6; Peter Abraham, "Calhoun Dedicates . . . ," *St.
Petersburg Times*, March 22, 1999, 10C; Weiss, "Freeman Arises . . . ," *Daily News*,
March 6, 1999, 44; Jacobs, "Little Wonder . . . ," *Hartford Courant*, March 6, 1999, C1.

The Big East tournament championship game: Rhoden, "Yes . . ."; O'Connell, "No.
3 UConn 82 . . . ," AP Online, March 6, 1999; Tara Sullivan, "UConn . . . ," *Record*,
March 7, 1999, S1.

Calhoun's quote about great players: Rhoden, "Yes . . ."

For McGinn's appearance in the UConn locker room, see Mark Kiszla, "Memory of . . . ,"
Denver Post, March 14, 1999, C4.

Details about the ACC's undefeated teams: University Wire and staff reports, "ACC
Streak . . . ," *Technician*, March 3, 1999.

UConn had the most NCAA tournament appearances without a trip to the Final Four: Arace, "Huskies Invited . . . ," *Hartford Courant*, March 21, 1998, C1; Brett McMurphy, "UConn Hopes . . . ," *Tampa Tribune*, March 8, 1999, 11.

"We've got one of the best programs . . . ," Jack Carey, "Hopes, Expectations . . . ," *USA Today*, March 8, 1999, 4E.

15. This One's for Joe

"Welcome to the Duke Invitational . . ." Steve Kelley, "Duke Is . . . ," *Seattle Times* for the *Florida Times-Union*, March 9, 1999, E3.

Duke's odds to win the NCAA tournament: Royce Feour, "Books, Fans . . . ," *Las Vegas Review-Journal*, March 9, 1999, 1C.

Information about Joe McGinn: Arace, "Game Time . . . ," *Hartford Courant*, March 11, 1999, C1; Plaschke, "UConn Believed . . ."; Fennelly, "Guy Named . . ."; Yantz, "Martin Touches . . ."; Lara, "Joe McGinn . . ."; Kiszla, "Memory of . . ."

Gonzaga game: John Harper, "What's in . . . ," *Daily News*, March 20, 1999, 54; John Smallwood, "For Gonzaga . . . ," *Philadelphia Daily News*, March 20, 1999, 45; Jon Wilner, "UConn Ends . . . ," *Los Angeles Daily News*, March 19, 1999; Arace, "Victory Bond?" *Hartford Courant*, March 22, 1999, C4; Blaudschun, "UConn's Final . . . ," *Boston Globe*, March 21, 1999, D1; John Smallwood, "Calhoun Finally . . . ," *Philadelphia Daily News*, March 22, 1999, 111; Les Carpenter, "Gone-Zaga," *Seattle Times*, March 21, 1999, D1; Brett McMurphy, "Finally Four . . . ," *Tampa Tribune*, March 21, 1999, 1; Jim Thomas, "UConn Secures . . . ," *St. Louis Post-Dispatch*, March 21, 1999, F1; Ernest Hopper, Sharon Ginn, and Darrell Fry, "Huskies Play . . . ," *St. Petersburg Times*, March 21, 1999, 10C; Dave Trimmer, "GU's No . . . ," *Spokesman Review*, March 21, 1999, C71; Les Carpenter, "It Takes . . . ," *Seattle Times*, March 23, 1999, D7; Lenn Robbins, "Nothin' but . . . ," *New York Post*, March 24, 1999, 74; Mark Murphy, "Final-ly, Calhoun's . . . ," *Boston Herald*, March 25, 1999, 110; Fennelly, "Guy Named . . ."; Jacobs, "Calhoun at Heart . . . ," *Hartford Courant*, March 21, 1999, E1; Brett McMurphy, "Finally Four . . . ," *Tampa Tribune*, March 21, 1999, 1; Peter Abraham, "Calhoun Dedicates . . . ," *St. Petersburg Times*, March 22, 1999, 10C.

Jim O'Brien, Ohio State, and national semifinal: Rusty Miller, "O'Brien Moves . . . ," AP, March 27, 1999; Ray Parrillo, "Redd, a Guard . . . ," *Philadelphia Inquirer*, March 25, 1999, E1; John Akers, "Duke-UConn," *San Jose Mercury News*, March 28, 1999, 1D; Shalin, "UConn Makes . . . ," *Boston Herald*, March 28, 1999, B16; Tony Barnhart, "Ohio State . . . ," *Atlanta Journal-Constitution*, March 28, 1999, 4G.

16. We Shocked the World!

The events before the national title game: Ray Parrillo, "UConn Confident . . . ," *Philadelphia Inquirer*, March 29, 1999, E4; Ed Graney, "UConn Refuses . . . ," *San Diego Union-Tribune*, March 29, 1999, D4; Tom Luicci, "UConn Ready . . . ," *Star-Ledger*, March 29, 1999, 37; Chris Dufresne, "We Are 33-2," *Charleston Daily Mail*, March 29, 1999, 1B; Darren Everson, "UConn Has . . . ," *Daily News*, March 29, 1999, 56; O'Connell, "Duke, UConn . . . ," AP Online, March 28, 1999; Tom Oates, "Blue Devils . . . ," *Wisconsin State Journal*, March 29, 1999, 1D; John Wilner, "UConn Can!" *Los Angeles Daily News*, March 30, 1999.

Calhoun's strategy against Duke: Vega, "This Peerless . . . ," *Boston Globe*, March 31, 1999, C6; Calhoun and Montville, *Dare to Dream*, 12–13, 15, 201; Weiss, "Came Down . . . ," *Daily News*, March 31, 1999, 61.

Details about Moore and Avery: John Akers, "Duke Taking . . . ," *San Jose Mercury News*, March 29, 1999, 1D; Frank Vehorn, "Student Goes . . . ," *Virginian-Pilot*, March 29, 1999, C6; Judy Battista, "Neighbors Travel . . . ," *New York Times*, March 29, 1999.

Shock the world quotes: Rudy Martzke, "CBS Team . . . ," *USA Today*, March 30, 1999, 2C; Sid Hartman, "El-Amin Makes . . . ," *Star Tribune*, March 30, 1999, 3C.

The national championship game: Bruce Lowitt, "Numbers Game . . . ," *St. Petersburg Times*, March 30, 1999, 5C; Wilner, "UConn Can!"; Calhoun and Montville, *Dare to Dream*, 202, 203; Jerardi, "UConn Believe . . . ," *Philadelphia Daily News*, March 30, 1999, 74; Brett McMurphy, "UConn's Hamilton . . . ," *Tampa Tribune*, March 30, 1999, 3; Dan Shanoff, "A Closer . . . ," Sportsillustrated.cnn.com, March 30, 1999; Weiss, "Came Down . . ."; Jim Baker, "UConn, CBS . . . ," *Boston Herald*, March 30, 1999, 72; *Hartford Courant*, "Coach's Calls."

Hamilton's NBA career: Ryan Pretzer, "To Get a Mask . . . ," Nba.com/pistons/news/ ripsmask.html.

El-Amin's arrest: Mike Allen, "Police Charge . . . ," *New York Times*, April 14, 1999, D1; Desmond Conner and Tom Puleo, "El-Amin Apologetic," *Hartford Courant*, April 16, 1999, A1.

17. I Wanted to Play for a Tough Coach . . .

Details about Butler: Liz Robbins, "Wizards' Butler . . . ," *New York Times*, February 18, 2007; Michael Lee, "The Great Escape," *Washington Post*, February 17, 2008; Neil Amato, "After a Rough . . . ," *Herald-Sun*, March 17, 2002, B4; Rhoden, "Butler Made . . . ," *New York Times*, March 18, 2002, 5; Elsberry, "Butler Continues . . . ," *Connecticut Post*, March 18, 2002; Paul Schwartz, "Huskies' Butler . . . ," *New York Post*, March 19, 2002, 81; Tony Barnhart, "UConn Star . . . ," Cox News Service, March 20, 2002; Jon Siegel, "From Isolation . . . ," *Washington Times*, April 21, 2006, C1; Tom D'Angelo, "Caron Butler . . . ," *Palm Beach Post*, October 30, 2002, 1H; Ed Miller, "Redemption Is . . . ," *Virginian-Pilot*, March 24, 2002, C7; Roscoe Nance, "Troubles Serve . . . ," *USA Today*, June 26, 2002, 7C; Tom Reed, "Wizards' Butler . . . ," Knight Ridder Newspapers, April 26, 2006; Mike Wise, "The Man . . . ," *Washington Post*, February 18, 2007, E1.

Butler's high school and prep school careers: Todd Rosiak, "Former Park . . . ," *Milwaukee Journal Sentinel*, August 5, 1999, 4; D. Orlando Ledbetter, "Ledbetter . . . ," *Milwaukee Journal Sentinel*, September 12, 1998, 2; Michael Smith, "Whatever It . . . ," *Boston Globe*, June 24, 2002, D1; Pete Thamel, "Second Chances," *Post-Standard*, March 22, 2002, C4; Amato, "After a Rough . . ."

Butler's recruitment: Nick Wishart, "UConn's Butler . . . ," *St. Louis Post-Dispatch*, March 22, 2002, D8; Sean O'Rourke, "Prep Star . . . ," *New Haven Register*, August 5, 1999, D1, D5

Brown and his recruitment: *Hartford Courant*'s Desmond Conner on September 10, 1999, C7; October 3, 1999, E13; October 13, 1999, C10; October 19, 1999, C2; November 17, 1999, C1; *Hartford Courant*'s Arace on August 22, 1999, E3; September 12, 1999, E2;

Daily News's Roger Rubin, January 9, 2000, 67; February 16, 2000, 70; March 30, 2000, 96; Mike DeCourcy, "Brown's Shot . . . ," *Sporting News*, November 27, 2000, 55; Alexander Wolff, "All Points . . . ," *Sports Illustrated*, November 20, 2000, 128; Julian Garcia, "Athlete of the Week . . . ," *Daily News*, February 2, 2000, 74; Waters, "Orange Seeking . . . ," *Post-Standard*, July 11, 1999, C4.

Calhoun and South Carolina: Desmond Conner, "Staying Power," *Hartford Courant*, November 8, 2001, H4; Weiss and Darren Everson, "Calhoun Nixes . . . ," *Daily News*, April 10, 2001, 74; AP State & Local Wire, "Report: Gamecocks Wooed . . . ," April 9, 2001; Adrian Wojnarowski, "Very Sweet . . . ," *Record*, March 18, 2002, S1.

18. If Maryland Is Number One in the Country . . .

Information on Okafor: *Hartford Courant*'s Desmond Conner, April 19, 2001, C2; April 20, 2001, C1; April 22, 2001, E10; Jim Litke, "An Advertisement . . . ," AP State & Local Wire, April 6, 2004; AP Online, "Knight Strikes . . . ," April 17, 2001; M. K. Bower, "Several Top . . . ," *Houston Chronicle*, April 11, 2001, 12; Marty Cook, "Houston Recruit . . . ," *Arkansas Democrat-Gazette*, January 25, 2001, C7; Sarah Hornaday, "Okafor Has . . . ," *Arkansas Democrat-Gazette*, February 27, 2001, C3; *Arkansas Democrat-Gazette*, "Okafor Commits . . . ," April 20, 2001, C1; Mike White, "Hoops Classic . . . ," *Pittsburgh Post-Gazette*, April 14, 2001, C2; Richard Oliver, "A Big-Time . . . ," *San Antonio Express-News*, February 2, 2004, 1D; Mark Babineck, "Houston Players . . . ," AP State & Local Wire, April 1, 2004; Joe Burris, "A Mind Game . . . ," *Boston Globe*, December 13, 2002, C1; Rob Harrington, "Building . . . ," *USA Today*, April 4, 2004.

The Pittsburgh Hoops Classic: Desmond Conner, "Spring . . . ," *Hartford Courant*, April 22, 2001, E10; Sean O'Rourke, "UConn Nabs . . . ," *New Haven Register*, April 20, 2001, E1, E5; White, "Hoops Classic . . ."

A "championship school with a championship coach" Jim Vertuno, "Okafor Left . . . ," AP State & Local Wire, March 28, 2003.

The story about Ben Gordon in the fifth grade: Mike Lupica, "Tops of . . . ," *Daily News*, March 30, 2004, 67.

The high school career and recruitment of Ben Gordon: Chuck Slater, *New York Times*, June 18, 2000, section 14WC, 3; August 13, 2000, section 14WC, 2; Pete Thamel, "Looking for . . . ," *New York Times*, January 2, 2004, 6; Jim Meehan, "Odd Couple . . . ," *Spokesman Review*, March 23, 2003, C1; Jim O'Donnell, "Bullish . . . ," *Chicago Sun-Times*, June 27, 2004, 96; Donna Tommelleo, "Huskies in . . . ," AP State & Local Wire, March 24, 2003.

Information about Duke and Gordon: Neill Ostrout, "Coach K's . . . ," *Connecticut Post*, April 3, 2004; Sarah Hornaday, "Recruiters Hit . . ." *Houston Chronicle*, November 18, 2000; Wire services, "Seton Hall . . . ," *Record*, August 15, 2000, S3.

Calhoun's shooting star quote: Matt Eagan, "In the End . . . ," *Hartford Courant*, March 27, 2002, G8.

Calhoun on Massimino: Adrian Wojnarowski, "Calhoun's Success . . . ," *Record*, March 31, 1999, S1.

Calhoun's desire for Butler to dominate in 2002: Alan Goldenbach, "He Does . . . ," *Washington Post*, March 24, 2002, D16.

St. Bonaventure game: Blaudschun, "Calhoun's Huskies . . . ," *Boston Globe*, December
14, 2001, C12; *Buffalo News*, "Bremer, Bonnies . . . ," December 29, 2001, C1; Ostrout,
"Huskies Lacked . . . ," *Connecticut Post*, December 30, 2001; Eagan, "In the End . . ."

The 2002 UNC team: Barry Svrluga, "UConn Fans . . . ," *News and Observer*, January 19,
2002, C7.

"Everyone, to a degree, needs to be convinced . . . ," Liesa Goins, "Build a Dream . . . ,"
Men's Health, posted January 6, 2004 (http://www.menshealth.com/best-life/
coaching-and-management-strategies).

UConn's win over Carolina: Frank Litsky, "After a Lecture . . . ," *New York Times*, January
20, 2002, section 8, 10; Ostrout, "UConn Runs . . . ," *Connecticut Post*, January 20,
2002.

The game at Arizona: AP, "UConn Swats . . . ," *Seattle Times*, January 27, 2002, C10;
Ostrout, "Fresh Stuff," *Connecticut Post*, January 27, 2002; Matt Eagan, "No. 25
UConn 100, No. 10 Arizona 98 (OT)," *Hartford Courant*, January 27, 2002, E11; UConn
Basketball, "2001–2002 Game No. 18"; Bob Baum, "No. 25 Connecticut 100, No. 10
Arizona 98, OT," AP, January 26, 2002.

UConn's victory over BC: Mike Cardillo, "Brown Fuels . . . ," *Daily Campus*, February
18, 2002; Michael Mutnansky, "UConn Extends . . . ," *Daily Campus*, February 18,
2002; Shalin, "UConn Clips . . . ," *Boston Herald*, February 17, 2002, B10; Matt Eagan,
"Brown Has BC . . . ," *Hartford Courant*, February 17, 2002, E1.

Villanova game: Michael Mutnansky, "UConn Freshman . . . ," *Daily Campus*, March
8, 2002; Joe Juliano, "Late Shot . . . ," *Philadelphia Inquirer*, March 8, 2002; Mark
Cannizzaro, "UConn Frosh . . . ," *New York Post*, March 8, 2002, 107; Weiss, "Gordon
Pulls . . . ," *Daily News*, March 8, 2002, 75; Elsberry, "Freshman Gordon . . . ,"
Connecticut Post, March 8, 2002.

Big East tournament finals: Michael Mutnansky, "UConn Defeats . . . ," *Daily Campus*,
March 11, 2002; Joe Drape, "In Classic . . . ," *New York Times*, March 10, 2002, section
8, 1; Shalin, "UConn Wins . . . ," *Boston Herald*, March 10, 2002, B12; Rubin, "UConn
Tops . . . ," *Daily News*, March 10, 2002; O'Connell, "No. 19 UConn 74 . . . ," AP
Online; Pete Thamel, "UConn Ousts . . . ," *Post-Standard*, March 10, 2002, C1; Greg
Mattura, "UConn's the Beast," *Record*, March 10, 2002, S4; Eagan, "In the End . . ."

N.C. State game: Al Featherston, "Another Recent . . . ," *Herald-Sun*, March 17, 2002,
B1; Steve Thompson, "Questionable Call . . . ," *Technician*, March 18, 2002; Michael
Mutnansky, "Butler, UConn . . . ," *Daily Campus*, March 18, 2002; Jerardi, "UConn's
Butler . . . ," *Philadelphia Daily News*, March 18, 2002; Paul Schwartz, "UConn
Gets . . . ," *New York Post*, March 18, 2002, 77; Ostrout, "UConn Men's Notebook,"
Connecticut Post, March 18, 2002; Blaudschun, "UConn Staggers . . . ," *Boston
Globe*, D1.

Calhoun describes Butler as one of the five best players in the country in Goldenbach,
"He Does . . ."

Second Maryland game: Jack Carey, "Maryland's Inside . . . ," *USA Today*, December 4,
2001, 7C; Michael Mutnansky, "Streak, Season . . . ," *Daily Campus*, March 25, 2002;
Steve Campbell, "Talent Needs . . . ," *Times Union*, March 25, 2002, D1; Rhoden,
"UConn Can't . . . ," *New York Times*, March 25, 2002, D5; Jack Carey, "Experience
Pushes . . . ," *USA Today*, March 25, 2002, 6C; John Smallwood, "Maryland

Shows . . . ," *Philadelphia Daily News*, March 25, 2002; Blaudschun, "Blake's
Shot . . . ," *Boston Globe*, March 25, 2002, D1; Rich Cimini, "UConn Can't . . . ,"
Daily News, March 25, 2002, 60; Michael Wilbon, "Mouton Holds . . . ," *Washington Post*, March 24, 2002, D17; Matt Eagan, "Butler's 26 . . . ," *Hartford Courant*, March 26, 2002, C1; Uconnhuskies.com, "UConn Falls . . ."; Alan Goldenbach, "Butler, a Forward . . . ," *Washington Post*, March 25, 2002, D12; Jacobs, "Caron Not . . . ," *Hartford Courant*, March 25, 2002, C1.

Butler's press conference: Uconnhuskies.com, "Statements from Caron Butler and Jim Calhoun."

Details about the nickname Tough Juice: Howard Fendrich, "Butler Brings . . . ," AP State & Local Wire, January 12, 2007.

19. We're Connecticut. We're Not Some Rinky-Dink Team

Details about UConn 2000 come from the University of Connecticut, Department of Chemistry, "The UConn Chemistry Building"; Rachel Z. Arndt, "Connecticut . . . ," *BusinessWeek*; *Connecticut Post*, "Continue the Work . . . ," March 26, 2002; Tommelleo, "Rowland Signs . . . ," AP, August 26, 2002; AP State & Local Wire, "UConn's Endowment . . . ," November 5, 2000.

Details about the money spent on UConn 2000 and the plans for UConn 21st Century: Peacock, "Building . . ."; Keith, "21st Century . . ."

Details about Okafor's rebounding and shot-blocking: Burris, "A Mind . . ."

UConn-UMass game: Jerry Spar, "UConn the Better . . . ," *Boston Herald*, December 11, 2002, 88; O'Connell, "UConn's Done . . . ," AP, December 13, 2002.

"We really aren't the same without Emeka" *Star-Ledger*, "Gordon, Okafor . . . ," January 12, 2002, 4.

Calhoun on the will to win: Jim Pignatiello. "UConn Fans . . . ," *Collegian*, December 11, 2002; Tommelleo, "UConn 59 . . . ," AP.

UConn's loss at Miami: Steven Wine, "Miami 77 . . . ," AP, January 21, 2003; Michelle Kaufman, "Rice Joins . . . ," *Miami Herald*, January 20, 2003; *Times* wires, "Canes Shock . . . ," January 21, 2003.

"We're getting better, and we're getting tougher" Clifton Brown, "With Strengths . . . ," *New York Times*, January 28, 2003, D1.

Loss to BC at Gampel: Adam Caparell, "UConn Has . . . ," University Wire and *Daily Campus*, February 3, 2003.

Calhoun's cancer and his response to it: UConn Men's Basketball, "Calhoun Press Conference Transcript," Monday February 3, 2003, Uconnhuskies.com; Sports Network, "UConn's Calhoun . . . ," February 9, 2003; Tommelleo, "UConn Coach . . . ," AP, February 3, 2003; Bob Becker, "UConn Coach Calhoun's . . . ," *Grand Rapids Press*, February 6, 2003, B5; *Telegram & Gazette* (Massachusetts), "Blaney to Take . . . ," February 4, 2003, D1; Weiss, "Cancer Jolts . . . ," *Daily News*, February 4, 2003, 53; Waters, "Problems Distract . . . ," *Post-Standard*, February 10, 2003, C1.

"We're Connecticut . . ." John Rowe, "Blaney in Tough . . . ," *Record*, February 11, 2003, S3.

Win over Syracuse: Drape, "UConn Answers . . ."; Uconnhuskies.com, "Okafor Helps . . ."

Calhoun's recovery: Sean Brennan, "How Sweet . . . ," *Daily News*, March 27, 2005, 88;

Ian O'Connor, "UConn's Calhoun . . . ," *USA Today*, March 23, 2003, 11C; Drape, "UConn Answers . . ."

Ben Gordon's arrest: Melissa Isaacson, "Ben Gordon . . . ," *Chicago Tribune*, April 19, 2007; AP Online, "Connecticut's Ben . . . ," February 14, 2003; Mike Jensen, "UConn Fractured . . . ," *Philadelphia Inquirer*, February 17, 2003, D2; AP, "Gordon Scores . . . ," February 15, 2003; AP State & Local Wire, "Gordon Starts . . . ," February 15, 2003.

"We're just stronger . . ." Jensen, "UConn Fractured . . ."

Calhoun's return: AP, "UConn's Coach . . . ," February 21, 2003; Tommelleo, "UConn Tops . . . ," AP Online, February 22, 2003; Uconnhuskies.com, "Calhoun Returns . . . ," February 22, 2003.

UConn's win at BC: Blaudschun, "No Focus . . . ," *Boston Globe*, March 9, 2003, E12; Uconnhuskies.com, "Huskies Trounce . . ."

Quote that UConn could beat any team: Paul Schwartz, "He's Conn-fident," *New York Post*, March 20, 2003, 95.

BYU game details: Josh Dubow, "UConn Outpaces . . . ," AP, March 21, 2003; Bill Finley, "Okafor's Blocks . . . ," *New York Times*, March 21, 2003, S6; Schwartz, "He's Conn-fident"; David Leon Moore, "UConn's Okafor . . . ," *USA Today*, March 26, 2003, 8C; Scott Taylor and Dick Harmon, "Cougars Question . . . ," *Deseret News*, March 21, 2003, D2.

Stanford game: Bill Finley, *New York Times*, March 22, 2003, section S, 6; March 23, 2003, section 8, 1; Carter Strickland, *Spokesman Review*, March 22, 2003, C1; March 23, 2003, C1; March 23, 2003, C9; Paul Schwartz, *New York Post*, March 22, 2003, 57; March 23, 2003, 102; Craig Hill, *News Tribune*, March 23, 2003, C7; March 28, 2003, C8. Bud Withers, "Nice Just . . . ," *Seattle Times*, March 23, 2003, D8; *Grand Rapids Press*, "Gordon, Okafor . . . ," March 23, 2003, D4.

Texas game: Herb Gould, *Chicago Sun-Times*, March 28, 2003, 162; March 29, 2003, 126; Adam Caparell, "UConn Men's . . . ," *Daily Campus*, March 28, 2003.

Details about Brown's critics: Mike Puma, "A National . . . ," *Connecticut Post*, March 21, 2004.

"I've never seen a player improve . . ." Moore, "UConn's Okafor . . ."

20. Emeka Okafor Comes along Once in a Lifetime

Boone's recruitment: Ostrout, *Connecticut Post*, October 19, 2002; October 22, 2002; November 15, 2002; Todd Jacobson, "Standardized Testing . . . ," *Washington Post*, October 31, 2002, D2; Mike Petersen, "New Recruits . . . ," *Daily Campus*, November 22, 2002; Uconnhooplegends.com, "Josh Boone."

Williams's recruitment: Ostrout, "Williams Picks . . . ," *Connecticut Post*, August 26, 2002; Andrew Jones, "ACC Schools . . . ," *Sunday Star-News* (Wilmington, N.C.), July 21, 2002, 1C, 4C; Rivals.com, "Marcus Williams . . ."

Villanueva's recruitment: Jim Benson, *Pantagraph*, November 6, 2002, B3; November 14, 2002, B3; Rivals.com, "2003 Rivals150"; Taylor Bell. 2006. *Glory Days: Legends of Illinois High School Basketball*, SportsPublishingLLC.com; Damon Seiters, "Big Time . . . ," *Las Vegas Review-Journal*, July 26, 2002, 1C; *State Journal-Register*, "Illini Still . . . ," July 31, 2002, 30; John Supinie, "Villanueva Makes . . . ," Copley News

Service, September 28, 2002; Jeremy Rutherford, "Illinois Gets . . . ," *St. Louis Post-Dispatch*, November 6, 2002, D1.

The expectations for UConn: Moran, *USA Today*, October 31, 2003, 1C, 4C; Tommelleo, "UConn Men . . . ," AP State & Local Wire, October 11, 2003; AP State & Local Wire, "Huskies Have . . . ," October 17, 2003; Waters, "Writers Say . . . ," *Post-Standard*, October 29, 2003, D1; Mike Cherry, "UConn Picked . . . ," *Charleston Daily Mail*, October 29, 2003, 42; *ESPN the Magazine*, November 24, 2003.

First Georgia Tech game: Ostrout, "Aching Back . . . ," *Connecticut Post*, November 26, 2003; Colin Stephenson, "Ga. Tech . . . ," *Star-Ledger*, November 27, 2003, 71; Hal Bock, "Georgia Tech 77 . . . ," AP, November 26, 2003; Robbins, "UConn Slips . . . ," *New York Post*, November 27, 2003, 68; Rubin, "Upset Stuns . . . ," *Daily News*, November 27, 2003, 84; Jack Wilkinson, "Tech Shoved . . . ," *Atlanta Journal-Constitution*, November 28, 2003, 1H.

Details about Thanksgiving 2003: Adam Caparell, "UConn No. 1 . . . ," *Daily Campus*, December 1, 2002; Robbins, "Huskies Fill . . . ," *New York Post*, November 29, 2003, 71; Moran, "UConn's Calhoun . . . ," *USA Today*, December 12, 2003, 13C.

Utah game: Steve Luhm, "UConn Gives . . . ," *Salt Lake Tribune*, November 29, 2003, D1; Mike Sorensen, "No Match . . . ," *Deseret Morning News*, November 29, 2003, D1; Hall Bock, "No. 1 UConn . . . ," AP Online, November 28, 2003.

Oklahoma game: O'Connell, AP Online, January 11, 2004; January 12, 2004; Bill Haisten, "OU Faces . . . ," *Tulsa World*, January 11, 2004, B1; Sports Network, "Oklahoma at Connecticut . . . ," January 11, 2004; Bill Haisten, "Okafor, Huskies . . . ," *Tulsa World*, January 12, 2004, B1; Dave Curtis, "UConn Runs . . . ," *New York Post*, January 12, 2004, 65; Pete Thamel, "Fast and Furious . . . ," *New York Times*, January 12, 2004, 1; Weiss, "Huskies Bark . . . ," *Daily News*, January 12, 2004, 66; Blaudschun, "UConn 86, Oklahoma 59," *Boston Globe*, January 12, 2004, C12.

Providence game: Ostrout, *Connecticut Post*, January 25, 2004; January 26, 2004; January 27, 2004; McNamara, "UConn Faces . . . ," *Providence Journal*, January 24, 2004, C1; January 25, 2004; Elsberry, "Gomes Has Calhoun . . . ," *Connecticut Post*, January 24, 2004; Tommelleo, "Providence Upsets . . . ," AP Online, January 24, 2004.

Details about Bobby Knight: *Indianapolis Star* library fact file, "Bob Knight: Former Indiana University Basketball Coach," Indystar.com/library.

The game at Pittsburgh: Cook, "Pitt-UConn . . ."

The game at Villanova: Rob Maaddi, "UConn's Okafor . . . ," February 28, 2004, AP Online; Ostrout, "Okafor Rescues . . . ," *Connecticut Post*, February 29, 2004; Matt Eagen, "Swats in . . . ," in *Top Dogs* (by *Hartford Courant*), Sports Publishing LLC, 2004, 88–91; Mike Jensen, "Huskies Escape . . . ," *Philadelphia Inquirer*, February 29, 2004, E6; *Grand Rapids Press*, "Okafor, UConn . . . ," February 29, 2004, E4.

Okafor's awards and statistics: John Rowe, "Okafor a Question . . . ," *Record*, March 10, 2004, S3; UConnhuskies.com, "Reviewing the 2003–2004 Season."

"I yell at my dog . . ." Rowe, "Okafor . . ."

Details about Okafor's back: AP Online, "UConn's Okafor . . . ," March 12, 2004; Rowe, "Okafor . . ."; O'Connell, "UConn Hopes . . . ," AP Online, March 9, 2004; Elsberry, "At Last . . . ," *Connecticut Post*, March 12, 2004.

Details about Brown: Puma, "A National . . ."; Janie McCauley, "UConn's Taliek . . . ," AP Online, March 26, 2004.

The Big East tournament finals: Shalin, "UConn Just . . . ," *Boston Herald*, March 14, 2004, B10; Don Burke, "Gordon's Jumper . . . ," *Star Ledger*, March 14, 2004, 3; J. P. Pelzman, "UConn Beast . . . ," *Record*, March 14, 2004, S1; Steve Serby, "Madison Sq. Gordon," *New York Post*, March 14, 2004, 99; Lisa Olson, "UConn Firmly . . . ," *Daily News*, March 14, 2004, 51; Kelly Whiteside, "UConn Relishes . . . ," *USA Today*, March 15, 2004, 10E; J. P. Pelzman, "UConn Is King . . . ," *Record*, March 14, 2004, S1.

21. Mike, Over the Years When We've Seen Teams Collapse . . . .

Lead-up to the Duke game: Michael Murphy, "NCAA 2004 . . . ," *Houston Chronicle*, March 28, 2004, 1; Tommelleo, "UConn Ready . . . ," AP Online, March 28, 2004; C. Lenox Rawlings, "UConn Job," *Winston-Salem Journal*, March 30, 2004, 1; Al Featherston, "Revelry, If . . . ," *Herald-Sun*, April 2, 2004, C1; Brian Hanley, "UConn Is . . . ," *Chicago Sun-Times*, April 2, 2004, 143; John Klein, "UConn Wants . . . ," *Tulsa World*, April 3, 2004, 4; Blaudschun, "On the Level . . . ," *Boston Globe*, April 2, 2004, E5; Mike Finger, "Let the Games . . . ," *San Antonio Express-News*, April 3, 2004, 1F; Jerome Solomon, "Basketball, Texas . . . ," *Houston Chronicle*, April 3, 2004, 1; Herb Gould, "Duke-UConn . . . ," *Chicago Sun-Times*, April 3, 2004, 94; Harrington, "Building . . ."

Calhoun's Hall of Fame rejection: Weiss, "Hall of Shame . . . ," *Daily News*, April 5, 2004, 56.

Duke game: *Hartford Courant*, *Top Dogs*, 138; Uconnhuskies.com, "Last Minute . . . ," April 3, 2004; Mike Lupica, "Calhoun's Gamble . . . ," *Daily News*, April 4, 2004, 57; Ostrout, "With Big Boost . . . ," *Connecticut Post*, April 4, 2004; Eddie Pells, "UConn Heads . . . ," AP Online, April 4, 2004; Luciana Chavez, "Duke Sent . . . ," *News & Observer*, April 4, 2004, C1; Jeremy Rutherford, "It's UConn . . . ," *St. Louis Post-Dispatch*, April 4, 2004, D1; Mike Harrington, "Okafor Leads . . . ," *Buffalo News*, April 4, 2004, C1; David Teel, "A Pair . . . ," *St. Paul Pioneer Press*, April 4, 2004, B7; Blaudschun, "Huskies Put . . . ," *Boston Globe*, April 4, 2004, E1; Mike Jensen, "UConn Edges . . . ," *Philadelphia Inquirer*, April 4, 2004, D1; Steve Carp, "Okafor Dominant . . . ," *Las Vegas Review-Journal*, April 4, 2004, 1C; John Delong, "It's Tech . . . ," *Winston-Salem Journal*, April 4, 2004, 1; Brett McMurphy, "Saving the Best . . . ," *Tampa Tribune*, April 4, 2004, 1; Todd Rosiak, "Down to the . . . ," *Milwaukee Journal Sentinel*, April 4, 2004, 1C; Mike Finger, "Okafor Leads . . . ," *San Antonio Express-News*, April 4, 2004, 1N; Craig Hill, "Ok Okafor," *News Tribune*, April 4, 2004, C1; Peter Finney, "Okafor Hands . . . ," *Times-Picayune*, April 4, 2004, 11; Ed Hardin, "In the End . . . ," *News & Record*, April 4, 2004, C1; Adrian Wojnarowski, "Okafor Wills . . . ," *Record*, April 4, 2004, S1; Michael Murphy, "Breaking Down . . . ," *Houston Chronicle*, April 4, 2004, 13; C. Lenox Rawlings, "Bitter End," *Winston-Salem Journal*, April 4, 2004, 1; Mark Kiszla, "Shock Waves," *Denver Post*, April 4, 2004, C1; Shalin and Michael Gee, "Coach K . . . ," *Boston Herald*, April 4, 2004, B13; Uconnhuskies.com, "Last Minute . . . ," April 3, 2004; Jon Milner, "It Was Different . . . ," *San Jose Mercury News*, April 5, 2004, 4D; Jim Litke, "Calhoun Misses . . . ," AP Online, April 5, 2004.

UNLV-Duke game from 1991: HBO presents "Runnin' Rebels of UNLV"; Bob Carter, "Coach K's . . . ," ESPN Classic, July 5, 2005, Espn.go.com/classic.

Georgia Tech game: Bob Cohn, "Huskies Are . . . ," *Washington Times*, April 6, 2004, C1; Ed Miller, "UConn Adventure," *Virginian-Pilot*, April 6, 2004, C1; Christine Brennan, "UConn Shows . . . ," *USA Today*, April 6, 2004, 6C; Brian Hendrickson, "UConn Turns . . . ," *Star News*, April 6, 2004, 1D; Ed Graney, "UConn-Quest," *San Diego Union-Tribune*, April 6, 2004, D1; Mike Jensen, "UConn Overpowers . . . ," *St. Paul Pioneer Press*, April 6, 2004, D1; Tom Kensler, "Hot Huskies . . . ," *Denver Post*, March 28, 2004, C15; Ostrout, "UConn's the 1," *Connecticut Post*, April 6, 2004; Jerry Sullivan, "Laughter Leads . . . ," *Buffalo News*, April 6, 2004, C1; Blaudschun, "Top Dogs," *Boston Globe*, April 6, 2004, C1; Shalin, "UConn Clinches . . . ," *Boston Herald*, April 6, 2004, 74; Jack Wilkinson, "UConn Wins . . . ," *Atlanta Journal-Constitution*, April 6, 2004, 7D; Eddie Pells, "UConn Easily . . . ," AP Online, April 6, 2004; Sarah Coffey, "UConn Fans . . . ," AP Online, April 6, 2004; Buck Harvey, "Where Does . . . ," *San Antonio Express-News*, April 6, 2004, 1D; Noreen Gillespie, "Fans Celebrate . . . ," AP State & Local Wire, April 6, 2004; Jerry Izenberg, "This Was . . . ," *Star-Ledger*, April 6, 2004, 41.

Details on Okafor and Gordon: *Basketball Digest*, September–October 2004.

22. I'm Just a Very Blessed Individual . . .

Rudy Gay's recruitment: Kim Baxter, "The League's . . . ," *Post-Standard*, November 10, 2004, F10; Ray Fittipaldo, "The Top Six," *Pittsburgh Post-Gazette*, November 12, 2004, E6.

NCAA's rules on exhibition games against noncollegiate opponents: Waters and Kim Baxter, "Rule Change . . . ," *Post-Standard*, November 1, 2004, C1.

A.J. Price's recruitment: Ostrout, *Connecticut Post*, September 30, 2003; November 17, 2003; David Borges, "Like Father . . . ," *New Haven Register*, April 3, 2009; Elsberry, "Price, Gay . . . ," *Connecticut Post*, September 22, 2003; AP State & Local Wire, "West 124, East 110"; Steve Tucker, "Big Crowd . . . ," *Chicago Sun-Times*, March 25, 2004, 124.

A.J. Price's illness: AP, October 5, 2004; October 12, 2004; October 19, 2004; Ostrout, *Connecticut Post*, October 6, 2004; October 7, 2004; November 11, 2004; Tommelleo, "Defending Champs . . . ," AP State & Local Wire, October 16, 2004.

Calhoun's quote after the game at Syracuse: Pete Thamel, "UConn's Search . . . ," February 8, 2005, *New York Times*, D1.

Rashad Anderson's illness: AP, February 9, 2005; February 12, 2005; Tommelleo, AP State & Local Wire, February 13, 2005; February 21, 2005; Weiss, "Huskies Need . . . ," *Daily News*, February 14, 2005, 58; Kathleen Nelson, "It's Just . . . ," *St. Louis Post-Dispatch*, March 18, 2005, C10; Adam Caparell, "Anderson Returns . . . ," *Daily Campus* online edition, posted February 22, 2005.

Calhoun's quotes after the N.C. State game: Kathleen Nelson, "UCan't . . . ," *St. Louis Post-Dispatch*, March 21, 2005, D1.

Villanueva turns pro: Christopher Lawlor, "Villanueva Set . . . ," *USA Today*, June 28, 2005, 10C; Pat Eaton-Robb, "UConn's Villanueva . . . ," AP, March 29, 2005; Voice of

America News, "NBA Names . . . ," Voice of America News, May 10, 2006; Benjamin Hochman, "Villanueva Growing . . . ," *Times-Picayune*, April 2, 2006, 21.

23. Calhoun Is Feared, but He Is Not Respected

Details about Andrew Bynum: Ostrout, *Connecticut Post*, August 29, 2004; October 28, 2004; November 19, 2004; AP, November 18, 2004; February 23, 2005; *Sporting News*, "College Basketball Inside Dish," July 19, 2004, 79; Guy Kipp, "St. Joseph's Bynum . . . ," *Star-Ledger*, October 28, 2004, 65; Rivals.com, "2005 Rivals150."

Andrew Bynum and the NBA: Elsberry, "Calhoun Must . . . ," *Connecticut Post*, March 30, 2005; *A Passion to Lead*, 40; Brian Lewis, "Bynum: I'm Ready . . . ," *New York Post*, June 25, 2005, 76; Bill Finley, "A Hoop Dream . . . ," *New York Times*, June 26, 2005, 4.

Details about Jeff Adrien: Ostrout, *Connecticut Post*, August 16, 2004; August 19, 2004; and November 19, 2004; Justin Young, Rivals.com, July 25, 2004; AP State & Local Wire, "UConn Announces . . ."; ScoutHoops.com, "Final AAU Top 25 Poll," September 23, 2004; RivalsHoops, "2005 Rivals150"; Jeff Goodman and Dave Telep, "Final AAU Top 25 Poll," ScoutHoops.com, September 23, 2004; BreakdownMagazine.com, "The Best . . . ," July 17, 2004; Travis Haney, "Top Coaches . . . ," *Augusta Chronicle*, July 14, 2004, Chardis, "Chief Warrior," JournalInquirer.com, January 27, 2009; Jeff Goodman, "Yo Adrien!" *Boston Herald*, January 30, 2006, 82; Jason Dunbar, "Adrien Commits . . . ," *Boston Globe*, August 20, 2004, F8.

Details about laptops: Tommelleo, "Second Player . . . ," AP, August 16, 2005; Ostrout, "UConn Suspends . . . ," *Connecticut Post*, August 18, 2005; Elsberry, "Calhoun Needs . . . ," *Connecticut Post*, August 21, 2005; *Boston Globe*, "UConn Player . . . ," September 14, 2005, E2; Ostrout, "Price Given . . . ," *Connecticut Post*, November 16, 2005; AP, "Price Out . . . ," Espn.com, October 28, 2005; Jane Gordon, "For UConn . . . ," *New York Times*, August 28, 2005, Nytimes.com.

Calhoun's induction into the Hall of Fame: Moran, "Calhoun Focused . . . ," *USA Today*, September 9, 2005, 11C; Elsberry, "Calhoun Spreads . . ."

Doyel's column: Greg Doyel, "(Bad) Business as Usual for UConn's Calhoun," CBS Sportsline.com, October 31, 2005.

Preseason polls: *Boston Globe*, "Duke No. 1 . . . ," November 8, 2005, E2; Bill Cole, "Can Top-Ranked . . . ," *Winston-Salem Journal*, November 11, 2005, F1; *Birmingham News*, "Duke Ranked . . . ," October 29, 2005, 12B; Jack Carey, "*USA Today*/ESPN Top 25 . . . ," *USA Today*, October 28, 2005, 10C; Waters, "Media Votes . . . ," *Post-Standard*, October 26, 2005, D1; Chris Licata, "Dick Picks . . . ," *Daily Campus*, November 16, 2005.

Marquette game: Sports Network, "Big East Splash . . . ," January 3, 2006; Colin Fly, "Marquette 94 . . . ," AP State & Local Wire, January 3, 2006; Todd Rosiak, "Marquette 94 . . . ," *Milwaukee Journal Sentinel*, January 4, 2006, C1; Ostrout, "Williams Returns . . . ," *Connecticut Post*, January 5, 2006.

LSU game: Mike Puma, "Calhoun Disappointed . . . ," *Connecticut Post*, January 8, 2006; Ostrout, "Armstrong Raises . . . ," *Connecticut Post*, January 8, 2006.

Jacobs's column and reaction to it: Jacobs, "From Now on . . . ," *Hartford Courant*, January 31, 2006; Jere Longman, "Calhoun Is . . . ," *New York Times*, February 11,

2006, D1; Elsberry, "Sadly, Jacobs-Calhoun . . . ," *Connecticut Post*, February 1, 2006;
Ashley Fox, "UConn's Calhoun . . . ," *Philadelphia Inquirer*, February 13, 2006; Seth
Davis, "Seth Davis's Hoop Thoughts," *Sports Illustrated*, February 20, 2006, vol. 104,
no. 8, 85; *Hartford Courant*, "Jacobs's Column . . . ," February 6, 2006, C2.
The loss at Villanova: O'Connell, "No. 4 Villanova Beats . . . ," AP, February 26, 2006;
Espn.com, "Nova Digs . . . ," February 26, 2006.
Second UConn-Villanova game: AP and Rivals.com, "UConn Avenges . . . ," February 26,
2006; Bill Finley, "Connecticut Reclaims . . . ," *New York Times*, February 27, 2006.
Details about UConn's senior class: Ostrout, "Before Departing . . . ," *Connecticut Post*,
March 5, 2006; *Connecticut Post*, "Big East Regular-Season Championships," March
5, 2006.

24. That Team Should Have Won the National Championship
Syracuse's play before the UConn game: Ethan Ramsey, "Is Gerry Overrated?" *Daily
Orange*, posted February 6, 2006.
Syracuse game in the Big East tournament: O'Connell, "Syracuse Stuns . . . ," AP
Online, March 9, 2006; Sports Network, "McNamara Does . . . ," March 9, 2006;
Sean Brennan, "Another Stunning . . . ," *Times Union*, March 10, 2006, C1; M. A.
Mehta, "McNamara-Led . . . ," *Star-Ledger*, March 10, 2006, 36; *St. Petersburg
Times*, "Syracuse Upsets . . . ," March 10, 2006, 2C; Wire reports, "McNamara,
Syracuse . . . ," *Richmond Times Dispatch*, March 10, 2006, E6; Erik Matuszewski,
"Syracuse Upsets . . . ," *National Post*, March 10, 2006, S7; *International
Tribune*, "Syracuse Upsets . . . ," March 10, 2006, 24; Tom Pedulla, "McNamara,
Syracuse . . . ," *USA Today*, March 13, 2006, 10E.
Albany game: Rich Cimini, "UConn Expresses . . . ," *Daily News*, March 17, 2006; Rob
Maaddi, "Albany Nearly . . . ," AP Online, March 18, 2006; Paul Schwartz, "Great
Escape," *New York Post*, March 18, 2006, 74; Marc Narducci, "UConn Avoids . . . ,"
Herald News, March 18, 2006, D1.
George Mason game: *Sentinel & Enterprise*, "GM Dethrones UConn," March 27,
2006; Paul Schwartz, "Dogs Are . . . ," *New York Post*, March 27, 2006, 89; Jerardi,
"By George . . . ," *Philadelphia Daily News*, March 27, 2006; Anthony, "George
Mason 86 . . . ," *Hartford Courant*, March 27, 2006, C6; Ostrout, "Out of Miracles,"
Connecticut Post, March 27, 2006; Desmond Conner, "Brown Gave . . . ," *Hartford
Courant*, March 27, 2006, C5; Sports Network, "The Slipper . . . ," March 26,
2006; Ralph Vacchiano, "No Comeback . . . ," *Daily News*, March 26, 2006; Weiss,
"UConn Has . . . ," *Daily News*, March 26, 2006, D7; Howard Fendrich, "Top-Seeded
Huskies . . . ," AP, March 26, 2006; Anthony, "UConn Moments: Top 10 Men's
Losses," *Hartford Courant*, November 8, 2009.
Details about the 2005 NBA draft: Ostrout, *Connecticut Post Online*, June 6, 2006; June
11, 2006; June 17, 2006; June 25, 2006; June 29, 2006; prospect rankings by Rivals
.com, Fred Kerber, "Nets Grab . . . ," *New York Post*, June 29, 2006, 100; Andy Katz,
"UConn Expects . . . ," Espn.com, November 8, 2004; Sports Network, "Huskies'
Boone . . . ," June 5, 2006; Benjamin Hochman, "Huskie Procession," *Times-Picayune*,
June 24, 2006, 1; Eaton-Robb, "Six Connecticut . . . ," AP State & Local Wire, June
27, 2006; Christopher Lawlor, "UConn's Williams. . . . ," *USA Today*, June 28, 2006,

3C; Robbins, "A Pick . . . ," *New York Post*, June 28, 2006, 64; Mark Murphy, "Future Is . . . ," *Boston Herald*, June 28, 2006, 88; *Mercury News* wire services, "Knicks Fans . . . ," *San Jose Mercury News*, June 29, 2006, 9; Al Iannazzone, "Nets Tap . . . ," *Record*, June 29, 2006, S7; *Grand Rapids Press*, "UConn Ties . . . ," June 29, 2006, D9; O'Connell, "UConn Ties . . . ," AP, June 29, 2006.

Details about Williams's pro career: AP, "Little-Used Williams . . . ," Espn.com, March 10, 2009.

25. It Won't Happen Again

Information about the 2006-2007 recruiting class: Rivals.com basketball recruiting staff, "Tar Heels, Buckeyes . . . ," June 1, 2006; Rivals.com, "Prospect Ranking: Final Rivals 150, Class of 2006."

Hasheem Thabeet's recruitment: Howie Lindsey, CardinalSports.com, May 25, 2006, May 30, 2006; Andrew Skwara, "Kingwood: Seven Foot Two Giant Appears," April 22, 2006, Basketballrecruiting.rivals.com; Scout.com, "Player Evaluation of Hasheem Thabeet"; Ostrout, "UConn Men's Notebook—[March 5]," *Connecticut Post*, March 5, 2006; Luke Winn, "Constant Rejection," *Sports Illustrated*, http://vault.sportsillustrated.cnn.com, December 25, 2006; Weiss, "And Thabeet . . . ," *Daily News*, November 9, 2008, 52; Harvey Araton, "UConn's Thabeet . . . ," *New York Times*, March 22, 2009; Adam Gorney, "Thabeet Tops . . . ," UConnReport .com, May 1, 2006; Rivals.com basketball recruiting staff, "African Center . . . ," Basketballrecruiting.rivals.com, May 10, 2006; Gerry Hamilton, "Visits for Thabeet," Orangebloods.com, May 30, 2006; Rivals.com basketball recruiting, "Thabeet Goes On," June 2, 2006; Eaton-Robb, "At Seven Foot Three . . . ," AP State & Local Wire, January 10, 2007; Marlen Garcia, "Dream Journey," *USA Today*, January 16, 2002, 1C.

"Keep your hands up" and the team's goal is to win the Big East: Kelley Whiteside, "Young UConn . . . ," *USA Today*, October 26, 2006, 8C.

Information about the Huskies of Honor: UConnhuskies.com, "2006-2007 University of Connecticut Basketball Media Notes," January 10, 2007.

Quote about breaking the backboard: Ostrout, "Calhoun Demands . . . ," *Connecticut Post Online*, March 1, 2007.

The statistic that UConn fell out of the AP top 25 for the first time in 67 polls: John Grupp, "UConn Forced . . . ," *Pittsburgh Tribune Review*, January 16, 2007.

Lack of linkage quote, ibid.

Information about the Orzechowski incident: Jeff Pearlman, "D-1 Can Be a Dangerous . . . ," Espn.com, January 17, 2007.

Lack of leadership information: Brett Orzechowski, *New Haven Register*, January 7, 2007; March 9, 2007; Ostrout, "Huskies Continue . . . ," *Connecticut Post*, February 19, 2007.

Information about A.J. Price: Brett Orzechowski, "Price Not Back . . . ," *New Haven Register*, January 14, 2007; Marlen Garcia, "Price Working Way . . . ," *USA Today*, January 16, 2007, 2C.

Information about Thabeet's season: Brett Orzechowski, *New Haven Register*, January 7, 2007; January 16, 2007; February 18, 2007; Eaton-Robb, AP State & Local Wire, January 10, 2007; April 12, 2007; Mike Puma, "UConn Freshman . . . ," *Connecticut*

Post, November 19, 2006; Zac Boyer, "UConn's Thabeet Struggles . . . ," *Daily Campus*, December 7, 2006; Marlen Garcia, "Dream Journey," *USA Today*, January 16, 2007, 1C; Ostrout, "Thabeet in No . . . ," *Connecticut Post*, February 15, 2007; Rich Elliott, "Thabeet Listens . . . ," *Connecticut Post*, April 26, 2007; Luke Winn, "Constant Rejection," *Sports Illustrated*, http://vault.sportsillustrated.cnn.com, December 25, 2006; Bill Sanders, "Sky's the Limit . . . ," *Atlanta Journal-Constitution*, February 20, 2007.

"It will never happen again" Weiss, "Calhoun Left . . . ," *Daily News*, March 8, 2007, 60.
Robbins's prediction: "Big East Battlers," *New York Post*, January 14, 2007, 80.

26. That's Why He's in the Hall of Fame

Calhoun on A.J. Price: Ostrout, "Price Is . . . ," *Connecticut Post Online*, January 24, 2008.
Indiana game: Espn.com news services, "UConn's Dyson . . . ," January 27, 2008; *Grand Rapids Press*, "Indiana Conned . . . ," January 27, 2008, D4; Wire dispatches, "UConn Surprises . . . ," *Pittsburgh Post-Gazette*, January 27, 2008, D3; Pete DiPrimio, "Indiana Falls . . . ," *News-Sentinel*, January 26, 2008; Ostrout, "Price Is Leader . . ."; Eaton-Robb, "Inconsistent UConn . . . ," AP State & Local Wire, March 22, 2008.
Details of the Wiggins-Dyson incident: Ostrout, *Connecticut Post Online*, January 27, 2008; January 31, 2008; AP State & Local Wire, "Wiggins Allowed . . . ," January 31, 2008.
For UConn's win streak, see Ostrout, "UConn Men's Streak . . . ," *Connecticut Post Online*, February 17, 2008.
Calhoun's quote after the West Virginia game: Weiss, "Calhoun Barks . . . ," *Daily News*, March 14, 2008, 84.
Thabeet's return: AP State & Local Wire, April 27, 2008; November 25, 2008; May 20, 2009. Ostrout, "Thabeet to Stay . . . ," *Connecticut Post Online*, April 27, 2008.
Details about Wiggins's transfer: Justin Verrier, "Wiggins Ends . . . ," *Daily Campus*, April 16, 2008; Ostrout, "Wiggins Decides . . . ," *Connecticut Post Online*, May 16, 2008.
Details about Kemba Walker: Kristie Ackert, *Daily News*, December 10, 2006, 92; January 5, 2007, 70; May 3, 2007, 6; February 24, 2008, 58; Dan Martin, *New York Post*, March 19, 2007, 69; March 24, 2007, 42; June 17, 2007, 75; April 20, 2008, 70; U.S. Fed. News, July 15, 2008; July 19, 2008; Ebenezer Samuel, *Daily News*, March 19, 2007, 62; June 17, 2007, 82; AP State & Local Wire, June 17, 2007; November 21, 2007; Espn.com basketball recruiting; Jay Gomes, "Walker Picks . . . ," Rivals .com, June 16, 2007; Justin Young, "Huskies Nab . . . ," Rivals.com, June 18, 2007; *New York Post*, "All-CHSAA Team," April 15, 2007, 93; Christopher Lawlor, "N.Y.'s Rice Topples . . . ," *USA Today*, January 15, 2007, 8C; Ostrout, "Walker Verbally . . . ," *Connecticut Post Online*, June 17, 2007; Justin Williams, "Guards Guide . . . ," *Augusta Chronicle*, July 16, 2007, C1; Denny Conroy, "Kemba Walker FIBA . . . ," ScoutNYPreps.com; Scout College Basketball Recruiting, Scouthoops.scout.com; Mike DeCourcy, "The Future of Hoops," *Sporting News*, June 18, 2007, 12.
Details about Stanley Robinson's hiatus: Dana O'Neil, "Robinson Picks . . . ," Espn .com, December 16, 2008; Aaron Torres, "Unsung Player," Hoopsaddict.com, April 6, 2009; Borges, "UConn's Robinson . . . ," *New Haven Register*, September 10,

2009; Eaton-Robb, "Robinson Takes . . . ," AP, January 16, 2010; Anthony, "The Stanley . . . ," Courant.com, August 4, 2008.

Thabeet's improvement: Donna Ditota, "Bigger and Better," *Post-Standard*, November 7, 2008, D12; Weiss, "And Thabeet . . ."

Thabeet's comments: Barker Davis, "UConn Represents . . . ," *Washington Times*, November 11, 2008, C5; Anthony, "Bergeron on Thabeet . . . ," Courant.com, November 10, 2008.

27. Not a Dime Back

Gonzaga game: Gregg Bell, "No. 2 UConn Rallies . . . ," AP Online, December 20, 2008; John Blanchette, "A Tough Win . . . ," *Spokesman Review*, December 21, 2008, C1; Greg Bishop, "Price Helps . . . ," *New York Times*, December 21, 2008, SP3.

Georgetown game: Ostrout, "UConn to Be Tested . . . ," *Connecticut Post Online*, December 28, 2008; Vega, "Hoyas Stun . . . ," *Boston Globe*, December 30, 2008, C6; Fiore Mastroianni, "Monroe Powers . . . ," *Hoya*, December 29, 2008.

UConn's number-one ranking: AP, "UConn Is Fourth . . . ," February 3, 2009.

Louisville game: Chip Cosby, "Fifth-Ranked Louisville . . . ," *Lexington Herald-Leader*, February 2, 2009.

Michigan game: Kevin Duffy, "UConn Forward . . . ," *Daily Campus*, February 9, 2009; Eaton-Robb, "No. 1 UConn . . . ," AP State & Local Wire, February 8, 2009.

Syracuse game: Waters, "Orange Rejected," *Post-Standard*, February 12, 2009, C1.

Dyson's injury: AP State & Local Wire, "UConn's Dyson . . . ," February 12, 2009.

Boeheim on Thabeet: Joey Johnston, "Thabeet Might . . . ," *Tampa Tribune*, February 14, 2009.

Pitt game: Espn.com, "Pittsburgh 76, Connecticut 68"; Davis, "Blair Helps . . . ," *USA Today*, February 17, 2009, 1C; Robbins, "Mosh Pitt," *New York Post*, February 17, 2009, 62; Blaudschun, "Blair, Pitt . . . ," *Boston Globe*, February 17, 2009, C5; O'Connell, "Blair's 20-20 . . . ," AP, February 17, 2009; Ray Fittipaldo, "Panthers Shrug . . . ," *Pittsburgh Post-Gazette*, February 20, 2009, D1; Tom Luicci, "UConn's Thabeet . . . ," *Star-Ledger*, February 14, 2009, 33.

Details about the cancerous tumor on Calhoun's neck: Reid Churner and Tom Weir, "UConn's Calhoun . . . ," *USA Today*, May 30, 2008.

Details about Calhoun's salary: Garber, " 'Dynamic Tension' . . ."; Desmond Conner, "Richer Contracts . . . ," *Hartford Courant*, July 31, 2004, C1; *Charleston Daily Mail*, "Connecticut Coaches . . . ," August 5, 1995; Jane Gordon, "Everyone Knows . . . ," *New York Times*, June 26, 2005, Connecticut Weekly section, 7.

Reaction to "Not a dime back" Ryan, "Calhoun Cashes . . . ," *Boston Globe*, March 3, 2009, C1; Eaton-Robb, "Auriemma Comes . . . ," AP State & Local Wire, February 22, 2009; Ron Cook, "Successful Coaches . . . ," *Pittsburgh Post-Gazette*, February 24, 2009, D1; Ron Chimelis, "Calhoun Wrong . . . ," *Republican*, February 26, 2009, B1; Elsberry, "Leave Calhoun . . . ," *Connecticut Post Online*, February 28, 2009; Frank Wooten, "Real Worth . . . ," *Post and Courier*, March 1, 2009, A11; Owen Canfield, "A Couple . . . ," *Hartford Courant*, March 2, 2009, B4; *Hartford Courant*, "Calhoun: Readers Weigh . . . ," March 4, 2009, A17; Chris Powell, "Coach Calhoun . . . ,"

Providence Journal-Bulletin, March 11, 2009, 7; John Murray, "Jim Calhoun Is . . . ,"
    Waterbury Observer, March 15, 2009.
Murray's article: "Jim Calhoun Is . . ."
UConn-Syracuse six-overtime game: Dave Skretta, "Syracuse Outlasts . . . ," AP State
    & Local Wire, March 13, 2009; Kevin Duffy, "UConn Stunned . . . ," *Daily Campus*,
    March 13, 2009; Mike Ogle, "UConn Is Stunned . . . ," *New York Times*, March 13,
    2009; Blaudschun, "Over Time . . . ," *Boston Globe*, March 14, 2009, C6; Mike Vaccaro
    "Long Memory," *New York Post*, March 15, 2009, 88.

28. Josh Nochimson . . . Became the Unofficial Go-Between

Calhoun's illness: CBSSports.com wire reports, "Huskies Crush . . . ," March 19, 2009;
    Brenda Sullivan, "Coach Jim . . . ," *Mansfield Today*, March 19, 2009; Weiss, "Jim
    Calhoun . . . ," *Daily News*, March 20, 2009.
Texas A&M game: John Branch, "Calhoun Rejoins . . . ," *New York Times*, March 22,
    2009.
Miles and possible NCAA violations: Adrian Wojnarowski and Dan Wetzel, "Probe:
    UConn Violated NCAA Rules," Yahoo! Sports, March 25, 2009; Ostrout, "UConn
    Faces . . . ," *Connecticut Post*, March 25, 2009; Dave Collins, "Calhoun Says . . . ,"
    AP State & Local Wire, March 26, 2009; Ian O'Connor, "Mount Calhoun . . . ,"
    Record, March 26, 2009, S1; Herb Gould, "UConn Downplays . . . ," *Chicago Sun-
    Times*, March 26, 2009, 61; Kevin Duffy, "UConn's Success . . . ," *Daily Campus*,
    March 13, 2009; Rhoden, "For Coaches . . . ," *New York Times*, March 30, 2009, D4;
    Anthony, "Ater Majok . . . ," Courant.com, April 23, 2009.
Details about Sampson's violations: Collins, "Calhoun Says . . ."
Calhoun on Nochimson: *Dare to Dream*, 103.
Graduation rates: Jacobs, "Degree of Difficulty," *Hartford Courant*, March 19, 2009;
    Scott W. Brown, "UConn Athletes . . . ," editorial, *USA Today*, April 2004, 22A; Brent
    Schrotenboer, "Athletic Powerhouses . . . ," *San Diego Union-Tribune*, March 18, 2008,
    D6; *Daily Edition*, "UNC Has Top . . . ," March 17, 2009, 4; *Connecticut Post Online*,
    "One Number . . . ," April 17, 2009; Cavanaugh, "Huskies, as Teams . . . ," *New York
    Times*, March 8, 1998, 15; Rick Telander, "Schoolyard Ball . . . ," *Chicago Sun-Times*,
    April 7, 2004, 150; Derrick Jackson, "Foul Play . . . ," *Boston Globe*, March 17, 2009;
    Amanda Falcone, "Graduation Stats . . . ," *Daily Campus*, October 8, 2002.
Reaction to the Yahoo! story after the Purdue game: Ostrout, "UConn's Calhoun . . . ,"
    Connecticut Post Online, March 27, 2009; Borges, "Calhoun: Make . . . ," *New Haven
    Register*, March 28, 2009.
Events leading up to the Final Four: Jacobs, "Brightest Spotlights . . . ," *Hartford Courant*,
    April 4, 2009, B1; Rhoden, "For Coaches . . ."; Michael Rosenberg, "Calhoun Has No
    Place . . . ," *Detroit Free Press*, April 2, 2009; Ostrout, "UConn Still . . . ," *Connecticut
    Post Online*, June 6, 2009; Blaudschun, "Top Dog . . . ," *Boston Globe*, April 4, 2009, 6.
National semifinal game: Nancy Armour, "Michigan State Defeats . . . ," AP State &
    Local Wire, April 5, 2009; Espn.com, "(2) Michigan State 82, (1) Connecticut 73";
    Andrew Bagnato, "Thabeet Struggles . . . ," AP State & Local Wire, April 5, 2009;
    Grand Rapids Press, "MSU Gets Feisty . . . ," *Grand Rapids Press*, April 5, 2004, C4;

Rubin, "Michigan St. Says . . . ," *Daily News*, April 5, 2009, 50; Mike Lupica, "Magic Night . . . ," *Daily News*, April 5, 2009, 50; AP State & Local Wire, "Connecticut's Jim Calhoun . . . ," April 5, 2009.

Calhoun's return: Ostrout, "Calhoun to Return . . . ," *Connecticut Post Online*, April 9, 2009.

Thabeet's NBA career: Mark Stein, "Thabeet Headed . . . ," Espn.com, February 26, 2010.

29. I Don't Get Defeated

Calhoun's bike crash and broken ribs: Weiss, "UConn's Calhoun . . . ," *Daily News*, June 14, 2009, 54; Fanhouse Newswire, "UConn Coach . . . ," June 13, 2009; Espn.com news services, "Calhoun Discharged . . . ," June 14, 2009.

Calhoun's medical leave: Borges, "Calhoun Returns . . . ," *New Haven Register*, February 12, 2010; Robbins, "Calhoun Calls . . . ," *New York Post*, January 20, 2010, 70; Gavin Keefe, "Calhoun Takes . . . ," *Day* (New London, Conn.), January 20, 2010; Davis, "Facing Another . . ."

UConn-Texas game: Kevin Armstrong, "UConn's Second-Half . . . ," *New York Times*, January 23, 2010.

Second UConn-Cincinnati game: AP, "Cincy Embarrasses . . . ," Espn.com, February 13, 2010; Anthony, "No Win . . . ," *Hartford Courant*, February 14, 2010, E8.

"For a team with its back to the wall . . ." Chardis, "All the Huskies . . . ," *Journal Inquirer*, March 5, 2010.

Alleged NCAA violations: Tim Dahlberg, "Not a Bad . . . ," AP, May 29, 2010; Filip Bondy, "As NCAA . . . ," *Daily News*, May 29, 2010, 46; Gary Parrish, "Calhoun Keeps . . . ," CBSSports.com, May 28, 2010; Les Carpenter, "Calhoun's Drive . . . ," Yahoo! Sports, May 28, 2010; Jacobs, "*If* Not . . . ," May 30, 2010; Chardis, "Answers Required . . . ," *Journal Inquirer*, May 29, 2010; Davis, "NCAA Allegations . . . ," DeCourcy, "NCAA Allegations . . . ,"; Paul Doyle and Anthony, "UConn's Testimony . . . ," *Hartford Courant*, October 16, 2010.

Criticisms of Calhoun's reaction to the NCAA violations: Dana O'Neil, "Jim Calhoun . . . ," Espn.com, October 8, 2010; Jacobs, "Isn't Jim . . . ," *Hartford Courant*, October 8, 2010; Charles P. Pierce, "Husky Don't," Boston.com, October 9, 2010.

30. From Maui . . .

Details about Jeremy Lamb: Espn.com basketball recruiting; Larry Hartstein, "Fast-Rising Norcross . . . ," *Atlanta Journal-Constitution*, September 16, 2009; New.kentuckysportsradio.com; Ostrout, "Calhoun at Middlesex . . . ," *Connecticut Post Online*; Borges, *New Haven Register*, "Calhoun in Bristol," June 10, 2010.

Details about Roscoe Smith: Espn.com basketball recruiting; Borges, "First Night . . . ," *New Haven Register*, October 16, 2009; Ken Tysiac, "Another Recruiting . . . ," *News Observer*, January 8, 2010; Matt Bracken, "Ex-Walbrook Star . . . ," *Recruiting Report*, January 8, 2010; Highschoolhoop.com; Ostrout, "Calhoun at Middlesex . . . ," Borges, "Calhoun in Bristol."

Details about Shabazz Napier: Espn.com basketball recruiting; Gavin Keefe, "Prep Guard . . . ," *Day*, April 3, 2010; Borges, "Calhoun in Bristol."

The trust comment: Ostrout, "Calhoun at Middlesex . . ."

Preseason predictions: Borges, "UConn Men Ranked 10th . . . ," *New Haven Register*, October 21, 2010.

Wichita State game: Espn.com; Anthony, "Kemba Walker . . . ," *Hartford Courant*, November 22, 2010; Brian McInnis, "UConn's Walker . . . ," *Honolulu Star-Advertiser*, November 23, 2010.

Michigan State game: John Marshall, "UConn Pulls . . . ," AP, November 24, 2010; Paul Suellentrop, "Maui Invitational . . . ," *Wichita Eagle*, November 23, 2010.

Kentucky game: John Marshall, "Walker Leads . . . ," AP, November 25, 2010; Brian McInnis, "UConn Handles . . . ," *Honolulu Star-Advertiser*, November 25, 2010.

UConn's movement in AP poll: Andrew Porter, "UConn Goes . . . ," Theuconnblog.com.

Pitt game: John Grupp, "Gibbs Leads . . . ," *Pittsburgh Tribune Review*, December 28, 2010.

Game at Notre Dame: Rick Gano, "Hansbrough Leads . . . ," AP, January 5, 2011; Espn .com.

Texas game: Jim Vertuno, "Walker's Jumper . . . ," AP, January 9, 2011; Mike Finger, "Win Twists . . ."; *Houston Chronicle*, January 9, 2011, 9.

Villanova game: Mike Kern, "Walker Is . . . ," *Philadelphia Daily News*, January 18, 2011, 47; O'Connell, "Walker Gives . . . ," AP, January 18, 2011.

31. To Mediocrity . . .

First Louisville game: Eaton-Robb, "Louisville Upsets . . . ," AP, January 29, 2011; Espn .com.

Walker's struggles: Anthony, *Hartford Courant*, January 30, 2011, E6; February 3, 2011.

Anthony's summary of UConn's struggles: "From Swagger . . . ," *Hartford Courant*, February 12, 2011, C1.

Oriakhi's benching: Anthony, "Alex Oriakhi . . . ," *Hartford Courant*, March 8, 2011.

Calhoun's suspension: Dan Gelston, "NCAA Suspends . . . ," AP, February 22, 2011; Joe Drape, "NCAA Bars . . . ," *New York Times*, February 23, 2011, 10; AP State & Local Wire, "Calhoun Says . . . ," March 10, 2011.

32. To Manhattan . . .

Win over Pitt in the Big East tournament: Dave Skretta, "Walker Leads . . . ," AP State & Local Wire," March 10, 2011; Mike Ogle, "Walker Carries . . . ," *New York Times*, March 11, 2011, 15; Mike Lupica, "A Bronx Tale . . . ," *Daily News*, 60; Kimberly Martin, "Buzzer Beater!" *Newsday*, A57.

Walker against NBA players: McInnis, "UConn's Walker . . ."

Syracuse win: Dave Skretta, "Walker Leads . . . ," AP, March 12, 2011; Mark Herrmann, "Walker Appears . . . ," *Newsday*, March 12, 2011, A46; Mike Ogle, "Everything Falls . . . ," *New York Times*, March 12, 2011, D1; Kevin Armstrong, "The Big Shot . . . ," *Daily News*, March 13, 2011, 58.

Calhoun-Pitino rivalry: Peter May, UPI, March 4, 1982; McNamara, "Pitino Returns . . . ," *Providence Journal*, October 30, 2005, C3; Desmond Conner, "Calhoun-Pitino . . . ," *Hartford Courant*, November 10, 2005; Borges, "Dunkin' on Rick . . . ," *New Haven Register*, February 1, 2009.

Walker's "Shock the world" quote: Jeffrey Martin, "UConn Edges . . . ," *Houston Chronicle*, April 2, 2011.

Louisville win: *Chronicle* news services, "March Madness," *Houston Chronicle*, March 13, 2011; Pete Thamel, "For a Fifth . . . ," *New York Times*, March 13, 2011, SP 1; Bigeast .org.

33. To Monday

San Diego State game: Greg Beacham, "Kemba Walker . . . ," AP, March 25, 2011; Tom Kensler, "Walker Takes . . . ," *Denver Post*, March 25, 2011; Randy Youngman, "Dream Season . . . ," *Orange County Register*, March 25, 2011; Borges, "UConn Facing . . . ," *New Haven Register*, March 24, 2011; Abbey Doyle, "Walker, UConn . . . ," *Herald Bulletin*, March 25, 2011.

Arizona game: Bruce Pascoe, "UConn Game Thread," *Arizona Daily Star*, March 26, 2011; Dan Fogarty, "Waving the Flag," Sportsgird.com, March 27, 2011; Greg Beacham, "UConn Earns . . . ," AP, March 27, 2011; Beth Harris, "Arizona's Scoring . . . ," AP, March 27, 2011; Randy Youngman, "UConn Run . . . ," *Orange County Register*, March 27, 2011; Jill Painter, "West's Top . . . ," *Los Angeles Daily News*, March 27, 2011, C1.

Calhoun-Calipari relationship: Ron Borges, "Clash of the Cals," *Boston Herald*, April 2, 2011, 34; Clay, "Revisiting . . ."; Art Stapleton, "Up Next . . . ," *St. Paul Pioneer Press*, March 28, 2011; Eddie Pells, "Calhoun, Calipari . . . ," AP, April 1, 2011.

Details about Knight and Doron Lamb: Ostrout, *Connecticut Post Online*, September 25, 2009; November 15, 2009; Borges, *New Haven Register*, June 27, 2009; March 31, 2011; Zach Braziller, "Lamb Picks . . . ," *New York Post*, April 18, 2010; Gavin Keefe, "How Do . . . ," *Day*, February 4, 2011; Espn.com; Anthony, "Brandon Knight . . . ," *Hartford Courant*, September 25, 2009; Davis, "Kentucky's Knight . . . ," April 1, 2011, Nbcsports.msnbc.com.

"We gonna shock the world" Eddie Pells, "UConn Holds . . . ," AP, April 3, 2011.

Pat Calhoun's quote: Tim Layden, "UConn's Drive . . . ," *Sports Illustrated*, 44, April 11, 2011.

Epilogue. Best Program Builder of All Time . . .

Boeheim's quote: Borges, "Calhoun Returns . . ."

Kentucky's problems: Jen Smith, "Decade of . . ."; *Kentucky Kernel*, November 2, 1998; Rhoden, "Kentucky's Basketball . . . ," *New York Times*, May 20, 1989.

Kansas and Roy Williams: Clifton Brown, "Getting along . . . ," *New York Times*, December 15, 1989.

McGuire and Smith: Art Chansky. 2006. *Light Blue Reign*, Thomas Dunne Books.

Pitino on Calhoun, Calipari, and Tarkanian: Conner, "Calhoun-Pitino . . ."

Details about Toraino Walker: Jacobs, "Walker Says . . . ," *Hartford Courant*, March 27, 1999.

Index

games vs. UConn, 200, 228; 1996
team, 92, 94; 1999 team, 117, 120, 121;
recruiting by, 71, 73, 144, 146, 189, 203;
vs. UConn in 2010 Maui Invitational,
239–240; vs. UConn in 2011 Final Four,
253–255

Kimball, Thomas (Toby), 40, 206, 217

King, Kirk, 67, 72, 90, 92, 94, 103

Knight, Bobby, 10, 13, 15, 25, 90, 147,
178, 220, 262; compared to Calhoun,
171–172

Knight, Travis, 87, 90, 92, 94, 94–95, 98

Krzyzewski, Mike, 13, 56, 135, 148, 178,
185, 220, 262, 264; and 2004 Final
Four, 181–183

Laettner, Christian, 56–57, 58–59, 65–66,
179–180, 264

Lamb, Jeremy, 237, 242, 251, 252,
247–250, 253, 255, 256

Leitao, Dave, 73, 78, 97, 116, 177;
recruiting by, 37, 43, 68, 71, 97, 148;
relationship with Calhoun, 58, 128,
136; as UConn assistant coach, 11, 18,
34, 53, 56

Lewis, Reggie, 8, 11, 27, 28, 66, 73, 237;
Calhoun on, 73, 79

Lobo, Rebecca, 79, 87, 88, 261

Louisiana State University (LSU): games
vs., 63–65, 196–197; recruiting by, 72,
195

Louisville, University of, 5, 28, 222, 224;
compared to UConn, 263–264; games
vs. UConn, 197, 211, 216, 230; at
UConn in 2011, 242–243; vs. UConn in
2011 Big East tournament, 247–250

Madison Square Garden, 82, 89, 151, 208,
221, 228; Big East tournament games
in, 2, 64, 153, 176, 246; NIT games
in, 33, 35–36; site of 1989 NBA draft,
39–40

Marshall, Donny, 60, 74, 78, 81, 83, 87,
96, 101, 138, 168; profile, 85–86

Marshall, Donyell, 91, 96, 102, 172–173;

vs. Boston College in 1994, 76–77;
Calhoun on, 79–90; on Calhoun,
77, 80; vs. Florida in 1994 NCAA
tournament, 78–79; play of, in
freshman year, 67, 69; play of, in junior
year, 67, 73–74; 79–80, 81; professional
basketball career of, 80; recruitment
of, 61–62, 75, 101; sophomore year of,
73–74; as a UConn superstar, 1, 74, 91,
150–151, 154, 162, 174, 219, 239

Maryland, University of, 30, 86; 1999
team, 117, 121; recruiting of, 61, 142,
168, 189–190; vs. UConn in 2002 NCAA
tournament, 154–156, 163, 260

Massachusetts, University of (UMass), 21,
101, 144, 163, 212, 238, 263; rivalry vs.
UConn in 1996, 89–90; vs. UConn in
2002, 159–160, 196

McGinn, Joe, 116; Calhoun and, 116–117,
125, 129; death of, 126–127

Miami, University of (Florida), 127; games
vs. UConn, 120, 151, 160; recruiting by,
40, 144, 194, 238; at UConn in 1999,
122–123; vs. UConn in 2003, 160, 200

Michigan State University, 30, 112, 169,
200; games vs. UConn, 206, 239, 251;
1999 team, 117, 118, 122, 125, 131–132,
136; at UConn in 1998, 118, 130

Miles, Nate, 222–224, 232–233, 264

Mississippi State University, 94–95, 260

Moore, Maya, 1, 84

Moore, Ricky, 90, 94, 103, 106–109, 112,
114, 119, 125; William Avery and,
133, 135; defense of, 118, 120, 123,
129–130, 135–137; vs. Duke, 133–138,
181; vs. Georgetown in 1996 Big East
tournament, 92–94

Moore, Tom, 127, 132, 161, 179, 194, 189,
205

Mullin, Chris, 29, 31, 110, 120, 149

Napier, Shabazz, 238, 240, 248, 252, 253,
254–255

National Collegiate Athletic Association
(NCAA): investigates UConn for Miles

recruitment, 222-224, 226, 231-233, 237, 239, 253; punishes UConn for low Academic Progress Report (APR), 268-269; punishes UConn for Miles recruitment, 243, 245, 264-265

NCAA tournament: *1978*, 5; *1981*, 8; *1982*, 58; *1990*, 52-58; *1991*, 63-65; *1994*, 78-79; *1995*, 85-86; *1996*, 94-95; *1998*, 111-114; *1999*, 127-138; *2000*, 140; *2002*, 152-156; *2003*, 164-167; *2004*, 177-184; *2005*, 192; *2006*, 200-202; *2008*, 211-212; *2009*, 224-227; *2011*, 252-256

National Invitation Tournament (NIT): *1988*, 32-36; *1989*, 39; *1993*, 67; *1997*, 105-106; *2001*, 144; *2010*, 230

Nochimson, Josh, 115, 222-223

Northeastern University, 2, 3, 18, 230, 233. *See also under* Calhoun, Jim

North Carolina, University of, 193, 222; compared to UConn, 13, 146, 262-263; games at UConn, 150, 191; recruiting by, 72, 168; vs. UConn in 1998 Elite Eight, 114, 251

North Carolina State University (NC State), 65, 95, 125, 190, 192; games vs. UConn, 95-96, 192; recruiting by, 30, 168, 253; vs. UConn in 2002 NCAA tournament, 152-153

Notre Dame, University of, 40, 75, 151, 215; games vs. UConn, 151, 173, 175, 184, 230; vs. UConn in 2011, 240, 242, 243, 253

Ohio State University, 35-36, 129-130, 251

Okafor, Emeka, 149, 159, 168-169, 178; blocked shots of, 150-151, 162, 164-165, 173, 207; Calhoun on, 159, 164, 171, 174; compared to Patrick Ewing, 174; vs. Duke in 2004 Final Four, 179-184; vs. Georgia Tech, 169-170, 184-185; injuries of, in 2003-2004, 169, 174-175; on loss to BC in 2003, 161-162; vs. Maryland in 2002 NCAA tournament, 154-155;

play of, in freshman year, 153, 156; play of, in junior year, 170-171, 173; play of, in 2003 NCAA tournament, 164-165; professional basketball career of, 185-186; recruitment of, 146-147; vs. Texas in 2003, 166-167; as UConn superstar, 1, 26, 174, 206

Ollie, Kevin, 67, 83, 86-87, 96, 175; on Calhoun, 60, 74-75; play of, in junior year, 74, 76, 81; recruitment of, 60-61, 101

Oriakhi, Alex, 237, 247, 250, 254, 255, 256, 268; play of, in 2010-2011, 239, 240, 242-243

Parcells, Bill, 32

Perkins, Lew, 89, 219

Perno, Dom, ix, 4, 8, 9, 10

Pikiell, Steve, viii, 25, 27, 50, 63, 169, 203

Pitino, Rick, 98, 147, 216, 231, 259-260, 263-264; rivalry vs. Calhoun, 247-248

Pittsburgh, University of (Pitt), 64, 151, 163; 200, 222, 224, 238, 252; games vs. UConn, 42, 69, 159, 161, 163, 211; recruiting by, 6, 101, 142, 194; vs. UConn in 1998, 119; vs. UConn in 2002 Big East tournament, 151-153; vs. UConn in 2004, 170, 173, 175-176, 184; at UConn in 2006, 197-198; vs. UConn in 2009, 217, 220; vs. UConn in 2011 Big East tournament, 2, 245-247, 249

Price, A. J., 205-207, 209, 222, 225; brain hemorrhage of, 190-191; laptop computer incident and, 194-196; play of, 210-211, 214-216, 219; six overtime game vs. Syracuse, 220-221

Providence College (PC): games vs. UConn, 39, 63, 67, 75, 75, 111, 118, 161; 1987 team, 24-25, 27, 127; recruiting by, 29, 194, 213, 238; vs. UConn in 1994, 74-76; at UConn in 2004, 170-171

recruiting, 5-7, 10; and Ray Allen, 68-72; 96-97; Amateur Athletic Union (AAU) and, 70, 195-196; and Taliek Brown,

143–144, 175; of Scott Burrell, 40–41; of Caron Butler, 143–144; Calhoun and, 11, 29–30, 37, 41, 60–61, 63, 68–69, 71–72, 75–76, 101, 103, 108–109; 144, 147–148, 194; class of 1991, 56, 60, 61–62, 101; class of 1993, 68–73; class of 1996, 101–103; class of 2006, 204–205; class of 2010, 1, 231, 237–238, 253–254, 269; Dickenman and, 23, 30, 37, 40, 68–70, 85; of El-Amin, 107–109; of Rudy Gay, 189–190, 195–196, 203; of Ryan Gomes, 170–171; Hobbs and, 102, 107, 143, 144; of Okafor, 146–147; of Chris Smith, 30, 37–38, 50; of Villanueva, 168–169; of Kemba Walker, 212–214

Robinson, Cliff, 24, 80, 109; ineligibility, 25–26, 30; 1989 NBA draft and, 39–40; play of, in junior year, 30–32, 34–35; as a UConn superstar, 40, 80, 81, 151, 206, 239

Robinson, Stanley, 204, 214, 219, 229, 237

Rowe, Dee, 4, 206

St. John's University, 49, 66, 91, 111, 198; dominance of, in pre-Calhoun era, 3, 12, 29; games vs. UConn, 111, 140, 162, 208, 230; recruiting and, 29, 43, 72, 144, 170, 190, 212, 213, 238; at UConn in 1990, 42, 45; vs. UConn in 1994, 77–80, 91; vs. UConn in 1999, 120–121, 124, 131; vs. UConn in 2002, 150, 151; vs. UConn in 2011, 242–243

San Diego, University of, 211–212

Sellers, Patrick, 231, 233, 243

Sellers, Rod, 35, 41, 42, 44, 50, 53, 57, 77, 224; on Clemson game, 54–55; Laettner and, 58–59; 65–66; vs. Shaquille O'Neal, 64–65

Seton Hall University, 61, 161; games vs. UConn, 42, 50, 81, 92, 122, 163, 212, 217; 1989 team, 21, 39, 49; recruiting by, 29, 101, 148, 170; at UConn in 1987, 25–26; at UConn in 1997, 104–105; vs. UConn in 1999 Big East tournament, 123–124

Shabel, Fred, 4

Sharpe, Joe, 105, 108, 134; on Calhoun 77–78, 133

Sheffer, Doron, 36, 74, 81, 89, 90, 92, 94, 98, 175; pre-UConn career of, 72–73

"The Shot," 54–57, 68, 181, 246, 249

Smith, Chris, 5, 39, 41, 63, 65–67; 77–79, 81, 206; Calhoun on, 44, 63; 1990 Big East Tournament, 51–52; 1990 NCAA Tournament, 53, 55–57; recruitment of, 30, 37–38, 50

Smith, Dean, 13, 220, 262–263, 267, 266; influence on Calhoun, 17, 20, 226

Solomon, Dave, 32, 129, 156, 171

Stanford University, 117; at UConn in 1998, 110–111; vs. UConn in 1999, 121–122; vs. UConn in 2003 NCAA tournament, 164–165

Storrs, Connecticut: as basketball capital of the United States, 185; influence of, on recruiting, 4–5, 29, 43, 60, 61, 71, 142, 205, 260, 263

Syracuse University: compared to UConn, 83, 123, 198; games vs. UConn, 92, 111, 140, 173, 206, 217; recruiting and, 3, 29, 60, 61, 103, 144, 189, 190; six overtime game vs. UConn in 2009, 220–222; vs. UConn in 1988, 30–32; vs. UConn in 1990, 42–43, 45, 49, 51–52; vs. UConn in 1995, 82, 85; vs. UConn in 1998 Big East tournament, 111; vs. UConn in 1999, 121–122, 123, 124, 130; vs. UConn in 2003, 161, 163; vs. UConn in 2004, 173–174; vs. UConn in 2005, 191, 192; vs. UConn in 2006, 197–200; at UConn in 2007, 205–206; vs. UConn in 2011, 2, 242–243, 247–248, 250

Taigen, Ted, 147

Tarkanian, Jerry, 197; compared to Calhoun, 263–264

Taurasi, Diana, 169, 185

Texas, University of: games vs. UConn, 140, 229; recruiting by, 239, 253;

Weiss, Dick (Hoops), 5, 63
West Virginia University, 32–33, 110, 121,
   206, 211, 230, 242
Williams, Gary, 35, 154, 190
Williams, Marcus, 168, 190, 194–196, 203

Williams, Roy, 104, 259–260, 264
Wooden, John, 68–69, 89, 265–266
Wright, Luther, 249

Yankee Conference, 3–4; 259; 266